Translation and Opposition

TRANSLATING EUROPE
Series Editors: Margaret Rogers, *University of Surrey, UK,* Gunilla Anderman[†] 2007

The emergence of English as the lingua franca of Europe as well as a global language has recently provided European nations, both large and small, with an international voice. The aim of the series, *Translating Europe*, is to cover aspects related to translation between English and the languages of Europe from among established, more recent and emerging members of the European Union, as well as giving voice to the speakers of more recent member states. Chosen topics will be wide ranging with each volume closely linked to a theme related to translation in its many multi-faceted functions. Translating Europe should be of interest to professional translators as well as scholars and students, not only in Translation Studies but also in Modern Languages, Linguistics and Comparative Literature.

Full details of all the books in this series and of all our other publications can be found on http://www.multilingual-matters.com, or by writing to Multilingual Matters, St Nicholas House, 31–34 High Street, Bristol BS1 2AW, UK.

TRANSLATING EUROPE
Series Editors: Margaret Rogers and Gunilla Anderman† 2007

Translation and Opposition

Edited by
Dimitris Asimakoulas and Margaret Rogers

MULTILINGUAL MATTERS
Bristol • Buffalo • Toronto

Library of Congress Cataloging in Publication Data
A catalog record for this book is available from the Library of Congress.
Translation and Opposition/Edited by Dimitris Asimakoulas and Margaret Rogers.
Translating Europe: 4
Includes bibliographical references and index.
1. Translating and interpreting--Social aspects. 2. Sociolinguistics.
I. Asimakoulas, Dimitris. II. Rogers, Margaret
P306.97.S63T726 2011
418'.02–dc23 2011028011

British Library Cataloguing in Publication Data
A catalogue entry for this book is available from the British Library.

ISBN-13: 978-1-84769-431-7 (hbk)
ISBN-13: 978-1-84769-430-0 (pbk)

Multilingual Matters
UK: St Nicholas House, 31–34 High Street, Bristol, BS1 2AW, UK.
USA: UTP, 2250 Military Road, Tonawanda, NY 14150, USA.
Canada: UTP, 5201 Dufferin Street, North York, Ontario, M3H 5T8, Canada.

Copyright © 2011 Dimitris Asimakoulas, Margaret Rogers and the authors of individual chapters.

All rights reserved. No part of this work may be reproduced in any form or by any means without permission in writing from the publisher.

The policy of Multilingual Matters/Channel View Publications is to use papers that are natural, renewable and recyclable products, made from wood grown in sustainable forests. In the manufacturing process of our books, and to further support our policy, preference is given to printers that have FSC and PEFC Chain of Custody certification. The FSC and/or PEFC logos will appear on those books where full certification has been granted to the printer concerned.

Typeset by Techset Composition Ltd, Salisbury, UK.
Printed and bound in Great Britain by the MPG Books Group.

Contents

Contributors vii

1 Systems and the Boundaries of Agency: Translation as a Site of Opposition 1
   D. Asimakoulas

Part 1: Rewritings

2 How Ibsen Travels from Europe to China: Ibsenism from Archer, Shaw to Hu Shi 39
   W. Zhao

3 Rewriting, Culture Planning and Resistance in the Turkish Folk Tale 59
   Ş.T. Gürçağlar

4 Where Have All the Tyrants Gone? Romanticist *Persians* for Royals, Athens 1889 77
   G. Van Steen

5 Oppositional Effects: (Mis)Translating Empire in Modern Russian Literature 93
   B.J. Baer

6 The Translator's Opposition: Just One More Act of Reporting ... 111
   E.E. Davies

Part 2: Dispositions and Enunciations of Identity

7 A Queer Glaswegian Voice 129
   D. Kinloch

8   Translating 'the shadow class [...] condemned to movement' and the Very Otherness of the Other: Latife Tekin as Author–Translator of *Swords of Ice* 146
    S. Paker

9   Translation and Opposition in Italian-Canadian Writing. Nino Ricci's Trilogy and its Italian Translation 161
    M. Baldo

10 Croker versus Montalembert on the Political Future of England: Towards a Theory of Antipathetic Translation 182
    C. O'Sullivan

11 Translation as a Means of Ideological Struggle 204
    C. Delistathi

12 'You say nothing; I will interpret': Interpreting in the Auschwitz-Birkenau Concentration Camp 223
    M. Tryuk

Part 3: Socio-cultural Gates and Gate-keeping

13 Dialectics of Opposition and Construction: Translation in the Basque Country 247
    I. Uribarri Zenekorta

14 The Translation of Sexually Explicit Language: Almudena Grandes' *Las edades de Lulú* (1989) in English 265
    J. Santaemilia

15 Serbo-Croatian: Translating the Non-identical Twins 283
    T.Z. Longinović

16 Translation as a Threat to Fascism 295
    C. Rundle

17 Censors and Censorship Boards in Franco's Spain (1950s–1960s): An Overview Based on the TRACE Cinema Catalogue 305
    C. Gutiérrez Lanza

Index 321

Contributors

Dimitris Asimakoulas is a lecturer in Translation Studies at the University of Surrey where he serves as Programme Director for the MA in Audiovisual Translation and the MA in Translation Studies with Intercultural Communication programmes. He holds a PhD in Translation Studies and teaches modules on translation theory, persuasive aspects of advertising discourse and intercultural mediation at undergraduate and postgraduate levels. Relevant publications on social movements, censorship, translation history and humour theory have appeared in the following journals: *Target*, *Meta*, *TTR* and *The Sixties: A Journal of History, Politics and Culture*. He is a member of the editorial board for the electronic journal *New Voices in Translation*.

Brian James Baer is Professor of Russian Language, Literature, and Translation Studies at the Institute of Applied Linguistics at Kent State University. He is the co-editor of Volume XII of the ATA (American Translators Association) Scholarly Monograph Series, *Beyond the Ivory Tower: Re-Thinking Translation Pedagogy*, and is the author of *Other Russias: Homosexuality and the Crisis of Post-Soviet Identity* (Palgrave Macmillan, 2009). He is the founding editor of the journal *Translation and Interpreting Studies* and is the general editor of the Kent State Monograph Series in Translation Studies. He is also the editor of *Contexts, Subtexts, and Pretexts: Literary Translation in Eastern Europe and Russia*, which appeared in John Benjamin's Translation Studies Library in 2011.

Michela Baldo graduated from the University of Padua (Italy) in Classics, Italian and Modern Greek in 2000 and she has a Masters degree (2004) and PhD in Translation Studies (2009) from the University of Manchester. Her PhD focused on migrant literature (Italian-Canadian writing) translated into Italian, and she has published articles on bilingualism, Italian-Canadian literature and translation, queer studies, film dubbing and subtitling. During her studies she taught Italian language and culture at the University of Manchester, where she has recently completed a post-doctoral research project funded by the Leverhulme Trust in collaboration with Dr Ludovica Serratrice (University of Manchester) and Professor Antonella Sorace (University of Edinburgh). The research aimed to study online language comprehension in English-Italian and Spanish-Italian bilingual school-age children. She is currently a Teaching Fellow in Translation Studies at the University of Birmingham and works occasionally as a freelance translator.

Eirlys Davies lectures at the King Fahd School of Translation, part of Abdelmalek Essaadi University in Tangier, Morocco, where she currently teaches courses in translation theory, French-English translation, research methodology, pragmatics and writing skills. She graduated in French and Linguistics from the University of Wales, Bangor, where she also was awarded a PhD in syntax and semantics. She was formerly a lecturer in the English Department of Sidi Mohammed Ben Abdallah University, Fez, Morocco, where she taught a variety of courses including semantics, pragmatics and stylistics. She has published one book (*The English Imperative*, Croom Helm, 1986) and numerous articles (in journals, books and encyclopaedias) on topics including translation, bilingualism, code-switching, intercultural communication, sociolinguistics and applied linguistics. Her translations from French into English have included literary, academic, journalistic and economic texts as well as the subtitling of films, documentaries and debates. Her current research interests include an examination of the role of translation in intercultural communication, a study of the medieval Andalusian songs known as *kharjas*, and an analysis of Moroccans' views of the Mediterranean.

Christina Delistathi is a Senior Lecturer in Translation at Middlesex University where she teaches translation theory and practical translation. She studied Politics and Political Science in Greece and Britain and completed her MA in Bilingual Translation at the University of Westminster. She has extensive experience as a professional translator and is currently completing a PhD on the translations of the *Communist Manifesto* into Greek.

Camino Gutiérrez Lanza graduated in English Studies (1993) and later was awarded her PhD in cinema translation and censorship in 20th century Spain (1999). She is an Associate Professor at the University of León, Spain, where she teaches English language and English-Spanish translation. She is currently leading two funded research projects on narrative, theatre and cinema translation and censorship in 20th century Spain. Her main areas of interest are descriptive translation studies, audiovisual translation, and cinema translation and censorship in 20th century Spain. She has published a number of articles, covering facets of these areas that range from methodological issues to specific case studies.

David Kinloch is Reader in English Studies at the University of Strathclyde, Glasgow, where he teaches Creative Writing and Scottish Literature. For many years he was a teacher of French, and his academic work includes *The Thought and Art of Joseph Joubert, 1754–1824* (Clarendon Press, 1992) and *4 Carnets de Joseph Joubert*, edited with Philippe Mangeot (Institute of Romance Studies, 1996) as well as articles on Mallarmé and translations of both Scottish and Quebecois theatre. He has published five books of poems to date: *Dustie-fute* (Vennel Press, 1992), *Paris-Forfar* (Polygon, 1994), *Un Tour d'Ecosse* (Carcanet, 2001), *In My Father's House* (Carcanet, 2005) and *Finger of a Frenchman* (Carcanet, 2011). He was a co-founder of the poetry journal *Verse* with Robert Crawford and Henry Hart, and of the nascent Scottish Writers' Centre.

Tomislav Lonvinović is Professor of Slavic and Comparative Literature at the University of Wisconsin-Madison. His books include *Borderline Culture* (1993), *Vampires Like Us* (2005), the co-edited and co-translated volume, with Daniel Weissbort, *Red Knight: Serbian Women Songs* (1992) and the translated volume edited by David Albahari, *Words are Something Else* (1996). He is also the author of several works of fiction, both in Serbian (*Sama Amerika*, 1995) and English (*Moment of Silence*, 1990). His forthcoming book *Vampire Nation: Violence as Cultural Imaginary* will be published by Duke University Press in 2011. His research interests include South Slavic literatures and cultures, Serbo-Croatian language, literary theory, Central and East European literary history, comparative Slavic studies, translation studies and cultural studies.

Carol O'Sullivan is a Senior Lecturer in Italian and Translation at the University of Portsmouth where she teaches on the MA in Translation Studies course and researches in the fields of translation history and audiovisual translation. She has published articles on a range of translation-related topics including censorship, subtitling, the translation of dialect poetry and translations of Irish literature from the Blasket Islands. Her monograph *Translating Popular Film* on translation and film storytelling will be published by Palgrave Macmillan in summer 2011. She recently held a British Academy small research grant for a project on translation publishing and censorship in 19th century Europe and is co-editing a volume of essays on this topic which was published by LIT Verlag in winter 2010.

Saliha Paker is Professor of Translation Studies and a translator of modern Turkish poetry and fiction, still teaching (part time) in Boğaziçi University, Istanbul (from which she retired in 2008), and Okan University, where she was Chair of the Department of Translation Studies from 2008 to 2010. Since the 1980s she has published her research on Ottoman literary translation history and the modern Turkish historiographical discourse governing it, in various international publications. Apart from her edition of *Ash Dîvan, Selected Poems of Enis Batur*, containing co-translations with Mel Kenne and Clifford Endres (Talisman House, 2006) and co-translations of Latife Tekin's fiction, her work in English includes an edited volume, *Translations: (Re)shaping of Literature and Culture* (Boğaziçi University Press, 2002), and articles on Turkish literature in English translation. She is the Director of the Cunda International Workshop for Translators of Turkish Literature (CWTTL), which she founded in 2006.

Margaret Rogers is Professor of Translation and Terminology Studies and Director of the Centre for Translation Studies at the University of Surrey, where she teaches terminology, translation and text analysis on the undergraduate and postgraduate programmes in Translation Studies. She initiated the Terminology Network in the Institute of Translation and Interpreting, UK, and is a founder member of the Association of Terminology and Lexicography. Her publications focus on terminology in text, particularly in LSP texts in translation.

Chris Rundle is a tenured researcher in Translation Studies at the Faculty for Interpreters and Translators (SSLMIT) of the University of Bologna, Italy. He is also Honorary Research Fellow in Translation and Italian Studies at the School of Languages, Linguistics and Cultures of the University of Manchester, UK. His main research interests lie in the history of translation and Fascism, with a special focus on the Italian Fascist regime, and in audiovisual translation, especially subtitling. He is the author of the monograph *Publishing Translations in Fascist Italy* (Peter Lang, 2010), and co-editor with Kate Sturge of the volume *Translation Under Fascism* (Palgrave Macmillan, 2010), a comparative study of translation in the Italian, German, Spanish and Portuguese fascist regimes. He is a coordinating editor of the online translation journal *inTRAlinea* (www.intralinea.it).

José Santaemilia is Associate Professor of English Language and Linguistics at the Universitat de València, as well as a legal and literary translator. His main research interests are translation, gender and language, sexual language and gender. He has published extensively on these topics, and is the author and editor of *Género, lenguaje y traducción* (Valencia University Press, 2003), *Gender, Sex and Translation: The Manipulation of Identities* (St Jerome, 2005), and *Gender and Sexual Identities: International Perspectives* (Cambridge Scholars Publishing, 2008). He has co-authored, with José Pruñonosa, the first critical edition and translation of *Fanny Hill* into Spanish (Editorial Cátedra, 2000).

Şehnaz Tahir Gürçağlar is associate professor of Translation Studies at Boğaziçi University in Istanbul. She has a PhD in Translation Studies from Boğaziçi University and an MA in Media Studies from Oslo University in Norway. She teaches courses on translation theory, translation history, translation criticism and interpreting. She has published numerous articles on translation history in Turkey and is the author of *Kapılar* (Scala 2005, a book exploring different approaches to translation history, published in Turkish), *The Politics and Poetics of Translation in Turkey, 1923–1960* (Rodopi, 2008) and *Çevirinin ABC'si* (Say 2011, an introduction to translation and translation studies, published in Turkish).

Małgorzata Tryuk received her MA and her PhD in Applied Linguistics (translation and interpreting) at the University of Warsaw, and later a DLitt degree from Adam Mickiewicz University in Poznań. She is currently Associate Professor at the Institute of Applied Linguistics at the University of Warsaw where she teaches courses on translation and interpreting studies. She has published several books and articles in Polish, French and English on conference and community interpreting and she was awarded the degree of DLitt (Habilitation) for her book *L'interprétation communautaire. Des normes et des rôles en interprétation* (Wydawnictwo TEPIS, 2004). She is particularly interested in the didactics of interpreting and is the local coordinator of the European Masters in Conference Interpreting (EMCI) at the University of Warsaw.

Ibon Uribarri Zenekorta graduated in Philosophy (1990) and Media Studies (1991) and later obtained his PhD in Philosophy (1996). He has undertaken extended research stays in Germany (Mainz, Marburg and Leipzig), the UK (St Antony's, Oxford) and Japan (Keio University). He has been a lecturer in Translation at the University of the Basque Country since 2002. He has written several books and articles on philosophy and translation issues (translation from German into Basque, translation of philosophy). He is now leading a funded research project on translation and censorship. He has translated main philosophical works by I. Kant, G.W.F. Hegel, C.S. Peirce, and L. Wittgenstein into Basque, as well as literary works by Yasunari Kawabata, Haruki Murakami, Thomas Bernhard and Herta Müller.

Gonda Van Steen earned a BA degree in Classics in her native Belgium and a PhD degree in Classics and Hellenic Studies from Princeton University. As the Cassas Chair in Greek Studies at the University of Florida, she teaches courses in ancient and modern Greek language and literature. Her research interests include classical drama, French travelers to Greece and the Ottoman Empire, nineteenth and twentieth-century receptions of the classics, and modern Greek intellectual history. Van Steen's first book, *Venom in Verse: Aristophanes in Modern Greece*, was published by Princeton University Press in 2000 and was awarded the John D. Criticos Prize from the London Hellenic Society. In her book of 2010, *Liberating Hellenism from the Ottoman Empire*, revolutionary uses of Aeschylus' *Persians* (1820s) and the Venus de Milo take center stage. Van Steen recently published another book titled *Theatre of the Condemned: Classical Tragedy on Greek Prison Islands* (OUP, 2011), which discusses the ancient tragedies that were produced by the political prisoners of the Greek Civil War (late 1940s through 1950s). She is currently working on a book manuscript that analyzes theatre life, performance, and censorship under the Greek military dictatorship of 1967–1974. She has also published articles on ancient Greek and late antique literature and on postwar Greek feminism.

Wenjing Zhao is Professor and Head of the Centre for Translation Studies at Henan Normal University, China. She obtained her PhD from the University of Manchester. She is the author of the monograph *Cultural Manipulation of Translation Activities: Hu Shi's Rewriting and the Construction of a New Culture* (2006) and of several articles in (translation history) related subjects: 'Literary Criticism and the Creation of Ibsen's Image in China' (2009, *Perspectives*); 'Study of Hu Shi's Marginalisation in Translation History in Light of Rewriting Theory' (2009, *Foreign Language Teaching*); 'Rethinking the Construction of Translation Studies as a Discipline' (2008, *Shanghai Journal of Translators*); and 'The Cultural Consideration of Interlingual Rewriting: Taking Hu Shi's Case as an Example' (2008, *Journal of Henan Normal University*). She is also a practising translator and has recently finished a translation of Mona Baker's book, *Translation and Conflict* (2006) which will soon be published by Beijing University Press.

Chapter 1
Systems and the Boundaries of Agency: Translation as a Site of Opposition

D. ASIMAKOULAS

Introduction

In December 2008 Athens became the centre of widespread protest, rioting and vandalism. With these dramatic events a motley crowd of angry youths, anarchists, anti-capitalist and anti-state groups, disenfranchised immigrants and politicized citizens in general shocked public opinion for the second time that month. The first poignant pang of shock arose with the event that triggered this unrest just after 9 am on 6 December 2008: after a verbal altercation with a group of young people in the restive Exarchia area in Athens, a policeman adopted a 'shoot-to-kill' approach when he randomly encountered a different group of youths, resulting in the death of Alexis Gregoropoulos, an unarmed 15-year-old high school pupil. Within hours, protest activities spiralled out of control in Athens, and over the next few days in every major Greek city. The source of such collective action can be traced back to pent-up discontent *vis-à-vis* crippling neoliberal policies, high-visibility financial scandals, widespread corruption, the lack of reform in 'free' public education (which actually comes with exorbitant costs), ideological splits, a very high unemployment rate among young people and 'party heteronomy' on all levels of life (see Mouzelis, 2009). More than 25 internet groups were formed immediately after Alexis' death, expressing reactions to the event, uploading reports 'from the ground', images and videos, while simultaneously coordinating action (Antoniade, 2010). Indeed, the orchestrated actions of this wave of acute resentment and the speed with which they rippled through the country can be attributed to the use of new technologies among young people: text messaging, (video) blogging, and other internet applications, such as YouTube. These were acts of 'political swarming' (Rheingold, 2002: 161–162), where *ad hoc* alliances, knowledge pooling about police movements and action alignment became possible through the use of mobile technologies. The uncannily concerted efforts of these 'smart mobs' left the older generation perplexed, muttering about conspiracy theories of various kinds.

Interestingly, and from an *intersemiotic translation* (Jakobson, 1959/2000) perspective, the December riots and Gregoropoulos' death are currently being refashioned into a forthcoming film by director Gerasimos Regas; this technique recalls such animated films as *Persepolis* (2007) and *Waltz with Bashir* (2008), both capturing political conflicts and conflicted identities in other contexts. Two years after December 2008, the stories of dramatic events surrounding the riots continue to be rewritten, all against the backdrop of the recent trials of the perpetrators.[1] At the time of the riots, however, accounts varied considerably, given the general confusion. The mass media struggled to keep up with the overload of information while simultaneously trying to offer their own analyses and evaluations of events. Mainstream television channels were unable to confirm immediately what had happened; the murder was first reported on the website of Indymedia Athens and a clearer image of the timeline then emerged. On 10 December 2008, the *Eleftheros Typos* broadsheet newspaper highlighted the gravity of the situation by using an outsize-font, black-background cover page which featured a translation. This translation 'had appeared' on the internet, in mailing lists and on blogs a few days earlier. The *Eleftheros Typos* cover text, which is an anonymously sourced translation of a quote by Isocrates into Modern Greek, is shown in Figure 1.1.

The text was subsequently commented upon on the personal website of Nikos Sarantakos[2] and in the IOS newspaper insert of the Sunday *Eleftherotypia* newspaper (20 December 2008).[3] With over 90,000 hits, according to IOS, the 'mutated' quote constitutes a *locus communis*; until the time of the riots, it had been variously used by the Deputy Minister for Education (G. Anthopoulos), a university dean (I. Gryspolakis), regional political party organizations, Hellenic–American associations, authors of 'letters to the editor' and bloggers (IOS, 2008: online). Sarantakos, a Greek polymath with degrees in Chemical Engineering and English Studies, is a published linguist/author and a seasoned translator (working for the European Parliament), as well as an active blogger. On his website, he promptly noted that the front page text did not exactly match the original ancient Greek text. A close back-translation of the *Eleftheros Typos* version

Systems and the Boundaries of Agency

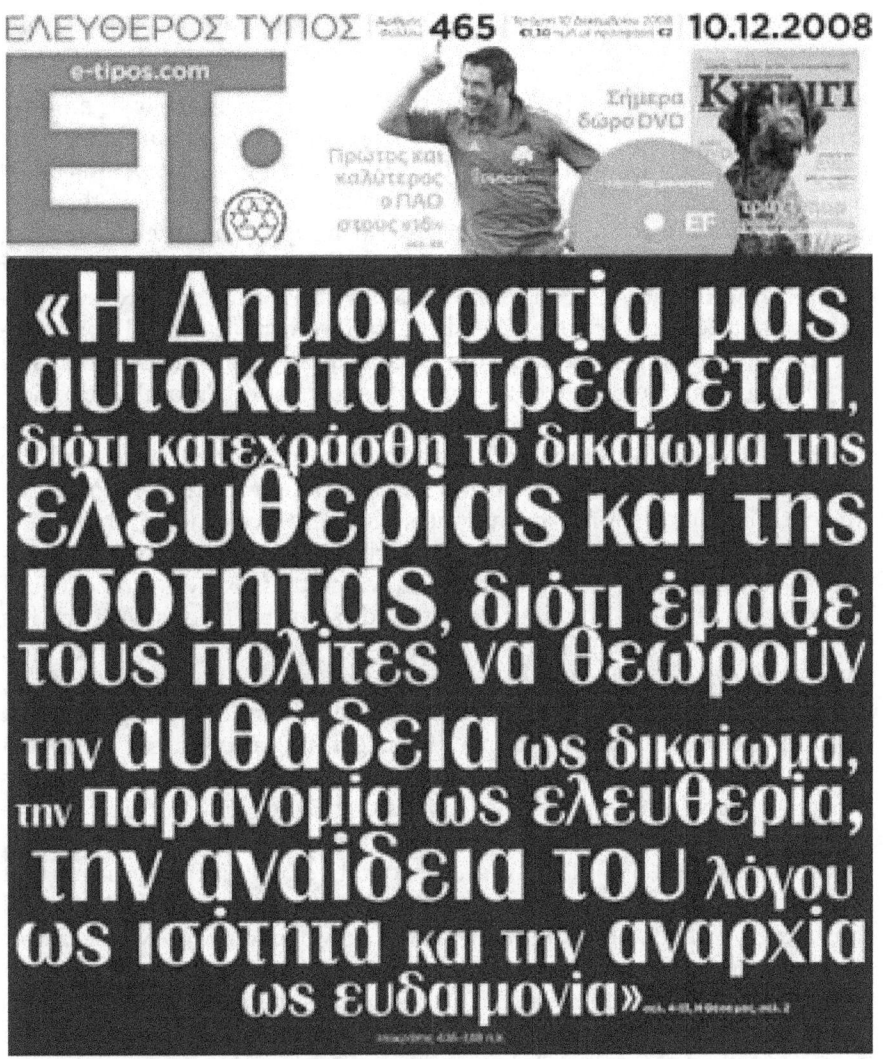

Figure 1.1 Front page of *Eleftheros Typos*, 10 December 2008

into English follows (bold lettering indicates the use of a larger font size in the title, as seen above in Figure 1.1):

> **Our democracy is self-destructing**, because it abused the rights of **freedom and equality**, because it taught citizens to consider **impertinence** as a right, lawlessness as freedom, **insolence in speech**

as equality and **anarchy** as happiness. (Isocrates 436–338 BC (*my translation*))

With the front page text, the editors captured what many saw as an orgy of destruction of public property, with banks, state-owned buildings, state universities, libraries, national theatres and shops being the primary targets of the vandals. The philological prowess of editors is not the only motivation for affording a translated text such high visibility. Resembling epigraphs in books (Genette, 1997: 157), that is, texts identifying and emphasizing the title as well as the content within, this intertextual reference constitutes an expanded headline, followed by a typical epigraph-like authorial stamp-cum-date. The composite headline adds gravitas to the evaluative statement made; it arguably shows how a 'morally superior' voice from the past admonishes and warns Greeks of contemporary surreptitious threats to democracy, a diachronically needed value and the matrix of a rule of law. Dramatic and serious though the translation of the Ancient Greek may sound, it constitutes a blithely modernized, shortened, skewed version of the source text (ST). Firstly, the context in which Isocrates composed his *Areopagiticus* speech, from which this text was culled, could not be more different. This speech was made some time before/during the Social War (357–353 BC), which left Athens with a weakened naval empire and with powerful city-state allies seceding from the Confederacy (Gagarin, 2000: 182). Isocrates readily maps the loss of political/military might against political and moral inadequacy. In his speech he caricatures the ills of a populist democracy and suggests a return to the 'ancestral constitution' as a means of rehabilitating Athens from its decadence and culture of litigation (which he saw as a direct result of the Janus-faced rhetoric of sophists) (Gagarin, 2000: 182, 183). This was a conservative political programme that required a restitution of the authority of the Areopagus Court, a council consisting of aristocrats and a subgroup of powerful citizens whose power had been stripped away by reforms as a response to the mismanagement of city affairs (Gagarin, 2000: 183). In Section 20 of *Areopagiticus*, Isocrates makes a comparison with the days when Areopagus protected Athenian laws, and thus decries the fact that the guardianship of laws was left in the hands of citizens. Yet, unlike the *Eleftheros Typos* front page, his speech never mentions 'anarchy', a 'self-destructing democracy' or the abuse of 'freedom and equality', points also mentioned by IOS and Sarantakos; the following constitutes my very literal rendition of the ancient Greek text (hence the use of interlingual glosses):

Those who governed the city then did not establish a system of government [*politeian*] only referred to in name [as] the most popular and benign, whilst in real practice appearing different to those who experience it, or which educated citizens in such a way that they perceived impunity [*akolasian*] as democracy, lawlessness [*paranomian*] as freedom, free speech [*parrhesian*] as equality-under-the-law [*isonomian*] and each person's license [*exousian*] to do anything as happiness [*eudainonian*], but [*a politeia*] which by showing hostility towards and punishing such men made all citizens better and more prudent.[4]

Existing English translations, such as the one by Lee Too for Texas University Press, are rather fluent and also contain some modernizations to facilitate comprehension (e.g. the use of the word 'populism' to render *koinotato prosagoreuomenin*). My purpose here was to achieve formal equivalence by following the syntax of the ancient Greek text, especially the use of the two 'complement' (*katigorimatikes*) participles in the first main clause and the string of relative clauses modifying the object, *politeian*. Leaving the contrastive analysis work to the reader, I need to note here that this example aptly illustrates how a translated text can channel and drastically modify the contextual implications of a temporally distant original, against the backdrop of a dominant *meta-narrative* (Baker, 2006: 44) with great communicative relevance and currency, namely, democracy. The 'revived' text in *Eleftheros Typos* is pressed into the service of reconfigured rhetorical effects: a fear appeal, or *pathos*, stirring up the fears of the audience who can see a Cassandra-esque voice from the past replaying a scenario of self-destruction that Greeks have been prone to throughout history; or an ethical appeal, or *ethos*, a flaunting of moral superiority on the part of 'wise ancestors' as well as the editors of the newspaper who ventriloquize them, and of the readers who align themselves with the stance expressed.

By way of showing the currency of the translated quote in December 2008, and the degree of layering to which its message was subject, it must be noted that the same text resurfaced, in English, when a journalist from *The Sunday Times* offered the explanation of Stratis Stratigis (former chairman of the Athens Olympics organizing committee) for the December riots:

> 'Our democracy is destroying itself because it misrepresented the right to liberty and equality,' says an e-mail circulating [sic] his [Stratigis'] friends. 'It taught the citizens to regard disrespect as a right, lawlessness as liberty, impertinence as equality and anarchy as enjoyment'.
>
> This is a quote from Socrates, the ancient philosopher who ended up being sentenced to death for voicing truths that nobody wanted to hear.

'It's funny,' said Stratigis. 'Those words have a ring about them today.' (Campbell, 2008)

Campbell's piece (dated 14 December 2008) is entitled 'Greek Riots Spark Fear of Europe in Flames' and the journalist evocatively concludes the entire article by using this translated quote. He also wrongly acknowledges the source as Socrates, whose name looks and sounds similar to Isocrates. Isocrates was allegedly 98 years old when he apparently starved himself to death in order to protest against the defeat of Athens by Philip (the father of Alexander the Great) in the Battle of Chaeronea (338 BC) (Gagarin, 2000: 3). The journalist from *The Sunday Times* foregrounds a disparate image of martyrdom by appending Socrates' tragic end to the quote, possibly in order to highlight a view of inconvenient truths being inhumanely repressed by the callous masses. Arguably, Campbell also hyperbolically allows a loose connection (of victimization) to be made between a representative of what is seen as Athenian success in the 21st century, Stratigis, and the *ethos* of one of the pillars of classic Athenian philosophy.

As the I-Socrates example shows, socio-cultural distinctions can give rise to or leave their imprint on the act of translation, a selective foregrounding of messages in its own right. This is precisely the topic that the present volume attempts to explore from various angles, as translation is often viewed in the popular mind as a facilitator and enabler of communication. The core concepts that underpin the discussion in each chapter of this book can be said to have great currency in Translation Studies (TS): issues of power brokering, agency, conflict (and conflicted subjectivities), cultural/linguistic hybridity and gate-keeping. If one of the main goals of theoretical approaches to translation is to observe, to rationalize and (even more boldly put) to predict different types of translation phenomena (see Chesterman & Wagner, 2002: 3; Shlesinger, 2009: 4), then contexts where oppositional effects of various kinds emerge feature as compelling and topical objects of study. Wars, important (inter)national events, or the increasingly diverse cultural constituencies brought together in a globalized world have cast into sharp relief clashes on the levels of social/professional practice, textual strategies, cultural identity and ideology. By shedding light on more such phenomena 'out there', researchers are increasingly encouraged to shy away from a view of translation as textual activity only, or as an activity that is purely the act of individuals, cut off from the environment in which they operate. More case studies conducted along these lines may allow a useful text-to-context and context-to-text negotiation, as originally suggested by

Hatim and Mason (1997: 16–19). Without wishing to expunge the intractable fuzziness of boundary lines between these levels, the book is divided into broad sections intended to reflect the foregoing concerns, sharpening the focus on either the textual or the agential aspects where appropriate.

Translation and Opposition consists of three sections. The section entitled 'Rewritings' focuses on 'refractions' of source material according to interests promoted by institutions of patronage (e.g. publishing houses or translation bureaux) and the dominant textual traditions in specific contexts as suggested by Lefevere (1982/2000: 234–235). The second section, 'Dispositions and Enunciations of Identity', examines translations as dynamic expressions of socio-political and linguistic self- and other-identification, that is, as interfaces where agency becomes manifest. The final section, 'Socio-Cultural Gates and Gate-Keeping', highlights even further the 'middle ground between translators and other agents' (Paloposki, 2009: 192). Thus the book comes full circle by placing translated products within the structure of society where the limits of freedom and control, alliances and competition, enter a constant game of shape-shifting. By the term 'opposition' I generally mean either potential clash or contingent consensus in texts and society. As the case of the December riots in Greece indicates, exchanges on a symbolic or a concrete level, be they friendly or hostile, become meaningful to constellations of recipients when they are seen against a backdrop, say, of a common (for those who agree) or an opposing (for those who do not) frame of reference. In the example of the December riots, this frame of reference was a ST with its translation. On a deeper level, it was the events/ideas that were constantly being re-voiced in order to mobilize potential participants or in order to endorse/condemn certain actions and attitudes. Translators, interpreters and subtitlers as mediators have a pivotal role to play in identifying dividing lines between 'us' and cultural and political 'others'. Dynamic groupings and (counteractive) regroupings of textual repertoires, of ideas and of social groups can be animated through translation. In what follows I explore such groupings on the mutually interactive levels of *society, individuals* and *cultural objects*.

Rewritings

In TS, the notion of opposition readily recalls systemic approaches to translation, especially because the latter offer explanations in terms of cultural semiosis and 'networks of oppositions', most notably along the lines of binaries such as primary (innovatory)/secondary (conservative) systems, centres/peripheries, canonized/non-canonized literary models and more/less strongly codified forms and genres (Even-Zohar, 1990: 15–21; Hermans, 1985: 11). Tensions and conflicts generated by such sets of oppositions bring a literary system forward, subjecting it to the imperatives of constant struggles for domination (Hermans, 1985: 11). A classic example from the relevant literature aptly showing how such interdependencies work is Clem Robyns' study of the transfer of Anglo-American detective stories into the French *série noire*. During the 1940s the centre of the French 'thriller system' was stagnant and a wholesale introduction of the new Anglo-American model took place, translations thus becoming vehicles of innovation (Robyns, 1990: 38). Such was the prestige of translations that subsequently originals not only conformed to Anglo-American conventions, but also often 'disguised themselves' as pseudo-translations (Robyns, 1990: 38). Domestic production diversified and developed during the 1950s, and French journalism, criticism, publishing houses and popular literary magazines contributed to the 're-conquering' of the centre of the literary system by domestic production, while translations were relegated to the periphery (Robyns, 1990: 38, 39). The extensive modifications that translations were subjected to reflect precisely that: every book contained a uniform number of pages so that production costs could be reduced; a single, coherent, bare-fact narrative line was adopted; and perceived plot/characterization inconsistencies were 'corrected' (Robyns, 1990: 27–29). Some changes were, however, of a more ideological nature, thus showing interactions between the literary system and that of politics or religion: the convention that violence is justified or even necessary to restore order was made explicit, while shocking sexual scenes, religious and anti-communist statements were blotted out (Robyns, 1990: 33, 34). Robyns does not make it clear whether the publishers or the critical establishment had an (in)direct influence on any of these decisions. Yet since translation is never a simple process, it could be argued that multiple, overlapping (and possibly clashing) agencies were at play.

The (poly)systemic strand of research in TS paved the way towards examining translation as both a cultural and social phenomenon, underscoring the role of competition and heterogeneity (Lambert, 1995: 111, 132). As seen above, literary devices within original or translated texts, the whole genre they represent, and their afterlife in a (target) system all function on the basis of interconnections and oppositions on a narrative, generic and socio-political level. One might say that this is by necessity the case, because the very essence of literary works cannot be seen in terms of the inherent meaning residing within them; instead, literary works serve an artistic and social purpose by means of patterns of antitheses. These patterns can thus be construed along the lines of Bakhtin's notion of *dialogism* (Roulet, 1996: 2), or in terms of *foregrounding* techniques, such as deviations from 'normal', standard forms and striking ways of describing an object or event (Boase-Beier, 2006: 91). Foregrounding and dialogism can, for example, be realized in metaphors, repetitions, sound plays, the strategic use of syntactic structures and 'marginal' discourses (e.g. dialects), the so-called 'remainder', poised to be exploited in translation (see Venuti, 1998a: 10–11).

Interdependencies/oppositions seen in this light are not a simple matter, nor are they limited to pairs of 'texts' or one source culture (SC) to target culture (TC) configuration only, where the needs of the receiving TC are the sole defining factor. Oppositions can be construed on a multiple-direction, global model. In relation to book production, for instance, Heilbron has suggested that levels of cultural importation and the role of translated texts in a national context vary considerably, depending on the (central) position of each (national) language and cultural production in an *international translation system* (Heilbron, 1999: 439–440). A similar perspective can be discerned in Zanettin's (2008) innovative volume on the 'semiotic mix' that comic books pose. Zanettin (2008) outlines the history of the comics industry, and although neither he nor any of the contributors to the volume explicitly describe comics as products in a polysystem, comic book production constitutes a prime example of how a complex, global system of cultural products evolves. The explosion of comic strips experienced in the United States in the 1930s, for example, 'jump-started' a global phenomenon, with European, South American and Asian producers subsequently filling in various niches in terms of aesthetic conventions and format (afforded with varying levels of prestige), age groups, and social class in each case (Zanettin, 2008: 2–5). Thus the 'glocal' (global-local) market of comic books can be seen to wax and wane under the pressures of competing pictorial and textual repertoires (Rota, 2008: 84–89), language policies, different literacies and financial or ideological concerns on the part of an extensive network of producers and consumers.

The relational logic of meaning-creation is not a feature of literature or the more creative types of texts only. It underpins all types of communication, translation included. Meaning-creation in translation is a dialectic process, requiring senders and recipients of messages to contextualize communicative intentions while using register in a meaningful way, with mediating translators always making judgements as to what the likely effects of conveying these intentions in a different context will be (Hatim & Mason, 1990: 57, 64–65). Misjudging intentions may give rise to oppositional effects, not least because messages are also semiotically embedded within a general system of values instantiated in genres, discourses and texts (Hatim & Mason, 1990: 69–75). The Isocrates example cited at the beginning of this chapter shows precisely how foregrounded typography (Van Leeuwen, 2006: 148), lexicalization/word selection (Van Dijk, 1995: 25; see inclusion of 'anarchy' in the Isocrates quote), and the staccato delivery of rhetorical structure (more specifically, of *parison* and *antithesis*, see Nash, 1989: 113, 114) in a very short text translated from ancient Greek can capture sharp distinctions between in-groups and dangerous others. Such kinds of oppositions have guided traditional research in ideology. As Verschueren suggests, the '[c]lose scrutiny of elements of contrast is one of the most powerful tools available to ideology research, because of its potential to reveal patterns of implicit meaning' (Verschueren, 1996: 594). The Isocrates example echoes Verschueren's argument that the set of contrastive elements, be they features of the lexical, sentential, or textual level, are not static, as they change intertemporally, intertextually and interlinguistically (1996: 596). Hierarchies of textual features and topics presented in texts reflect social hierarchies, with both being subject to changes over time.

Bearing glocal interactions in mind, Wenjing Zhao in this volume focuses on a rather common but largely under-researched phenomenon: how foreign writers and their works travel to target contexts through literary criticism, a form of translation in the broad sense. The author uses André Lefevere's (1992) concept of rewriting in order to examine issues of form and content as well as contextual variables affecting translation. The case study sheds light on the importation of Henrik Ibsen's plays in China by Hu Shi, a US-educated scholar and consequently a key figure in the New Culture Movement in China (1915–1923).[5] Hu Shi, a prestigious cultural producer inclined to press for literary/cultural reforms, opposed established norms in China at the time; he went on to introduce what was until then a peripheral genre (drama) into China and interpreted Ibsen's ideas according to the ideological needs of Chinese society – for example, the need to oppose women's subjugation and feudalistic values. Zhao traces the trajectory of this migration of ideas by looking at two Western scholars who in their time were engaged in oppositional views in their respective literary establishments and societies. Firstly, William Archer 'rewrote' Ibsen focusing on the functionality of style/language and making Ibsen's works known in the US and the English-speaking world in general. Secondly, George Bernard Shaw adopted a 'didactic drama' approach and realistic writing, injecting his own socialist views into the plays. Hu Shi's critical work echoes such attempts at selectively localizing

Ibsen, and his rewriting activity was consequential for the further development of the Chinese literary field. Hu Shi's influential rewriting project found an outlet in a radical Chinese literary journal. Through his essay-writing, Hu Shi presented Ibsen as, for instance, an internationalist, and along with other ideological interventions his work constituted a subtle – yet in some cases very visible – re-working of the discourse of 'Ibsenism'.

Şehnaz Tahir Gürçağlar's chapter focuses on intralingual translations (also described as 'rewrites') of traditional folk stories in Turkey. Folk stories remained part of the oral Turkish literary system until the 19th century and were intended for largely illiterate populations in rural areas. As folk stories started to be printed for mass circulation in the Ottoman Empire, their profile began to change and various writers penned different versions. Seen from a historical perspective, these rewrites reflect different concerns and offer different visions of a society going through drastic cultural and political transformation. The culture planners of the newly founded Turkish republic attempted to control and even tame folk story rewrites by systematically excluding them from the literary canon they envisaged for the young readers; they also encouraged a certain type of rewriting activity that would comply with the themes and styles they regarded as appropriate for the emerging Turkish nation. The chapter examines such rewrites published throughout the 19th and 20th centuries, and addresses the issues of anonymity, authorship, ideology, culture planning and cultural resistance that they raise. As is shown, folk stories evolved thematically, stylistically and lexically. These diachronically observed changes constitute the imprint of shifting and often oppositional ideological, literary, political and cultural norms in the emerging modern Turkish nation.

Gonda Van Steen's chapter discusses the perspectival interpretation of an ancient, canonized text with high literary and political visibility: Aeschylus' *Persians*. Starting from the present, it is argued that recent productions of *Persians* have become vehicles of outspoken opposition through translation and adaptation. This recent tendency must be placed in the historical and questioning perspective fostered by studies of performance *histories*, to be unmasked as just that: a new and unusual phenomenon, as well as a product of modern sensibilities inspired by the Iraq War. Van Steen's key example of an older Greek translation and production of Aeschylus' *Persians* (staged in Athens, 1889) offers a necessary counterweight: her study analyses how a (then credible) translation became a platform of (now offensive) conformism. Her discussion of the 1889 Romanticist translation and production also sheds light on the broader and longer-term modern Greek reception of Aeschylus' tragedy and outlines the contours of a receptive trend that lasted from the early 19th century through the mid-1960s (or up until the revisionist work in Greek tragedy by the avant-gardist theatre director Karolos Koun). In 1889, on the occasion of the state visit of Kaiser Wilhelm II to Greece, the Athenian production of Aeschylus' *Persians* wooed the goodwill of the German emperor and of the Greek royals, and grew into a display of Germanophilia, even as it implicitly identified the young and ambitious emperor with Xerxes. Also, the translation became a metaphorical act that marked the translator's and the director's move from agency to collusion. Van Steen's study answers lingering questions such as: who was responsible for making the ancient tragedy undergo this peculiar transformation? How was the 1889 production received? To which historical and theatrical context did it respond? How did the translator mediate the lack of Greek political and artistic self-confidence when adapting the play that was, for some, *the* cultural reminder of the Greeks' stance of opposition against the foreign invader of the 5th century BC?

Brian Baer's chapter focuses on the pivotal role of translation in cases of literary heteroglossia, in which, to quote Meylaerts (2006: 95), translation can accentuate 'ideological sociocultural faultlines' and potentially constitute 'a statement about cultural identity'. Baer discusses translation and (mis)translation in the literature of the Russian Empire, which is characterized by the opposition between two codes, the prestigious languages of Western Europe versus the languages of the colonized peoples of the Russian empire. To explore this phenomenon of heteroglossia, Baer proposes a typology of translation effects that capture the way in which readers negotiate meaning. His typology is a scale, ranging from 'total translation' to 'zero translation'. In cases of 'total translation' the reader is provided only with the target utterance, and is invited to believe that translation reflects a smooth exchange, with both languages and cultures converging. At the other end of the scale is 'zero translation', in which no translation of the source utterance is provided, thereby highlighting a gap between the two languages and cultures. Between these two poles of the scale there is a range of translation effects. Baer gives the example of code-switching in Tolstoy's *War and Peace* where the society hostess Anna Sherer speaks to her guests in French but inserts Russian words and phrases. Baer's main focus, however, lies in the phenomenon he calls '(mis)translation'; as he argues, (mis)translation uncovers contradictions and myths of official imperial discourse and as such can be used to expose issues of power that are often taken for granted or 'mystified' in both total and zero translation. Baer discusses (mis)translations within three different contexts: firstly, within the context of romantic irony, with examples taken from Mikhail Lermontov's *A Hero of Our Time* (1840), a 'commentary on Russia's imperial project'; then within the context of Soviet dissent where translation played a key role in the official policy of *druzhba narodov* (friendship of Soviet peoples), he analyses Roziner's *A Certain Finkelmeyer*, a novel that debunks this policy; and finally in relation to the fall of the Soviet Empire, with Iskander's novella *Pshada*. Iskander's novel shows a man who is disoriented between two languages and two identities, a man who benefited from the empire but is also its victim. Acts of (mis)translation, Baer argues, set up an opposition between a 'desire for a commonality that would transcend language and ethnicity', exposing that same desire as the 'colonialist's dream'.

In the chapter contributed by Eirlys Davies, the issue of opposition is approached from a more reflective angle. As is shown, views of how translation should be carried out vary greatly; some argue that the translator must always remain subservient to the ST and its author, while others defend translators' freedom to introduce their own input, to manipulate and oppose the source material as they see fit. This chapter examines a number of examples of translators' opposition and the different ways in which such opposition has been perceived, sometimes as dishonest and unjustified distortion, yet in other cases as a valid strategy in the interests of adaptation, improvement or new creation. It looks at some attempts to set down general rules for what is acceptable, which have led some to try and establish clear distinctions between different types of text requiring different treatments by the translator. As is argued, these divisions (such as those drawn between literary and professional translation, or between translation, adaptation and rewriting) rarely prove to be watertight or convincing. Translation may less counterintuitively be seen as one instance of a broader activity, that of reporting or reproducing previously existent texts, which also covers acts such as quotations, indirect speech, summaries and reviews. Indeed, comparisons can be and are made between translations and some other acts of reporting; parallels are drawn and some apparent differences are shown to be less than crucial. Finally, as Davies argues, the continuum between total subservience and freely chosen opposition can be seen in these other forms of reporting too; the possibility of reducing, elaborating, distorting or transforming the original text is available to all reporters, not just translators. Instead of focusing on the specific issue of fidelity versus freedom in translation, then, it may be more profitable to take a broader view and recognize that these choices are faced by all those who are called upon to report the discourse of others.

Dispositions and Enunciations of Identity

The systemic frameworks alluded to in the previous section seem to take the linguistic and the cultural context as points of departure but they still morph into the sociological. As Chesterman (2006: 11) argues, internal frames of reference and action, such as values, ideologies, traditions, that is, 'ideas', more readily encompass the cultural, whereas 'actions', that is, social behaviour (here we may add observable linguistic behaviour) or the function of institutions concern the realm of sociology. And as is expected, so Chesterman (2006: 11) argues, both ideas and actions are causally related to each other. We can add here that this interaction is constitutive of identities, too. The issue of who we are is based, first of all, on *ideas* held as dear or poised to change due to external influences, namely, imitation (or avoidance of imitation), criticism, coercion and persuasion. Secondly, our identity configuration depends on how we all switch on our linguistic or other *skills* and *behave* in real situations when material resources or other symbolic, cultural or political opportunities allow it.

The concept that comes to mind the moment 'causality', 'tradition' and 'identity' are mentioned is 'agency'. It is a topic that has attracted increased attention, just as definitions of agency proliferate in various areas of the social sciences. Translation, as a service offered by people for people, constitutes fertile ground for this multifaceted concept. Kinnunen and Koskinen (2010: 6) economically define agency as 'willingness and ability to act', where 'willingness' refers to internal dispositions, relating to issues of intentionality, reflexivity and ethics, and 'ability', on the other hand, refers to interactive dyads of power (dominant-dominated), as well as to choice and action in time and space (Kinnunen & Koskinen, 2010: 6, 7). In other words, agency only makes sense in the context of a constant dialogue between individuals or between individuals and structures in society. Koskinen follows up this point by exploring the issue of causality, a problematic notion in the humanities, given that causal links are notoriously difficult to establish. As Koskinen (2010: 183) argues, the binarism of agency on the one hand, and structure/causality on the other is counterintuitive because 'causality in human behaviour is often agent-based, cognitive and motivated, whereas agency is limited in many ways and causally constrained by the structural positions where the agents are located' (Koskinen, 2010: 183). Both agency and structure need to be examined by TS researchers if they are to offer even modest explanations about translation behaviour in certain contexts.

Searching for answers to such pertinent questions for TS led a growing number of researchers to turn to the work of the French sociologist Pierre

Bourdieu. From the first models of describing cultural fields in the early 1990s (see Lambert, 1995) to Simeoni's (1998) seminal article on habitus and the 2005 special issue of *The Translator*, a methodological toolkit was (re)discovered in order to better understand agency, power and cultural evolution. The debate on Bourdieu's compatibility with other systemic approaches notwithstanding (Hermans, 1999: 131–132), relevant concepts have been readily introduced in translation with a view to exploring the links between the individual and the collective, the conscious and the unconscious (Lambert, 1995: 121). Of great interest here is the concept of habitus; its usefulness is summarized by Gouanvic (2005: 148), who argues that the usual object of research in TS boils down to an analysis of habitus, namely: (a) the two-way relation between the habitus of various (interacting) translation agents and their respective target fields; and (b) the study of STs and target texts (TTs) as instantiations of habitus traits. Gouanvic adds that, in essence, a translator becomes the agent of an author, first being drawn to specific authors and then conveying their 'discourse', wording, syntax and rhythm, but in a way that conforms to this particular translator's habitus, as formed in the TC literary (or other) field (Gouanvic, 2005: 158, 159).

Various oppositional effects can be explored when visiting the concept of habitus. This is a notion that allowed Bourdieu to place individual agency within the powerful matrix of social conditioning, thus opposing both structuralist determinism (societal objectivity) and a purposeful action model (individual subjectivity). Habitus can help to explain how agents in society come fully equipped with a feel for the game (Bourdieu & Wacquant, 1996: 115–116) or a facility for unconscious strategizing in every form of social activity (Bourdieu & Wacquant, 1996: 128–129). Bourdieu's definition is as follows:

> [Habitus is a system] of durable, transposable dispositions, structured structures predisposed to function as structuring structures, that is, as principles which generate and organize practices and representations that can be objectively adapted to their outcomes without presupposing a conscious aiming at ends or an express mastery of the operations necessary in order to attain them. (Bourdieu, 1999: 53)

The acuity of Bourdieu's model of social practice allowed him to make the extraordinary claim that a set of basic dispositions can cut across a great range of social practices, ranging from the physical (posture) to the discursive (manner of speaking). These dispositions could also be seen to operate across a swathe of fields intra- and inter-socially (say from the field of the economy to the field of culture and from the cultural field in one area of the world to that of another). It then comes as no surprise that TS readily adopted the notion for two main reasons: firstly, because translation is a global action influenced by various areas of activity beyond the state–national sphere; and secondly, because habitus may counter the apparent bias of notions such as 'norms' towards the 'structured' aspect of agency (Simeoni, 1998: 21, 22), possibly providing a clearer picture of a translator's identity, the interaction of their overt behaviour and internal, organized principles. As Simeoni argues, translation developed historically through 'coercion' (external economic, political and religious pressures) to become a profession of an 'internalized subservience' to the language, the ST author, the client, the requirements of the target setting and so on (Simeoni, 1998: 12). Yet there is a more active, 'structuring' angle here, because translation is equally defined by sanctions and voluntary emulation, based on a translator's professional experience and social trajectory (Simeoni, 1998: 23). All translators start with a general, 'social' habitus, as Simeoni argues, and they eventually hone it to a specialized habitus; hence the tension felt when a translator needs to comply with not-as-yet-internalized norms of operation or, conversely, a feeling of ease when the repertoire of acquired skills is varied enough to facilitate their 'guided encounter' with the specifications of a given translation task (Simeoni, 1998: 27). The act of translation seems to be a constant negotiation, acceptance and rejection of modes of working. To recall the Bourdieusian model, a habitus is in constant flux; it is formed under specific opportunities and constraints giving rise to categories of perception and appreciation; thus, it may produce practices that tally with existing societal structures, or it may be modified as those structures gradually change, and, occasionally, it may be in direct opposition to them (Swartz, 1997: 212, 213). Contingent regularities/oppositions can be seen in all three cases, as the chapters of this volume illustrate.

In the field of queer studies and translation, research has focused on key techniques of identity formation. For example, it has been suggested that strongly parodical textual acts in fiction, also known as 'camp talk', link communities of homosexual men and create the context for opposition to hegemonic structures and values (Harvey, 2003: 70). This is perhaps achieved in subtle, complex ways in poetry, an area where the semiotic potential of language for subversion/inversion can reach a high level of diversification. A good example is the pervasive metaphor of 'the closet', as a semi-hidden performance of gay identity. Habitus instantiations of the closet (e.g. in images or ambiguous grammatical gender) can be used to signal both hiding from the forces of order that seek to contain homosexuality – which give rise to the act of hiding in the first place – and an act of injecting mainstream societal norms with the viewpoint of those oppressed by them (see Papanikolaou (2005: 254) on the poetry of Cavafy or 'Kavafis'). This is a 'structured' event, because ambivalent moves are the mainstay of minority identities, but also a 'structuring' act: readers of poems are unsettled and made complicit, so that 'an impeded spectacle' becomes an 'enforced viewpoint' (Papanikolaou, 2005: 253).

Such identity issues are at the centre of David Kinloch's chapter. This becomes apparent from the very first lines where the authorial 'I' is visible and serves as a preamble to the competing origins that form a backdrop against which the author constructs his own voice. The chapter discusses this authorial trajectory by revisiting the fragments of local and global voices that merge into a distinct queer Glaswegian poetic persona. This trajectory reveals various oppositional networks and collective 'assemblages of forms that make up a semiotic regime' (Venuti, 1998b: 136), revealing tensions between and re-evaluations of a minoritarian and majoritarian habitus. A corollary of this process, of course, is the extension of the meaning of the concept 'translation'. Broadly defined, then, translation entails the following conditions (see Zethsen, 2007: 299): a ST exists or has existed at some point in time; a transfer into another language, genre or medium has taken place and the resulting products bears some similarity to the original that depends on the 'skopos' of the derived text. Both oppositional networks and the broader definition of translation can be seen in the sources of inspiration Kinloch has identified. First, the Glaswegian poet Tom Leonard, who produced intralingual translations of, say, American poems, into the Glaswegian dialect. Since poetry is said to have the potential to foreignize without the actual influence of the foreign (Barbe, 1996: 334), the effect of Leonard's approach is one of blurring the boundaries between foreignization and domestication. In this way, the TT creates multiple oppositions to the perception of language as a transparent medium, to aesthetic values and to the dominant ideology of the mainstream middle class ('hardmen'). Edwin Morgan, the second source of inspiration for Kinloch, and the late Scottish poet laureate, exhibits a deft use of ambivalences and silences, thus capitalizing on the conditioned/conditioning function of the 'closet', as discussed above. Morgan both ventriloquized in his own poems and directly translated the work of eastern European poets, paying special attention to STs with conflicted figures. The use of Scots and English and of silences signals (political) censorship and the homoerotic experience. Finally, Kinloch further sharpens the focus on the process of writing as an act of translation by analysing a long poem by the 20th-century Scottish poet Hugh McDiarmid. Although on the surface McDiarmid's modernist poem

A Drunk Man Looks at the Thistle (1926) seems like an odd option for exploring queer voices, this poem is, according to Kinloch, ideal owing to its constant Derridean deferral of meaning. An engaged reading of the poem generates the 'enforced viewpoint' of ambiguities and oppositions that are the hallmarks of an exploration of sexuality. The poem is, literally and metaphorically, hovering between 'languages': the alternating use of Scots and English, the play between enunciation and opacity, the transvestic ventriloquizing narrator, the residues of crib translations of other European poets' work, the use of adaptations and footnotes. This is a complex imbrication of major and minor discourses, hetero- and homosexual identities, original production and reiteration/translation.

Examining the translation of prose, Saliha Paker's chapter focuses on similar fault lines of aesthetic conventions, creativity and authorial intervention. The work examined is Latife Tekin's *Buzdan Kılıçlar* and its translation into English as *Swords of Ice* by Saliha Paker and Mel Kenne. As Paker argues, Tekin remains Turkey's foremost experimental novelist, a questioning, provocative voice preoccupied by the dynamics of poverty and marginality. In a habitus-enacting and self-effacing manner, Tekin presents herself not as a writer, but as a translator who channels a dispossessed world into the mainstream. It is because of this, Paker argues, that the novel in its Turkish original can be interpreted as a translation in which there is a tension between dispossession and possession, between the mute and those who have a voice. The novel focuses on the 'shadow community', a group of 'ragged men' who are 'hapless players controlled by economic and social forces' in unnamed neighbourhoods in a nameless city, which is taken to be İstanbul. Paker's discussion centres on the 'shadow words' in the novel, a term which she uses to describe the words that have been stolen from 'the others' since the dispossessed do not have words of their own, and which, Paker argues, constitute the actual medium of translation. In addition, Paker suggests that *Buzdan Kılıçlar* instantiates a style which can be taken as a manifesto for literary-political and ideological opposition, as it comes in the wake of and is framed against Tekin's earlier novels that had been severely criticized. Paker makes use of paratextual discourse such as interviews with the author and the Prologue to *Buzdan Kılıçlar* to analyse this manifesto. A contrast to the 'author as translator' figure is provided in the final section of her chapter, where Paker explores the role of the English translators of this work. There, a parallel can be drawn between Paker as translator talking about the translation she herself has produced (with Mel Kenne) of a novel that was written/translated by a woman who identifies with the poor and dispossessed she is writing about. In an act of double translation/intervention, the translators have attempted to foreground the universal otherness of the 'shadow class' as well as an expected Turkish otherness in the translation. This is a chapter about making the marginal the central, a potentially uncomfortable opposition which is played out in what Paker calls the 'original translation' and the English translation.

Issues of authorial–translatorial and interlingual–translatorial agency are also problematized in Michela Baldo's chapter, in which translation is seen as a heuristic tool of self-discovery, evident both in original writing as well as in translation. This is possible in literary texts where hybrid identities are portrayed and/or reworked. Baldo uses a case study that illustrates this point rather well: a trilogy of novels by Nino Ricci, an author who operates in the cultural space of second-generation Italian-Canadian immigrants. The trilogy was particularly successful in Canada and was subsequently 'repatriated' by Italian translator Gabriella Iacobucci in 2004 (and also adapted by Jerry Ciccoritti for a TV mini-series in the same year). It can be argued that mobile, temporally discontinued communities, such as the Italian-Canadians, feature prominently as cultural groups of 'translated beings' (Cronin, 2006: 45); in other words, they are forced to constantly negotiate observed (linguistic) behaviour and (indirectly experienced) cultural values around them. The texts examined by Baldo represent a field in which a semi-assimilated community find themselves in a state of incongruity between their recent past in the host country and their own inherently Italian traditions, between the old world (and its idyllic representation) and the new world (with its own cultural stereotyping practices). The hybridity of identities in the textual tradition represented by Ricci's work is signalled in the ST habitus, the special admixture of minority 'codes'; such codes are normally constitutive of these communities and in literature they acquire the additional function of mimesis, or representation of a mode of communicating. Baldo borrows the notion of code-switching as a contextualization cue in spoken communication (Gumperz, 1982) and adapts it to the specificities of written communication, that is, the cognitive and narrative requirements of novels. Baldo argues that contextualization can be linked to the notions of focalization and voice, as evidenced in the subtle and meaningful interaction of linguistic features within the matrix of the text. Both direct speech and narrative sequences in Ricci's trilogy are interspersed with linguistic fragments that collide, serving as icons or indices of ideological positioning (outgroups/ingroups): Canadian English, French, Standard Italian, *italiese* (a blend of *italiano* and *inglese*), and features of the Molisan dialect in Italian. Seen in this light, code-switching is an act of translation/interpretation in the original that brings the plot forward and facilitates a critique of domestic and foreign values alike. Iacobucci's translation into Italian retains only some of these features in the text, trying to compensate for the inevitable loss in distinct ways (yet not consistently so). As Baldo illustrates, with the texts coming a full linguistic and cultural circle, the needs of the publishing house and a new audience are addressed, causing translation loss and a shift in focalization. The final product can be seen as a site of opposition with respect to the age-old ethical imperative to represent accurately the cultural other. The effacement of the superimposition of codes in Ricci's translated work echoes Berman's suggestion that there is a need to be both conscious of and in the position to examine actively the 'tendencies or *forces* that cause translation to deviate from its essential aim', which is what he also calls the 'negative analytic' of translation (Berman, 2000: 286, original emphasis).

Carol O'Sullivan explores the issue of oppositional agency in a case in which the translator's ideological position clashes with the content/references of the original. Taking Lawrence Venuti's notion of 'simpatico' in literary translation as the point of departure, O'Sullivan problematizes the ethical assumption of ST author–translator ideological/cultural alignment and suggests two 'agential modes' in translation: concessionary and preventive. The former refers to translation contexts where the agents of translation generally espouse the socio-cultural load of the original, and allow it to be channelled as such in the TC, making sure that it undergoes undertranslation (modifications and omissions) in the parts that are less palatable in the TC. A preventive translation mode, on the other hand, entails overtranslating, in an attempt to protect the target readership from the perceived deleterious content of the ST. The case study that the author presents to illustrate this point is the English translation of Comte Charles Forbes de Montalembert's *De l'avenir politique de l'Angleterre* (1855) [*The Political Future of England*]; the text, a political tract praising the English socio-political status quo and suggesting further democratic reforms as well as the re-adoption of Roman Catholicism, constituted covert critical political commentary against repression in France at the time. O'Sullivan traces the complex trajectory of the translation as well as the debate it caused. The initiator and translator of the first version in English was John Wilson Croker (1780–1857), an Irish lawyer and Tory politician. In the introduction and a series of footnotes that Croker prolifically added in this first edition, he attacked Montalembert's political and religious views, as well as the consistency, argumentation and style of the text, always spelling out the fact that the comments made in the ST concerned France and not England. The ensuing debate (with the involvement of the ST author, by proxy) resulted in a second edition, where the paratextual material was whittled down. The remaining main body of the text, however, throws up interesting questions with respect to the *antipatico* role in translation. Omissions were kept to a minimum, but the translator effected a repositioning of participants by employing such devices as cohesion shifts, additions for explicitation purposes, and shifts of (grammatical) agency. Thus a preventive translation mode in this instance (and beyond) can mean channelling the 'dangerous' material accurately, but with subtle 'improvements' that lay bare the specificities of the original, possibly effecting a change in the TT audience design, from 'addressees' to 'eavesdroppers' (Mason, 2000: 4). Such agential interventions in paratextual and textual material can be extended beyond political texts, to politicized literature (see Von Flotow, 1997: 28, 44), to journalistic texts (see Bielsa & Bassnett, 2009: 124–131), and historiography (see Mason, 2000: 7–16), to name but a few. They also highlight the importance of linking translation techniques to certain effects, but only by considering how these effects are likely to arise in specific habitus-forming contexts, something that Venuti's classic foreignization/domestication framework lacks (see Bennett, 1999: 131).

A dual structure-agency perspective allows a more holistic approach to translation, often revealing interesting opposition effects. For example, tension may be felt when (TC) circumstances do not tally with a habitus already formed under different opportunities and constraints. The chapter by Christina Delistathi explores this phenomenon among 'competitive peers' in translation, by focusing on a moment of political crisis. The approach adopted recalls views on discourse as an ideological practice, in that it sustains or changes 'significations of the world from diverse positions in power relations' as well as political practice, namely both as a site as well as a stake in power struggles (Fairclough, 1992: 67). Translation is, of course, an organic part of this process, because it serves as a channel of 'the migration and transformation of discursive elements between different discourses' (Robyns, 1994: 408). Looking at dynamic interactions of power within political minorities, Delistathi investigates processes of legitimation and political identity-formation in Greece in the first half of the 20th century. Her case study concerns the attempts of the newly formed, counter-hegemonic Greek Communist Party (KKE) to control the political scene of the Left. As part of this agenda, translations and retranslations became the sites of maintaining party orthodoxy and of eliminating competition from rival Trotskyist groups or individuals that did not fully conform to the KKE's world view. This discursive battle can be simultaneously placed in a broader global context of political developments at the time as well as significant socio-political shifts in Greece. It was a precedent-setting struggle that was to become one of the most influential conceptual frames for the social movements that developed in the second half of the 20th century. As Delistathi argues, the height of this activity can be traced back to the early 1930s. A key text that captures very aptly the dispositions at that time is the Greek translation of the *Communist Manifesto*. The KKE attempted to promote its own interpretation of this seminal political text and to become the sole arbiter of Marxist ideology in Greece. The focus of the analysis is the 1933 version of the *Communist Manifesto*. The text is seen as an emblematic text, representing entire political groupings and advancing 'enthymemes', that is, evaluative reminders of political provenance in three ways: in the paratextual configuration of the book, in the authenticity of the translation (as evidenced in ST glosses, temporal/social dialect options), and in accompanying reviews/debates that contested the quality of each translation and what was perceived as the skewing of Marxist ideals by previous translations.

The concept of opposition in language transfer is considered from a dual perspective in Małgorzata Tryuk's chapter: exploring aspects of community interpreting work in the Auschwitz-Birkenau concentration camp, she examines the role of the interpreter as one that shifts between opposition to the SS camp guards and sometimes to the inmates themselves; she also shows how interpreting under conditions where terror and an aggressively monolingual environment prevail can be understood as opposing the specialized habitus of community interpreting. The fact that the information about camp interpreters in the Auschwitz-Birkenau Memorial and Museum Archives, from which Tryuk draws her material, is sparse shows that the function of the camp interpreters was perhaps one that was often overlooked or underestimated. Tryuk's chapter serves to bring these individuals to the fore and argues that interpreting in such extreme conditions was frequently more than just transferring information from one language to another; it was often a means of survival. Surviving in the concentration camp without any knowledge of German was practically impossible, as information was crucial for obtaining – illegally – the bare necessities, such as food and clothing, and for avoiding illness, overwork and the brutality of SS soldiers. Tryuk focuses her profiling on the *Lagerdolmetscher*, prisoners who were used as interpreters in the camp, with interpreting mainly required from German into Polish, but also from German into French, Czech and Russian. The *Lagerdolmetscher* did not have any additional privileges or exemptions from work, yet they had access to information which could be used to help others in the camp. This uneasy position as go-betweens acting in a space between the oppressors and the oppressed that Tryuk highlights shows the best and worst of human behaviour. The recollections from the Archives that she uses show interpreters who themselves were beaten by the SS guards, interpreters who relished the job and 'carried out all the [guards'] orders with zeal', interpreters who hoped that they would be rewarded by the inmates for their services if they ever survived the camp, and interpreters who simply hoped to help other inmates and ease, no matter how trivially, their existence in the camp. The *Lagerdolmetscher* were required not only to interpret camp orders, rules and directions, but also to interpret at hearings, when new prisoners arrived at the camp, and also to interpret during interrogations. It is perhaps in the interpreting during interrogations that the opposition to the professional habitus of interpreting really comes to light: one inmate says that he addressed his answers during an interrogation to the female inmate who was interpreting, rather than to the camp official; another interpreter says he 'tried to frame the answer to favour the defendants'. This is interpreting where the outcome could be the difference between life and death, where, Tryuk argues, the role of the interpreter is 'a deeply human role' that cannot be 'unbiased' or 'neutral', and as such the generally accepted principles of community interpreting simply cannot apply.

Socio-cultural Gates and Gate-keeping

Structured and structuring dispositions are indissolubly linked with the very environment that feeds into them, Bourdieu's fields. As a metaphor, 'field' refers to a circumscribed 'space' of structured societal networks where agents occupy different positions. There, they confront each other using strategies that maintain or change the balance of forces, that is, the distribution of economic, cultural, social and symbolic capital at their disposal (Bourdieu & Wacquant, 1996: 101). Each field is in essence circumscribed by the specific species of capital that is contested within it, such as cultural capital and economic capital in the case of the intellectual and the business fields respectively. Yet despite their differences, fields have some common properties. Without wishing to oversimplify Bourdieu's intricate conceptual apparatus here, we can concentrate on two, *homology* and *autonomy* (Bourdieu, 1995: 72–77), because they can be directly linked to the research carried out by contributors to this volume (and beyond).

All fields exhibit structural and functional *homologies*. Put differently, they develop isomorphic properties, such as positions of dominance and subordination, struggles for exclusion and usurpation, and mechanisms of reproduction and change (Bourdieu & Wacquant, 1996: 106). And such homologies 'travel' intra-socially. For example, in the field of cultural production, producers compete with each other and pursue personal interests linked to their position of dominance or subordination, with the ensuing patterns of opposition resulting in the constant change of cultural products (and the formation of schools of thought, ingroups and outgroups); then the supply of cultural products meets another taste-forming force (without necessarily having to seek it), and that is demand which, in turn, is shaped by the competitive struggles between different classes or class factions over material or cultural goods (Bourdieu, 2002: 230, 231). Homologies explain why individuals with dominant positions in society tend to consume luxury goods, or 'emblems of class', which producers, in turn, produce and showcase, striving towards senior positions in the field of cultural production (Bourdieu, 2002: 232). Struggles in the cultural field become euphemized class struggles, simply because the habitus of agents instructs them to perceive things around them in terms of durable oppositions, such as 'high' versus 'low'.

Bourdieu has only occasionally dealt with the way homologies 'match' inter-socially, using the English term 'gate-keepers' for agents facilitating cultural transfer (Meylaerts, 2005: 279). In the very few instances where he does address this issue, however, an opportunity is missed to actually explain initial (adequacy/acceptability), text-linguistic (formulation) and preliminary (translation policy) norms with the rigour that a 'field model' could afford (Meylaerts, 2005: 282). This gap did not escape the attention of TS researchers. Gouanvic, for example, examined the ways in which American science fiction was grafted onto the French context in the 1950s. Cultural production and the production of science fiction in particular were fields where agents assumed their positions and took part in a struggle for prestige. This genre, defined against the backdrop of more canonical literature in the US cultural field, successfully caught on in France at the time, because there was a group *homologous* to that of the technophile lower middle class in the US, a group that sought to acquire greater social power. French translators became the main 'gate-keepers' for the counterpart of this group in France. By translating and essay writing, they succeeded in institutionalizing the genre, especially since, as cultural producers, they happened to enjoy a high degree of legitimacy at that time (Gouanvic, 1997: 145). Both in the USA and in France science fiction texts were 'classified' under specific *socio-discursive models*, stories which 'instantiate ideological positions in the social space of a given period by means of relatively homogeneous thematics' (Gouanvic, 1997: 139). By translating certain texts (and not others), agents of translation (including publishers) were able to promote a specific point of view (e.g. social criticism through the presentation of utopias). Such a 'move' became instantly comprehensible and was well received by the readership, also in pursuit of their own interests in the struggle for power (Gouanvic, 1997: 144). The grafting was complete when editorial structures in France (magazines, series titles, publishing outlets) homologous to those in the USA were created, supporting models which determined the (marginal) position of such cultural goods in the market (Gouanvic, 1997: 137).

The second property of fields, *autonomy*, concerns defining the 'inside' and 'outside' margins of fields, that is, the stakes of the game involved. All fields tend to rely on their own principles of organization, resisting outside influences to a greater or lesser extent. A prime example is the 'literary and artistic field', which is contained within the field of power, the latter being contained within the field of class relations (Bourdieu, 1993: 37, 38). When the laws of these external fields 'reign unchallenged', the field of cultural production becomes more *heteronomous*; it is subject to the laws prevailing in the field of power (political/economic profit) (Bourdieu, 1993: 38). When it is (relatively) impervious to such influence from the outside, the cultural field is *autonomous*; it strives to define itself in its own terms, forming hierarchies on the basis of symbolic ('prestige', 'art for art's sake') and not economic capital (Bourdieu, 1993: 38–39). Such oppositions explain why certain genres have short or long production cycles, why they secure greater or lesser profits, and why they are 'sanctioned' or even simply 'understood' by restricted socio-cultural elites, institutions or mass audiences (Bourdieu, 1993: 48, 51). They are also indicative of the performative ambiguity of cultural producers both as servants of dominant groups and as experts who are in a position to defend the autonomy of their field and probably intervene in political matters (Bourdieu, 1990: 145).

When specifically considered for the area of translation, autonomy creates theoretical doubts but also methodological opportunities. Simeoni sounds rather sceptical about whether translation can be seen as a field in its own right. As he argues:

> The real proof of belonging to the field is found when the relevant decisions made by the stakeholders are taken with an eye on what their peers are doing, either to go along with them, or to oppose them. As things stand, only very restricted fields of this kind (usually identified by the presence of literary retranslations, or polemical translations), fit the description. (Simeoni, 1998: 26)

Translation is by default hetero-circumscribed, a professional area of service to whichever field wishes to use the translated document. Autonomy can only be seen in the self-contained area of translation criticism, as the quote above implies. Yet as a part of the field of cultural production or economic activity, translation can be seen to contribute actively to the development or even genesis of such fields, occasionally allowing views on heteronomy to transpire. For example, Gouanvic has shown how the autonomy of the French literary field was strengthened further by the emergence of an autonomous literary field of foreign literature in the early 20th century. This occurred after a generic 'gate' was opened, that is, establishing a special series, and when various heteronomy-related 'facts of publication' came into play, that is, censorial interventions and signed contracts (Gouanvic, 2005: 152–157). Interestingly, calls for resistive translations can be seen in nations which, according to Simeoni, feature as 'highly coercive decision centres' with respect to contractual agreements and where, therefore, translators can be seen at the bottom of the pyramid in the document creation business (Simeoni, 1998: 13). Thus translation can be seen as a rather influential yet diffuse field, with different gate-keepers intervening at different times and from various positions.

In this volume, the chapter that traces the parallel course of homologies in an ethnos (or relevant social groups therein) and its language/culture is Ibon Uribarri Zenekorta's overview of nascent literary fields in the Basque country. Through a chronological account of translation activity stretching from the 16th century to the present, the author highlights the oppositional patterns that shaped the field of translation, patterns that were conditioned by different variables: the selection of works to be translated *vis-à-vis* original production in Basque, the translation directionality (including pivot translations), and the translation strategies utilized for individual works. All these variables were under the constant influence of socio-political gate-keeping, the pressing need for the creation of a national and linguistic identity, as well as the shifting centres of power within and beyond the Basque regions. Thus in the 16th and 17th centuries translation activity (mainly carried out in the French regions) and interdialectal translations in Basque fluctuated in tandem with political patronage; thematics was restricted and a frozen style prevailed in the TT, reflecting the lack of linguistic standardization. The 18th and 19th centuries were marked by shifting values and thematics, mainly due to the influence of the Enlightenment movement as well as the rise of Basque exceptionalism; this resulted in nationally minded, domesticating translations and linguistic purism. The beginning of the 20th century witnessed the rise of original production in Basque as well as translation, the main concern being the enrichment of the national repertoire with great European classics and the adoption of genres and thematics that supported a nationalistic agenda. This trend continued after the Spanish Civil War with the return to linguistic purism and the construal of translation as an act of recreation or of repairing blemished originals. Francoist suppression followed the Civil War and the Basque language and culture were banned from public life until the *apertura* ('opening up') of the 1950s and 1960s when a distinct generation gap emerged: the older Basque generations still sought to elevate the level of their indigenous culture with specific translations and purist language, while the younger, Marxist-minded generation sought to oppose both Francoist homogenizing discourse and the older establishment of their own regions. The chapter concludes with the ongoing changes in Basque since the return to democracy: the broader administrative and educational use of Basque (this time a language with an official status), as well as the crucial role of academia, translation projects, and 'good quality translations' in the creation of intracommunal cohesion and greater visibility of a minoritarian culture in the international arena.

In some cases, field heteronomy and the oppositions it generates take on a concrete, socially relevant and divisive meaning. This is shown in José Santaemilia's chapter on the translation of sexually explicit language. The author looks at a very under-researched area inhabiting the margins of literary systems, that is, works with an erotic content. Such works throw up significant issues with the complex interrelations between pornography, obscenity and eroticism in art. According to Winick (2001: 1907), 'obscenity' usually has a legal content, 'pornography' is more subjective and indicates personal disapproval, and 'erotica' signals sensuality. Both pornography and obscenity are tied to oppositions between mass-market commodities and 'real' art, depending on an array of factors, including 'a country's economy, degree of industrialization, the role of religion, gender roles, politics and government, literacy level, socioeconomic class structure, involvement in the threat or reality of military action, relative access to communication technology, cultural history, legal system and national character' (Winick, 2001: 1907). As a result, the thematics or function of works with sexually explicit content may polarize a society or acquire an oppositional appeal or lose this oppositional appeal as new media and new social constituencies emerge in interrelated, homologous fields. The subversive role of Western erotica in Eastern Bloc countries, or the division of opinion between different strands of feminism *vis-à-vis* the dehumanizing/empowering role of pornography are good examples of this (Winick, 2001: 1909–1910). The complex diachronic or synchronic development of such debates can be captured in specific works of art and then transferred (or muted) in translations that travel across space and time. Santaemilia indicates precisely that, by focusing on Aldudena Grandes' *Las edades de*

Lulú, first published in 1989. This is a work that outlines the relationship between Lulú, a middle-class young woman, and Pablo, a close family friend who seduces her into the world of sexual hedonism. *Las edades de Lulú* in essence constitutes a barometer of current trends in Spain as it captures the full transition from Spain's Francoist past to a democratic society where the position of women as authors, narrators and characters, and the value of individuals in society in general were rapidly transforming. Thus the whole novel can be seen as a palimpsest of oppositional loads: an opposition to the literary mainstream, to expectations on 'proper' language usage (especially for women – see also Coates, 2004: 97), to gender roles (sexual experimentation), and to publishing practices (commodification of literature). *Las edades de Lulú* tapped into a market that was ready to accept subversive material along these lines and achieved a great degree of 'mainstreaming' and recognition. The book was consequently translated into English in 1993 by Sonia Sotto, an experienced translator working for a prestigious publisher. Santaemilia concentrates on what he perceives to be the common denominator in works with erotic content, namely, sexually explicit language, and more specifically on how two of the functional categories of sexually explicit language fared. The first, the depiction of sexual urges/actions, was in the main desexualized in the TT. The second, emphatic intensifiers and swear words, were less diverse in the TT. Ultimately, Santaemilia's case study problematizes the notion of equivalence by looking at different literary, linguistic and value systems and their complex interaction, as arenas where opposition brings literary evolution and the potential for expression forward.

Perhaps the most extreme case of heteronomy and social polarization can be seen in contexts of war. These are cases where 'split or even strained loyalties' are not tolerated and where 'one's identity is almost completely constructed and enforced by other actors' (Baker, 2010: 200). Tomislav Longinović explores the political and linguistic fragmentation that came in the wake of the Wars of Yugoslav Succession (1991–1995). This is an extreme example of abrupt shifts in hegemonic and subaltern sociocultural positions for an area that formerly remained cohesive under the guise of a unitary communist state. Serbo-Croatian as a lingua franca of the region was violently 'dethroned' and challenged after the dissolution of Yugoslavia. Seen through a nationalistic and religious prism, Serbo-Croatian was divided up into languages that Longinović describes as 'non-identical twins' and which today lack the symbolism of orthographic hyphenation. As Longinović argues in his chapter, this act might appear counterintuitive on historical/linguistic grounds. Regional varieties that had historically sprawled over ethnic group constellations were subject to standardization a long time ago, as a result of the political impetus of all ethnic groups to oppose the rule of the Hapsburgs and the Ottomans; this constituted a way of promoting a narrative of a united Slavic ethnos. Even today, minor variations on the lexical, graphological and grammatical levels sprawl over isogloss enclaves that usually defy the geo-political boundaries of ethnic disparities. The ways of conveying meaning linguistically have remained similar, yet lines of division have become more distinct with the contribution of political and cultural elites that serve a public narrative of exceptionalism in each community. In this context, translation serves as a tool of alterity, a distancing practice that takes place even in cases where the codes used are mutually intelligible. A striking example used by Longinović is the first screening of a Serbian film after the Serbo-Croatian war in (intralingual) subtitles for the Croatian audiences. Such tactics have also been employed in the area of literary translation, where individual Serbian works are presented to readers after minimal interventions are made to re-fashion them into Croatian texts.

The inner workings and opposition effects within fields become more apparent in contexts of social policy interventions and cultural questioning, as the last two chapters of this volume indicate. As Chris Rundle argues in his chapter on the 1930s Fascist regime in Italy, when looking at the history of translation in totalitarian contexts, it is easy to assume that this will be a history of rigid repression and closure. Rundle sets out to show how the Fascist regime's attitude towards translation, especially the translation of literature, actually evolved from a relative tolerance to one of increasing hostility in direct relation to certain key events, namely, the creation of an Italian empire in Africa and then the introduction of anti-Semitic legislation. What emerges is that, as long as translation could be interpreted as a form of positive cultural exchange, then it posed no ideological problem and the regime took no concrete action to obstruct it – even when it became clear that Italy was actually more receptive and published more translations than any other country. But once the cultural debate came to be dominated by the rhetoric of imperial dominance and racial superiority, translation then came to be perceived as a form of cultural weakness in the first instance, and as a form of cultural pollution in the second. It was at this relatively late stage that the regime actually introduced concrete measures designed specifically to restrict the number of translations being published. What also emerges, in Rundle's opinion, is that the regime felt far more threatened by the symbolic value of translation as an indicator of its own cultural failure, than it did by any specific texts and their perceived impact.

In her chapter, Camino Gutiérrez Lanza looks at the censorship for dubbed and subtitled films that was in place – and evolving – in Spain during the 1950s and 1960s. Gutiérrez Lanza provides a detailed overview of the conservative censorship board that saw itself as a moral guardian for cinema goers, and then tracks the *aperture* ('opening up'), as a widespread liberalism began to take hold and institutional readjustments were made, generating opposition between the pro- and anti-regime groups. Using the TRACE cinema catalogue, unpublished reports, ministerial decisions and reports written by cinema censors, Gutiérrez Lanza shows that the 'the moral threshold was gradually being raised'. The new 'Cinema Classification and Censorship Board' was created in 1962 and was headed up by José María García Escudero, whose role in the new liberal and more lenient board Gutiérrez Lanza explores in some detail. The new board approved many of the dubbed films which had been banned by earlier authorities on the grounds of poor moral standards, and Gutiérrez Lanza uses the data in the TRACE project to demonstrate that films classified as 'seriously dangerous' by religious censors could still be given approval for showing. These changes to censorship and moral arguments had a practical effect on the work of translators who dubbed and subtitled foreign films for distribution in Spain: 'to avoid the film being banned, both translators and distributors made changes to the screenplay before seeking approval of the censorship board' while 'dialogue left unaltered in the translated version were, however, later revised and changed by the censors'. The case study of the film *The Best of Everything* (Negulesco, 1959) serves to highlight the negotiations that took place not only between censors and distributors but also between the censors themselves. Changes to the dubbed screenplay are presented, clearly showing the elimination, or at least 'toning-down', of any morally dubious content. Despite the changes and its subsequent approval by the censorship board (the film was eventually classified in April 1963 as a film for adults over the age of 18), some censors were still in favour of banning it; the film's saving grace, however, was that it presented a depiction of American society and not Spanish society. This chapter constitutes an insightful analysis of how opposing views *vis-à-vis* censorship were formed and negotiated during a period of change.

Conclusion

All contributors to this volume have indicated, directly or indirectly, that an uncomplicated view of (audiovisual) translation and interpreting as acts of mechanical transfer does not hold. The practices and effects investigated here go against a 'super-meme', to use Chesterman's term (1997: 8): "'the path schema", with the translation itself being the "trajector" moving along this path [...] the idea that translation "carry across" something from A to B'. This is a view arguably sustained by the metaphors that the etymology of the word 'translation' in many languages triggers: 'carry/lead across' in many European languages (e.g. 'cross over', or *prevođenje* in Croatian; Longinović, personal communication, 17 February 2010). The same schema remains dormant in standard terminology used in TS (source and target language/culture). Yet, as Chesterman aptly observes, although translation is directional, there is no 'moving' involved, simply because the source is no longer a source or might become redundant after the translation (Chesterman, 1997: 8). It is more useful to think of translation as a transformation (Chesterman, 1997: 8), a message in one language or mode 'evolving' into a different entity, to play on Chesterman's sustained genetic metaphors. A text is routinely pressed into 'evolution' to satisfy the needs of translators, clients, audiences, publishing industry intermediaries, literary-aesthetic conventions and socio-cultural formations in probably both 'A' and 'B' contexts.

If translation is a matter of transformation/evolution, oppositional effects can ripple through the entire life cycle of each instance of communication and every area of identity formation that translation agency affects. The following interrelated, constituent areas of identities have been singled out in this volume:

- The deeper levels of beliefs and ideas, which are fed both by personal traits, needs or views of individual translators, interpreters, audiovisual translation experts, as well as by the great social structures they are part of; the latter are responsible for allowing relatively consistent patterns of value-formation to emerge.
- The cultural products/texts themselves, each semiotically attached to networks of other texts and being characterized by its own distinctive features and level of complexity; some STs may already be 'translations' in the literal or metaphorical sense to start with; more importantly, 'ideas' inhabit them, which necessitate a minimal or considerable transformation, in (mis)translation in the narrow sense or more broadly in rewriting, reviewing, paratextual mediation and performance.
- The interacting social fields involved; these are the greater forces that provide the context for competitive struggles and collaboration. Interpreters and (audiovisual) translators participate in multiple

fields and the limits of their actions are circumscribed by the (tacit) rules, conditions and censorial attitudes of each field.
- The active agency of translators; since translators intra- and inter-socially participate in multiple fields, be they social or specifically translational, they experience various performative ambiguities and dilemmas. They can choose or be forced to align themselves with the structures around them or, alternatively, to insulate themselves. They can also serve as gate-keepers of 'foreign material' in a preventive or concessional way.
- The 'switching on' of abilities; given various opportunities and constraints, the professional (Chesterman, 2001: 141), the linguistic/semiotic, and the ethical competence (see Kadric & Kaindl, 1997: 138, 139–140) of translators is often put to the test; the way the translation is carried out ultimately depends on prior internalization and negotiation of codes of practice, personal experience, as well as on the level of freedom or duress under which individuals operate.

Perhaps it is fitting to end this chapter with a quote closer to the UK reality and which can show, yet again, how the very act of translation can evoke oppositional perspectives. A 2006 article by the BBC entitled 'Translation Costing Public £100m' reported the following:

> Phil Woolas, Communities Minister, said: 'She [Communities Secretary Ruth Kelly] has already made clear that public services need to give far greater priority to promoting social cohesion and shared values rather than supporting separateness and we are examining the issue of translation in this context.' (BBC News, 12 December 2006: online)

Translation and public service interpreting at the time of this report were seen by officials as an expensive luxury that threatened the integrity of a shared value of unity. In his statement, Woolas obscures the fact that the fabric of society may be multilingual to start with and that integration may be happening in tandem with translation. If we leave the unity-in-diversity argument to one side, there are more fundamental issues at stake here. Given the current state of affairs, properly trained translators/interpreters could be seen to prevent incalculable (financial) damage to society when miscommunication ensues (work-hours lost to incomprehensible/confusing instructions, safety issues and miscarriages of justice). Expecting translation to be a force of division without weighing up the outcome throws up significant ethical questions. As it seems, opposition effects encompassing all the identity levels listed above continue to reverberate in our everyday lives.

Acknowledgement

Here I must personally give my special thanks to Dr Catherine Slater, the copy-editor, whose sharp eye for detail, professionalism and flair are uniquely informed by her academic interest in translation. The completion of this chapter was made easier and speedier, especially because Catherine contributed summaries for the pieces by Saliha Paker, Małgorzata Truyk, James Baer and Camino Gutiérrez Lanza. I am grateful to her for her advice and help.

Notes

1. On 11 October 2010, two policemen, Epameinondas Korkoneas and Vasilis Saraliotis, were sentenced to over 25 years and 10 years in prison respectively for the murder of Alexis Gregoropoulos.
2. See http://www.sarantakos.com/isocrat.htm.
3. See http://archive.enet.gr/online/online_fpage_text/id=46806532,60989316,67495172.
4. The full ST can be found online at the Tufts University *Perseus Project*, at http://www.perseus.tufts.edu/hopper/text?doc=Perseus%3Atext%3A1999.01.0143%3Aspeech%3D7%3Asection%3D20. Accessed 8.6.10.
5. For an excellent overview of the staging and reception of Ibsen in Europe, see Chapter 3 in Anderman (2005: 75–119).

References

Anderman, G. (2005) *Europe on Stage. Translation and Theatre*. London: Oberon Books.
Antoniâde, K. (2010) Το Ίντερνετ, Πηγή Συντονισμού και Έκφρασης. Οι Εξεγερμένοι του Διαδυκτίου [Internet, a source of coordination and expression. The insurgents of the world wide web]. *Eleftherotypia* 6 April 2010. On WWW at http://archive.enet.gr/online/online_text/c=112,id=14123492. Accessed 26.7.10.
Baker, M. (2006) *Translation and Conflict: A Narrative Account*. London/New York: Routledge.
Baker, M. (2010) Interpreters and translators in the war zone. Narrated and narrators. *The Translator* 16 (2), 197–222.
Barbe, K. (1996) The dichotomy *free* and *literal* translation. *Meta* 41 (3), 328–337.
BBC News (2006) Translation costing public £100m. *BBC News* 12 December 2006. On WWW at http://news.bbc.co.uk/1/hi/uk/6174303.stm. Accessed 15.10.10.
Bennett, P. (1999) Book review. *The Scandals of Translation. Towards an Ethics of Difference*. *The Translator* 5 (1), 127–134.
Berman, A. (2000) Translation and the trials of the foreign (L. Venuti, trans.). In L. Venuti (ed.) *The Translation Studies Reader* (pp. 284–297). London/New York: Routledge.

Bielsa, E. and Bassnett, S. (2009) *Translation in Global News*. London/New York: Routledge.
Boase-Beier, J. (2006) *Stylistic Approaches to Translation*. Manchester: St Jerome.
Bourdieu, P. (1990) *In Other Words. Towards a Reflexive Sociology* (M. Adamson, trans.). Oxford: Polity Press.
Bourdieu, P. (1993) *The Field of Cultural Production. Essays on Art and Literature*. Oxford: Polity Press.
Bourdieu, P. (1995) *Sociology in Question* (R. Nice, trans.). London: Sage.
Bourdieu, P. (1999) *The Logic of Practice* (R. Nice, trans.). Oxford: Polity Press.
Bourdieu, P. (2002) *Distinction. A Social Critique of the Judgement of Taste* (R. Nice, trans.). London: Routledge.
Bourdieu, P. and Wacquant, L.J.D. (1996) *An Invitation to Reflexive Sociology*. Cambridge: Polity Press.
Campbell, M. (2008) Greek riots spark fear of Europe in flames. *The Sunday Times* 14 December 2008. On WWW at http://www.timesonline.co.uk/tol/news/world/europe/article5337633.ece. Accessed 20.1.10.
Chesterman, A. (1997) *The Memes of Translation. The Spread of Ideas in Translation Theory*. Amsterdam: John Benjamins.
Chesterman, A. (2001) Proposal for a Hieronymic oath. *The Translator* 7 (2), 139–154.
Chesterman, A. (2006) Questions in the sociology of translation. In J. Duarte, A. Assis Rosa and T. Seruya (eds) *Translation Studies as the Interface of Disciplines* (pp. 9–27). Amsterdam/Philadelphia: John Benjamins.
Chesterman, A. and Wagner, E. (2002) *Can Theory Help Translators? A Dialogue Between the Ivory Tower and the Wordface*. Manchester: St Jerome.
Coates, J. (2004) *Women, Men and Language. A Sociolinguistic Account of Gender Differences in Language*. Harlow: Pearson Longman.
Cronin, M. (2006) *Translation and Identity*. London: Routledge.
Even-Zohar, I. (1990) Polysystem studies. Tel Aviv: Porter Institute for Poetics and Semiotics/Durham: Duke University Press. Special issue of *Poetics Today*, 11 (1).
Fairclough, N. (1992) *Discourse and Social Change*. Cambridge: Polity Press.
Gagarin, M. (2000) *Isocrates* (Vol. I) (M. Gagarin, introduction; D. Mirhady and Yun Lee Too, trans.). Austin: University of Texas Press.
Genette, G. (1997) *Paratexts. Thresholds of Interpretation* (J.E. Lewin, trans.). Cambridge: Cambridge University Press.
Gouanvic, J-M. (1997) Translation and the shape of things to come: The emergence of American science fiction in post-war France. *The Translator* 3 (2), 125–152.
Gouanvic, J-M. (2005) A Bourdieusian theory of translation, or the coincidence of practical instances: Field, 'habitus', capital and 'illusio'. *The Translator* 11 (2), 147–166.
Gumperz, J. (1982) *Discourse Strategies*. Cambridge: Cambridge University Press.
Harvey, K. (2003) *Intercultural Movements. American Gay in French Translation*. Manchester: St Jerome.
Hatim, B. and Mason, I. (1990) *Discourse and the Translator*. London/New York: Longman.
Hatim, B. and Mason, I. (1997) *The Translator as Communicator*. London/New York: Routledge.
Heilbron, J. (1999) Towards a sociology of translation: Book translation as a cultural world-system. *European Journal of Social Theory* 4 (2), 429–444.

Hermans, T. (1985) Translation studies and a new paradigm. In T. Hermans (ed.) *The Manipulation of Literature. Studies in Literary Translation* (pp. 7–15). London/Sydney: Croom Helm.
Hermans, T. (1999) *Translation in Systems*. Manchester: St Jerome.
IOS (2008) Η Κυριότητα της Αλήθειας [The mastery of truth]. *Eleftherotypia* 20 December 2008). On WWW at http://archive.enet.gr/online/online_fpage_text/id=46806532,60989316,67495172. Accessed 10.10.10.
Jakobson, R. (1959/2000) On linguistic aspects of translation. In L. Venuti (ed.) *The Translation Studies Reader* (pp. 113–118). London/New York: Routledge.
Kadric, M. and Kaindl, K. (1997) Asterix – Vom Gallier zum Tschetnikjäger: Zur Problematik von Massenkommunikation und übersetzerischer Ethik. In M. Snell-Hornby, Z. Jettmarová and K. Kaindl (eds) *Translation as Intercultural Communication: Selected Papers from the EST* (pp. 135–145). Amsterdam: John Benjamins.
Kinnunen, T. and Koskinen, K. (2010) Introduction. In T. Kinnunen and K. Koskinen (eds) *Translators' Agency* (pp. 4–10). Tampere: Tampere University Press.
Koskinen, K. (2010) Agency and causality: Towards explaining by mechanisms in translation studies. In T. Kinnunen and K. Koskinen (eds) *Translators' Agency* (pp. 165–187). Tampere: Tampere University Press.
Lambert, J. (1995) Translation, systems and research: The contribution of polysystem studies to translation studies. *Traduction, Terminologie, Redaction* 13 (1), 105–152.
Lefevere, A. (1982/2000) Mother Courage's cucumbers: Text, system and refraction in a theory of literature. In L. Venuti (ed.) *The Translation Studies Reader* (pp. 233–249). London: Routledge.
Lefevere, A. (1992) *Translation, Rewriting and the Manipulation of Literary Fame*. London/New York: Routledge.
Mason, I. (2000) Audience design in translating. *The Translator* 6 (1), 1–22.
Meylaerts, R. (2005) Revisiting the classics. Review article. Sociology and interculturality. Creating the Conditions for Inter-National Dialogue Across Intellectual Fields. *The Translator* 11 (2), 277–283.
Meylaerts, R. (2006) Literary heteroglossia in translation. When the language of translation is the locus of ideological struggle. In J. Duarte, A. Assis Rosa and T. Seruya (eds) *Translation Studies as the Interface of Disciplines* (pp. 85–98). Amsterdam/Philadelphia: John Benjamins.
Mouzelis, N. (2009) On the December events. In S. Economides and V. Monastiriotis (eds) *The Return of Street Politics? Essays on the December Riots in Greece* (pp. 41–44). London: LSE, The Hellenic Observatory.
Nash, W. (1989) *Rhetoric: The Wit of Persuasion*. Oxford: Blackwell.
Paloposki, O. (2009) Agency, choice and constraints in the work of the translator. In J. Milton and P. Bandia (eds) *Agents of Translation* (pp. 189–208). Amsterdam/Philadelphia: John Benjamins.
Papanikolaou, D. (2005) Words that tell and hide: Revisiting C.P. Cavafy's closets. *Journal of Modern Greek Studies* 23 (2), 235–260.
Rheingold, H. (2002) *Smart Mobs. The Next Social Revolution. Transforming Cultures and Communities in the Age of Instant Access*. Cambridge, MA: Basic Books.
Robyns, C. (1990) The normative model of twentieth century belles infidèles: Detective novels in French translation. *Target* 2 (1), 23–42.
Robyns, C. (1994) Translation and discursive identity. *Poetics Today* 15 (3), 404–428.

Rota, V. (2008) Aspects of adaptation: The translation of comics formats. In F. Zanettin (ed.) *Comics in Translation* (pp. 79–98). Manchester/Kinderhook, NY: St Jerome.
Roulet, E. (1996) Polyphony. In J. Verschueren, J-O. Östman, J. Blommaert and C. Bulcaen (eds) *Handbook of Pragmatics* (pp. 1–18). Amsterdam/Philadelphia: John Benjamins.
Shlesinger, M. (2009) Crossing the divide: What researchers and practitioners can learn from one another. *Translation and Interpreting* 1 (1), 1–16.
Simeoni, D. (1998) The pivotal status of the translator's habitus. *Target* 10 (1), 1–39.
Swartz, D. (1997) *Culture and Power, the Sociology of Pierre Bourdieu*. Chicago/London: University of Chicago Press.
Van Dijk, T.A. (1995) Discourse analysis as ideology analysis. In C. Schäffner and A. Wenden (eds) *Language and Peace* (pp. 17–33). Aldershot: Dartmouth Publishing.
Van Leeuwen, T. (2006) Towards a semiotics of typography. *Document Design* 14 (2), 139–155.
Venuti, L. (1998a) *The Scandals of Translation. Towards an Ethics of Difference*. London/New York: Routledge.
Venuti, L. (1998b) Introduction. *Translation and Minority. Special Issue. The Translator* 4 (2), 135–144.
Verschueren, J. (1996) Contrastive ideology research. Aspects of a pragmatic methodology. *Language Sciences* 18 (3–4), 589–603.
Von Flotow, L. (1997) *Translation and Gender. Translating in the Era of Feminism*. Manchester: St Jerome.
Winick, C. (2001) Pornography. In D. Jones (ed.) *Censorship: A World Encyclopedia* (Vol. 3, L–R) (pp. 1907–1912). London: Fitzroy Dearborn.
Zanettin, F. (2008) Comics in translation: An overview. In F. Zanettin (ed.) *Comics in Translation* (pp. 1–32). Manchester/Kinderhook, NY: St Jerome.
Zethsen, K. (2007) Beyond translation proper – extending the field of translation studies. *Traduction, Terminologie, Redaction* 20 (1), 281–308.

Part 1
Rewritings

Chapter 2
How Ibsen Travels from Europe to China: Ibsenism from Archer, Shaw to Hu Shi

W. ZHAO

Introduction

In Translation Studies (TS), the so-called manipulation school, and rewriting theory[1] in particular, initiated what can be described as a revolution in translation circles. Arguably, it generated developments that greatly enlarged the scope of TS and enabled the field to include activities that 'complement' translation in the broad sense of the term, as an intercultural and actual physical transfer of messages; these activities include '[t]exts that rewrite the actual text in one way or another, such as plot summaries in literary histories or reference works, reviews in newspapers, magazines, or journals, some critical articles' (Lefevere, 1992: 6). All these rewritings, according to Lefevere (1992: 6), are less obvious forms of translation compared with translation in its 'traditional' sense. In addition, the target ideology, poetics and patronage[2] constitute significant prerequisites for the success or failure of such acts of rewriting and render translation itself a highly mediated social act: '[r]ewriting and refraction (the latter a term used in Lefevere's earlier work) refer to the *projection of a perspectival image* of a literary work (novel, play, poem)' (Asimakoulas, 2009: 241, my emphasis). Lefevere was among the first to concretely address sociological variables in TS by putting forward the notion of rewriting and various 'control factors' that shape such 're-imaging' of literature (Zhao Wenjing, 2006). However, some forms of rewriting, literary criticism being one, have remained relatively under-researched (see, for example, Gaddis Rose, 1997). By examining the way in which Henrik Ibsen's plays travelled from Europe to China, this chapter argues that literary criticism plays a very significant role in establishing the image of foreign writers and/or their works against the backdrop of the ideological and poetological specificities of the target culture, especially when critics are famous and academically influential. Hu Shi's critical essay 'Ibsenism' has been taken as a case study here to illustrate how aesthetic and ideological norms from the two cultures involved converged or were in opposition to each other.

It has been widely acknowledged that the popularity of the Norwegian dramatist Henrik Ibsen in China owed heavily to Hu Shi (胡适, 1891–1962),[3] a distinguished Chinese scholar who gained his doctorate in the US under John Dewey's supervision and who is acknowledged as 'a central figure in 20th-century Chinese academic and ideological history' (Yu Yingshi, 1983/2000: 76). It was Hu Shi's critical essay 'Ibsenism'[4] that played a pioneering role in introducing Ibsen to the Chinese reading public and to Chinese literary and dramatic circles and greatly facilitated the popularization and naturalization of Ibsen's plays. Indeed, this highly influential work assessed the significance of Ibsen's work and its value for Chinese society. Hu Shi's rewritings of Ibsen profoundly affected his own thinking and writing, which in turn indirectly (but significantly) influenced Chinese literary developments. In fact, Hu also practised other forms of rewriting in making Ibsen known to a Chinese audience, publicizing Ibsen's works and establishing Ibsen's image as a social critic rather than an artist with works such as his one-act play *Life's Greatest Event* (1919), an obvious imitation of Ibsen's *A Doll's House* and his co-translation of *A Doll's House* (1918) which alerted the Chinese reading public to homologous social issues in the Chinese context. Thus Hu Shi's rewriting activity had an impact on ideological and poetological reforms in China.

The concept of rewriting can be highly productive for the analysis of Hu's work. It is widely acknowledged that all 'conventional' translations alter the imported message to varying degrees, to meet the perceived needs of new audiences and localities. Theoretical concepts, from Walter Benjamin's 'afterlife' and 'the continued life' of the original (1923/2000: 16, 19), Jacques Derrida's 'transformation' (1979), Edward Said's 'travelling theory' (1978), and Lawrence Venuti's 'foreignizing and domesticating translations' (1995) to Gideon Toury's 'descriptive translation studies' (1985) and Lefevere's 'refraction/rewriting' (1985, 1992), all emphasize this effect of transferring information into a new context. Rewriting theory perhaps more explicitly acknowledges the value of adaptation, imitation, critical work and anthologizing in TS. Thus it can more accurately capture the creative itinerary of an influential cultural producer such as Hu Shi, including his 'original' articles.

Obviously, Hu Shi used English as a pivot language in reading and interpreting Ibsen and his plays. Therefore, it is essential to have an overview of the entire communication chain between Ibsen and the Chinese readership, the channels and agents through which Ibsen travelled to the English world, and how these first translators or rewriters interpreted Ibsen; as will be shown, Hu Shi's interpretation of Ibsen in the Chinese context was an organic part of this communication chain.

Channels and Agents: Ibsen Travelling to China

Hu Shi's selection of Ibsen was by no means accidental. Hu had an explicit goal: importing models for Chinese literary circles so as to facilitate a literary and cultural reform. Early in 1915, while still in the United States, Hu commented in a letter to the editor of *Tiger Magazine* (甲寅) on issues of translation that drama had become the most popular genre in European literature, while poetry and fiction had dropped to a secondary status (Hu Shi, 1915/1993: 1). Hu Shi cited seven European dramatists whom he considered world-famous, and stated that Chinese literary circles were facing a transitional period and needed to learn from world famous works. Ibsen is a focal point in this letter. Not only is he the first dramatist in Hu's list, but he was the only one Hu selected for translation; Hu told the editor of his plan to translate Ibsen's *A Doll's House* and *An Enemy of the People*, although at the time he had no idea when he would put his plan into practice (Hu Shi, 1915/1993: 1).[5] The letter reveals Hu's strong awareness of the social and poetical function of translation and his purpose in selecting a dramatist rather than a poet or a novelist.

In fact Hu shows a strong interest in the subject matter in Ibsen's plays, which he summarizes as individuality and individualism in his essay 'Ibsenism' (Hu Shi, 1918/1987b). In the 1910s, when Hu was in the USA, many dramatists were popular in the English-speaking world, including famous dramatists whose works had been translated into English, as Hu stated in his abovementioned letter to the editor (Hu Shi, 1915/1993: 1). The question that arises here is why Hu singled out Ibsen from among so many possible candidates. To answer this question, it is important to revisit the channel(s) through which Hu accessed Ibsen and how his sources rewrote Ibsen.

Obviously, Hu Shi's access to Ibsen was based not on the original Norwegian – a language Hu did not know – but on English translations. Hu Shi was very familiar with the English tradition but chose a Norwegian writer instead, even if indirect translation could potentially compromise translation quality and authenticity.[6] By making such a decision, Hu must have attached more significance to the ideological function than to the fidelity of the original content at textual level.

Thus, relevant data that may help shed light on this chain of communication between Ibsen and the Chinese public include introductory comments, reviews and criticism, by both Hu and other authors. On the basis of this approach, the amalgamation of material that gave rise to Hu's rewritings can be identified. For example, his essay 'Ibsenism' bears the traces of George Bernard Shaw's commentary work *The Quintessence of Ibsenism* (1891/1913), and also quotes from *The Correspondence of Henrik Ibsen* (1905), edited and translated by Mary Morison from the Norwegian (see Eide, 1987: 186, note 34). William Archer is another important figure who is considered a prolific translator, critic, editor and director of Ibsen's plays (see Lingard, 2000a). According to Tam (2001: 178), Hu Shi's translation of *A Doll's House* was based on the 1906 edition of William Archer's English version (Ibsen, 1892/1906). Because of the limited space here, this chapter focuses mainly on Shaw and Archer's analysis of Ibsen, and on whether Hu Shi and his critical work interpret Ibsen in the same way or differently and why.

Influences on Hu Shi: Ibsen According to Archer and Shaw

Translators or rewriters are not innocent bystanders or conduits of messages in other languages. Shaw and Archer as well as Hu Shi had their own agendas when they introduced Ibsen into their respective target cultures. According to Lingard, Ibsen was introduced to the English-speaking world in the 1890s 'primarily through William Archer's translations' (Lingard, 2000b: 689). Archer was deeply impressed by Ibsen's plain prose which lent itself to aesthetically satisfying performance and he intended to introduce it as a model for the English theatre. This explains why he attached much more importance to the aspects of language and performance in Ibsen's plays. This contrasts with the approach adopted by Hu Shi, who attached more significance to thematics, and the issue of modernizing plays along Ibsenian lines. Next, we come to Archer and Shaw's interpretation of Ibsen. William Archer, a famous translator and director of Ibsen's plays, is well known for producing rather literal translations (Postlewait, 1986). Arguably, the so-called literalness of Archer's translations derives not from any lack of skill, but from his personal translation philosophy. Archer paid much more attention to functional aspects of poetics or 'what literature should be like' (see Lefevere, 1992: 14) rather than to 'what society should be like' (1992: 14), that is, ideology. Also, being a drama critic, Archer was more inclined to see plays from a poetological angle, and was very sensitive to the aesthetic and theatrical potential of language. For example, writing on *The Master Builder* in 1893, he described it as 'a great piece of music, [...] with its rhythms and harmonies, not only of speech but of structure'. He called it 'unquestionably the greatest *poem* Ibsen has produced since *Peer Gynt*' (Archer, 1893; cited in Postlewait, 1986: 10, original emphasis). Although many contemporary critics, including Shaw, took issue with Archer and accused him of being ignorant of the social elements in Ibsen's plays (Archer, 1893; cited in Postlewait, 1986: 9), such criticism does not seem to hold water, as Archer's priorities explicitly lay elsewhere: he simply aimed to mimic the form of Ibsen's texts.

This is closely linked to Archer's personal approach. As a staunch advocate of Ibsen, Archer admired above all the aesthetic and theatrical features of Ibsen's plays. While most contemporaries regarded Ibsen as a social theorist and studied his plays mainly from the perspective of problem issues and ideological elements (see, for instance, Shaw, below), Archer insisted on a poetic and symbolic Ibsen, focusing on the 'intricacies of the plot' and the 'introspective' method of characterization for the symbolic power of Ibsen's drama (Postlewait, 1986: 10). In addition, he maintained that Ibsen was not simply writing about so-called social problems (see, for example, his essay 'Henrik Ibsen: philosopher or poet?' (Archer, 1905)). In an age when almost every critic tried to present Ibsen as a reformer, Archer opposed such views. As Postlewait puts it:

> Archer ends his 'Ibsen and English Criticism' with his typical pessimism, to such an extent that he states that Ibsen's plays will be antiquated before the great public is ripe for a thorough appreciation of them. (Postlewait, 1986: 46)

Shaw's subsequent comment that, although Archer was a devoted Ibsenite, he was 'never in the least an Ibsenist' (Shaw; cited in Postlewait, 1986: xvii) then comes as no surprise. This seems to be an exaggeration, but Shaw astutely identifies the difference between himself and Archer in interpreting Ibsen. Hu Shi, in this sense, can be categorized as an active Ibsenist. All his life, he was advocating Ibsenism and individualism, as will be shown below.

Perhaps it was a novelty at the time to see Ibsen from this poetic perspective, which is markedly different from that of most of Archer's contemporaries. However, unlike his translations, Archer's criticism does not seem to have been given enough attention in even such authoritative anthologies as *Penguin Critical Anthologies: Henrik Ibsen* and *Oxford Ibsen*. It seems that complex processes of rewriting, selective appropriation and exclusion were at play at the time. Postlewait, for example, mentions

Shaw's marvellous reviews and criticism, whose style 'neither Archer nor anyone else can match' (Postlewait, 1986: 11). Yet this can hardly be a convincing explanation for the absence of Archer in critical anthologies. Even Shaw acknowledged Archer's greater importance as a theatre critic (Postlewait, 1986: 11). I would like to argue here that the compilers' agenda could be the major factor in 'rewriting Archer out', as it were. For example, some compilers of the two above-mentioned collections did not consider Archer to be the one 'who set the *correct way* for understanding Ibsen' (Postlewait, 1986: 9, my emphasis). However, it is beyond the scope of this essay to discuss the factors behind this phenomenon: our focus here is on how Archer presents Ibsen's aesthetic charm to the English world (and beyond) and on Archer's standing in the interpretation of Ibsen. As will be shown below, Hu Shi's approach to Ibsen was in opposition to such an interpretation. Whereas Archer sought to establish new dramatic conventions, Hu Shi tried to use drama to attack traditional ideologies.

Archer was a qualified translator and director. This can be identified by the sharp contrast between the attacks on Ibsen's subject-matter and the glorification of Archer's translations and productions. While denouncing the alleged immorality of the plays, critics acknowledged that '[o]ur stage history – at any rate, that of the present generation – furnishes no record of another such vivid combination of the realistic and the imaginative side of the histrionic art' (Postlewait, 1986: 75); the translations were regarded as beautiful, and the performances as products of high quality (Postlewait, 1986: 107). Without Archer's elegant translation and his direction on the stage, Ibsen would not have become known to the English world in the first place, and there would not have been any criticism on Ibsen and his plays at the turn of the 20th century. It is no exaggeration to state that Archer is the single reason why Ibsen's plays became highly popular in both Britain and the US within the space of a few years. It can be assumed that Ibsen's popularity in the US may have attracted Hu Shi's attention[7] to this Norwegian playwright and, in turn, Hu's complex rewritings enabled Ibsen to become well known in China.

In addition to Archer, Ibsen also owed his reputation to another critic, George Bernard Shaw, who has become better known as a dramatist than a literary and translation critic. Shaw's critical work *The Quintessence of Ibsenism* (1891) contributed significantly to the popularity of Ibsen in the English-speaking world and vestiges of this work can be traced in Hu Shi's essay entitled 'Ibsenism'.

Shaw's book created controversy when it was launched. Numerous critics would agree with Dukore's claim that Shaw's work should more appropriately be called 'The Quintessence of Shavinism' (Dukore, 1980:

xi). Many critics have assumed that *The Quintessence of Ibsenism* is more about Shaw than about Ibsen, and to some extent 'assimilated Ibsen to the Shavian sphere: the only quarrels have been about the legitimacy of the process and how far it misrepresents the Norwegian' (May, 1985: 117). Huntley Carter went so far as to say that in *The Quintessence* Ibsen had been 'butchered to make a Fabian holiday', thus identifying Shaw's Fabian socialist leanings as a central reason of such a distortion (Carter, 1912; cited in May, 1985: 117). Yet these criticisms are not entirely justified. For instance, the accusation that Shaw 'butchered' Ibsen is excessive, because Carter seems to argue that there had existed a standard interpretation of Ibsen's text. Such claims smack of the 'intentional fallacy', whereby the author's intention or the text itself makes an interpretation possible (Boase-Beier, 2006: 33). Carter's view cannot be reconciled with the less counterintuitive assumption that what Ibsen says depends on what the reader – here the translator – understands, as well as on the translator's provenance/position in the literary system. After the publication of the book, the author is in essence dead, and the translator/rewriter negotiates norms and discourses according to perceived needs in target culture systems. Shaw was merely rewriting literature according to or because of her/his own poetological and discursive position in the literary field. We cannot blame Shaw for foregrounding his own viewpoint, or Shavinism as they call it, in his commentary on Ibsen. Most critics do rewrite originals in similar ways and, as we will see below, Hu Shi also routinely resorts to this practice – injecting Hu-Shi-ism into his 'Ibsenism'.

The debate on authorial intentions and differing perspectives is a very complex one. Even Ibsen himself proclaimed his opinion differently at different stages. Those who have read Ibsen's statement in 1898 (see below) may argue that Shaw's viewpoint seems to disagree with what Ibsen stated. However, a wider examination of Ibsen's public speeches and correspondence in the 1870s and 1880s, as well as in 1898 (see, e.g. McFarlane, 1970), soon reveals some obvious self-contradictory statements. For example, Ibsen in his later years, around 1898, tended to deny the presence of conscious social and didactic elements in his works. Thus, in a speech he delivered in 1898, he claimed:

> Whatever I have written has been without any *conscious thought* of making propaganda. I have been *more* the poet and *less* the social philosopher than people generally seem inclined to believe. (Ibsen, 1965: 337, my emphases)

Some critics might take this remark as a total denial of didacticism (and perhaps a vindication of Archer). However, closer analysis shows a rather different claim. Ibsen is not totally denying the propaganda function in his plays, or his role as a 'social philosopher'. What he claims explicitly is that he was not consciously making propaganda, and that he was more concerned with aesthetics and less with social issues than was often assumed. His statement postdates (it appeared seven years after) the publication of *The Quintessence of Ibsenism* (1891) which, as will be shown below, stressed the social and ideological analysis of the plays rather than the theatrical aspects. Perhaps, upon perceiving that Shaw's *The Quintessence of Ibsenism* became very influential, Ibsen sought to redress the balance and discourage critics from following Shaw's example in ignoring the aesthetic elements in his work. Moreover, the apparent intentions of an author are often not a complete guide to the meaning of their work. Therefore, assessment of critical works cannot be made solely on the basis of the original author's personal statements. For instance, when speaking to the Norwegian Women's Rights League in 1898, Ibsen denied that his plays advocated women's rights: 'I must decline the honour of being said to have worked for the Women's Rights movement. I am not very sure what Women's Rights actually are' (Ibsen, 1898/1970a: 169). Yet 13 years earlier, in 1885, Ibsen claimed in a speech to a workers' procession:

> The transformation of social conditions which is now being undertaken in the rest of Europe is very largely concerned with *the future status of the workers and of women*. That is what I am hoping and waiting for, *that is what I shall work for*, all I can. (Ibsen, 1885/1970b: 105, my emphases)

Should we, therefore, believe in the Ibsen of 1885 or the Ibsen of 1898 when we read and interpret his plays? Apparently Shaw chose the politicized Ibsen and therefore stressed the social elements of his works rather than their aesthetic charm.

It is worth noting that more than one of Shaw's plays echoes the work of Ibsen. For instance, Shaw's *Mrs Warren's Profession* bears traces of Ibsen's *Ghosts*. Both playwrights use plays to condemn social ills. In *Ghosts*, marriage is no different from prostitution, and in *Mrs Warren's Profession*, prostitution is a form of business not unlike any other kind of business (Dukore, 1980: 48). In his 1913 edition of *The Quintessence of Ibsenism*, after recording how critics attacked Ibsen's *Ghosts* in newspapers and journals, Shaw recounts how a similar reaction was directed against *Mrs Warren's Profession* in New York in 1905. This, claimed Shaw, demonstrated the hatred of profiteers, since both plays expose the 'regular commercial industry', prostitution, which yields huge profits for the 'pillars of society' (Shaw, 1891/1913: 90). As a Fabian socialist, Shaw further condemns capitalist society, where exploitation is necessary for the survival of elites; he links prostitution to the system of capitalism. Because of his world view, Shaw read Ibsen from this social and ideological perspective, thus constructing what he called Ibsenism. Shaw's notion of Ibsenism influenced not only English readers, but also a worldwide reading public. It set up the refracted 'image' of Ibsen for Hu Shi, the Chinese scholar who would become a lifelong Ibsenist. Because of the popularity of Shaw's book, Ibsen became identified with Ibsenism in the minds of many readers of the time, including Hu Shi, who borrowed the very term Ibsenism as the title of his essay. To analyse how far Hu Shi followed Shaw in his work 'Ibsenism', it is, therefore, crucial to briefly discuss Shaw's *The Quintessence of Ibsenism*.

The social and ideological importance attached to Ibsen in Shaw's critical work is closely associated with Shaw's own ideology in literary writing. *The Quintessence of Ibsenism* was first published in 1891, and revised both in 1913 and 1922. For Shaw, drama was a means of communicating propaganda: not only did he describe his own drama as propagandist, but he also argued in his preface to *Pygmalion* (Shaw, 1965) that the purpose of all drama was didactic. His viewpoint, which is quite similar to Hu Shi's, inevitably affected not only Shaw's own writing but also his literary interpretation of others. In *The Quintessence of Ibsenism*, the social and didactic function of Ibsen's plays is accentuated. Ibsen's poetic innovation, by contrast, is not adequately illustrated, although Shaw was neither unaware of nor uninterested in Ibsen's theatrical aesthetics. Indeed, he explicitly stated in the preface to the first edition that what follows 'is not a critical essay on the poetic beauties of Ibsen, but simply an exposition of Ibsenism' (Shaw, 1891/1913: xix). So, at the very outset, Shaw already signalled his conscious selection and intentional manipulation in interpreting Ibsen: while underscoring the social function of the plays, he purposely ignored Ibsen's poetic technique and innovation.

Shaw's views as a Fabian socialist and his attitude towards capitalist society undoubtedly affected his outlook. Unlike Archer, Shaw regarded Ibsen's plays as exposing problems in the reality of capitalist societies. Shaw introduces Ibsen's plays by summarizing the plots, in a manner that recalls the technique of Charles and Mary Lamb (1978) in *Tales from Shakespeare* (1807/1909). However, whereas *Tales from Shakespeare* merely retells Shakespeare's plots in contemporary English and changes the genre from play to short story, Shaw's plot summaries were written as narratives interspersed with comments, in which he explicitly gave voice to many of his personal views.

It was Archer's competent presentation both in written form and in performance and Shaw's knowledgeable critique of Ibsen that greatly influenced Hu Shi, a Chinese PhD candidate in the US around that time. We can trace the similarities in Hu's essay 'Ibsenism' and Shaw's *Quintessence*. For instance, Shaw's advocacy of tragedy and realistic writing might have influenced Hu Shi greatly since his critical essays, including 'Ibsenism', emphasized these two aspects (see Jiang Yihua, 1993). Shaw's influence can also be seen elsewhere. Towards the end of the section 'The Lesson of the Plays', Shaw claims that 'What Ibsen insists on is that there is no golden rule; that conduct must justify itself by its effect upon life and not by its conformity to any rule or ideal' (Shaw, 1891/1913: 172). This, we should admit, is true of Ibsen, who displays problems but never offers solutions. At the very end of this section, Shaw informs his readers, who might expect him to reduce Ibsenism to a formula, that 'its quintessence is that there is no formula' (Shaw, 1891/1913: 172). This appears to be the source of a similar expression in Hu Shi's essay 'Ibsenism', in which Hu claimed:

> Society and countries are changing all the time, so we cannot prescribe for them. [...] Moreover, societies and countries are different. Medicines fit for Japan may not cure China; those for Germany may not be good for the United States. [...] Ibsen is a wise man. He knows that just as there is no 'universal' prescription, there is no 'universally applicable' truth. (Hu Shi, 1918/1987b: 167, my translation)

In other words, the cure, which Hu intends to provide for social ills in China, is a prescription of no prescription.

Shaw's emphasis on the social aspects of drama is not tantamount to ignoring Ibsen's theatrical technique in *The Quintessence*. In a section entitled 'The technical novelty of the play', Shaw illustrates Ibsen's new technique of inserting discussions into his plays and justifies it through comparisons with Shakespeare's plays. Contemporary critics and playwrights were opposed to the use of discussions in plays. According to Shaw, *A Doll's House* 'might be turned into a very ordinary French drama' if there is no discussion in the last act (Shaw, 1891/1913: 192). Indeed, there would be nothing striking about it if there is no such discussion between Nora and her husband in the third Act. Nevertheless, what Shaw stresses in Ibsen's dramatic technique is still its didactic function – and this constitutes a prime example where the inventory (motifs, techniques) and the functional (views on the role of literature) components of poetics merge (see Lefevere, 1992: 26, 27). According to Shaw, the inserted discussion is intended to reinforce the theme of the play. Viewed from this angle, Hu Shi's 'Ibsenism' goes even further than Shaw's and mentions nothing of the writing technique.

Hu Shi's Presentation of Ibsenism

Ibsen did not become well known to the Chinese reading public until 1918, when Hu Shi published his critical essay 'Ibsenism' (Tam, 2001: 30). But why did Chinese readers so readily accept Hu Shi's Ibsen? According to Lefevere, professionals operating within the literary system, and institutions of patronage within or outside the literary system (state authorities, institutes, journals etc.), are important control factors in either facilitating or hindering the dissemination of literature (Lefevere, 1992: 15). The issue of whether a work can be publicized and become influential depends primarily on who wrote it, and where it was published. As a prestigious professor at Beijing University, Hu Shi had status. He set a precedent in literary circles and in the public imagination by being the first influential scholar who 'transplanted' Ibsen to China and drew attention to his work; his (subjective) presentation or 'image' of Ibsen in his subsequently very frequently quoted essay has been a point of reference for critics and laymen alike. In addition, the essay was published in a special issue on Ibsen of *New Youth* (1918),[8] a radical literary journal at that time. The journal published high quality academic articles and was extremely popular among the avant-garde. This essay has been widely acknowledged as the first comprehensive critical work in Chinese, 'the first time that Ibsen was seriously and systematically presented to the Chinese reader' (Tam, 2001: 30). Hu's description of Ibsen in 'Ibsenism' serves as a pioneering introduction as well as a 'framing device' (see Baker, 2006: 105) for the interpretation of Ibsen and his plays. This special issue was a landmark in Chinese journalism. For the first time in Chinese journalistic history (Wang Jinhou, 1996: 211), an entire journal issue was devoted to a single foreign literary figure. This issue actually carried a serious and comprehensive rewriting of Ibsen in both obvious and less obvious forms of translation. Since Hu Shi was a well-known, influential and authoritative scholar with a large readership at that time, his essay had a special impact on the Chinese intellectual community and proved even more effective in establishing a 'rebellious' image of Ibsen. The following quotation from Shen Yanbing (1925), one of the most famous writers and critics in contemporary Chinese literature, indicates the light under which Ibsen was represented:

> The Special Issue on Ibsen in New Youth six or seven years ago made this Norwegian playwright an incarnation and a symbol of literary revolution and women's liberation, and a rebel against traditional ideas [...]. At that time, Ibsen's name was as famous as, if not more

famous than, those of Marx and Lenin today. (Shen Yanbing, 1925; cited in Wang Jinhou, 1996: 213, my translation, my emphases)

Although Ibsen's popularity is partly justified by the artistic quality of his works, it was undoubtedly Hu Shi's pioneering introduction of Ibsen to the Chinese public that played an extremely significant role in popularizing Ibsen and his works, also creating Ibsen's enduring image for the target readers.

Hu Shi's rewriting influence can perhaps be seen in such figures as Hong Shen (洪深) and Tian Han (田汉) who would later become famous dramatists; both aspired to become the 'Ibsen of China' (Wang Jinhou, 1996). In his introduction to an *Anthology of New Chinese Literature on Drama* (中国新文学大系·戏剧集), Hong Shen, who had studied drama in the United States, also acknowledged enthusiastically that Hu Shi's 'Ibsenism' greatly influenced the development of Chinese drama, especially in terms of the selection of thematics (Hong Shen, 1935: vi). The character of Nora became a popular symbol of the struggle for gender equality. Consequently, Chinese writers showed a special interest in this Norwegian playwright and attached importance to social problems.

The instant popularity of 'Ibsenism' and issues pertaining to Ibsen's works raises several important questions. On the surface, the situation in the Chinese literary tradition as well as Hu Shi's own scholarship would suggest that any other author/genre except Ibsen's work would be a more plausible choice. Traditionally, there existed a deep-seated contempt of drama[9] among Chinese intellectuals. Hu Shi had studied philosophy in the United States for seven years (1910–1917); thus he had easier and more direct access to, and a greater familiarity with, philosophical works from the English-speaking world. Why, then, did Hu Shi choose a Norwegian dramatist rather than English philosopher as other famous rewriters such as Yan Fu did?[10] And why was a dramatist so well received?

China in the beginning of the 20th century is an apt example of poetological and ideological concerns of rewriters and the target culture being key variables in the way 'foreign' material was channelled into another country. The overthrow of the feudal regime in China (1911) had not expunged deep-seated norms or socio-political values generated under such a regime. Hu Shi and other cultural reformers sought to disrupt this feudal tradition and to forge a new cultural space by means of introducing foreign works. To gain popular grassroots support they needed to find a suitable medium. Drama was precisely that, a convenient means of disseminating anti-feudal ideology to a wide swath of the population, including the illiterate. Another issue of *New Youth* (October 1918) on the reform of Chinese drama constitutes a good indication of this agenda. Articles in this issue explicitly demonstrate why drama should be selected and how to improve this genre. New themes were needed if the old literature promoting traditional feudal values was to be relegated to the margins of the literary system. The individualism and iconoclasm identified in Ibsen's dramas met these needs perfectly. Thus, Ibsen's powerful attack on the evils of society and his unremitting struggle against the 'majority' made him the most suitable literary figure for the New Culture Movement that was in opposition to the 'doxa' of his time. The ideological prejudice in China against women at the time constituted yet another significant factor. Perhaps no English writers could replace Ibsen in reflecting women's individualism.

At that time, Chinese women's status in families and society was as low as it could be. In another essay, 'On the issue of chastity' (贞操问题), Hu Shi (1918/1987a: 53–60) mirrors this social reality, exposing the extremely unequal social status of men and women, and how the traditional ethical values of chastity as well as governmental policies encouraging women to make sacrifices resulted in an unfulfilling life for women. Thus it is not only Hu Shi's political agenda that is inscribed in this essay, but also the social and ideological context at the time that is reflected in it; the state of affairs that Hu Shi deplores points to the need for a revolution to secure women's liberation; conditions were right for the introduction of Ibsenism to China. Hu Shi's opposition to inhuman behaviour is coupled with protest-mode comments, namely, the need to develop public awareness, in order 'to form a public opinion against it' (Hu Shi, 1918/1987a: 54).

Re-Imaging Ibsen

According to Lefevere, rewriters create images of the source writer and text (Lefevere, 1992: 4). Ezra Pound, for example, created the image of Chinese poetry for the West with his anthology *Cathay* (Lefevere, 1992: 5). Going in the opposite cultural direction, Hu Shi shaped Ibsen's image by selectively presenting his plays in his seminal essay 'Ibsenism'. Out of Ibsen's 26 plays, only nine were referred to in Hu's essay: *When We Dead Awaken, A Doll's House, Ghosts, Rosmersholm, Pillars of Society, John Gabriel Borkman, An Enemy of the People, The Wild Duck* and *The Lady from the Sea*. This is not because of Hu Shi's lack of familiarity with the remainder of Ibsen's repertoire. Recalling his life in the United States in his essay 'My credo and its evolution', Hu Shi asserted '[m]y reading of Ibsen [...] taught me the importance of honest thinking and honest speaking. I read all of Ibsen's plays and was particularly pleased by *An Enemy of the People*'

(Hu Shi, 1931/2001: 245). This demonstrates that Hu Shi's essay was based on an extensive reading of Ibsen. Indeed, Yuan Zhenying's article 'Ibsen's biography' in the same special issue of *New Youth* on Ibsen was divided into three main sections, with one subsection. 'The three main divisions were on Ibsen's youth, his middle years, with a subsection on *Brand* and *Peer Gynt*, and his later years' (Eide, 1987: 132). Neither of these two plays was mentioned in Hu Shi's essay. Hu introduced Ibsen merely as a realistic writer and was most interested in his ability to diagnose social problems. His selection of materials reflects this theme: *Brand* and *Peer Gynt* appear to have been excluded because they do not correspond to these priorities. Compared with Shaw's selection of 16 of Ibsen's plays to comment on in his *The Quintessence of Ibsenism*, Hu Shi seems much more selective in this respect; he focused on nine.

For quite a long period afterwards, Ibsen came to symbolize a revolutionary fighter and a social reformer rather than an artist. Most of the critical literature in China focused on Ibsen's rebellious spirit and praised him highly as a liberator of women while the aesthetic qualities of his plays have hardly foregrounded, as if Ibsen had become famous only because of his ideological significance. A closer look at Hu Shi's rewritings would explain why Ibsen impressed his readers in this way. Compared with other translations of Ibsen's plays in the same issue of *New Youth* on Ibsen, 'Ibsenism' focuses more on Ibsen as the social reformer. Since Hu Shi's academic status and authority (supervisee of John Dewey, professor at Beijing University and co-editor of *New Youth*) earned him discourse power, his essay was frequently quoted.

The opening section sets the tone for the whole article: 'Ibsen's literature, or his philosophy, converges on realism' (Hu Shi, 1918/1987b: 153). It should be noted that Hu Shi's concept of realism here is not limited to its literary definition. By 'realism', Hu also refers to Ibsen's insight and courage in exposing social evils in a straightforward way. To demonstrate this, Hu Shi constantly quotes either Ibsen's letters or his characters, reflecting thereby a tendency for most Chinese critics and readers to regard characters as mouthpieces of authors. At the same time, Hu Shi loses no opportunity to insert his comments on realistic writing and his interpretation of Ibsenism:

> Ibsen described actual social and familial conditions in order to move readers, to make us feel how dark and corrupt our families and society are and to make us understand that our families and society must be reformed – this is what is meant by Ibsenism. (Hu Shi, 1918/1987b: 160, my translation, my emphases)

Arguably, Ibsen's plays are not merely realistic. Even his contemporary critics interpret Ibsen in symbolist terms (see Postlewait, 1986: 136), a point that will be taken up below.

The repeated use of 'us' and the possessive adjective 'our' in the above statement shortens the distance between Ibsen and Chinese readers, and mutes the foreign origin of the material discussed. It is not clear to readers whether Hu Shi is referring to Norwegian or Chinese society and families, which leaves the message open-ended, and portrays what Ibsen is describing as a universal phenomenon. Hu Shi continues:

> However, Ibsen, like doctors, describes what is wrong in the body, but he never prescribes. He knows that human society is a very complex organization with various different situations and contexts. Therefore there are various illnesses. And there is no panacea. That is why he just describes the illness, and lets the patients seek prescription elsewhere. (Hu Shi, 1918/1987b: 163, my translation)

This foregrounds Ibsen's image as a doctor to diagnose social illness rather than as a skilful playwright. According to Hu Shi's interpretation, Ibsenism reveals that society and families have been corrupted; reforms are urgently needed. The constant backdrop of this reimaging is the Chinese feudal social system. It comes as no surprise that, operating within it, Hu Shi offers significant nodes in his writing which could facilitate contextual transposition, creating points of contact between the original plays and the target social reality. Ibsen's 'problem plays'[11] (问题剧) in essence are turned into social corrective tools for the Chinese.

According to Lefevere, the ways in which the original writers and their works impress the target readers depend heavily on how they are rewritten since '[t]he non-professional reader increasingly does not read literature as written by its writers, but as rewritten by its rewriters' (Lefevere, 1992: 3). This was particularly true of Chinese practices in the early 20th century, when the majority of people were 'non-professional readers', who read for entertainment. Elizabeth Eide argues that the Chinese never read the original to find aesthetic solutions to literary problems. They relied on commentary works which determined how the original work should be interpreted and received (Eide, 1987: 151).

Injecting Hu-Shi-ism into Ibsenism

It is obvious that, in rewriting Ibsen, Hu Shi tried to insert Hu-Shi-ism into Ibsenism. Generally speaking, Hu's connection between the original plays and the target social reality is seamless and effective. Nevertheless, occasionally, Hu tends to become highly visible in his interventions. For instance, in his assessment of Ibsen's political philosophy, Hu Shi asserts that 'Ibsen never advocated narrow-minded nationalism, he was never a narrow-minded patriot. [...] I believe Ibsen in his later years before he died certainly progressed to the stage of internationalism' (Hu Shi, 1918/1987b: 163). This argument is rather arbitrary and not very convincing. That 'Ibsen never advocated narrow-minded nationalism' does not mean that he necessarily opposed it. On what basis could Hu Shi assume that Ibsen would advocate internationalism? Whenever such generalizing statements appear, they in all likelihood constitute cues of Hu Shi's ideas and, by extension, of his desire to prove his own point. Hu Shi consistently disputed nationalist propaganda and advocated internationalism. This explains why 'Ibsenism', apparently gratuitously, presents Ibsen as an internationalist: Hu Shi is mobilizing a prestigious playwright to support his agenda.

Ibsen's work cannot be reduced to social realism. What Ibsen presented in his plays is much more complex and richer than what mere realism can cover. The various plays lend themselves to different categorizations (see Durbach, 1991; Haugen, 1979; Shaw, 1891/1913). Moreover, Ibsen's plays certainly possess some outstanding artistic features which allow his writings to endure time and exceed geographical boundaries. When the social problems outlined in the plays no longer exist, his plays remain popular. This phenomenon per se confirms their lasting artistic beauty, an issue barely touched upon by Hu Shi. In his '"On drama translation" a reply to T.F.C.', Hu explicitly claims that:

> our intention [in translating and introducing foreign plays] is to make use of the plays to import the ideas in them. If you read our Special Issue on Ibsen, you would know our focus on Ibsen is not his being an artist but his being a social reformer. (Hu Shi, 1919/1993: 487, my translation)

Indeed, Hu Shi makes use of Ibsen's work to promote his own philosophy. As he later acknowledged in his essay 'Introducing my ideology' (介绍我的思想) '"Ibsenism" represents my philosophy and my religion' (Hu Shi, 1930; cited in Wang Jinhou, 1996: 214, my translation). Ibsenism becomes a vehicle of Hu-Shi-ism.

Conclusion

Rewriters are never innocent code-switchers. Their rewritings always serve a special purpose (Lefevere, 1992: 15). Literary criticism of foreign works, a type of rewriting, plays a significant role in assimilating the original writers and their works, whose images do change in their migration to the target context. The way in which translation and/or rewritings function in the target culture relies more on the manner in which the target-culture environment accepts or acculturates the imported knowledge than on the original text itself. For instance, the translation, assimilation and often improvement of ancient Greek philosophy and scientific discourse by Arab rewriters and consequently by Europeans resulted in dramatic achievements in the respective target cultures. Kong Huiyi (1999: 1–2) shows the different direction of these achievements, even though knowledge was drawn from the same sources. The difference, Kong asserts, must have been caused by differences in the receiving socio-political environments (Kong Huiyi, 1999: 2). In a similar vein, Yu Guifen (2001) compares the completely different results of the absorption of Western civilization in China and in Japan at the turn of the 20th century. She draws a similar conclusion. Here it is not my intention to comment on the plausibility of their arguments, or on the possibility of factors other than translation being at play. These case studies converge to the same assumption: the socio-political needs of the target context can affect the selection, production and the reception of the original text. The translators'/rewriters' agenda and ideologies, their selection of materials, their use of available channels to diffuse their material, and their strategies to make the works agreeable to the audience and to guide readers' interpretation are key factors that can make a difference in the ways in which a translated work is produced and consumed. 'Ibsenism' is an effective piece of rewriting to reinforce this assumption. It is safe to say that Hu Shi's purpose to introduce Ibsen to Chinese society was more to provide a cure for social ills than to introduce a new dramatist to the intellectual community. Both the production and the reception of the 'rewritten' texts are determined by various ideological factors such as the target culture needs, the academic prestige of the rewriters and the literary tradition in the target context. It is all of the above that have made Ibsen what he is today and what he stands for in China while Hu Shi's legacy continues, until further rewriting takes place to reflect the needs of shifting socio-political and poetological environments.

Notes

1. Rewriting theory put forward by André Lefevere greatly extends the translation research domain to cover criticism, imitation, biography and encyclopaedia entry authoring (see also Asimakoulas, 2009; Lefevere, 1985, 1992).

2. The three notions of ideology, poetics and patronage are significant, known as control factors in Lefevere's rewriting theory.
3. Returning to China in 1917, Hu Shi became the youngest professor at Beijing University and one of the key figures of the epoch-making New Culture Movement (1915–1923) who would become an oriental cultural giant in the 20th century with 35 honourable doctor degrees granted by famous universities in the USA, Canada and Britain, including such universities as Cambridge and Oxford.
4. To distinguish between Ibsenism as Ibsen's own ideology and 'Ibsenism', the critical essay by Hu Shi, I use single quotation marks for the latter.
5. In the same letter, Hu also mentioned Gerhart Hauptmann from Germany, Eugene Brieux from France, Johan August Strindberg from Sweden, George Bernard Shaw and John Galsworthy from Britain, and Maurice Maeterlinck from Belgium.
6. For interesting case studies on the modalities and function of indirect translations, see Toury (1995: Chapter 7).
7. Hu Shi was in the US during 1910–1917, at the time when Ibsen was highly popular there.
8. Hu Shi was then one of the six general editors for *New Youth* and he edited this special issue (Song Jianhua, 1996: 136).
9. In Chinese tradition, intellectuals looked down upon drama. Both playwrights and actors, even novelists, were regarded as lowbrow. Novelists in ancient China tended to conceal their real identity by using pennames. Poetry and essay writing were considered highbrow.
10. Yan Fu (严复) is famous for his translation of English philosophical works at the turn of the 20th century, slightly before Hu Shi.
11. 'Problem plays' refers to plays exposing social problems and were thus given the name by Chinese literary critics during the New Culture Movement, in Chinese '问题剧'.

References

Archer, W. (1905) Henrik Ibsen: Philosopher or poet? *Cosmopolitan Review* (NY), February.
Asimakoulas, D. (2009) Rewriting. In M. Baker and G. Saldanha (eds) *Routledge Encyclopaedia of Translation Studies* (pp. 241–245). London/New York: Routledge.
Baker, M. (2006) *Translation and Conflict*. London/New York: Routledge.
Benjamin, W. (1923/2000) The task of the translator. In L. Venuti (ed.) *The Translation Studies Reader* (pp. 15–23). London/New York: Routledge.
Boase-Beier, J. (2006) *Stylistic Approaches to Translation*. Manchester: St Jerome.
Derrida, J. (1979) The supplement of Copula: Philosophy *before* linguistics. In J.V. Harari (ed.) *Textual Strategies Perspectives in Post-structuralist Criticism*, (pp. 82–120). London: Methuen & Co.
Dukore, B.F. (1980) *Money & Politics in Ibsen, Shaw and Brecht*. Columbia: University of Missouri Press.
Durbach, E. (1991) *A Doll's House: Ibsen's Myth of Transformation*. Boston: Twayne Publishers.
Eide, E. (1987) *China's Ibsen: From Ibsen to Ibsenism*. London: Curzon Press.
Gaddis Rose, M. (1997) *Translation and Literary Criticism*. Manchester: St. Jerome.

Haugen, E. (1979) *Ibsen's Drama: Author to Audience*. Minneapolis: University of Minnesota Press.
Hong, S. (1935) 中国新文学大系：戏剧导言 (Introduction to anthology of new Chinese literature on drama). In Hong Shen (ed.) 中国新文学大系：戏剧集 (*Anthology of New Chinese Literature on Drama*). Shanghai: Shanghai liangyou tushu yinshua gongsi.
Hu, S. (1915/1993) 给《甲寅》编者的信 (A letter to the Editor of *Tiger Magazine*). In Y. Jiang (ed.) (1993) 胡适学术文集：新文学运动 (*Collection of Hu Shi's Academic Essays: New Literature Movement*) (pp. 1–2). Beijing: Zhonghua shuju.
Hu, S. (1918/1987a) 贞操问题 (On the issue of chastity). In Z. Yi (ed.) (1987) 中国现代作家选集：胡适 (*Selection of Modern Chinese Writers: Hu Shi*) (pp. 53–60). Hong Kong: Joint Publishing Company.
Hu, S. (1918/1987b) 易卜生主义 (Ibsenism). In Z. Yi (ed.) (1987) 中国现代作家选集：胡适 (*Selection of Modern Chinese Writers: Hu Shi*) (pp. 153–167). Hong Kong: Joint Publishing Company.
Hu, S. (1919/1993) '论译戏剧'答T.F.C. ('On drama translation': A reply to T.F.C.). In Y. Jiang (ed.) (1993) 胡适学术文集：新文学运动 (*Collection of Hu Shi's Academic Essays: New Literature Movement*) (pp. 487–488). Beijing: Zhonghua shuju.
Hu, S. (1931/2001) My credo and its evolution. In Ouyang Zhesheng and Liu Hongzhong (eds) (2001) *The Chinese Renaissance* (pp. 226–254). Beijing: Foreign Language Teaching and Research Press.
Ibsen, H. (1885/1970b) From a speech to A Workers' Procession. In J. McFarlane (ed.) *Henrik Ibsen: A Critical Anthology* (p. 105). Baltimore: Penguin.
Ibsen, H. (1892/1906) *Ibsen's Prose Dramas* (W. Archer, ed. and trans.). London/Newcastle-upon-Tyne: Walter Scott Publishing Co.
Ibsen, H. (1898/1970a) From a speech to the Norwegian Women's Rights League. In J. McFarlane (ed.) *Henrik Ibsen: A Critical Anthology* (p. 169). Baltimore: Penguin.
Ibsen, H. (1965) *Ibsen: Letters and Speeches* (E. Sprinchorn, ed.). London: MacGibbon & Kee.
Jiang, Y. (ed.) (1993) 胡适学术文集：新文学运动 (*Collection of Hu Shi's Academic Essays: New Literature Movement*). Beijing: Zhonghua shuju.
Kong Huiyi (1999) 翻译文学文化 (*Translation, Literature and Culture*). Beijing: Beijing University Press.
Lamb, M. and Lamb, C. (1978) *Tales from Shakespeare*. Beijing: Chinese Youth Press.
Lefevere, A. (1985) Why waste our time on rewrites? The trouble with interpretation and the role of rewriting in an alternative paradigm. In T. Hermans (ed.) *The Manipulation of Literature: Studies in Literary Translation* (pp. 215–243). London: Croom Helm.
Lefevere, A. (1992) *Translation, Rewriting and the Manipulation of Literary Fame*. London/New York: Routledge.
Lingard, J. (2000a) William Archer: British literary translator, critic, editor and journalist. In O. Classe (ed.) *Encyclopaedia of Literary Translation into English* (Vol. I) (pp. 70–73). London/Chicago: Fitzroy Dearborn Publishers.
Lingard, J. (2000b) Henrik Ibsen: Norwegian dramatist and poet. In O. Classe (ed.) *Encyclopaedia of Literary Translation into English* (Vol. II) (pp. 688–694). London/Chicago: Fitzroy Dearborn Publishers.
May, K.M. (1985) *Ibsen and Shaw*. London: MacMillan.
McFarlane, J. (ed.) (1970) *Henrik Ibsen: A Critical Anthology*. Baltimore: Penguin.

Postlewait, T. (1986) *Prophet of the New Drama: William Archer and the Ibsen Campaign*. Westport/London: Greenwood Press.

Shaw, B. (1891/1913) *The Quintessence of Ibsenism*. London: Constable and Company.

Shaw, B. (1965) *The Complete Prefaces of Bernard Shaw*. London: Paul Hamlyn.

Song, J. (1996) 胡适与中国文化转型 (*Hu Shi and the Transformation of Chinese Culture*). Harbin: Heilongjiang jiaoyu chubanshe.

Tam, K. (2001) *Ibsen in China 1908–1997: A Critical-Annotated Bibliography of Criticism. Translation and Performance*. Hong Kong: The Chinese University Press.

Toury, G. (1995) *Descriptive Translation Studies – and Beyond*. Amsterdam/Philadelphia: John Benjamins.

Wang Jinhou (1996) 五四新文学与外国文学 (*May Fourth New Literature and Foreign Literature*). Chengdu: Sichuan University Press.

Yi, Z. (ed.) (1987) 中国现代作家选集：胡适 (*Selection of Modern Chinese Writers: Hu Shi*). Hong Kong: Joint Publishing Company.

Yu, G. (2001) 西风东渐 – 中日摄取西方文化的比较研究 (*Western Learning Eastwards – A Comparative Study Between China and Japan in Absorbing Western Culture*). Beijing: Commercial Press.

Yu, Y. (1983/2000) 中国近代思想史上的胡适 (Hu Shi's position in modern Chinese intellectual history). In Z. Ouyang (ed.) (2000) 解析胡适 (*Analysing Hu Shi*) (pp. 73–131). Beijing: Shehui kexue wenxian chubanshe.

Zhao, W. (2006) *The Cultural Manipulation of Translation Activities: Hu Shi's Rewriting and the Construction of a New Culture* (翻译的文化操控 – 胡适的改写与新文化的建构). Shanghai: Fudan University Press.

Chapter 3
Rewriting, Culture Planning and Resistance in the Turkish Folk Tale

Ş.T. GÜRÇAĞLAR

Introduction

The present chapter tackles the different versions of *Kerem ile Aslı*, a well-known folk story in Turkey, in relation to the concepts of rewriting, retranslation and culture planning. I argue that a study of the various versions of the story serves as an instrument which touches upon two distinct practices of early republican Turkey, one being literal and the other political. The chapter will set out to demonstrate the close links between these two practices and show how a certain literary attitude became indicative of political resistance, or endorsement, on a deeper level.

Folk stories are an important part of the Ottoman–Turkish literary tradition, occupying a major place in the reading experience of the population. Some of these stories were born out of popular imagination and have no known provenance. These texts circulated among the population as part of the oral storytelling tradition and were later written down by various writers and publishers. Other folk stories have recognized authors whose manuscripts were printed in the 19th century and started to circulate among the population, serving as a point of departure for other manuscripts, as well as numerous oral performances. In the Ottoman Empire, folk stories were 'born' at various times in what one can call an Ottoman intercultural space (Paker, 2002). The geographical space where these stories flourished mainly covered the eastern parts of the current territory of the Turkish Republic, expanding into the neighbouring territories of Azarbeijan, Iran and Armenia. It is therefore difficult to attribute these stories to specific cultural or ethnic groups, and variants of the stories have survived within the national boundaries of other countries. On the other hand, some folk stories of Ottoman–Turkish literature, including romances especially, originate from the classical Arabic and Persian literatures. These usually have a different style and form and their manuscripts formed a basis for later oral renderings (Boratav, 2002: 72).

The present chapter explores the way folk stories were transformed and rewritten with the transition to the republican period.[1] It contextualizes these rewrites *vis-à-vis* the culture planning efforts of the young Turkish Republic, which covered a wide range of areas, including translation. My discussions on culture planning owe a debt to Itamar Even-Zohar who defines culture planning 'as a deliberate act of intervention, either by power holders or by "free agents", into an extant or a crystallizing repertoire' of culture (Even-Zohar, 2002: 45). Elsewhere I have taken up how the Turkish state exerted systematic efforts towards creating a new cultural repertoire in Turkey in the 1923–1946 period (Tahir Gürçağlar, 2008a). In the present chapter, I will specifically delve into the repercussions of these efforts in the field of folk literature. I will especially focus on the debate created around a proposal by the Directorate General of Publications under the Ministry of Interior Affairs in 1937, which included a call for modernizing and rewriting traditional folk tales. The debate triggered by this proposal offered an opportunity for various writers to express their views on traditional folk stories. However, the debate was not limited to the folk tale, and provides clues about the feelings of the writers and intellectuals in early republican Turkey regarding the government's culture planning efforts. It also hints at various issues surrounding these culture planning efforts, such as the rigid classification of the population as 'urban' and 'rural' by intellectuals in the country and a vision of what good literature was and how it could be used to further political goals. The case study included in this chapter will offer a brief analysis of three rewrites of a well-known Turkish folk story: *Kerem ile Aslı* ('Kerem and Aslı') printed in various editions throughout the republican period. The three specific rewrites chosen for this chapter were all published in the 1930s and display a series of strategies which reflects certain political and cultural issues unique to the period.

The rewriting of folk tales to suit specific socio-political goals is not uncommon. Mette Rudvin provides an overview of the various amendments introduced to fairy tales and folk tales in 19th-century Europe while these were being transferred from oral to written literature by famous collectors such as the Grimm Brothers or Asbjørnsen and Moe (Rudvin, 2000: 79–88). What Rudvin writes about German or Norwegian stories holds equally true for Turkish rewrites of folk tales:

> Not only were the published editions significantly changed in respect to the manuscripts, but the revisions of the subsequent published

editions saw many amendments too. The amendments to the tales carry strong ideological implications concerning developments in social and sexual hierarchies. (Rudvin, 2000: 81)

The Provenance and Types of Folk Stories in Ottoman-Turkish Culture

Researchers have classified the Turkish folk story in different ways using different criteria. A frequent criterion is to classify these stories in relation to their theme or generic features, which are defined either by their content and characters (such as heroic stories with a leading warrior as the main protagonist) or by the bards to whom they are attributed and who are presumed to have created these stories out of lived experience (Artun, 2006: 122–132). Various studies have been published regarding the Turkish folk tale since the 1940s. However, researchers have largely adopted Pertev Naili Boratav's approach and classifications. Boratav, a major folklorist of the 20th century, classified the folk story genre into two main thematic types: the heroic story and the folk romance (Boratav, 2002: 18). The folk romance is especially pertinent to the theme of the present chapter as the famous *Kerem ile Aslı* story taken up in this chapter is one of the leading narratives in this group. Some folk romances are products of the popular imagination, while others have been derived from the biographies and works of renowned travelling bards from the past. Aşık Kerem, the alleged composer and writer of the prose and verse parts of *Kerem ile Aslı*, was one such bard (Boratav, 2002: 18). His life and work have been dated back to the 16th century (Boratav, 2002: 25).

In Turkey, the oral storytelling tradition had largely become extinct by the republican period starting in 1923. In some regions, however, especially in Eastern Turkey in towns like Kars, this tradition seems to have survived longer; Boratav, for example, published his observations of public storytelling sessions in the 1930s and 1940s (Boratav, 2002: 30). It can be safely argued that by the 20th century the main distribution channel for these stories had become the printed book. Yet even before the 20th century, manuscripts had started to replace oral storytelling, serving as the standard version of the stories. Nevertheless, it would be impossible to have an 'authoritative' version recorded in a single manuscript, and manuscripts reflected the variety and individuality present in oral renderings (Boratav, 2002: 147). Even manuscripts of stories with known sources featured various amendments, demonstrating an indifference to issues of provenance and authorship.

The study of these different versions of folk tales, first in manuscript and then in printed format, provides an opportunity for a discussion of a number of issues that are relevant to Translation Studies (TS) today. From a theoretical and methodological perspective these versions can be studied as cases of 'intralingual translation' as defined by Roman Jakobson (1958/2000: 114)[2] as they were all spoken and written in the Turkish language. Nevertheless, the intralingual character of the rewrites of folk tales does not eliminate the possibility that some of these stories have existed and continue to exist in other languages and cultures. The best known example is perhaps *Leyla ile Mecnun*, the provenance of which goes back to an Arab legend. In this case, one also needs to consider the fact that the initial introduction of this story into the Ottoman–Turkish literary system was the product of an act of an interlingual transfer – perhaps not in the modern understanding of translation as an act of linguistic and cultural transfer of a particular source text to a new culture and language, giving rise to a specific target text that has close correspondence to its source, but as the result of intercultural and intertextual contacts involving two separate languages. Furthermore, many folk tales have served as source texts for film and stage productions. As popular texts circulating among the readership in various forms and formats, these stories have become a part of the popular imagination and have inspired works in different art forms, such as painting, theatre, film and the opera, to mention but a few. In that sense, the texts and themes which have migrated to such different media can be studied as cases of 'intersemiotic translation' (Jakobson, 1958/2000: 114). This illustrates that the multifaceted character of the operations of intertextual and intercultural transfer in the folk tale defies clear-cut definitions and classifications, opening up a large field marked by a complex network of relations among the various rewrites. This chapter mainly deals with the rewrites of Turkish folk tales, that is different versions by different writers, printed in book form in the republican period in Turkey. Therefore its scope excludes other forms of art, which are no less exciting to explore.

It is impossible to claim the existence of individual and uniform original texts from which various rewrites have emerged. The rewrites co-exist simultaneously with complex sets of links among them. Some written versions are based on different oral renderings of the same stories, while others have been derived from written texts that are accepted as more or less standard. These complex links bring forth the question of intertextuality. The question is not whether there are intertextual links and references among the different rewrites beyond an inspiration provided by a theme or character – by now this is firmly established – but rather the degree and nature of this intertextuality. Some rewrites have strict relations of kinship. This is especially evident in the printed versions in the republican period. Some manuscripts are acknowledged as the most complete versions of the story, which legitimizes their use as source texts by writers and publishers who, in their turn, amend, 'improve', or sometimes transform the texts. Some of these texts acknowledge their source, while most need a textual comparison to reveal their reliance on a specific printed source text. Although this lack of regard for the source text reflects a permissive attitude to literary appropriation, it contradicts, or even opposes, a more modern view of literary originality and authorship which came to Turkey as a by-product of cultural and literary Westernization. Although rewriters of folk literature have traditionally been termed *musannif* ('compiler' or 'classifier') (Boratav, 2002: 108), most popular printed rewrites did not use this designation to describe their writers and either published the book anonymously or credited the work to a writer.

On the other hand, canonical literature in the republican period, largely shaped and guided by translations well into the 1950s, came to be associated with a view of literature as original creation as exemplified by the rising attention given to source texts and source authors by publishers in the field of translated canonical literature starting in the first half of the 1940s (Tahir Gürçağlar, 2002, 2008a). Folk tales, however, were held to be outside the canon by the literary establishment and remained immune to the evolution of a new understanding of literary provenance, becoming increasingly dominant in the field of canonical literature translated from Western languages. In fact, folk tales were widely criticized and various attempts were made to tame, control, or at least 'guide' the writing and rewriting of these stories. The main reason for these attempts (on the part of both the government and independent intellectuals) did not entail literary or aesthetic concerns, but rather consisted of a critique of the themes, characters and events treated by the folk tales. The example of an official proposal to reshape the Turkish folk tale and the discourse formed around it in the 1930s offers clues regarding this interesting intervention by the government and the response it evoked among writers, publishers and other intellectuals.

An Attempt at Shaping the Field of Folk Tales

The proposal to modernize traditional folk tales was prepared by the General Directorate for Publications under the Ministry of the Interior, dated 11 May 1937 and signed by the Secretary General of the ruling Republican People's Party and the Minister of the Interior, Şükrü Kaya (see Elçin, 1997 for the full text of the proposal in Turkish). The proposal had developed around the assumption that books addressing 'intellectual' (*münevver*) readers only had a circulation of around 1000–2000 copies, while the wider public read popular books which were printed in much greater numbers, up to 50,000 copies per edition (Elçin, 1997: 62). A list of the 65 most popular titles was offered in the proposal: the titles included well-known anonymous folk tales with both heroic and romantic themes, such as *Aşık Garip, Köroğlu, Kerem ile Aslı, Yusuf ile Züleyha* and *Şahmeran* as well as popular novels with known authors, such as *Kürkçü Dükkanı* by Muharrem Zeki (published in 1933) and novels published anonymously but which are not a part of the Turkish folk tradition, such as *Kaçırılan Kadın* (published in 1934) and *Sihirbaz Kadın* (published in 1932).

The proposal criticized popular books based on a number of points, and suggested that the language, style and illustrations in these books were of a poor quality. These books were said to be 'the products of an ideology and tradition that does not comply with the new human idea'[3] that the government aspired to create (Elçin, 1997: 62). The books were also criticized for pursuing commercial aims. In addition, the proposal also mentioned that some popular books featured superstitious and fundamentalist characteristics (which did not fit the early republican ideology created and upheld by the officials in the Republican People's Party who specifically emphasized secularism and positivism).

The proposal stated its intention in very clear terms: 'we want to commission the writing of new popular stories and novels in order to meet the needs of a wide readership both in villages and towns in order to facilitate their national and cultural education' (Elçin, 1997: 63).

The proposal included 10 works as the initial list of titles to be rewritten and stated its criterion as using the conventional protagonists of these books in new themes and adventures 'which uphold the goals of the new Turkish reforms and civilization' (Elçin, 1997: 63). Authors were invited to submit the themes and plots of their choice for selection by a committee to be formed specifically for this purpose.

The proposal is a telling example of attempts made by the ruling elite to shape popular culture in the early republican period as part of their larger culture planning efforts. They saw an opportunity in folk tales to convey the concepts and principles of the republican regime to a wide audience. This audience was conceptualized as a large group of people who needed to be taught about specific ideas and principles without necessarily intending to learn them. This deliberate yet discrete intervention in culture is indicative of two oppositional attitudes visible in early republican Turkey. The first type of opposition displayed here is that shown by the government to the popular literary poetics they obviously wished to channel to serve their interest. The second type is the passive opposition of the publishers who continued to print folk tales despite the criticism coming from the government. Evidently, these publishers did not adopt the cultural policies of the government which obviously wished to disseminate a specific type of literary disposition. The positive attitude shown by various writers to thematic, literary and ideological aspects of the established forms of the folk tales came to lend further support to this opposition and will be illustrated with examples from the *Kerem ile Aslı* narrative.

There was a diversity of opinions raised by writers and publishers regarding the proposal. İbrahim Hilmi, a major publisher of the time, saw a commercial opportunity in the proposal and asked in a letter to cooperate with the Directorate General of Publications (Elçin, 1997: 65–66). The İkbal publishing house boasted of having undertaken such an endeavour prior to the government initiative and wished to join forces with the government (Elçin, 1997: 67–68). The kind of approval extended by these two publishers was not shown by a number of intellectuals who either actively opposed the proposal or hinted at a more subtle type of resistance in their arguments. A book written on the subject of books published for the popular market (*Halk Kitaplarına Dair* by Faruk Rıza Güloğul, 1937) compiles the views of a number of writers on the topic and shows that writers had mixed feelings about the government proposal.

The famous poet, critic, writer and translator Behçet Kemal Çağlar fully endorsed the government proposal and named it a 'wonderful opportunity' ('en isabetli fırsat') for writers who wanted to serve their country. He further maintained that it would be a 'glorious and excellent' ('muhteşem ve mükemmel') idea to save characters of folk literature from 'an idle oriental atmosphere' ('miskin şark havasından sıyırıp') and bring them to modern times (Güloğul, 1937: 62–63). The negative description used by the writer about the Orient creates another type of opposition inherent in Çağlar's thinking (the East versus the West).

A famous literary figure of the time, Peyami Safa, also appeared to approve the proposal and suggested that the government had every right to request the publication of 'better' ('daha iyi') people's books (Güloğul, 1937: 46). However, he was critical of the proposal to modernize the stories, and pointed out the difficulty in preparing new rewrites which could attract the attention of the peasants (Güloğul, 1937: 47). The difficulty of producing such rewrites was a point often emphasized by writers. Although this objection is not a form of open opposition to the proposal, the discourse emphasizing the challenges of rewriting can also be interpreted as a covert display of resistance. For instance, in his critical essays on the subject, the celebrated translator and critic Nurullah Ataç started out by acknowledging the 'good intentions' ('hüsnüniyet') behind the proposal (Güloğul, 1937: 48), but argued that Turkish writers who had been invited to prepare new editions of folk stories were not fit for the task. He further maintained that Turkish writers had not understood and adopted the ideology of republican reforms sufficiently to be able to disseminate them in their rewrites (Güloğul, 1937: 50). Both of these writers stressed the point that the government had made a good proposal, but their resistance is voiced in their emphasis on the difficulty of the task and appears more passive than active (Even-Zohar, 2002: 48–49).

There were also writers who were explicitly opposed to the proposal, indicating that not everyone felt compelled to appreciate a proposal made by the government. The journalist and popular novelist Bürhan Cahit openly raised his opposition by saying that there was 'no possibility, furthermore no need to modernize' these stories (Güloğul, 1937: 43). He suggested that popular folk tales had the crucial function of creating the habit of reading in people, arguing that instead of modernizing the existing stories, the government needed to encourage the writing of new popular stories which would spontaneously replace the older ones if they were written with enough force (Güloğul, 1937: 43). Hüseyin Cahit Yalçın, an eminent writer and politician of the time, was even more explicit in his opposition and wrote, 'in principle I am opposed to all such initiatives' (Güloğul, 1937: 53). He was especially opposed to the government's attempt to define what is best for readers and to identify what good literature is.

These mixed responses shown to the government proposal indicate that not every initiative taken by the government would be readily accepted by the intelligentsia. Nevertheless, even though the initiative was not met with much enthusiasm, it triggered substantial debate among literary figures regarding folk literature, a field otherwise not so visible in public debates. In Even-Zohar's terms, the proposal created some 'energy' in a literary field whose repertoire was still in the making (Even-Zohar, 2002: 47). The proposal did not lead to a great deal of publication activity as the Directorate General had hoped. There are only a few books identified by researchers as having been triggered by the proposal. Alpay Kabacalı writes that the Directorate General of the Press published only a few rewrites after it launched the rewriting campaign, and that these were not popular among readers (Kabacalı, 1994: 89). Duymaz argues that the proposal also led to the publication of one particular rewrite of *Kerem ile Aslı* by Besim Atalay in 1939 (Duymaz, 2001: 13). In my own research, I could find no 1939 edition of the story. The only available rewrite by Atalay had actually been written and published earlier in 1930. The following case study provides a brief analysis of this rewrite, as well as two others from the 1930s.

A Case Study on Rewrites of *Kerem ile Aslı* in the 1930s

Kerem ile Aslı is known to have existed in the oral Ottoman–Turkish storytelling tradition since the 16th century (Boratav, 2002: 25; Elçin, 1949: 64). Like all stories in the tradition, it comprises both prose and verse sections performed by travelling bards where prose offers the general outline of the plot while the verse serves to enrich the work stylistically (Boratav, 2002: 36–38). My case study concentrates on the prose parts of the stories, which are especially indicative of manipulations carried out by rewriters of the story.

Kerem ile Aslı is attributed to a bard named Aşık Kerem who allegedly lived in the 16th century. In his 1949 study of the story, Şükrü Elçin argues that Kerem's hometown is Erzurum in Eastern Turkey, offering evidence from place names mentioned in the narrative (Elçin, 1949: 64). Although the provenance of the story is largely attributed to the Ottoman–Turkish tradition, various versions were printed in the languages of Turkey's neighbouring countries which are thought to derive from a single Turkish source (Duymaz, 2001: 253–254). Known versions include Azarbaijani (various versions exist in today's Azarbaijan and among the Azeri-speaking population in Southern Iran), Armenian, Crimean, Turkmen, Georgian and Bulgarian (Duymaz, 2001: 24–35). A comparative approach to these versions would no doubt reveal invaluable data regarding notions of literature, culture, religion and ideology in the various languages. Among these, the Armenian versions are especially interesting since in almost all of the Turkish versions, Aslı's Armenian background serves as the main obstacle preventing the union of the two lovers. According to a study carried out by Ali Duymaz, the best known Armenian versions of the story are translations from the printed Ottoman version by the İkbal Publishing House (Duymaz, 2001: 34–35), which will also serve as a basis for my analysis in this chapter. Duymaz reports that these translations often change the storyline and eliminate the religious difference between Kerem and Aslı, also domesticating the names of people and places (Duymaz, 2001: 35).

In the following paragraphs, three rewrites of *Kerem ile Aslı* which appeared in Turkey in the early republican period are discussed. For this analysis, I have chosen to adopt the printed version (published for the first time in 1913 by the İkbal Publishing House) which served as a point of departure for most of the rewrites published after that date (*Tevatür ile Meşhur ve Mütearef Olan Kerem ile Aslı Hikayesinin Tekmil Nüshası* (1913) and *Kerem ile Aslı* (1934)). Several earlier manuscripts of *Kerem ile Aslı* from the 19th century can also be found in various libraries and archives, including the earliest versions of the story printed by lithograph press (Duymaz, 2001: 6–7). The first publisher to print the story was İkbal; the book became a success and was printed three times before the republican period (Özege, 1977: 1846). It started to be printed in Roman script after the alphabet reform of 1928, replacing Ottoman script. The 1934 edition is designated as the 9th edition. None of the subsequent İkbal editions carries the name of the rewriter, while Boratav has confirmed Süleyman Tevfik, a well-known journalist and writer of the time, as the writer[4] of the İkbal version (Boratav, 2002: 150). It is evident that İkbal published one version among many and also introduced changes to the lithograph pressed copy upon which it drew. The criteria which guided the owner/editor to choose that specific version are unknown and may well have been coincidental. Nevertheless, the success of the 1913 İkbal version of *Kerem ile Aslı* established it as the authoritative 'source text', serving as an inspiration and point of departure for many rewrites to follow. It also served as a source for one particular Armenian version, which was published in Turkish with Armenian characters in Istanbul in 1925 (Elçin, 1949: 1).

An academic study published in 1949 refers to the İkbal version as valuable for having remained as faithful to its original as possible (Elçin, 1949: 1). This suggests that a previous manuscript was seen as the 'original', although the author does not mention what he means by the term 'original', and neither does he indicate which manuscript he considers to be the 'original'. This status of the İkbal text seems to have continued until nowadays as illustrated by a new edition of *Kerem ile Aslı* published by one of the major publishers in Turkey, İş Bankası Kültür Yayınları, in 2006 (Öztürk, 2006). This edition includes two different versions of the story, which are the Anatolian (Turkish) and the Azarbaijani versions. The Azarbaijani version has been translated into Turkish by Öztürk with no mention of the source text, whereas the Turkish version is a nearly verbatim copy of the 1913 İkbal text. As I will illustrate in the following paragraphs, many writers and editors acted in a similar way and reprinted the İkbal version with amendments. These amendments, carried out in various forms and to varying degrees, demonstrate some interesting positions taken towards the İkbal version, both thematically and stylistically. Moreover, the changes introduced to *Kerem ile Aslı* by some rewriters foregrounded certain ideological issues and passed on political messages to the readership.

According to the plot of *Kerem ile Aslı*, Kerem and Aslı are destined for each other but are prevented from uniting due to the fact that Kerem is Muslim and Aslı is an Armenian Christian. In what follows I will offer a brief summary of the plot based on the İkbal version:

Plot summary (after the İkbal version):

There was once a fair and kind-hearted sultan in Isfahan who had a Christian monk as his treasurer. After much anticipation each had a child, whom they promised to marry to each other. The sultan had a baby boy (Kerem) and the monk, a baby girl (Aslı). After a few years the monk broke his promise and fled the country since he did not want to give away his daughter to a Muslim man. The children grew up separately but met again in their teenage years. They fell in love, but Aslı was taken away by her father to a remote part of Anatolia. Desperate to find his beloved, Kerem set out on the road with his best friend Sofu. This was the beginning of a journey which took them many years while they travelled through numerous towns in Eastern Turkey to find Aslı. Kerem finally found Aslı in Aleppo where the Pasha forced the monk to allow their marriage. Still determined to stop them, the monk cast a spell on Aslı's bridal gown. On their wedding night, Kerem started unbuttoning Aslı's dress, but the dress buttoned itself back up. He struggled with the buttons for hours and finally started burning in flames due to his unconsummated passion. He burnt to death and Aslı followed him when her hair caught fire, drawing the story to a close.

This plot is more or less common to most rewrites of *Kerem ile Aslı*, with a few exceptions. Although each rewrite introduces a number of lexical and matricial[5] changes to the İkbal version for various reasons, this chapter will take up only three rewrites, all coming from the 1930s, which are indicative of some ideological issues and offer clues regarding their vision of literature and the expectations of the readers.

The first rewrite to be considered is by Besim Atalay, published in 1930 by Istanbul Devlet Matbaası. Atalay was a member of parliament from Aksaray at the time, which is stated on the title page, both elevating the status of the rewrite and offering us clues about the importance attributed to folk literature as a means of ideological dissemination. The title of the book is *Aşık Kerem* (Kerem, the bard) although the content is the same as the İkbal version, entitled *Kerem ile Aslı*. The reason why this particular rewrite is included in the present chapter is the way in which Atalay inserted additions into the first few pages of the text which are of a strikingly ideological nature. The first addition comes on the first page of the story as Kerem's father is being introduced. The addition reads:

> All of the old sultans were stupid people who had no concern for their subjects. The fact that this sultan appointed himself a treasurer belonging to another religion strengthens this argument. (Atalay, 1930: 1)

The additions continue in the second and third pages in the form of paragraphs and two footnotes, again inserted at points where the Sultan is depicted. All these additions pertain to the cruelties and egocentricism of monarchs. One particular paragraph shows how the sultans spent all their money for their own pleasure, while they let their subjects suffer, and one of the footnotes claims that monarchs could even order the execution of their closest friends and supporters (Atalay, 1930: 2–3). The intention of these additions only becomes clear when they are contextualized within the political circumstances of Turkey in 1930. The last Ottoman sultan was ousted in 1922 and the Turkish Republic was established in 1923. One of the aims of replacing the Ottoman script by the Roman alphabet in 1928 was to separate the people from their Ottoman past, which was associated with a strong Muslim heritage. By making these additions, Atalay portrayed the monarchic system, which was still fresh in the minds of the readers, as bad. This is especially interesting when we consider the fact that most of the rewrites represent the Sultan as a fair and clever ruler, something they owe to the İkbal version. The Atalay version was not popular among scholars and critics. For instance, Şükrü Elçin calls it 'propagandistic' ('propaganda') (Elçin, 1949: 1).

A *Kerem ile Aslı* rewrite by the famous rewriter of folk stories, Muharrem Zeki (Korgunal), who produced a total of over 40 rewrites in the 1930s and 1940s, was published in 1931 (Muharrem Zeki, 1931). This rewrite did not have the same kind of ideological intentions as the Atalay version. In fact, its cover illustration features a glamorous Aslı stretched out invitingly on a divan, depicted in a setting that is more fitting for a story from the Arabian Nights, and anchors the story in the fantastic tale tradition with slightly erotic associations. The tale is a rough retelling of the İkbal version where Muharrem Zeki has omitted a large proportion of the verse sections, apparently foregrounding the romance and adventure elements of the story. One addition he makes to the tale is interesting as it offers some clues regarding the expectations of the readership from such popular publications and how the rewrites were manipulated for all kinds of purposes. The addition comes in the episode where Kerem and Aslı meet for the first time as adults. In terms of the physical contact between the two lovers, the İkbal version has Kerem kiss Aslı on the eye, as is customary as a noble display of brotherly or friendly affection. Muharrem Zeki's Kerem, however, is much more daring and approaches Aslı in a much more passionate way:

> The prince started feeling weak in his knees, felt faint and his heart started burning with the fire of love.
>
> [...]
>
> He jumped on her and kissed her eyes, cheek and lips fully.
>
> The girl was overwhelmed and let herself be embraced by this stranger. Then she came to her senses. She wanted to run away on the grass with her tiny bare feet but this would not be possible. Mirza's[6] fingers of steel had clasped her delicate wrist. [...] He united his lips with hers with a sudden thrust. He kissed her until she passed out. (Muharrem Zeki, 1931: 15)

Rather than the poetics of the folk tale, this addition with sexual overtones can be associated with popular romantic or melodramatic novels of the day which Muharrem Zeki had also been writing throughout his long career. This kind of rewriting was probably not the kind of modernization that the government wanted to see in the folk tales. Nevertheless, it is indicative of the way Muharrem Zeki tried to please his readers. We do not know how many copies this particular edition sold. However, it was republished three times in 1940, 1945 and 1954, indicating its popular success. The Muharrem Zeki version thus shows us that particular styles of rewriting could make folk tales cross generic boundaries. It also enables us to trace the links among various agents who operated at the crossroads of folk literature and urban popular literature such as Muharrem Zeki.

The third rewrite to be taken up from the 1930s is marked by an interesting omission. While the plot and dialogue remain very similar to the İkbal version, this rewrite by Orhan Seyfi (1938a) plays down the role of religion in *Kerem ile Aslı* by omitting a key moment in the story relating to the conversion of Aslı to Islam. This moment of conversion is present in most rewrites deriving from the İkbal version, but some rewriters like Orhan Seyfi who digress from the İkbal text prefer to omit it. This section of the tale comes towards the end and gives an account of the reunion of the two lovers in Kayseri. In the İkbal version, Kerem starts singing a tune whose lyrics invite Aslı to convert to Islam. As Aslı confesses her great love for Kerem she also agrees to convert, lifting the biggest barrier to their marriage for the Muslim readership. The rewrite by Orhan Seyfi omits both the song and Aslı's conversion, considerably shortening and reducing their encounter to a romantic meeting only (Orhan Seyfi, 1938a: 135). The elimination of the religious element at that specific point in the story was no doubt a deliberate act which needs to be considered within the context of the republican reforms that aimed to reduce the weight of religion in the making of a new national consciousness. By keeping Aslı's Christianity intact, Orhan Seyfi evidently gave a message of tolerance and permissiveness towards interreligious marriages. This is a specific manipulation that some current rewrites of the story also carry out today, perhaps to appear more politically correct (examples include Binyazar, 2007: 83–84; Yalsızuçanlar, 2001: 120). Orhan Seyfi is introduced as the 'compiler and corrector' of the story which brings to mind the possibility that he was creating a slightly 'corrected' version which was brought in line with the general ideology of the state.

Interestingly enough, there is also some evidence indicating that Orhan Seyfi was against the modernization of folk tales and the proposal made by the government for revising folk tales. He published another rewrite in 1938 called *Asri Kerem* ('The Modern Kerem') (Orhan Seyfi, 1938b) which was a humorous take on *Kerem ile Aslı*. Orhan Seyfi used the plot and the characters as satirical elements to criticize the press and publication circles of the 1930s. Orhan Seyfi wrote a preface to this book where he referred to the government proposal and introduced this version as an attempt to modernize the folk tale. He concluded by writing that he promised to continue writing modernizations of folk stories if the Directorate General of Publications liked that first attempt (Orhan Seyfi, 1938b: Preface). His ironic tone in the preface implied that he was not at all keen on the proposal. This resonates with people like Hüseyin Cahit Yalçın who opposed the proposal, condemning the government for trying to become a self-proclaimed judge of 'good' literature (Güloğul, 1937: 53).

Another interesting aspect of these rewrites was the attitude they displayed towards the issue of authorship. Although all three writers were engaged in a similar type of effort, they were all given different titles in their respective versions. Atalay was called 'tasnif eden', which was a term often used for rewrites of folk stories and means 'one who re-arranges'. As mentioned previously, Orhan Seyfi was called 'compiler and corrector', foreshadowing the amendments in the book. Both of these titles imply a source text which precedes the two rewrites, although nothing is mentioned regarding the identity of that text. On the other hand, Muharrem Zeki's *Kerem ile Aslı* is attributed to him as the writer. While the other two versions acknowledged the fact that they were not the 'original' story, the Muharrem Zeki version appropriated *Kerem ile Aslı* as one *originally* written by the rewriter, although the readership would not have been deceived, as *Kerem ile Aslı* was one of the best known folk tales in the Ottoman tradition. Nevertheless, this appropriation points to a different way of writing and reading literature, mainly marked by an indifference to issues of authorship and literary provenance.

Kerem ile Aslı as Retranslation

This brief excursion into Kerem and Aslı's world should only be considered an introduction into this fascinating work and its many manifestations in the Turkish literary field. *Kerem ile Aslı* continues to be published today but in shifting contexts. The rewrites published in the 2000s regard the work more highly and place *Kerem ile Aslı* in a relatively revered folk tradition. Some publishers, for instance, include the work in their series of 'Turkish classics' ('Türk klasikleri') (Öztürk, 2006), while the Ministry of Education includes the book, without mentioning any specific versions, in a list of 100 books recommended for secondary education.

The database of the Turkish National Library has 56 entries for *Kerem ile Aslı*, while there are 11 different contemporary rewrites available in the book market today. The conceptual framework supplied by TS to explore retranslations can also be instrumental in thinking about the numerous rewrites of *Kerem ile Aslı*. The most common definition of retranslation is 'the act of translating a work that has previously been translated into the same language, or the result of such an act, that is the retranslated text itself' (Tahir Gürçağlar, 2008b: 233). The implications of this concept for contextualizing the different versions of *Kerem ile Aslı* are considered below.

The current view on retranslations suggests that they are not the products of any inherent value in the source text; rather, they are a product of their context (Paloposki & Koskinen, 2004: 29). Furthermore, retranslations do not come about in an isolated and haphazard way. All too often, they feature explicit or implicit references to previous translations. A study of emerging patterns reveals that many retranslations are in competition with the translations which precede them and try to establish their difference in one way or another (Venuti, 2003: 25). My findings on rewrites of *Kerem ile Aslı* largely overlap with the findings on retranslations.

All three rewrites analysed in this chapter are clearly products of their immediate socio-political and cultural contexts, rather than being products whose aim is to perpetuate *Kerem ile Aslı* by adding to the stock of already numerous versions of the story. I have already shown how ideological manipulations have found their way into two of these rewrites. However, it would be wrong to conclude that all rewrites of *Kerem ile Aslı* have been written for ideological purposes. Some rewrites were printed to challenge previous rewrites, and perhaps increase their sales figures through this trick. Throughout the years, certain rewrites have openly declared themselves 'complete' (*Aşık Kerem ile Aslı Han*, 1954) or 'supplemented with new parts taken from old manuscripts dating back 200–300 years' (*Resimli Büyük Kerem ile Aslı Hikayesi*, 1960) and thus have pointed out the inaccuracies or shortcomings of previous rewrites. One should also add commercial factors into the equation. In the 1930s and 1940s, folk tales sold about 50,000 copies per edition. The Atalay version includes this particular number in its inside cover. In an environment where canonical books sold about 3000 copies each, this was a huge figure. The place of commercial concerns is also apparent for the rewrites printed in the 21st century. While some new rewriters mainly use *Kerem ile Aslı* as a source of inspiration and fabricate their own stories in a relatively more distant relationship to the İkbal version (Binyazar, 2007; Yalsızuçanlar, 2001), many are reprints of the İkbal version. Some publishers, such as İlya, Damla and Metropol, have put a label on their covers, indicating the status of the book in the 100 essential books list. This automatically attracts students and their parents as the main target group for the book. For these rewrites, among other things, *Kerem ile Aslı* means guaranteed sales.

One can then argue that rewriters have different reasons for preferring the activity of rewriting over 'original' writing and choosing *Kerem ile Aslı* from among a large repertoire of folk tales. This obvious conclusion comes with a caution. In a study of rewrites of folk tales, the concerns and roles of publishing houses, and the various agents involved in the production of the rewrites such as general editors, proof-readers and distributors should be taken into consideration. Commercial strategies are often decided upon by people involved in the management of publishing companies, rather than rewriters themselves, while ideological, socio-cultural, linguistic or stylistic amendments made to the text of the folk tales are probably at the discretion of the rewriter or a product of his/her interaction with various parties involved.

Notes

1. The terms 'rewriting', and its nominal form 'rewrite', are used in a narrower sense in the present chapter than the wider use of the term by André Lefevere, who referred to a diversity of acts of textual transfer such as criticism, interlingual translation and anthologizing under the umbrella term 'rewriting' (1992). For the purposes of this chapter, I define rewriting in a more literal sense and use it to imply the writing of different versions of the same stories by different writers.

2. Jakobson's definition of this phenomenon as 'rewording' and 'an interpretation of verbal signs by means of other signs of the same language' (1958/2000: 114) has been criticized as being too linguistic, notably by Toury (1986; also see Eco & Nergaard, 1998: 220). My treatment of the different rewrites of folk tales should be regarded as an approach that has a focus on the socio-cultural contextual factors alongside textual ones. Özlem Berk has problematized the same point in her study exploring the modernized editions of Turkish novels as cases of intralingual translation (Berk, 2005).
3. All translations from the Turkish are mine.
4. Please note that none of the versions published in Turkey is attributed to a 'rewriter'. 'Rewriting' and 'rewriter' are not terms used in Turkish literature. In this chapter I employ them as methodological concepts to refer to the writing and writers of the different versions of folk stories.
5. I use the term 'matricial' with reference to Gideon Toury's matricial norms as omissions, additions, syntactic changes and reshuffling of textual units (Toury, 1995: 58–59).
6. The original name of Kerem according to some rewrites.

References

Artun, E. (2006) *Anonim Türk Halk Edebiyatı Nesri*. Istanbul: Kitabevi.
Aşık Kerem ile Aslı Han (1954) Istanbul: Maarif Kitaphanesi.
Atalay, B. (1930) *Aşık Kerem*. Istanbul: Devlet Matbaası.
Berk, Ö. (2005) Diliçi Çeviriler ve *Mai ve Siyah. Dilbilim* 14, 139–150.
Binyazar, A. (2007) *Kerem ile Aslı*. Istanbul: Merkez Kitaplar.
Boratav, P.N. (2002) *Halk Hikayeleri ve Halk Hikayeciliği*. Istanbul: Türkiye Ekonomik ve Toplumsal Tarih Vakfı.
Duymaz, A. (2001) *Kerem ile Aslı Hikayesi Üzerinde Mukayeseli Bir Araştırma*. Ankara: T.C. Kültür Bakanlığı.
Eco, U. and Nergaard, S. (1997) Semiotic approaches. In M. Baker (ed.) *Routledge Encyclopedia of Translation Studies* (pp. 218–222). London/New York: Routledge.
Elçin, Ş.M. (1949) *Kerem ile Aslı Hikayesi*. Ankara: Milli Eğitim Basımevi.
Elçin, Ş. (1997) *Halk Edebiyatı Araştırmaları II*. Ankara: Akçağ.
Even-Zohar, I. (2002) Culture planning and cultural resistance in the making and maintaining of entities. *Sun Yat-Sen Journal of Humanities* 14, 45–52.
Güloğul, F.R. (1937) *Halk Kitaplarına Dair*. Istanbul: Bozkurt Matbaası.
Jakobson, R. (1958/2000) On linguistic aspects of translation. In L. Venuti (ed.) *The Translation Studies Reader* (pp. 113–118). London/New York: Routledge.
Kabacalı, A. (1994) Halk Kitapları. *Müteferrika* 4, 83–90.
Kerem ile Aslı (1934) 9th edn. Istanbul: İkbal Kitabevi.
Lefevere, A. (1992) *Translation, Rewriting and the Manipulation of Literary Fame*. London/New York: Routledge.
Muharrem Zeki (1931) *Kerem ile Aslı*. Istanbul: Kurtuluş Matbaası.
Orhan Seyfi (1938a) *Kerem ile Aslı*. Istanbul: Kanaat Kitabevi.
Orhan Seyfi (1938b) *Asri Kerem. Mizahi Destan*. Istanbul: Hilmi Matbaası.
Özege, S. (1977) *Eski Harflerle Basılmış Türkçe Eserler Kataloğu* (Vol. 4). Istanbul: Fatih Yayınevi.
Öztürk, İ. (2006) *Kerem ile Aslı*. Istanbul: İş Bankası Kültür Yayınları.

Paker, S. (2002) Translation as *Terceme* and *Nazire*, culture-bound concepts and their implications for a conceptual framework for research on Ottoman translation history. In T. Hermans (ed.) *Crosscultural Transgressions. Research Models in Translation Studies II: Historical and Ideological Issues* (pp. 120–143). Manchester: St. Jerome.

Paloposki, O. and Koskinen, K. (2004) A thousand and one translations. Revisiting translation. In G. Hansen, K. Malmkjaer and D. Gile (eds) *Claims, Changes and Challenges in Translation Studies* (pp. 27–38). Amsterdam/Philadelphia: John Benjamins.

Resimli Büyük Kerem ile Aslı Hikayesi (1960) Istanbul: Halk Kitapçılık.

Rudvin, M. (2000) *The Role of Oral Narrative in Shaping National Identity*. Modena: Edizioni II Fiorino.

Tahir Gürçağlar, Ş. (2002) Translation as conveyor: Critical thought in Turkey in the 1960s. *Works and Days* 20 (1–2), 253–278.

Tahir Gürçağlar, Ş. (2008a) *The Politics and Poetics of Translation in Turkey, 1923–1960*. Amsterdam/New York: Rodopi.

Tahir Gürçağlar, Ş. (2008b) Retranslation. In M. Baker and G. Saldanha (eds) *Routledge Encyclopedia of Translation Studies* (pp. 233–236). London/New York: Routledge.

Tevatür ile Meşhur ve Mütearef Olan Kerem ile Aslı Hikayesinin Tekmil Nüshası (1913) Istanbul: İkbal Kütüphanesi [in Ottoman script].

Toury, G. (1986) Translation. A cultural-semiotic perspective. In T.A. Sebeok (ed.) *Encyclopedic Dictionary of Semiotics* (Vol. 2) (pp. 1111–1124). Berlin/New York/Amsterdam: Mouton de Gruyter.

Toury, G. (1995) *Descriptive Translation Studies and Beyond*. Amsterdam: John Benjamins.

Venuti, L. (2003) Retranslations: The creation of value. *Bucknell Review* 47 (1), 25–38.

Yalsızuçanlar, S. (2001) *Kerem ile Aslı. Aşıklık Ne Müşkil Haldir*. Istanbul: Timaş Yayınları.

Chapter 4
Where Have All the Tyrants Gone? Romanticist Persians for Royals, Athens 1889

G. VAN STEEN

Introduction

During the Greek revolutionary period of the 1820s, the *Persians*, Aeschylus' oldest extant play, became the direct link with and expression of the military and other 'national' glories of the classical era. This 'historical' tragedy was first staged at the Great Dionysia festival of 472 BCE as a theatrical reflection of the battle of Salamis, which the Greeks had won against the Persians in 480 BCE. To the 19th-century Greek revolutionaries and to many philhellene supporters, Aeschylus' unique play seemed to hold up the supreme analogic model of a Greek triumph in the struggle for liberation from the Ottoman Turkish occupiers. At the start of its new lease of life in the emerging nation-state of Greece, this tragedy was not the critical, disquieting and empathetic play that modern theatre practitioners and scholars have uncovered, but *the* exemplum of a soothing genre of patriotic (self-)assurance and moral confirmation.

In its pre-revolutionary modern Greek reception, Aeschylus' *Persians* turned from a tragedy into a heroic–patriotic drama. It posed time-specific as well as long-lasting challenges of translation and performance, both of practical performance on stage and of the demands of performativity implied in the presumed patriotic script and in the victorious to triumphant message. The earliest modern Greek version of the *Persians* already probed and extended the conventional limits of patriotism and memory and of performance and performativity. The record of an 1820 closed reading of the play (written up by Comte de Marcellus, 1859, 1861; Van Steen, 2007), which was held in Turkish-occupied Constantinople, delivers a close-up of how the Greek cultural and military past was explored by and through liberal performance. Thus the tragedy made its timid debut as a voice of Greek nationalism and patriotism in the face of well-defined enemies, the Ottoman Turks, who 'reincarnated' the ancient Persians. With such a revolutionary voice, the play stood for the generative forces of modern Greek history and destiny rather than of theatre. The desire of Greek intellectuals and Western philhellenes to engage in a direct comparison of the contemporary Greek nation with ancient Greece tapped into an emotional definition of heroism and patriotic action – which may still be among the main impulses driving the current interest in the *Persians* as a manual for modern 'historical' analogies, or for explorations of the present through the past and its supposed time-hallowed lessons.

In the decades after 1821, liberated Greece erected physical theatre buildings, but it did not extend or honour the early patriotic struggle of the Greek performance culture: theatre practitioners and patriotic plays could not always be sure to find the hard-won freedom of speech (Chatzepantazes, 2006: 64–67; Delveroude, 1988: 299–300, note 27). Rather, neoclassical adaptations and melodramas enjoyed official Greek approval and occasional financial sponsorship, often to the detriment of 'authentic' revivals of ancient plays and native modern Greek stagings, whose patriotism was then deemed exaggerated or offensive by the foreign (Bavarian) royal house and the Greek aristocracy (Van Steen, 2000: 44–50).[1] The nominal or grand modern Greek premiere of Aeschylus' *Persians* came in 1889 and was heavily charged with the expectations of the court.[2] The sea change, then, in the tragedy's modern Greek stage tradition occurred in 1965, with a strikingly self-reflexive production created by the avant-gardist Greek theatre director Karolos Koun (1908–1987).[3]

In this chapter, I argue that the 1889 Greek appropriation of Aeschylus' *Persians* illustrates the nature and purpose of late 19th-century official conservatism. The question of how Greek patriotism versus officialdom in its various hues played out in the 1889 reworking of the tragedy commands special interest. I do not aim, however, to provide an exhaustive account of the play's early modern Greek reinterpretations. Instead, I will highlight how important threads of a representative revival production were interwoven with historical Greek notions of translation and conformism as they were enacted on stage. This brief study touches on many issues, but it can only aim to achieve a concerted foray, with attention to detail, into topics such as translation and (the lack of) opposition to conservative officialdom. It cannot attempt complete coverage of many aspects and dimensions of translation and opposition, even when these dimensions marked modern Greek theatre as a theatre of political and cultural memory in its earliest formative, destabilizing, or solidifying operations. Yet each drama performance that touched the Greek nerves of nationalism and patriotism also metaphorically stood for what was happening to performance and translation in a broader temporal context (Chatzepantazes, 2006). This is precisely the focus that this analysis brings to the 1889 modern Greek production of Aeschylus' *Persians*.

All the King's Patriots ...

In October 1889, the royal wedding of Konstantinos, the crown prince of Greece, to Sophia of Prussia, the sister of Kaiser Wilhelm II, supplied the celebratory occasion for a production of Aeschylus' *Persians*. The emperor himself was expected to attend and Athens was filled with anticipation. The choice of this tragedy to mark a celebratory event may today seem an odd one, given that the *Persians* is a work in which loss and fear figure as prominent themes. Director Demetrios Kokkos staged the 'gala' production at the newly opened Municipal Theatre of Athens with a company of aristocratic dilettanti, the *kosmikoi erasitechnes*, or the 'worldly amateurs', as the Greek theatre historian Giannes Sideres referred to them (Constantinidis, 1987: 20; Glytzoures, 2001: 49–50, 54; Sideres, 1976: 76, 87–91; 1990: 216). This 1889 production was hailed as a Greek premiere and as the return of Aeschylus to his native soil. But what Sideres and the Greek public expected to be a broad-popular patriotic occasion turned into a display of subservience to the Germans, or into stage diplomacy for the sake of courting Western goodwill.

Kokkos selected the translation by Alexandros Rizos Rankaves (1809–1892), a scholar-diplomat, writer, critic and editor, and perhaps the best known philologist-translator of ancient drama in the formal Kathareuousa or classicizing Greek language (Athanassopoulou, 2002: 296–298; Garantoudes, 2000; Van Steen, 2000: 68–72). Rankaves had published his archaicizing translation of Aeschylus' *Persians* in 1885. Of prestigious Greek–Phanariot stock, Rankaves spent many years of his life residing abroad, where he exhibited great curiosity about the international theatre scene (Sideres, 1976: 31). He believed, however, that he could present classical drama in the way in which the ancients would have seen and experienced it (Sideres, 1976: 25). Therefore, he did not yield easily to foreign pressures, especially not when those affected the formal aspects of language and text (Glytzoures, 2001: 54, note 92). Despite his confident investment in Greek continuities, Rankaves also believed that European fashions and ideals could be grafted onto the ancients and their literary forms. With the latter conviction, he and many of the contemporary Greek intelligentsia represented a Romanticizing classicism movement (Chasape-Christodoulou, 2002: I-327; Chatzepantazes, 2002: 243, 244).

Thus Rankaves attuned his translation of Aeschylus' *Persians* to the grand orchestral musical score written by another German royal, the philhellene Prince Bernhard of Saxe-Meiningen (cf. Sideres, 1990: 216).[4] This preferred musical composition, which the Greek court insisted on hearing, had fashioned – and made fashionable – the 1881 German production of an adaptation of the *Persians* by Hermann Koechly (published 1876) (Flashar, 1991: 108, 397; Sideres, 1976: 88). Prince Bernhard, whose father Georg II, the Duke of Saxe-Meiningen, produced many plays with his own company and thereby influenced Greek and other European conceptions of court theatre (Osborne, 1988), participated actively in the Greek staging of the *Persians*. The Prince also attended the dress rehearsal of the play, where he was welcomed by Rankaves (anonymous Greek newspaper report in *Akropolis*, 15 October 1889; Glytzoures, 2001: 54–55, 60, 499). He even imposed some of his own ideas for a historicizing stage design, and in particular for the tomb of Darius, Xerxes' father (Glytzoures, 2001: 59, 490).

After the model of Koechly's German adaptation, Rankaves went on to produce a new, 'happy' ending to the classical tragedy. He had published this alternative finale, or the last exchange between Xerxes, his mother Atossa, and the chorus (from Aeschylus, *Persians*, 1014 onward), as an appendix to his 1885 translation (Rankaves, 1885: 271–274). This drastic intervention subverted the sombre and apocalyptic ending of the original: the new ending cut short the protracted lamentations of the Persian king, who arrived in rags, and of the elders over the devastating loss of their forces. Now the tragedy made an unexpected, pro-monarchist and optimistic turn. Calling on Xerxes' life-long servants for assistance, Queen Atossa welcomes her son as King and promptly re-invests him with the regalia of – despotic – power:

Χαῖρε Βασιλεῦ παντάναξ ...
Δοῦλοι, ἄρατε τὰς πύλας. Ὁ δεσπότης ἔφθασε.
Πορφυροβαφῆ τὸτ (sic) δρόμον στρώσατε θεράπαιναι.
Ἄνδρες, γέροντες, γυναῖκες, παῖδες, προσκυνήσατε.
(Rankaves, 1885: 271–272)

Welcome King who rules all ...
Slaves, open the gates. The despot has arrived.
Servants, spread purple carpets out on the road.
Men, elders, women, children, prostrate yourselves.[5]

Xerxes utters meek reservations against the 'typical' Persian display of power (in Rankaves' Orientalizing exaggeration of the more discreet portrayal by Aeschylus):

> "Οχι, ὢ ἁγνή μου μῆτερ. Τί συνέβη ἀγνοεῖς.
> . . .
> Τί μοὶ λέγεις μῆτερ; Μήπως εἶμαι πλέον Βασιλεύς;
> Βασιλεὺς λαὸν μὴ ἔχων, Βασιλεὺς χωρὶς στρατοῦ!
> (Rankaves, 1885: 272)

> No, my innocent mother. You do not know what has happened.
> . . .
> What are you saying to me, mother? Perhaps I am still King?
> A king who does not have a people, a king without army!

Atossa, however, is quick to override her son's objections and to invoke 'the people', on whose behalf she presumes she speaks:

> . . . μένει ἔτι ὁ λαὸς,
> . . .
> Μένουσι τῆς γῆς οἱ ὅροι, μένει καὶ τὸ κράτος σου,
> κ' οἱ ὑπήκοοί σου πάντες πειθαρχοῦσιν ὡς τὸ πρίν.
> (Rankaves, 1885: 272–273)

> . . . There are still the people,
> . . .
> The bounds of the land remain, and also your rule remains,
> and all of your subordinates obey you like before.

Atossa promises, and the chorus instantly concurs, that the 'obedient' people of Xerxes' land, which he may still call his own, will produce a new race to replace the army that he has lost and to bestow future victories upon him (Eliade, 1999: 167; Symvoulidou, 1998: 48). Koechly had his chorus console Xerxes by assuring him of the ever-obedient nature of his subjects in the closing lines:

> Denn von Anfang her
> Bis an's Ende der Tage gilt dieses Gesetz
> Für Persia's (sic) Volk:
> Dass mit seinem König es Eins ist!
> (Koechly, 1876: 13)

> For from the beginning
> until the end of days, this law holds true
> for the people of Persia:
> that it is agreed with its King!

Rankaves' adaptation of the adaptation rendered the closing lines as follows:

> ἐπειδὴ ἀπ' ἀρχῆς μέχρι τέλους τῶν χρόνων
> αὐτὸς παρὰ Πέρσαις κρατεῖ ὁ Θεσμός·
> Βασιλεὺς καὶ λαὸς ὅτι ἓν εἰσί.
> (Rankaves, 1885: 274)

> Indeed, from the beginning until the end of times
> this law holds among the Persians:
> that King and people are one.

Rankaves' Germanophile adaptation conformed to the contemporary aesthetics of Romanticist melodrama in the pursuit of grand orchestral music, a 'happy' ending, psychological sensitivity, and the exaggeration of emotions – including the hyperbolic promise of popular support. Instead of the bleak and threnodic finale of Aeschylus' original, Rankaves conveyed the hopeful prospect of moderate and respected governance through a humbled and changed Xerxes. His stage character of Atossa, however, did not abjure the historical legacy of the hubristic Persian despot, nor did it dislodge the political background of tyrannical oppression and military aggression. These ambivalent anti-tyrannical as well as pro-dynastic components that Rankaves projected onto the Persian – or on the German – monarchs made for ceremonial and symbolic theatre or for official and diplomatic state ritual.

Greek aristocrats and intellectuals allowed their court's foreign policy considerations to dictate the form, style and objective of their dramatic art. They rewrote history and tragedy to offer an emperor, monarch and monarchists a more palatable version of Aeschylus' play with its prior reputation for championing Greek patriotic liberation and territorial integrity. The newly polished, revamped tragedy was put to political work and vouched for Greek loyalty: it ensured the obeisance of Greece to Germany and, in particular, the Greek aristocracy's willingness to confirm the hegemony of the Western court imported into their country. Rankaves' act of smoothing over the original's 'rough spots' for rulers proved that he knew well enough how to identify the foreign enemy whom the popular classes perceived to have infiltrated Greece. Thus far, the modern reception history of Aeschylus' *Persians* had targeted foes beyond national borders. In the pre-revolutionary performance of 1820, for example, the enemy had been – *per* definition – without and not within the conspiratorial Greek circles of Constantinople. In 1889, the opponent within, i.e. the Western-leaning court and aristocracy, posed an ideological, cultural and artistic threat, as well as a political danger.

The transformation of the 1889 *Persians* into a Romanticist, melodramatic play of political conformism explains why the production was perceived as a setback for the cause of Greek patriotism. Sideres regarded the altered script and the entire production as public acts of 'submission' to the palace on the part of the amateur company (Sideres, 1976: 91, 94). The theatre historian's stated disappointment with a production that failed to be 'patriotic' and that 'diminished' a historical Greek victory, points up the extraordinarily hefty modern Greek expectations that rested on this early public revival of Aeschylus' *Persians*. Other ancient plays, too, underwent processes of adaptation that corresponded with the 18th- through 19th-century neoclassical and Romanticist fashions. These fashions determined the mode in which the plays premiered in post-revolutionary Greece, before audiences consisting of the upper classes, with cosmopolitan interests and aspirations. Ambitious calls for a 'national' theatre that would draw on the ancients in their undiluted form or pay homage to the heroes of the Revolution followed; they were answered by the more conservative intelligentsia, including students and professors at the University of Athens. Some of the resulting antiquarian productions of classical drama, however, imparted a staged nationalism and cultural chauvinism that was voiced by – mostly amateur and student – theatre groups that could not otherwise compete with foreign, mainly Italian, professional companies or with Western European plays and adaptations of ancient themes (Chatzepantazes, 2002: 49–50, 138, 139, 155, 181–182, 274, 633).

Rankaves' pro-monarchic Persians of 1889, or his tribute to the German emperor, must be explained in the light of his – literary as well as political and ideological – engagement with the project of empire. Rankaves took an active interest in the Greek imperial future, or in the possible restoration of the Byzantine Christian empire (Skopetea, 1988: 277–280). He had been urging the Greeks to become (culturally) more Western European by striving to establish – paradoxically and in true Orientalist vein – an eastern empire, which would include the Levant (Gotsi, 2006: 40–41). Some of his lesser-known exoticizing fiction and publications in the periodical press deal with imperial policies, colonial practices and the Greek 'civilizing' mission (Gotsi, 2006: 23, 38–44). Thus Aeschylus' *Persians* became emplotted in Rankaves' long-time negotiations with the European imperial enterprise as well as with his mediation of the Greek imperial vision.

The 'Repatriation' of Classical Tragedy to Greece

The pro-dynastic makeover of the 1889 *Persians* points up fault-lines in the complex dependencies between Greek revival tragedy and translation practice. It also unmasks the pressures to establish a modern Greek theatre and repertoire of manifest political as well as cultural capital – to use Pierre Bourdieu's categories (1993). The immediate relevance of these relationships and their general importance as building blocks of Greek identity are confirmed by the Greek efforts to revive Sophocles' *Antigone* in Athens ... belatedly. The Greek reception history of this tragedy, too, reveals a rather uncritical but widespread 19th- through early 20th-century fascination with foreign-imported models. It was the compelling combination of a German adaptation and a Romanticist musical score that steered the *Antigone*'s early Western European reception. The choral music composed by Felix Mendelssohn-Bartholdy launched the *Antigone* of director Ludwig Tieck as *the* 'classical' production ever since its grand opening performance in Potsdam in 1841. The translation was by Johann Jakob Christian Donner and the production enjoyed the patronage of Friedrich Wilhelm IV of Prussia, who dreamed of a 'renaissance of Greek tragedy in the heart of the Kingdom of Prussia', and whose actions expressed growing nationalist, pro-dynastic, and didactic fervour (Hall & Macintosh, 2005: 319).[6]

The 'Mendelssohn *Antigone*', as the production became known, caused many *Antigone* performances to spring up throughout Western Europe. These performances were well intentioned attempts to smooth over the 'intractable' aesthetics and conventions of Greek tragic theatre with the aural and visual delights of Romantic drama, to which the mid-19th-century upper classes of theatregoers had grown accustomed. The tremendously influential model provoked a sense of belatedness in the Greek theatre world, because the Greeks had failed to revive the *Antigone* before the German adaptation stole the show and also because they had not embraced the modern success version as quickly as other countries had done. By wasting such valuable opportunities, the Greeks, some thought, had failed to prove the authenticity of their own descent from the ancients. The search for historical continuity and classical ancestry inspired many of the first modern Greek revival productions of ancient tragedy. Few saw the bold liberties that neoclassical and Romanticist adaptations took, however, as encroaching upon the broad claim to continuity.

The Romanticist Greek staging of Sophocles' *Antigone* of 1867 was modelled closely after the 1841 German version (Rankaves, 1895: II-164–165; Sideres, 1976: 42–45). The Athenian production proudly showed off Mendelssohn's celebrated music: a full 15-member chorus of students sang the choral passages in Rankaves' translation in Kathareuousa Greek (Chasape-Christodoulou, 2002: I-340–341; Chatzepantazes, 2002: 634; De Herdt, 2003: I-98, 191; Glytzoures, 2001: 45). This staging, too, amounted to a cosmopolitan and aristocratic tribute to the Greek king and the elite (Chatzepantazes, 2002: 138–140, 273–274, note 41, 633). With this first complete *Antigone* production of 1867, the semi-professional Greek actors and director celebrated another ritual of state: the royal wedding of King George I and the Russian princess Olga. The 'patriotic' tragedy was staged at the Herodes Atticus Theatre, which was newly excavated and fitted out, though not yet restored (Sideres, 1976: 43). An archaeology professor from the University of Athens, Athanasios Rousopoulos, was in charge of the direction. This academic basis – a common feature of mid-19th- through early 20th-century revival productions – demonstrates how willing some Greek intellectuals were to participate in the disciplined training in foreign-imported aesthetics and, in particular, in Western choral or orchestral music, especially when courtly performances were at stake. Sideres characterized the rage for the Mendelssohn *Antigone* as the phenomenon of *'Antigonismos'*, with a pun on the modern Greek word for 'antagonism' or 'rivalry' (*antagonismos*) (Sideres, 1976: 82, with reference to a Greek newspaper report in *Ephemeris*, 22 October 1888). In the competitive struggle to bring the first revival of Sophocles' *Antigone* to Greek soil, be it in its 'authentic' form or in adaptation, the German version held pride of place. For several decades to come, *Antigone*-mania marked the tragedy and its author as vehicles of foreign-imported Romanticism through the Siren call of music. The same infatuation impacted on other classical plays as well, including Aeschylus' *Persians*.

A case in point was that of Sophocles' *Philoctetes*. In the same year, 1889, in which Rankaves offered up his Germanized translation of Aeschylus' *Persians*, amateurs and students of the Drama School of the National Drama Association (Ethnikos Dramatikos Syllogos, under the directorship of Professor Antonios Antoniades) staged a repeat performance of the *Philoctetes* in ancient Greek but divided into three acts. This production, which had seen its Greek premiere in late November 1887, also accommodated a symphonic musical score, albeit by minor German composers. Still celebrating the Greek–German marital union of 1889, the *Philoctetes*, staged at the Municipal Theatre of Athens, even opened with the German national anthem. Some critics and scholars, however, continued to argue that any choral music or other modern accretions should be subordinated to the original text and not vice versa. In other words, in Greece, revival tragedy should be owned by the Greeks.

The 19th-century Greek Romanticist tradition in revival tragedy came to a rude awakening when it ran into the vocal protests of Georgios Mistriotes, a Classics professor from the University of Athens and the controversial standard-bearer of a line of conservative philologists turned amateur stage directors. Mistriotes loudly questioned the key position of Romanticist revivals in Greek repertory and court-serving theatre, albeit with his keen, personal focus on affirming the unity and purity of Greek lineage, which manifested itself in his insistence on classical Greek for his own performances. Mistriotes' Society for Staging Ancient Greek Drama, active from 1896 until 1906, specialized in classical-language revivals of Sophoclean tragedy, which marked a decade of protectionist cultural activity that purported to be 'patriotic' in the name of the inherited Hellenic civilization (see, for instance, Chasape-Christodoulou, 2002: I-513; Chatzepantazes, 2002: 139–140; Chatzepantazes, 2006: 175–176, 184, 219, note 47; Sideres, 1976: 101–105, 113–128, 210–226, *passim*). Mistriotes was one of the last to defend tenaciously the linguistic ideal that rejected modern Greek translations of the ancient Greek texts. Non-translation of the plays, however, meant limited dissemination and narrowed the potential for viable stage production. In March 1889, or a mere few months before the production of the *Persians* took place, Mistriotes had publicly declared that it was the 'mission' of the modern Greek playwright, 'like another Heracles, to tear down the gates of Hades and to bring back up to the light of day the heroes of [ancient] Greek history' (translated from the Greek quotation by Chatzepantazes, 2006: 175, with references to Mistriotes' published speeches in the Greek journal *Palingenesia*, 28, 29, and 30 March 1889). Greek dramaturgy, nationalism and didacticism had to join forces in a 'patriotic', historicizing theatre that functioned as a school for the nation – an ideal with roots in the Western Enlightenment and with a long-lived but charged history in modern Greece.[7]

In the early 1890s, or shortly after the Romanticist staging of Aeschylus' *Persians*, Mistriotes announced an 'authentic' production of the *Ajax* of Sophocles. The latter was more and more frequently being hailed as *ethnikos*, or a 'national' playwright (Chasape-Christodoulou, 2002: I-521–522; Sideres, 1976: 105, note 1). With a great sense of urgency, Mistriotes reclaimed Sophocles, the public persona from among the classical dramatists, for the cause of Greek nationalism and patriotism. Sophocles' reception was in need of proper redirection, so the professor asserted, because the overwhelming success of the Mendelssohn *Antigone* had badly Romanticized it. Before Mistriotes staged his own *Antigone* in 1896 – a terrible flop – the play's recent Greek history had led revival tragedy's deliberate show of Western 'progress' and modern urban sensibility. The shadow of the 1896 Olympics heightened the pressure on any modern Greek revivals of ancient Greek culture as well as on productions of classical drama, to meet the standards set by the state's investment in Greece's cultural capital and also in the 'sacred' nature and ideological potential of mass gatherings in monumental open-air sites. Before increasing numbers of foreign visitors to Greece, modern Greek revival productions of ancient theatre had to labour to build patriotic reverence, domestically as well as internationally, for a young nation with huge internal and external, political, social, economic and financial problems. Critics carped that some of these productions, as well as some of the rituals associated with the Olympic Games, amounted to costumed pageantry and propagandistic manipulation of the masses. In the process, however, modern Greek identity and the concomitant stage identities were being politically and ideologically defined and negotiated under the pressures of the volatile global political landscape of the late 19th century and the turn of the 20th century.

Conclusion

The pro-dynastic Greek production of Aeschylus' *Persians* of 1889 was used as a vehicle for the nation's 'Western-style' advancement and to legitimate its claims to modernity. A treatment of the play that conversed with Greek ideas of translation, Romanticism and revival tragedy raised many questions, some of which led to the conclusion that translation that resisted popular resistance was – perhaps unfairly – perceived as doubly imitative or, under a political spotlight, as doubly humbling. This chapter has therefore explored some additional instances of pressure placed on classical tragedy, not to be dissident but to conform, and to deliver feel-good, comfort solutions for particular, often celebratory occasions, audiences and classes. These cases exhibited a new kind of partisanship, not that of the Greek revolutionary age, but that of scoring political points with the power-holders and of succumbing to palace tastes and caprices. They supply benevolent to patronizing performance histories with which to question the tenet that reliance on tragic models from antiquity was necessarily a radical or dissident move. This tenet has inflected the reception histories of Aeschylus' *Persians* and of Sophocles' *Antigone*, in particular. What tied together various Romanticist productions of ancient plays in the later 19th century was the recurring interest in imported German music, which was expected to secure their success. Reading the 1889 *Persians* and its context anew allowed us to explore the ever-evolving Greek dynamics of theatre adaptation and translation, patriotic politics, and 'national' language and literature. Also, the Greek production may serve as a healthy reminder that the reception history of Aeschylus' *Persians* has not excluded reactionary treatments. It may thus provide a longer historical background to some revisionist resistance versions of the play which have recently emerged to question perceived imperialist behaviour of the United States in Iraq. We tend to forget just how recent a phenomenon this 'revision/reversal' is and how it is forging a reception of the *Persians* that, with its strength of conviction, makes it nearly impossible to set the clock back.

Aeschylean drama may strike us as an unlikely and unexpected vehicle of the drive toward conformism or of the pressure to live up to the ideal of upper-class 'patriotism'. Was Aeschylus a conformist, then? No, he was turned into the icon that the unstable, late 19th-century Greek society was then seeking. For a translation/adaptation, however, to work in the political terms of 1889 as well as on the official stage, it had to comply with certain public norms as defined by upper-class Greek identity. Laden with the baggage from antiquity and overcharged with philhellene and Western expectations, revival tragedy thus became the late 19th-century proving ground for the triumph, not of liberalism and democracy, but of modest degrees of political utility and compliance. The 1889 Romanticist makeover and courtly manipulation of Aeschylus' *Persians* was sanctified by the enthusiasm among Greek aristocrats for fashionable Western European dramaturgical aesthetics, which expressed Western civic values. It was also this imported aesthetic that further contaminated any proclaimed translation of the ancient tragedy and that amplified the translation's potential for political mixing. Formerly a locus of anti-tyrannical opposition, the *Persians* became a platform for the diplomacy of flattery and alliance building, or for subservient peace offerings instead of defensive or defiant wars. That classical drama was expected to build for Greece a vital reserve of international goodwill is perhaps harder to comprehend today. Modern sensibilities measure and esteem ideological 'authenticity' in the representation of ancient plays as a component of their success. They value the timeless works' permeability to current ideological trends and radical appropriations, and they weigh revivals against each other by their degree of revisionism and openness to adaptation and transformation – which often amounts to their potential for opposition.

Acknowledgements

The author is indebted to Dimitris Asimakoulas and Margaret Rogers for their responsible work as editors, benefitting greatly from their sensitive comments and suggestions.

Notes

1. A typical example of sponsored 19th-century student and amateur productions was the school production of Sophocles' *Antigone*, which was staged in

Athens in 1858. For many more examples, see De Herdt (2003, *passim*) and Sideres (1976). De Herdt (2003) provides data on several late 19th-century translations of Aeschylus' *Persians*, some of which were written with a student clientele in mind. Stagings at this time were typically conducted either in the original ancient Greek language or in the formalist Kathareuousa. Productions of classical tragedy in Demotic appeared in the early 20th century and then only after several incidents had occurred that made the Language Question (*Glossiko Zetema*) notorious, such as the Euangelika and the Oresteiaka, or the outcry over translations of the Gospels and of Aeschylus' *Oresteia* respectively (Van Steen, 2008). For a brief summary of these events in light of the modern Greek revival history of ancient Greek drama, see Constantinidis (1987).

2. Eliade summarizes the production data on three late 19th-century student and amateur productions of Aeschylus' *Persians*, including this nominal premiere (1991: 115).
3. See further Hall, in her aptly entitled section 'Making *Persians* topical again' (2007: 185–186). Koun's production is one of those pioneering stagings that have, overall, received far too little attention in Anglo-Saxon scholarship. Hall rightly identifies Koun's *Persians* of 1965 as one of three revisionist performances that engendered the strong sentiment and self-doubt provoked by the wave of politically critical revivals which started in 1993, with the provocative new stage version of Aeschylus' *Persians* by the American trail-blazing director Peter Sellars. Sellars let empathy with the victims speak loudly in his *Persians*, staged in Salzburg, Edinburgh, Los Angeles and other venues, in an adaptation by Robert Auletta (1993). Sellars and Auletta replaced the ancient Persians with the modern Iraqis of Baghdad, who had suffered both the regime of Saddam Hussein and defeat in the 1991 Gulf War. They transformed the tragedy into a window on the East and turned the play into a very critical mirror held up to the United States. They asked American audiences to rethink their own imperialism and their incomplete image of the adversaries whom their government punished. Without being blind to the faults of the enemy, they transformed Aeschylus' drama into a prime example of controversial and at times disturbing theatre (Hall, 2007: 185, 191–194). Another more recent and revisionist stage adaptation of Aeschylus' *Persians* was written by Ellen McLaughlin (2005: 251–309) and directed by Ethan McSweeney (2003) (Hall, 2007: 192–194).
4. With the production at hand and the musical score becoming the focus of attention, Rankaves' work inspired three more translations in the year 1889 (cf. De Herdt, 2003: I-44, 158–160, 175, note 315; II-33, 36–37, 47, 90; Sideres, 1976: 91). The increasing interest which Greek 'philological' translators took in Aeschylus' *Persians* did not achieve much to reappropriate the tragedy for Greece or to remedy the anaemic condition of Greek dramaturgy at large. The boost in translations was, if anything, the *result* of the mid- through late 19th-century craving for Western European acceptance through adopting its values and aesthetics: some modern Greek translators merely hoped to get a piece of the action (cf. De Herdt, 2003: II-105–106).
5. All translations from either modern or ancient Greek are my own.
6. The Mendelssohn *Antigone* is the subject of discussion in many sources (e.g. Fischer-Lichte, 1999: 253–255; Flashar, 1991: 60–81, 85, 90–91, 110; Flashar, 2001: 36–44; Macintosh, 1997: 286–289). The celebrated production also gave impetus

to literary and philosophical discussions of Sophocles' original play from the mid-19th century onwards. Steiner (1984) provides an insightful and eloquent introduction to the many theatrical, operatic, cinematic and psychological reworkings of Sophocles' *Antigone*.

7. Chatzepantazes positions Mistriotes at the source of the exalted public promulgation of the patriotic, religious, moral and family values that found their formal rhetorical expression in the notoriously reactionary triptych of 'Fatherland, Religion, and Family' (*patris, threskeia, oikogeneia*) (2006: 178, note 14, 185 [quotation]).

References

Athanassopoulou, E.F. (2002) An 'ancient' landscape: European ideals, archaeology, and nation building in early modern Greece. *Journal of Modern Greek Studies* 20 (2), 273–305.

Auletta, R. (1993) *The Persians by Aeschylus*. Los Angeles: Sun and Moon Press.

Bourdieu, P. (1993) *Pierre Bourdieu. The Field of Cultural Production: Essays on Art and Literature* (R. Johnson, ed. and introduction). New York: Columbia University Press.

Chasape-Christodoulou, E. (2002) *Η ελληνική μυθολογία στο νεοελληνικό δράμα· από την εποχή του Κρητικού θεάτρου έως το τέλος του 20ου αιώνα* [*Ancient Greek Myth in Modern Greek Drama: From the Era of the Cretan Theatre until the End of the Twentieth Century*]. 2 vols. Thessaloniki: University Studio Press.

Chatzepantazes, Th. (2002) *Από του Νείλου μέχρι του Δουνάβεως· το χρονικό της ανάπτυξης του ελληνικού επαγγελματικού θεάτρου, στο ευρύτερο πλαίσιο της Ανατολικής Μεσογείου, από την ίδρυση του ανεξάρτητου κράτους ως τη Μικρασιατική καταστροφή* [*From the Nile to the Danube: The Chronicle of the Development of the Greek Professional Theatre, within the Broader Framework of the Eastern Mediterranean, from the Foundation of the Independent State to the Asia Minor Catastrophe*]. Heraklion, Crete: Panepistemiakes Ekdoseis Kretes.

Chatzepantazes, Th. (2006) *Το ελληνικό ιστορικό δράμα· από το 19ο στον 20ο αιώνα* [*The Greek Historical Drama: From the Nineteenth to the Twentieth Century*]. Heraklion, Crete: Panepistemiakes Ekdoseis Kretes.

Constantinidis, S.E. (1987) Classical Greek drama in modern Greece: Mission and money. *Journal of Modern Greek Studies* 5 (1), 15–32.

De Herdt, K. (2003) 'Je crains que vous ne me trouviez trop moderne pour un Grec.' Over Griekse vertalingen van Oudgriekse teksten, ca. 1860–1910 ['I fear that you might find me too modern for a Greek'. About Greek translations of ancient Greek texts, c. 1860–1910]. 2 vols. PhD thesis, University of Ghent, Belgium.

Delveroude, E-A. (1988) *Η καλλιέργεια του πατριωτικού αισθήματος στη θεατρική παραγωγή των αρχών του 20ου αιώνα* [Cultivating the patriotic sentiment in early twentieth-century theatrical production]. In G.Th. Maurogordatos and Ch.Ch. Chatze-ioseph (eds) *Βενιζελισμός και αστικός εκσυγχρονισμός* [*Venizelism and Urban Modernization*] (pp. 287–314). Heraklion, Crete: Panepistemiakes Ekdoseis Kretes.

Eliade, M. (1991) Παραστασιογραφία [List of productions]. In K. Topouzes (ed. and trans.) *Αισχύλου Πέρσαι* [*Aeschylus' Persians*] (pp. 113–126). Athens: Epikairoteta.

Eliade, M. (1999) Έρευνα και καταγραφή των νεοελληνικών παραστάσεων αρχαίου ελληνικού δράματος· απρόοπτα και ζητούμενα [Researching and recording modern Greek productions of ancient Greek drama: The unpredictable and the desirable]. In P. Mauromoustakos (ed.) *Παραστάσεις αρχαίου ελληνικού δράματος στην Ευρώπη κατά τους νεότερους χρόνους* [*Productions of Ancient Greek Drama in Europe during Modern Times*] (pp. 161–169). Athens: Kastaniotes.

Fischer-Lichte, E. (1999) Invocation of the dead, festival of peoples' theatre or sacrificial ritual? Some remarks on staging Greek classics. In S. Patsalidis and E. Sakellaridou (eds) *(Dis)Placing Classical Greek Theatre* (pp. 252–263). Thessaloniki: University Studio Press.

Flashar, H. (1991) *Inszenierung der Antike: Das griechische Drama auf der Bühne der Neuzeit, 1585–1990.* Munich: Beck.

Flashar, H. (2001) *Felix Mendelssohn-Bartholdy und die griechische Tragödie: Bühnenmusik im Kontext von Politik, Kultur und Bildung.* Leipzig: Verlag der Sächsischen Akademie der Wissenschaften.

Garantoudes, E. (2000) Η αναβίωση της αρχαίας ελληνικής μετρικής τον 19° αιώνα· η μετρική θεωρία και πράξη του Αλέξανδρου Ρίζου Ραγκαβή [The revival of ancient Greek metrics in the nineteenth century: The metrical theory and practice of Alexandros Rizos Rankaves]. *Μολυβδοκονδυλοπελεκητής* [*Molyvdokondylopeleketes*] 7, 28–74.

Glytzoures, A. (2001) *Η σκηνοθετική τέχνη στην Ελλάδα· η ανάδυση και η εδραίωση της τέχνης του σκηνοθέτη στο νεοελληνικό θέατρο* [*The Stage Director's Art in Greece: The Emergence and the Establishment of the Art of the Stage Director in Modern Greek Theatre*]. 2 vols. Athens: Hellenika Grammata.

Gotsi, G. (2006) Empire and exoticism in the short fiction of Alexandros Rizos Rangavis. *Journal of Modern Greek Studies* 24 (1), 23–55.

Hall, E. (2007) Aeschylus' *Persians* via the Ottoman Empire to Saddam Hussein. In E. Bridges, E. Hall and P.J. Rhodes (eds) *Cultural Responses to the Persian Wars: Antiquity to the Third Millennium* (pp. 167–199). Oxford: Oxford University Press.

Hall, E. and Macintosh, F. (2005) *Greek Tragedy and the British Theatre 1660–1914.* Oxford: Oxford University Press.

Koechly, H. (trans.) (1876) *Die Perser, Tragoedie des Aeschylos.* Heidelberg.

Macintosh, F. (1997) Tragedy in performance: Nineteenth- and twentieth-century productions. In P.E. Easterling (ed.) *The Cambridge Companion to Greek Tragedy* (pp. 284–323). Cambridge: Cambridge University Press.

Marcellus, M.-L.-J.-A.-C. Demartin du Tyrac (Comte de Marcellus) (1859) Une lecture d'Eschyle à Constantinople en 1820. *Le Correspondant* 48, 301–331.

Marcellus, M.-L.-J.-A.-C. Demartin du Tyrac (Comte de Marcellus) (1861) Les Perses d'Eschyle à Constantinople. Scène orientale. In *Les Grecs anciens et les Grecs modernes* (pp. 225–289). Paris: Michel Lévy Frères.

McLaughlin, E. (2005) The Persians. In *The Greek Plays* (pp. 251–309). New York: Theatre Communications Group.

Osborne, J. (1988) *The Meiningen Court Theatre 1866–1890.* Cambridge: Cambridge University Press.

Rankaves, A.R. (1895) *Απομνημονεύματα* [*Memoirs*] (Vol. 2). Athens: G. Kasdones.
Rankaves, A.R. (trans.) (1885) Αισχύλου *Πέρσαι* [Aeschylus' *Persians*]. In *Άπαντα τα φιλολογικά Αλεξάνδρου Ρίζου του Ραγκαβή* [*The Complete Philological Works of A. R. Rankaves*] (Vol. 12), Μεταφράσεις [*Translations*] (pp. 221–274). Athens: Perres Brothers.
Sideres, G. (1976) *Το αρχαίο θέατρο στη νέα ελληνική σκηνή 1817–1932* [*The Ancient Theatre on the Modern Greek Stage, 1817–1932*]. Athens: Ikaros.
Sideres, G. (1990) *Ιστορία του νέου ελληνικού θεάτρου 1794–1944* [*History of Modern Greek Theatre, 1794–1944*] (Vol. 1), 1794–1908. Athens: Kastaniotes.
Skopetea, H. (1988) *Το «Πρότυπο Βασίλειο» και η Μεγάλη Ιδέα· όψεις του εθνικού προβλήματος στην Ελλάδα (1830–1880)* [*The 'Model Kingdom' and the Great Idea: Perspectives on the National Problem in Greece (1830–1880)*]. Athens: Polytypo.
Steiner, G. (1984) *Antigones*. Oxford: Oxford University Press.
Symvoulidou, Ch. (1998) Μετάφραση και θεατρική κριτική (1889–1990). (Ano Teleia) μία διαχρονική προσέγγιση με αφορμή τις νεοελληνικές παραστάσεις των έργων του Αισχύλου [Translation and theatre criticism (1889–1990): A diachronic approach based on the modern Greek productions of the plays of Aeschylus]. In H. Patrikiou (ed.) *Η μετάφραση του αρχαίου ελληνικού δράματος σε όλες τις γλώσσες του κόσμου* [*The Translation of Ancient Greek Drama in All the Languages of the World*] (pp. 47–63). Athens: Centre for Research and Practical Applications of Ancient Greek Drama 'Desmoi', 1998.
Van Steen, G.A.H. (2000) *Venom in Verse: Aristophanes in Modern Greece*. Princeton: Princeton University Press.
Van Steen, G.A.H. (2007) Enacting history and patriotic myth: Aeschylus' *Persians* on the eve of the Greek War of Independence. In E. Bridges, E. Hall and P.J. Rhodes (eds) *Cultural Responses to the Persian Wars: Antiquity to the Third Millennium* (pp. 299–329). Oxford: Oxford University Press. [Revised and expanded in Van Steen, G. (2010) *Liberating Hellenism from the Ottoman Empire: Comte de Marcellus and the Last of the Classics*. New York: Palgrave MacMillan.]
Van Steen, G.A.H. (2008) 'You unleash the tempest of tragedy': The 1903 Athenian production of Aeschylus' *Oresteia*. In L. Hardwick and C. Stray (eds) *A Companion to Classical Receptions* (pp. 360–372). Oxford: Blackwell.

Chapter 5
Oppositional Effects: (Mis) Translating Empire in Modern Russian Literature

B.J. BAER

Introduction

The first major works to introduce postcolonialism to Translation Studies, such as Eric Cheyfitz's *The Poetics of Imperialism: Translation and Colonization from The Tempest to Tarzan* (1991) and Tejaswini Niranjana's *Siting Translation: History, Post-Structuralism, and the Colonial Context* (1992), presented translation as deeply implicated in the colonial project, serving as a vehicle to carry out, justify and naturalize colonial oppression. However, since those seminal works appeared, scholars have increasingly focused on the ways translators and interpreters from colonized cultures, despite the asymmetrical power relations involved, have nevertheless managed to 'talk back to empire', using translation to resist, subvert and oppose colonial domination (Alvarez & Vidal, 1996; Bassnett & Trivedi, 1991; Tymoczko, 2010; Tymoczko & Gentzler, 2002; Venuti, 1992).

The Russian, then Soviet, empire is a rich source for the study of translation and power although it is often ignored in postcolonial writing in favour of the traditional theatres of European colonization – Africa, Asia and the Americas – and by Russianists themselves who typically conflate the Russian empire and Russia. 'Within the agreed-upon conceptual framework of literary scholarship on Russia', Eva Thompson argues, 'Russian colonialism faded from view' (Thompson, 2000: 2). Nevertheless, Russia has been a large, multilingual, multi-ethnic empire since 1547 when Ivan IV first assumed the title *tsar*, a somewhat mangled form of *caesar*, the Latin term for 'emperor'. Later, Peter the Great would recognize his own imperial expansion by assuming another borrowed title, *imperator*, making him *tsar i imperator* or, in back translation, 'emperor and emperor'. At the same time, Peter the Great's policy of forced Westernization created a bilingual if not polyglot elite. In fact, many members of Russia's elite in the 18th and 19th centuries learned French as their first language.

Peter's turn to the West also encouraged the translation of Western European scholarship and literature into Russian, which soon made translation a very visible and much-respected art in Russia. At the same time, however, this reliance on translation underscored Russia's 'belated entry' onto the European cultural scene and instilled a profound sense of cultural inferiority in many Russians. As the Romantic poet Vilíam Kiukhelbekher lamented in the early 19th century, 'Who translates translators?' (Greenleaf & Moeller-Sally, 1998: 8). And so, while the members of Russia's elite were the beneficiaries and protectors of a vast empire, they often felt themselves to be victims of the cultural imperialism of the West. This victimization, Thompson argues, has often overshadowed or even erased the victims of Russia's own colonial legacy.

This split colonial identity has in turn shaped the rather unique manifestation of multilingualism in Russian literature, where basically two forms of multilingualism developed: the one characterized by the prestige languages of Western Europe and the other by the languages of the colonized peoples of the Russian empire. The first form of multilingualism consists largely of phrases with low semantic content that suggest cosmopolitanism and worldliness. A small sampling of such phrases from Fyodor Dostoevsky's *Crime and Punishment* (1866) includes: *Ich danke, c'est de rigeur, en toutes lettres, assez causé, adieu, mon plaisir*. The second form of multilingualism consists largely of nouns describing culture-specific items or practices of Russia's colonized peoples, such as the many Ossetian words that appear in Mikhail Lermontov's *A Hero of Our Time* (1840): *arkalyk*, 'a short overcoat', *beshmet*, 'a waisted garment', *gurda*, 'a high quality blade', *kunak*, 'friend', and *yashmak*, 'a veil worn by Muslim women', among others.

Rainier Grutman (2002) has attempted to categorize the various functions of multilingualism in literary texts by adapting the categories developed by the Russian formalist Boris Tomashevsky (1925) to describe the major functions of literary devices: realist, compositional and aesthetic. Grutman's use of these categories is productive, but like most formalist models, the categories function within the closed system of the literary text. I would propose instead a typology of translation effects that reach beyond the text to describe the ways in which readers negotiate meaning. To the extent that an imperial identity transcends the various languages and cultures of empire, such translation effects can support the illusion of such a transcendent identity, question or even oppose it.

Translation Effects

If we imagine this typology as a scale, one end of that scale would be represented by what I refer to as 'total translation', produced when the source utterance is suppressed and the reader is provided only with the target utterance. In such situations, the reader is given to believe that the translation represents an unproblematic exchange, a perfect mapping of the two languages and cultures. This may be accomplished by indicating that the speaker's utterance was spoken in the source language, that is, 'he said in French', or by providing a description of the speaker's ability as in the following passage from Leo Tolstoy's *War and Peace*:

> He spoke that refined French in which our grandfathers not only spoke, but also thought, and with the gently modulated, patronizing intonation that was natural to a man of consequence who had grown old in society and at court. (Tolstoy, 2007: 5)

Total translation typically produces the 'effect of equivalence', similar to what Lawrence Venuti (1992: 4) described as an 'effect of transparency' or George Lakoff (1987: 322) as 'total commensurability'. In his essay 'The effects of translation' (2004), Phillip Lewis describes how this effect is produced in the English translation of Jacques Derrida's essay 'Mythologie blanche' [White mythology]. 'The text of [Derrida's] "White mythology" sometimes drops the words in brackets [German source terms]', Lewis notes, 'making do with just the English words. One effect of this kind of omission is to reduce the attention paid to translation that is sustained in the original' (Lewis, 2004: 265). By removing the source terms, the translator de-problematizes their translation. He denies the reader an opportunity to evaluate the translation against the original, thereby creating an effect of equivalence where there was none in Derrida's original.

In an essay entitled 'L'effet du reel' (1968), Roland Barthes explores the effect produced by descriptive passages in realist fiction. Examining the short story *Un coeur simple* by Gustave Flaubert, Barthes focuses on the description of a room that included, among other things, a piano, above which hung a barometer. The barometer, however, never again appears in the story and plays no role in the plot. What then, Barthes asks, is the purpose of such 'useless details', of which 'every narrative, at least every Western narrative of the ordinary sort nowadays, possesses a certain number' (Barthes, 1986: 142). It is the very randomness or uselessness of these details, he concludes, that allows them to produce the intended effect: the effect of reality. In such cases, the signified (the specific object mentioned) is downplayed in favour of a larger referent: reality. Similarly, in translation the effect of equivalence is produced when the signified of the utterance (message content) is downplayed in favour of a larger referent, such as equivalence, perfect fluency or ideal cosmopolitanism.

At the other end of the scale of translation effects is 'zero translation', a situation in which no translation of the source text or utterance is provided,[1] suggesting a problematic or impossible mapping of two languages or cultures. For example, in Dostoevsky's *Crime and Punishment*, the hero Raskolnikov encapsulates the continental philosophy of social Darwinism, which he condemns, in a statement in French: *Crevez, chiens, si vous n'êtes pas contents* ('Die, dogs, if you're not happy'[2]). By delivering the statement in French, Dostoevsky suggests the incompatibility of this philosophy with Russian cultural values: it is untranslatable. Along the same lines, Raskolnikov refuses translation work offered him by his friend Razumikhin. The text for translation is a socially progressive treatise in German entitled 'Is woman a human being?'[3] Raskolnikov rejects the offer, telling Razumikhin: 'I don't need ... translations!' (Dostoevsky, 1999: 108).

Of course, between these two extremes, there is a wide variety of translation effects. For example, in the opening paragraph of Tolstoy's *War and Peace*, the society hostess Anna Sherer, speaking to her guests in French, code-switches twice, introducing Russian words and phrases:

> Eh bien, mon prince, Gênes et Lucques ne sont plus que des apanages, des поместья de la famille Buonaparte. Non, je vous préviens, que si vous ne me dites pas, que nous avons la guerre ... je ne vous connais plus, vous n'êtes plus mon ami, vous n'êtes plus мой верный раб comme vous dites. (Tolstoy, 1961: 7)

> (So, my prince, Genoa and Lucca are now just estates, the private estates of the Buonaparte family. No, I warn you, if you don't say this means war ... I no longer know you, you are no longer my friend, you are no longer, as you put it, my loyal slave.)

While overall Sherer's use of French suggests her fluency, her linguistic code-switching implies a mismatch between the French and Russian. Moreover, in the following paragraph her Germanic surname is provided, as well as the fact that she was a lady in waiting, designated in Russian by the German borrowing *freilina*, which only serves to complicate further the relationship between the Russian language and Russian cultural identity. As the translator Richard Peaver insists, the multilingualism in Tolstoy's novels is not gratuitous, but serves a variety of purposes:

> Tolstoy used French for a reason, or for several reasons: to give the tone of the period; to play on the ironies of a French-speaking Russian aristocracy suddenly finding itself thrown into war with France; to suggest a certain frivolity and uprootedness in characters like Prince Vassily and the witty Bilibin. ... (Remnick, 2005: 109)

Eva Thompson (2000: 93) suggests that 'such a state of affairs implies a culture's deep discomfort about itself'.

(Mis)Translation Effects

The representation of acts of (mis)translation produces its own particular effects. While (mis)translation is related to zero translation insofar as they both attest to the complex relationship that obtains between languages and cultures, the representation of acts of (mis)translation goes further by staging that incompatibility, exposing in the process the ignorance or deception of the translator. And so, whereas zero translation suggests resistance to foreign ways, as in the above-mentioned example from *Crime and Punishment*, (mis)translation implies a more oppositional stance, for it lays bare the contradictions and myths of Russia's official imperial discourse. In that sense, it is not merely a rejection of that discourse; rather, it functions to deconstruct it, exposing issues of power that are often rendered invisible or 'mystified' in both total and zero translation.

Much interesting work has been done exploring representations of (mis)translation in the context of exile, specifically in the work of Vladimir Nabokov. As Juliette Taylor comments, 'throughout his œuvre, Nabokov's fictional treatment of translation tends to highlight the incommensurability of different languages, and the failure of complete and effective interlingual communication' (Taylor, 2005: 266). Nabokov's exiles are often lost in a maze of false equivalents, led astray by the superficial equivalence of homophones. For example, consider the Russian heroine of Nabokov's short story *Krasavitsa*, translated into English as *Russian Beauty*. A Russian émigrée living in Berlin, her speech is described in the following way:

> She spoke French fluently, pronouncing *les gens* (the servants) as if rhyming with *agence* and splitting *août* (August) in two syllables (*a-ou*). She naively translated the Russian 'grabezhi' (robberies) as *les grabuges* (quarrels) and used some archaic French locutions that had somehow

survived in old Russian families, but she rolled her r's most convincingly even though she had never been to France. (Nabokov, 1973: 4)

Her language, somehow out of sync with her time and place, reflects the disorientation of the émigré experience.

Far less work, however, has been done in exploring representations of (mis)translation in the context of empire. Consider, for example, Nikolai Karamzin's claim, put forward in Volume 1 of his monumental *History of the Russian State* (1993), that the root of Slav (Slav'ianin) is *slava*, meaning 'glory'. Then in a footnote he admits that this is probably not the case and that a more likely explanation is that the word was derived from the word *slovo*, meaning 'word' (Karamzin, 1993: 129). Juxtaposing the two etymologies can be seen as oppositional in that it exposes the tension between truth and myth-making at the heart of Karamzin's historiographic project. Far more mischievously oppositional is the (mis)translation offered by Alexander Pushkin at the beginning of Part 2 of his novel in verse, *Evgenii Onegin*. There he presents the following 'translation': O rus!, the Latin for countryside, which he attributes to Horace, followed by O Rus'!, the medieval, poetic term for Russia. The translation signals his characters' move from the capital to the countryside, while lampooning the imperial pretensions of Alexandrine Russia and perhaps mocking German Romantic nationalism, which situated the spirit of the nation in the folk.

(Mis)translation and Romantic Irony

The motif of (mis)translation is deployed in a more sustained way in Mikhail Lermontov's *A Hero of Our Time* (1840) as a commentary on Russia's imperial project. The novel has a complex structure consisting of three narrative frames and five stories, and the action takes place in the Caucasus region of the Russian empire. In the first story 'Bela', Maksim Maksimych, a simple Russian soldier who has risen to the rank of junior captain, relates to the story's first person narrator, a would-be writer travelling in the Caucasus, of how Pechorin, the elusive 'hero' of the novel, traded a horse for a Tartar princess, who then died of neglect in the Russian fort. While recounting the tale, the narrator tells the readers they might want to skip a few pages to the end of Bela's tale, but then adds: 'Only I don't advise you to do this because the passage over the Mountain of the Cross (or, as the scholar Gamba calls it, *le mont St. Christophe*) is worthy of your curiosity' (Lermontov, 2004: 29).[4] The Russian reader immediately understands that Gamba has mis-translated the mountain's Russian name for *krestovaia*, an adjective derived from the word *krest*, meaning 'cross', which has nothing to do with St. Christopher, or *St. Christophe* in French. Vladimir Nabokov, who translated the novel with his son Dmitry, apparently felt the (mis)translation was so important to the novel's thematics, he translated the Russian verb *nazyvat'*, 'to call', as 'to mis-call'. He also added a footnote, describing Gamba's (mis)translation as a 'blunder' (Lermontov, 1992: 179). The incident is indeed significant in that it cues the reader to interpret the passage ironically, putting Gamba's scholarly credentials into question. Interestingly, Lermontov was well aware of the connection between the Mountain of the Cross and Russia's colonization of the region, for in a preface to the first publication of 'Bela' in *Notes of the Fatherland* in 1839, he offered 'a description of the journey past the Mountain of the Cross and a scholarly gloss on the legend that the cross was placed there by Peter the Great' (Binyon, 1992: xv).

The theme of (mis)translation continues in the next paragraph, in which the narrator recounts his travels:

> And so, we were descending Mount Gud into the Chertova Valley. There's a romantic name! You could already see the evil spirit's nest among the inaccessible precipices – but that wasn't true. The name Chertova Valley comes from the word *cherta* – line – not *chert* – devil – for here at one time ran the border with Georgia. (Lermontov, 2004: 29–30)

Here the romantic (mis)translation of the valley's name obscures colonial reality by substituting a fictitious spirit for the border of a once independent Georgia. The passage then concludes with the narrator's observation that: 'This valley was buried in snow-drifts that reminded me rather vividly of Saratov, Tambov, and other dear spots of our fatherland' (Lermontov, 2004: 30). Nabokov suggests the narrator's comment regarding Saratov and Tambov should be read ironically as the cities 'connote backwood, in-the-sticks provincialism' (Lermontov, 1992: 179). However, in keeping with the passage as a whole, the irony here more likely involves the notion that a comparison between these Caucasian villages and good old Russian cities is predicated on their being covered in snow.

Throughout the novel Lermontov associates Russia's empire with (mis) translation insofar as almost all the stories involve some sort of failed or foiled border crossing: Pechorin's native bride Bela, won for a horse, dies, but not before performing a blatant act of resistance by refusing to convert to Russian Orthodoxy; the 'honorable smugglers' in 'Taman' steal Pechorin's belongings; and Pechorin himself in his journal confesses that his cynicism is the result of society having mis-interpreted his shyness as haughtiness. Eva Thompson reads the novel as a prime example of the complicity of Russian literature with Russian imperial expansion, but her reading largely ignores the oppositional effects of Lermontov's irony, which complicate any simple relationship – or complicity – between the novel and empire. In fact, the theme of (mis)translation or misinterpretation in the novel exposes the colonial politics lurking behind romantic notions of the exotic East and provides the novel with a thematic unity that compensates for the disunity of its plot.

(Mis)translation and Soviet Dissent

Translation played an important and very visible role within the Soviet empire through the official policy of *druzhba narodov*, or friendship of Soviet peoples, which cast the translator as, in the words of the Soviet-era translator and theorist Vladimir Rossels, 'a propagandist of friendship among the peoples of our country, called upon as a writer, as an active figure of Soviet literature, to struggle against all manifestations of bourgeois nationalism' (quoted in Leighton, 1991: 18). The translation of works among the various peoples of the Soviet Union provided a good deal of work for translators as there were at least 100 different linguistic groups within the USSR. Some of them, such as the indigenous peoples of north Siberia and the Soviet Far East, were given an alphabet and, as a consequence, access to the literatures of the world through translation as part of a government initiative to spread literacy and to encourage cultural exchange.

While the idea was noble, the actual practice was often much less so, involving translation from an interlinear 'trot' (*podstrochnik*) and the selection of texts for translation based on ideological correctness. Rather than commission the translation of works of oral literature that reflected a traditional religious world-view, the Soviet literary establishment sought out new works that exhibited class consciousness and modern, secular values. As Werner Winter put it, 'the use of translation as a tool in political strategy' left a dubious legacy (Winter, 1964: 295). The quality of many of these translations was lampooned by the poet Arsenii Tarkovskii in his poem 'The Translator' ('Perevodchik') which included the refrain: 'Oh, those eastern translators! How you make my head hurt' ('*Akh, vostochnye perevodchiki, kak bolit ot vas golova*') (Tarkovskii, 1982: 69). The much-vaunted policy of friendship of Soviet peoples also served to conceal the unsavoury realities of life for Russia's non-Russian peoples living in Siberia, who enjoyed a significantly lower standard of living than Russians:

> In 1989, only 3 percent of native dwellings had gas, 0.4 percent had water, and 0.1 percent had central heat. Most had no sewage disposal,

and their size was half of that of Russian dwellings. The native villages were often destroyed by fiat of the Moscow government, and the natives were forced to move to larger settlements, which made it difficult or impossible for them to provide for themselves. (Thompson, 2000: 137)

The central government's official translation policy then was a kind of Potemkin village, concealing, albeit rather shoddily, the real situation of non-Russian peoples.

Felix Roziner represented official Soviet translation policy in an utterly absurd and tragic light in his novel *A Certain Finkelmeyer* (*Nekto Finkel'meier*), which circulated in the Soviet Union in samizdat in the late 1970s until it was finally published in the West, in Russian in 1981 and in English translation in 1984. The eponymous hero of the novel is Aaron-Chaim Mendelevich Finkelmeyer, a Jewish poet who is unable to find a publishing venue for his original poetry in the Soviet Union and so takes a job with the Ministry of Fisheries in Siberia. Finkelmeyer is patterned in many obvious ways on the poet Joseph Brodsky, whose trial as a social parasite was a cause célèbre for the Soviet intelligentsia in the 1960s. In fact, Finkelmeyer's trial on the same charge contains actual quotations from Brodsky's trial. Roziner, however, refuses to portray Finkelmeyer in a hagiographic light, presenting him instead in comical terms as a complex, thoroughly flawed individual with an extraordinary poetic gift.

The novel opens when Leonid Nikolsky, an engineer and Moscow intellectual, first discovers Finkelmeyer's poems on a flight to Siberia while paging through the journal *Friendship*, which 'specialized in translations from literatures of the non-Russian nationalities' (Roziner, 1991: 11). Nikolsky notes the abysmal quality of the poetry:

> One after the other [the poems] proved to be silly, high-flown bouts of rhetoric coerced into a meter and surrounded with empty, unnecessary rhymes by the cold calculation of their translators. As a poetry lover Nikolsky felt something akin to revulsion. (Roziner, 1991: 11)

From the very start the novel exposes the contradictions and absurdities of the official Soviet policy of friendship of peoples, for while Finkelmeyer's editor in Moscow encourages him to bring back a 'native poet' (Roziner, 1991: 83) from Siberia, Finkelmeyer himself is unable to attend university or to publish under his own name because he is a Jew. Similarly, his lover Danuta is a Lithuanian who is exiled to Siberia. Nikolsky, an ethnic Russian, comments rather nonchalantly that 'he had heard some vague reports about nationalities being shuffled about, but he hadn't remembered which ones they were' (Roziner, 1991: 212). The brutal reality was that 'the deportations from Latvia, Lithuania, and Estonia that took place at that time [1939–1941] destroyed some 20 percent of these small nations' citizens' (Thompson, 2000: 134). The Soviet policy of friendship of peoples did not, it seems, extend to all the peoples of the Soviet Union.

It turns out that, while on official business in Siberia, Finkelmeyer had met Danil Manakin, a cultural representative of a small ethnic people, the Tongors. Finkelmeyer, who had published a collection of military verse – he had been named the regimental poet while serving in the army – under the Russified pseudonym A. Yefimov, concocts the scheme to publish his poems as translations of Tongor originals; he finds Manakin to be the perfect dupe to pose as the first poet of the Tongor people. The premise of Roziner's novel is not entirely absurd if one considers the case of Dzhambul Dzhabaiev, a Kazakh, who became a factory of 'pseudotranslations'. A number of Russian poets created poems as translations of non-existent Kazakh originals by Dzuabayev (Toury, 1995: 44).[5] Or consider the experience of the prose writer Sergei Dovlatov while on a trip to the Kalmyk city of Elista. There a local poet greeted Dovlatov and presented the Russian writer with what he said was an interlinear translation of one of his poems and asked Dovlatov to provide a poetic Russian translation. It turned out, however, that there was no original (Friedberg, 1997: 179).

The scheme is successful and Manakin is offered a contract for an entire volume of verse. But Finkelmeyer grows uncomfortable with the arrangement, and consults his mentor, referred to throughout the novel as the 'Master', an avant-garde poet in the 1920s who turned to literary translation from the French when he was no longer permitted to publish his own original work. As a translator, the Master is adept at 'elevating' the interlinear translations he was given:

> All the Master had to do was make a twist here, a turn there, and suddenly the poem would work. The poets he thus rendered into Russian wrote articles about problems of translation, naively admitting that the Russian version surpassed the original and thanking him for guiding their 'mountain streams into the ocean of Russian poetry'. (Roziner, 1991: 83)

The Master tries to convince Finkelmeyer to continue to use Manakin as his 'double', explaining that:

> Manakin has given you the chance of a lifetime. No Finkelmeyer could publish these poems. No Ivanov for that matter. They're too removed from reality – asocial, idealistic, pantheistic. That's what any editor

> would tell you in his rejection note. But poets from national minority groups have a certain leeway. They don't need to satisfy rigorous socialist standards. So long live Danil Manakin! (Roziner, 1991: 86)

Once he explains to Finkelmeyer what he must already have known – that because of the content of his poems and because he is a Jew, he could never publish his work in the Soviet Union – Finkelmeyer agrees to continue as Manakin's translator. Finkelmeyer finally acknowledges that there are many ways to live as a poet under the Soviet regime, 'the most honorable being translation' (Roziner, 1991: 182).

Nikolsky, in turn, encourages Manakin to remain in his arrangement with Finkelmeyer by posing as an official in the realm of culture and aping official Soviet-ese:

> 'The cultural front is important now', said Manakin slowly and clearly. 'We are a small minority. The party says we need national forms of socialist culture to ... so we can ...'
>
> '... take your place in the multinational socialist state, isn't that it?'
>
> Manakin wiped his forehead with a handkerchief.
>
> 'Well, if that's what the Party says, then of course it's important.' (Roziner, 1991: 73)

Nikolsky, entertaining himself at the expense of both Manakin and Soviet literary policy, encourages the Tongor 'poet' to continue the ruse for the sake of the Party.

However, their arrangement – they agree to split all royalties – falls apart when Finkelmeyer is brought up on the charge of 'social parasitism' for having quit his job with the Ministry of Fish Production so as to devote himself entirely to writing poetry. He planned to live off the advance from the volume, half of which Manakin had already transferred into his bank account. Manakin, too, was dissatisfied with playing Finkelmeyer's double, especially now that he was celebrated throughout the USSR as 'the first Tongor poet' (Roziner, 1991: 171). In a gesture of independence, he decides to discard his pseudonym, Aion Neprigen, which means good fortune in Tongor, in favour of his real name. He also employs the hack poet Prebylov to 'modify' Finkelmeyer's 'translations'. However, when Manakin is unable to produce the originals, it becomes clear to the court that the translations are Finkelmeyer's original work. As a consequence, Manakin is stripped of his post as cultural representation of the Tongor people and sent back to Siberia. There, in a plot twist reminiscent of Nabokov's *Lolita*, Manakin tracks down his 'double', now serving a four-year sentence with compulsory labour, and shoots him. A very drunk Manakin, whom the local Russians refer to as 'walrus-face', pointing once again to the social reality behind official Soviet ethnic policy, freezes to death in a Siberian snowstorm.

(Mis)translation and the Fall of the Soviet Empire

In 1993, two years after the collapse of the Soviet empire, Fazil' Iskander's novella *Pshada* appeared in the Russian journal *Znamia*. Iskander was in many ways an imperial success story. Born in Abkhazia, a region located in the northwest corner of the Republic of Georgia, Iskander attended university in Moscow where he continues to live today. Set against the backdrop of the dissolution of the Soviet empire and the Abkhazian battle for independence, *Pshada* explores the complex relationship between ethnic – in this case Abkhazian – and imperial identities. The hero of the novella is a retired general in the Soviet army who, like Iskander and his most famous literary character, Sandro, is a native Abkhazian from the village of Chegem. However, as N.N. Shneidman notes, this novella differs significantly from Iskander's other Abkhazian prose not only because it has a straightforward third-person narrative but also because 'there is no humour, hyperbole, or fantasy in the story' (Shneidman, 1995: 77). In addition, the novella's commentary on imperial identity is far darker than in his Sandro tales.

The novella opens with the recollection of a brutal incident from the Second World War. The general, then a colonel, is facing two German soldiers who have killed his beloved Abkhazian aide-de-camp. Now captive, the Germans plead for mercy, *pashchada* in Russian, but the colonel is unmoved and summarily executes the two men. This memory is only the first in a string of memories from the war, all involving encounters with fellow Abkhazians. A beneficiary and protector of the Soviet empire, the general recalls confronting Abkhazians who were collaborating with the Nazis, seduced by the promise of an independent Abkhazia following the war. The general's loyalty to the Soviet Union, it appears, does not waver: his allegiance is to the empire over his nation. However, interwoven with these war memories are thoughts of 'the lost world of his childhood in Abhazia' (Laird, 1999: 22), which constitute a kind of counter-narrative.

The juxtaposition of the general's nostalgic reminiscences of Abkhazia and his brutal memories of war points to cracks in the ideal of a Soviet imperial identity. Moreover, the general speaks Russian with an accent and 'has suffered professionally because of it' (Haber, 2003: 66), while he has almost entirely forgotten the Abkhazian language. Like Nabokov's exiles, he is permanently dislocated between two languages and two identities, unable to fully inhabit the one or to return to the other. Moreover, the empire that made him a general and which he defended throughout his career is crumbling around him. As a result, Haber points out, 'he feels lost, rootless, and without an identity' (Haber, 2003: 66). In the final pages of the story, the general recalls his childhood in Abkhazia and in particular the happy time he spent in the village of Pshada which, in the general's memory, is a place 'where peace always reigns' (Shneidman, 1995: 77). However, the general cannot remember the meaning of the village's name, which is 'shelter'. He wracks his brain until he is suddenly stopped by a severe pain in his chest and dies of a massive heart attack, 'a lonely death among strangers' (Shneidman, 1995: 77). Like Iskander himself, the general is an imperial success story, rising from the periphery of empire (Abkhazia) to the very centre (Moscow). However, he is unable to survive the collapse of the imperial myth that gave his life significance and made him a success; he dies not the death of a Soviet hero, but that of a stranger.

Sigmund Freud, in his work *The Psychopathology of Everyday Life* (1966), focuses on various slips and misinterpretations produced in the subconscious through the mechanism of repression. The second chapter he devotes to 'forgetting of foreign words' for 'depending on our own general state and the degree of fatigue, the first manifestation of functional disturbance evinces itself in the irregularity of our control over foreign vocabulary' (Freud, 1966: 41). Freud then goes on to illustrate this by narrating a conversation he had on a train with a gentleman, who like Freud is Jewish and, 'being ambitious, bemoaned the fact that his generation, as he expressed it, was destined to become stunted, that it was prevented from developing its talents and from gratifying its desires' (Freud, 1966: 41). He then attempts to conclude his speech with a quotation from Virgil 'in which the unhappy Dido leaves her vengeance upon Aeneas to posterity' (Freud, 1966: 41), but he cannot remember the end of the quotation. Freud supplies him with the missing word, after which the man asks him to explain why it is he should have forgotten the word – the Latin indefinite pronoun *aliquis*. He eventually admits to Freud that he is worried his lover may be pregnant. His hope that she was not, Freud concludes, contradicted the desire for progeny expressed in Dido's curse. This contraction, Freud suggests, caused him to forget the word *aliquis*, which the gentleman associated with liquid and so with his lover's period.

Read in the light of Freud's concept of everyday psychopathology, the general's inability to recall the meaning of the word *pshada* may point to a repression. It is no coincidence, I would argue, that the Abkhazian word which means 'shelter' echoes the Russian word *pashchada*, mercy, mentioned twice in the opening paragraph in reference to one of the German soldiers who held his hands behind his head 'as if asking for mercy' (Iskander', 1993: 3). The general, however, showed the soldier no mercy and shot him in the back of the head – precisely where his hands were clasped together. This traumatic incident, associated in his memory with the word *pashchada*, may have blocked his recollection of the meaning of *pshada*. And so, paradoxically, the Abkhazian word for shelter becomes a site of repression and conflict through a metonymic association with the general's brutal execution of the German soldiers.

Lawrence Venuti, in a discussion of psychoanalysis and translation, describes as the fundamental dream of the translator

> that a translation will restore the foreign text in its entirety, in its materiality, without loss or gain, that the translation will establish such a similarity to the foreign text as to overcome the irreducible differences between languages and cultures. (Venuti, 2002: 221)

By analogy, I would argue, the colonialist dreams that empire, too, can overcome the irreducible difference between languages and cultures. In Iskander's novella, however, the general's (mis)translation of *pshada* through the false equivalence of homophones (*pshada/pashchada*) disrupts both dreams, revealing that 'the signifying chain created by the translator doesn't translate any dream embodied in the foreign text [and, as I contend, in empire], but rather replaces it with the translator's own unconscious desire' (Venuti, 2002: 221). Rather than overcoming differences between languages and cultures, the (mis)translation represents the return of the repressed: the general's awareness of the irreducible difference between his imperial Soviet and his national Abkhazian identities.

In an interesting symmetry, Freud's ambitious young Jew worries that his minority ethnicity might stand in the way of his career, while Iskander's ambitious old Abkhazian wonders if he was wrong to sacrifice his minority ethnicity for the sake of his career in the Soviet army. The general's subconscious, it would seem, is literally denying his conscience shelter (*pshada*): there is no escape from Soviet history. And with the fall of the Soviet empire, how can he now justify his actions? This tale of (mis)translation then offers, in Shneidman's words, 'a perceptive elaboration of the relationship between different nationalities in the allegedly happy family of Soviet nations' (Shneidman, 1995: 77), pointing to the incommensurability of an ethnic identity and an imperial Soviet one, particularly for non-Russian citizens of the USSR.

Conclusion

In his 1882 lecture 'What is a nation?' Ernst Renan asserts that 'the essence of a nation is that all individuals have many things in common and also that they have forgotten many things' (Renan, 1990: 11). As he goes on to explain:

> no French citizen knows whether he is a Burgundian, an Alan, a Taifale, or a Visigoth, yet every French citizen has to have forgotten the massacre of Saint Bartholomew, or the massacres that took place in the Midi in the thirteenth century. (Renan, 1990: 11)

In the context of empire, the acts of (mis)translation discussed above are predicated on a desire for a commonality that would transcend language and ethnicity, while exposing that desire as the colonialist's dream. In other words, these (mis)translations reveal precisely those things that must be forgotten in order to imagine the Russian empire as a happy family, and in doing so challenge Eva Thompson's rather broad claim that

> not a single Russian writer of note has questioned the necessity or wisdom of using the nation's resources to subjugate more and more territory for the empire or to hold on to territories that are not Russian, or even Slavic. Not one has questioned the moral ambiguities of colonial violence. (Thompson, 2000: 33)

By representing scenes of (mis)translation, the authors discussed above point to the fictional basis of the Russian, then Soviet, empire and of the violence committed in its name.

Notes

1. 'Zero translation' is often used to describe one of the unusual cases of translation compiled by G.C. Kálmán (1986), specifically case number three, in which a source text has no target text. What I refer to as 'total translation' is related to Kálmán's first case, in which a target text has no source text. While this case is often referred to as pseudotranslation, I use 'total translation' to refer also to cases in which the source text is, for whatever reason, unavailable, and so the reader cannot check the accuracy of the target text. In other words, case number one need not always be a ruse. In any case the effect of withholding the source text is that the reader is unable to verify the accuracy of the target text and so is led to believe the translation was unproblematic, transparent, unworthy of comment.
2. All translations are my own.
3. Dostoevsky does not provide the German title of the article. The Russian translation of the title, however, sounds like a parody of an article by Dostoevsky's

contemporary G.Z. Eliseev, 'Various opinions on the question: Are women people? Ancient and modern opinions. Our is on the side of women' [Raznye mneniia o tom: zhenshchiny – liudi li? – Mneniia drevnikh, mneniia noveishie. – Nashe predubezhdeniie v pol'zu zhenshchin], which was published in the journal *Sovremennik* in 1861 (Dostoevskii, 1973: 371n). Of course, by making the article German, Dostoevsky ties this progressive debate to foreign influences. And so, it is interesting that when Raskolnikov, on the road to repentance, begins to read the Bible, no mention is made of the fact that this text too is a translation. Fully consonant with Russian cultural values, this text reads 'like an original'.
4. The original Russian reads: 'Только я вам этого не советую, потому что переезд через Крестовую гору (или как называет ее ученый Гамба, le Mont St. Christophe) достоин вашего любопытство.'
5. Of course, with representations of pseudotranslation – as opposed to pseudotranslations themselves – the mystification is exposed or, in Gideon Toury's words, 'the veil has been lifted' (1995: 40).

References

Alvarez, R. and Vidal, C. (eds) (1996) *Translation, Power, Subversion*. Clevedon: Multilingual Matters.
Barthes, R. (1968) L'Effet de réel. *Communications* 11, 84–89.
Barthes, R. (1986) The reality effect. In R. Howard (trans.) *The Rustle of Language* (pp. 141–148). New York: Hill and Wang.
Bassnett, S. and Trivedi, H. (eds) (1991) *Post-Colonial Translation*. London/New York: Routledge.
Binyon, T.J. (1992) Introduction. In M. Lermontov (ed.) (V. Nabokov in collaboration with D. Nabokov, trans.) *A Hero of Our Time* (pp. xi–xxii). New York: Alfred A. Knopf.
Cheyfitz, E. (1997) *The Poetics of Imperialism: Translation and Colonization from the Tempest to Tarzan*. Philadelphia: University of Pennsylvania Press.
Dostoevskii, F.M. (1973) Prestuplenie i nakazanie. Rukopisnye redaktsii. In V.G. Bazanov (ed.) *Polnoe sobranie sochinenii v tridstati tomakh* (Vol. 7). Leningrad: Nauka.
Dostoevsky, F. (1999) *Crime and Punishment* (S. Monas, trans.). New York: Signet Classic. Originally published in 1866.
Friedberg, M. (1997) *Literary Translation in Russia. A Cultural History*. University Park: Penn State Press.
Freud, S. (1966) *Psychopathology of Everyday Life*. In A. Brill (ed. and trans.) *The Basic Writings of Sigmund Freud* (pp. 35–178). New York: The Modern Library.
Greenleaf, M. and Moeller-Sally, S. (1998) Introduction. In M. Greenleaf and S. Moeller-Sally (eds) *Russian Subjects. Empire, Nation and the Culture of the Golden Age* (pp. 1–17). Evanston, IL: Northwestern University Press.
Grutman, R. (2002) Les motivations de l'hétérolinguisme: Réalisme, composition, esthétique. In F. Brugnolo and V. Orioles (eds) *Eteroglossia e plurilinguismo letterario. II. Plurilinguismo et letteratura* (pp. 329–349). Rome: Il Calamo.

Haber, E. (2003) *The Myth of the Non-Russian: Iskander and Aitmatov's Magical Universe*. Lanham: Lexington Books.
Iskander', F. (1993) Pshada. *Znamia* 8, 3–36.
Kálmán, G.K. (1986) Some borderline cases of translation. *New Comparison* 1, 117–122.
Karamzin, N.M. (1993) *Istoriia gosudarstva rossiiskogo* [*History of the Russian State*]. Moscow: Zolotaia alleia.
Laird, S. (1999) *Voices of Russian Literature: Interviews with Ten Contemporary Writers*. Oxford: Oxford University Press.
Lakoff, G. (1987) *Women, Fire and Dangerous Things: What Categories Reveal about the Mind*. Chicago/London: University of Chicago Press.
Leighton, L. (1991) *Two Worlds, One Art*. DeKalb, IL: Northern Illinois University Press.
Lermontov, M. (1992) *A Hero of Our Time* (V. Nabokov in collaboration with D. Nabokov, trans.). New York: Alfred A. Knopf.
Lermontov, M. (2004) *A Hero of Our Time* (M. Schwartz, trans.). New York: The Modern Library.
Lewis, P. (2004) The effects of translation. In L. Venuti (ed.) *The Translation Studies Reader* (2nd edn) (pp. 256–275). London/New York: Routledge.
Nabokov, V. (1973) A Russian beauty. *A Russian Beauty and Other Stories* (S. Karlinsky and D. Nabokov, trans.) (pp. 1–8). New York: McGraw-Hill.
Niranjana, T. (1992) *Siting Translation: History, Post-Structuralism, and the Colonial Context*. Berkeley: University of California Press.
Remnick, D. (2005) The translation wars. *The New Yorker* (7 November), 98–109.
Renan, E. (1990) What is a nation? In H. Bhabha (ed.) *Nation and Narration* (pp. 8–22). London/New York: Routledge.
Roziner, F. (1991) *A Certain Finkelmeyer* (M. Heim, trans.). New York: W.W. Norton.
Shneidman, N.N. (1995) *Russian Literature, 1988–1994: The End of an Era*. Toronto: University of Toronto Press.
Tarkovskii, A. (1982) *Izbrannoe: Stikhotvoreniia, poemy, perevody (1929–1979)*. Moscow: Khudozhestvennaia literatura.
Taylor, J. (2005) 'A distortive glass of our distorted glebe': Mistranslation in Nabokov's Ada. *Linguistica Antverpiensia* 4, 265–278.
Thompson, E. (2000) *Imperial Knowledge. Russian Literature and Colonialism*. Westport, CT: Greenwood Press.
Tolstoy, L. (1961) *Voina i mir*. In L.N. Tolstoi (ed.) *Sobranie sochinenii v dvadtsati tomakh* (Vols 4–7). Moscow: Khudozhestvennaia Literatury.
Tolstoy, L. (2007) *War and Peace* (A. Bromfield, trans.). New York: HarperCollins.
Tomashevsky, B. (1925) *Teoriia literatury* [*Theory of Literature*]. Moscow/Leningrad: Gosizdat.
Toury, G. (1995) Pseudotranslations and their significance. In G. Toury (ed.) *Descriptive Translation Studies and Beyond* (pp. 40–52). Amsterdam: John Benjamins.
Tymoczko, M. (2010) *Translation and Resistance*. Amherst: University of Massachusetts Press.
Tymoczko, M. and Gentzler, E. (2002) *Translation and Power*. Amherst: University of Massachusetts Press.

Venuti, L. (1992) Introduction. In L. Venuti (ed.) *Rethinking Translation: Discourse, Subjectivity, Ideology* (pp. 1–17). London/New York: Routledge.

Venuti, L. (2002) The difference that translation makes: The translator's unconscious. In A. Riccardi (ed.) *Translation Studies: Perspectives on an Emerging Discipline* (pp. 214–241). Cambridge: Cambridge University Press.

Winter, W. (1964) Translation as political action. In W. Arrowsmith and R. Shattuck (eds) *The Craft and Context of Translation: A Critical Symposium* (pp. 295–301). Garden City, NY: Anchor Books.

Chapter 6
The Translator's Opposition: Just One More Act of Reporting

E. E. DAVIES

Introduction

Descriptions of translators' roles have often suggested that they are by definition subservient agents, whose job requires them to submit to the greater authority of the source text and its author, working invisibly to produce a faithful representation of this source. Hermans is thus moved to ask: 'Are translators born subservient, do they acquire subservience, or do they have subservience thrust upon them?' (Hermans, 1999: 134). Yet others have proclaimed the right of translators to display a certain opposition, manipulating the content of the source text at will, projecting their own identity onto the text they produce and exploiting it to convey their own message. The literature on translation abounds in sweeping generalizations reflecting these contrasting views. Thus we read that 'good translation is invisible' (Chesterman & Wagner, 2002: 80) and yet that 'no translation should ever be taught as a transparent representation of that text' (Venuti, 1995: 312); that 'the person who desires to turn a literary masterpiece into another language has only one duty to perform, and this is to reproduce with absolute exactitude the whole text, and nothing but the text' (Nabokov, 1992: 134) and yet that 'it is essential to take many liberties in order to create a text in a target language that truly speaks through our cultural context' (Zeller, 2000: 138).

Rather than offering any more such generalizations, the present chapter will survey some specific instances of unfaithful, or what could be called 'oppositional', translation, which have inspired reactions ranging from stern retribution to wholehearted admiration. And instead of attempting to draw finer distinctions between the contexts where fidelity or freedom may be valid, it will suggest that the possibilities may be more usefully viewed in a broader context, placing translation itself within a wider category of communicative acts.

Opposition and Subservience

Extreme subservience is often expected when the text to be translated is viewed with particular respect, as with sacred texts. For instance, the Second Vatican Council's *Liturgiam Authenticam* (2001) portrays translation as a dangerous enterprise, and requires that in translations of the Bible and church liturgy 'the original text, as far as possible, must be translated integrally and in the most exact manner, without omissions or additions in terms of their content, and without paraphrases or glosses' (2001, §20) and that 'translators should therefore allow the signs and images of the texts, as well as the ritual actions, to speak for themselves; they should not attempt to render too explicit that which is implicit in the original texts' (2001, §28). According to Delisle (2005: 843), the recommendations require translators to translate literally even passages which they do not themselves understand. While few translation specialists espouse this extreme position, many insist that a literal approach is often preferable, implying that this achieves a certain type of equivalence between source and target texts. Thus Newmark (1981: 39) remarks: 'In communicative as in semantic translation, provided that equivalent effect is secured, the literal word-for-word translation is not only the best, it is the only valid method of translation'.

Yet the notion of equivalence resists definition and seems to remain ultimately an intuitive concept. Certainly, the effect of a literal translation is sometimes far removed from that of its source, as is the case with the word-for-word interlinear translations often used by anthropologists in presenting their data. Sturrock (1990), for instance, looks at the translations provided by Malinowski (1935) and objects that they have the effect of making the source language, Kiriwinian, appear 'a crude, even contemptible linguistic instrument' (Sturrock, 1990: 1003), doing 'the reputation of his natives much disservice' (1990: 1004). More generally, it is often judged undesirable for a translation to read like a translation, yet the ideal of a perfectly natural, fluent and idiomatic translation is often difficult to reconcile with that of fidelity.

Others consider total fidelity quite simply impossible. Thus Fawcett (1995: 177) writes with scepticism of how translation may 'masquerade as an "innocent" activity in which an honest translator communes with the original author and passes on undistorted the message of the source text', and for Weinberger (2000: 2), 'translation is change'. Translation is recurrently described as a process of production rather than reproduction, by Bastin (1993: 474), Godard (1990: 91), Pym (2004a: 18) and Wallace (2002: 69), while others describe it as 'manipulation' (Lefevere, 1990: 26), 'intervention' (Niranjana, 1992: 173), 'transformation' (Rabassa, 1989: 2) or 'a critical act' (Levine, 1991: 3).

Of course, some unfaithful translations are not conscious acts of opposition but merely the result of translators' incompetence. For instance, in January 2006, CNN was temporarily barred from working in Iran after its translation of a speech by President Ahmadinejad mistakenly used the term 'nuclear weapons' where the original referred only to nuclear technology. Only after CNN had made public apologies to all concerned, and declared that the guilty interpreter would not be used again, was the agency reinstated (CNN News, 2006).

A still greater furore erupted when Ahmadinejad was widely reported in the Western press as declaring that Israel should be wiped off the map. Specialists hastened to point out that this was a mistranslation, his words being more accurately rendered as 'the regime occupying Jerusalem must vanish from the page of time' (Cole, 2006; Norouzi, 2007). A change of metaphor in such a sensitive context had far-reaching effects, making what was apparently a call for regime change sound more like an appeal for genocide. And yet in many other contexts such a substitution of one metaphor for another would have passed without comment.

Other divergences appear to be ideologically motivated. In a translation provided by MEMRI (the Middle East Media Research Institute) of an article by Halim Barakat, remarks originally referring to Zionists became remarks about Jews, with the result that criticism of a specific political movement became in translation an attack upon a religion, and Barakat's name was tarnished (Barakat, 2002). For more discussion of MEMRI's exploitation of translation for propaganda purposes, see Baker (2006) and El Oifi (2005).

Yet elsewhere the points of view of source text authors are regularly distorted with the approval of all concerned. Hjort (1990: 42) reminds us that, in order to meet target audience norms, translators are often obliged to make their texts conform to ideological values far from those of the original author, as when articles for publication in scholarly journals are required to avoid discriminatory formulas: 'Many are the non-Anglophone authors known to espouse sexist and antiquated views who, in this respect, have been presented to North American audiences as socially correct'.

Cases like this, where the translator's opposition to the source author's position is motivated by a concern to make this author's image more acceptable to the target audience, are commonplace and may often pass unnoticed by one or both parties. For instance, as Mason (2002: 140) notes, 'interpreters are often tempted to "round off the edges" of unpleasant utterances they are required to convey'. A concern for intercultural understanding, in particular, often takes precedence over any sense that subservience to the source author's tone is required (Davies, forthcoming). Davies (2001) shows how Ed Emery's English translation of a French article by Ignatio Ramonet weakens the original's aggressive and highly critical tone, yielding a text more palatable to British readers than a faithful translation would have been. In this instance, the mitigating translation seems to have been approved by the original author, but attempts to mitigate may also be perceived as dishonest distortions. Helmreich (2001), for instance, accuses Associated Press of a lack of integrity in its translation of Yasser Arafat's Al Naqba speech of 15 May 2002, in which, he claims, 'entire sentences and clauses had been excluded; moderating words had been added; fiery attacks – like a slur on the United States – had been cleaned out; statements had been condensed, enhanced, or otherwise altered'. In this case, the translator's opposition to the tone of the original is seen as a dishonest attempt to hide what others may want to see.

There is, moreover, a long tradition of censorship in translation, with questionable passages being left untranslated, translated into a third language unlikely to be understood by the target audience, or simply omitted (see Ó Cuilleanáin, 1999, and the papers in Merkle, 2002). Such strategies could be seen as the most extreme form of opposition to part of a source text: the view that it does not merit translation. Critical judgements may also lead to other strategies, as when translators make improvements to a text. Professional translators regularly remove discrepancies, inaccuracies and clumsy phrasings, and indeed Pym argues that 'to translate is to attempt improvement' (Pym, 1992: 162). But here again it is dangerous to generalize: in some cases preserving the defects of the source may be crucial, as in the case, cited by Chesterman and Wagner (2002: 20–21), where the text to be translated is a job application full of errors and the translation is commissioned by the potential employer.

The policy of withholding parts of the source text may be contrasted with that of amplifying the source material, adding supplementary detail which manipulates the way the target audience receives the translation. Appiah (1993: 817) emphasizes the value of an '"academic" translation, translation that seeks with its annotations and its accompanying glosses to locate the text in a rich cultural and linguistic context'. Von Flotow (1997: 41), however, notes the danger that such a didactic approach may 'lead to curious forms of misinterpretation, with emphasis placed on semantic or cultural items the source text does not stress at all'. O'Sullivan (2006: 106–108) cites a telling example where a German translation of *Alice in Wonderland* is at such pains to clarify a reference to the Mock Turtle that the result is 'heavy-handed and pedantic', totally destroying the fantasy element which gives the original its charm; here the translator opposes the whimsical, possibly mysterious effect of the source, presumably out of a conviction that the content of a translation must be transparent and accessible. Yet it must after all be recognized that there are contexts where full comprehension of a translation is not a prime consideration. Nida (1988: 301) observes that 'many people prefer a translation of the Scriptures which they only partially understand', while Jasper (2005: 112), also discussing Biblical translation, remarks that 'perhaps all a translator can do is remind us that we do not understand'.

Some of the most empowering views of translators are expressed in discussions of literary translation. It is sometimes claimed that a successful translation of a poem constitutes a new poem (for instance, by Mathews (1966: 67)), and when song lyrics are translated, the result is often perceived as a new song (Davies & Bentahila, 2008). Wallace (2002: 66) describes translators as 'active [...] shapers of texts with the potential to catalyze literary and even social change'. From this perspective, drastic divergence from the original text may be perceived as a valid creative act. Zeller (2000: 137), for instance, applauds the decision of Augusto D'Halmar, in translating a poem by Oscar V. de Lubisz Milosz, to omit the last eight lines of the original, praising the new ending of the Spanish version and even conjecturing that the original might also sound better without these eight lines. Particularly vociferous defences of the translator's right to opposition have come from feminist critics and translators; thus Godard notes the replacement of the 'modest, self-effacing translator' by 'an active participant in the creation of meaning' (Godard, 1990: 94). Levine calls herself a 'translator-collaborator' (1991: xi) and describes translation as 'a more advanced stage of writing' (Levine, 1992: 79), while Zeller (2000: 139) seems to give the translator equal status with the author, referring to a work 'emanating from another author's context and brought in to the readers' universe by its other author, the translator'.

This brings us to views about the translator's own profile, some arguing that this should remain unobtrusive, others that it can be flaunted. While the authorship of many translations is never officially acknowledged, the identity of a translator may on occasion have an important effect on how a work is received. The Vatican insists that Biblical translators should remain anonymous members of a team, yet it also requires them to be believers displaying 'not only a rare degree of expertise, but also a spirit of prayer and of trust in the divine assistance' (Second Vatican Council, 2001: §75). Similar requirements are commonly laid down for other sacred texts; thus, according to Greenspoon (2005: 60), Max L. Margolis insisted that 'only Jews could produce a Bible translation for Jews', and Kidwai (1987) recounts how translations of the Koran by hostile Christian missionaries forced Muslims to provide their own versions. Outside the religious domain, too, translations may be rejected if their authors' attitudes or loyalties are suspect. Grees (2003) comments that while Nagi Naguib's translations into German of works by Naguib Mahfouz and Yahya Haqqi by Nagi Naguib were praised in the Arabic media, a German who had translated the same books would have been accused of seeking to promote negative stereotypes about the Arabs. Evidently a translator whose background suggests less than total commitment to the values of the source culture may at times be suspected by members of this culture of what is to them unacceptable opposition.

On the other hand, the active collaboration of the source text author with the translator may make divergences from the original more acceptable. And of course, when authors translate their own works, no matter how far such self-translations depart from the original text, they will hardly be criticized for distorting or subverting this original as an independent translator might well be. Rather than an opposition to the original work, the translation may be seen as an extension of, or indeed even an improvement on it. Clearly the notion of ownership of the text intervenes here; the same process of producing a new language version of a source text is perceived differently depending on whether the one who produces it can claim to own the source text or not.

Narrowing the Field

The range of examples and reactions surveyed above illustrates the difficulty of generalizing about fidelity and freedom, submission and opposition. Those wishing to acknowledge this range of possibilities therefore sometimes try to relate them to different categories of translation or different text types. For instance, the contrast between professional and literary translation is often evoked. As observed above, many literary translators claim for themselves a high degree of freedom, whereas the translation of informative texts is usually expected to stay closer to the original; for Reiss (2000: 30), what she calls content-focused texts 'require *invariance in transfer of their content*' (original emphasis). On the other hand, Sturrock (1990: 1011) takes the opposite view; he refers to day-to-day translation which is 'hackwork, of sources themselves perishable whose integrity is thought scarcely worthy of defence', but goes on to argue that 'the principles of translation derive not from this low kind of translation but from the highest kind, from the translation of masterworks whose claims to integrity are paramount and certainly come before any assuagement of the tastes of readers'.

Others have contrasted translation theorists and translation practitioners; thus Fawcett (1995: 187) alludes to 'the dispute between the mystics and the craftsfolk', while Chesterman and Wagner (2002) offer us 'a dialogue between the ivory tower and the wordface', in which Wagner dismisses much theory as irrelevant to the concerns of the practising translator, remarking that resistant translation would not go down well in an EU brochure (Chesterman & Wagner, 2002: 33). In a similar vein, Pym (2004b: 9) observes that Venuti, Schleiermacher and Berman would hardly be successful as translators of scientific reports. Certainly opposition does not seem a valid option in such contexts.

Another relevant distinction might be that between prescriptive and descriptive approaches to translation theory. While translation manuals tend to stress the value of fidelity, descriptions of what happens in actual translations often show this principle being repeatedly violated. Holmes (1994: 109) emphasizes the need to provide students with norms to follow, yet at the same time to draw their attention to the fact that these norms are sometimes very successfully broken. Newmark (1988: 12) solves the problem of conflicting norms by identifying a category which he terms restricted translation, which includes information translation, interlinear translation, plain prose translation and the translation of metalingual texts, simply concluding that 'translation theory [...] is not concerned with restricted translation'.

This last suggestion illustrates another way of handling the conflicting positions, by distinguishing further categories such as adaptations, imitations, rewritings, and so on. However, there seems to be no clear agreement on the distinctions proposed. For some, such as Nabokov (1992), anything less than a perfectly literal rendering is not to be considered a translation at all; for others, adaptation is a process aimed at solving problems created by translation (Bastin, 1993), while for Gambier (1992), all translation is ultimately adaptation.

Snell-Hornby (1988: 26) laments the fact that 'all the theorists, whether linguists or literary scholars, formulate theories for their own area of translation only; no attempt is made to bridge the gap between literary and "other" translation'. Twenty years later, there still seems to be much truth in this remark. Tymoczko (2005) argues convincingly that translation is best treated as an open, fuzzy concept, a cluster concept rather than one based on a prototype, and she advocates a framing approach to translation, which situates it within other areas of enquiry. In the remainder of this chapter, therefore, rather than attempting to deal with the issue of submissive fidelity versus the translator's freedom to oppose by drawing finer distinctions between categories of translation, I would like to set translation within a broader category of texts: those which involve the act of reporting on already existent texts.

A Broader Perspective: Translation as an Act of Reporting

The parallel between translation and reported speech has been suggested by a number of theorists. It is, for instance, evoked in Jakobson's (1972) classification, which sets what he calls 'intralingual translation', reformulating a message in the same language, beside interlingual translation, involving a change of language. Of the second type, Jakobson remarks that 'such a translation is reported speech: the translator recodes and transmits a message received from another source' (Jakobson, 1972: 162). Wienold (1981) proposes that translation be set within a more general theory of text processing, which deals with 'communication in the form of texts which have their ground in other texts' (Wienold, 1981: 98), while Gutt (1991) classifies most instances of translation within the interpretive use of language, which serves to represent what someone has already said or thought. Robinson (2003) also groups translation with other uses of language which rely on pre-existent texts, applying to translation Derrida's (1988) concept of iterability, the idea that 'all language use is the reperforming of past performances' (Robinson, 2003: 66). Others have taken the opposite tack, emphasizing the extent to which other forms of writing resemble translation. Chan (2002: 69) claims that 'all texts can ultimately be considered translations', and Bannet (1993: 586) that there is 'no original which is not also a translation'.

Everyday life is indeed full of recycled texts. In the course of a day, we may listen to gossip about what others have said, read a summary of a commission's findings, peruse a film review, scan abstracts of scholarly articles, enjoy a joke involving mimicry, or appreciate an advertisement's intertextuality. We can likewise use the words of others for our own ends; a poem can be quoted to convey a declaration of love, the words of an authority to reinforce our own arguments. And of course we may also reiterate our own earlier discourse. For Barthes (1977: 46), every text is 'a tissue of quotations'. Formally, reports range from direct quotation, which reproduces exactly the original words, through the strictly regulated *oratio obliqua*, to reproductions which may not preserve any formal elements of the original. Lucy (1993: 18) suggests that direct quotations 'imitate' the original speech event, while an indirect quotation '*analyzes* or interprets the event' (original emphasis): an opposition which may recall the fidelity/freedom continuum. Indirect quotation, like free translation, may add or omit content, make changes of emphasis or style, mitigate or intensify original claims. Consider, for instance, such cases of reporting as newspaper articles popularizing scientific reports, retellings of the classics for children, updated versions of older texts, censored works, and parodies. A book review, for example, need not be exhaustive or objective; it may highlight some aspects of the book and gloss over others, make its content more accessible or more obscure, stress its strengths or its shortcomings, reject or endorse its arguments – in short, it may serve the interests of the original author or oppose them.

In other words, the contrast between opposition and subservience observed in translation choices is just as evident in other forms of reporting. Yet the controversies do not seem to rage with such fierceness over different ways of reporting. Discussions of reporting do not tend to assume a dichotomy between fidelity and freedom, implying that what is not one must be the other, and arguing vehemently in favour of one or the other approach. Viewing translations as examples of reporting, then, may help to avoid unnecessarily rigid distinctions and over-general endorsements of one approach or another.

It might be argued that translation is nevertheless distinct from other acts of reporting. Wienold, for instance, argues that translation seeks to preserve the meaning of the original text, whereas most other types of text processing 'involve serious alterations in the meaning and structure of the original' (Wienold, 1981: 97). On the other hand, Robinson feels that translation is no exception to the rule that iteration always involves change: 'We always modify what we perform. We always introduce new elements into our performances' (Robinson, 2003: 66). In fact, the extent to which accuracy is expected in the relaying of a prior text surely depends more on contextual factors than on whether the relay is accomplished via translation or some form of intralingual report. The accuracy of certain types of translation is taken for granted; the world's great physicists and philosophers do not feel the need to read Einstein in German or Aristotle in Greek, just in case translators may have distorted the original texts. But the same is true of certain reports; one imagines that many people were content to trust a summary of Iraq's statement on its weapons programme in December 2002, rather than perusing the original's 12,000 pages. And while reports on important documents may be inaccurate or misleading, this is as true of translations as of intralingual versions; consider, for instance, the inaccuracies in the English translation of Simone de Beauvoir (Grosholz, 2004; Von Flotow, 1997), and the mistranslation of Da Vinci's diary which led Freud into error (Bass, 1985). Ultimately, the possibility of opposition via deliberate reduction, elaboration or distortion seems open to translators and other reporters alike.

Many of the other generalizations made about translation do not distinguish it from reports of other types. For instance, descriptions which present translation as 'a cross-cultural event' (Snell-Hornby, 1988: 26) or as 'transporting one entire culture to another' (Álvarez & Carmen-África Vidal, 1996: 5) remain overgeneralizations, for a change of language does not always coincide with a change of culture. The documents of a single bilingual community are often produced, via translation, in two languages, its members having a choice of which to use. On the other hand, cross-cultural communication may very well take place without translation; a shared language does not preclude otherness, and an outsider to a community may nevertheless use its language.

Similarly, while translation is often said to entail a shift of audience, this too is an overgeneralization. Certain texts are from the start addressed directly and specifically to addressees who will read them only in translation (as when one head of state addresses another who does not share his/her language). Nor is a translation always motivated by the fact that its intended readers are unable to understand the source text; García González (2005) surveys a range of examples where this is not the case. In these respects translations do not contrast clearly with other kinds of report, whose audience likewise may or may not be distinct from that of the source text, and may or may not be able to consult the original document as well as the report.

A translation is often characterized as involving a change in the context of a text. Again, however, this does not distinguish it from other acts of reporting. In reproducing a historical document or literary work centuries after it was written, or borrowing someone else's phrase and reusing it in an entirely different sense, we likewise extract discourse from its original context and deliver it to an audience possibly quite ignorant of this source.

A further characteristic of translation is the fact, noted by Pym (2004c: 116), that a translated text may have a dual status, functioning both as a translation, seen as deriving from a prior text, and as a text in its own right. Literary critics have explored the extent to which a translation may acquire a life of its own, unrelated to its source (see, for instance, Brisset's (1991) examination of the Quebecois translation of Macbeth by Michel Garneau). But again, the same may be said of certain types of reporting.

A review article may at the same time be a presentation of its author's own views, and a commentary on an earlier scholar's text may be read as an original piece of research.

Indeed, the line between a translation and a text reporting on a work which originated in another language is not clear either. As noted by Holman and Boase-Beier (1999: 3), when Shakespeare incorporates Ovid's story of Pyramus and Thisbe into *A Midsummer Night's Dream*, this is not viewed as an instance of translation, whereas when Ted Hughes includes the story in his anthology of tales from Ovid, it is. Ultimately, of course, it is often the label assigned to a text which determines how it is read and received. Yet reports, like translations, are sometimes not explicitly labelled as such, and labels can also be false; writers may present their own original work as a pseudo-translation (as James Macpherson did with his Ossian poems) or as merely a report of someone else's text (as Joseph Conrad did in *Lord Jim*), while plagiarism, as the unauthorized appropriation of another's work, can be carried out with or without translation.

In fact, then, the parallels between translation and other types of report seem more striking than the differences. In both cases, the source text is an object to be processed, explored and re-presented in a new form. While this original text may be a fluid entity, open to differing interpretations, the translator/reporter is expected to put forward at least one possible interpretation and make this available to the target audience. As Janowitz (1993: 395) suggests: 'The translation implicitly asks what is this text – a series of words? And most importantly, it asks and [...] answers the question, how are we to read the text?' The decisions made in translations/reports will vary according to the extent to which their authors feel enabled and inclined to make this new text their own or, on the contrary, obliged to defer to the original; and the choice between subservience and opposition is not an issue specific to translators, but one faced by all those who are called upon to report the discourse of others.

Conclusion

Translators may indeed be submissive mediators whose only concern is to transmit as accurately as possible the message conveyed by a source text – just as a reporter may faithfully transcribe a speech delivered by someone else. Yet translators and other reporters may also adopt an oppositional stance. They may modify the content, organization, style or tone of all or part of the original message for any of a variety of motives: to make it more acceptable, to demonstrate its shortcomings, to subvert its ideology or to enrich it with further input, to facilitate the task of their target audience, or to challenge and provoke this audience. Drawing divisions between faithful and free translation, between translation and adaptation, imitation or rewriting, may ultimately be less useful than simply recognizing the translator as one type of reporter and acknowledging that, like other reporters, a translator may have more or less room for manoeuvre depending on the nature of the source text, the purpose of the report, and the identity of its potential readers.

Lambert (2006: 97), writing of 'the distinction between translation, imitation, adaptation, etc.', argues that 'rather than the conceptual borderlines between these parallel intertextual operations, it is their common basis, origin and function that deserves our attention'. I have here taken this reasoning a step further, suggesting that translation even in its broadest sense may profitably be set within a larger frame. Rather than focusing on the precise principles governing a particular type of translation for a particular purpose, it may sometimes be helpful to take a wide angle view, and consider the controversies of translation theory within the context of a more general examination of reporting. I would agree with Hermans (2002: 22) that Translation Studies 'needs to look beyond its own borders'. What is needed is not so much sweeping generalizations and equally sweeping counterclaims about what 'a translation' should be like, but rather an acknowledgement that translation, as one among many means whereby texts may be reiterated, reformulated and reframed, is open to the full range of possibilities available for other such reporting activities. The requirement of submissive fidelity is not imposed only on translators, nor is the freedom to oppose available only to the authors of intralingual reports; either approach may be justified or rejected in a translation or any other type of report. The chapters in this volume illustrate a few of the ways in which translators may exercise their right to mediate or manipulate, to submit or to oppose.

References

Álvarez, R. and Carmen-África Vidal, M. (1996) Translating: A political act. In R. Álvarez and M. Carmen-África Vidal (eds) *Translation, Power, Subversion* (pp. 1–9). Clevedon: Multilingual Matters.
Appiah, K.A. (1993) Thick translation. *Callaloo* 16 (4), 808–819.
Baker, M. (2006) *Translation and Conflict: A Narrative Account*. London/New York: Routledge.
Bannet, E.T. (1993) The scene of translation: After Jakobson, Benjamin, de Man and Derrida. *New Literary History* 24 (3), 577–595.
Barakat, H. (2002) The story of an article. On WWW at http://www.halimbarakat.com/publications/articles/onmemri_1.html. Accessed 10.11.10.
Barthes, R. (1977) *Image–Music–Text*. London: Fontana.

Bass, A. (1985) On the history of a mistranslation and the psychoanalytic movement. In J. Graham (ed.) *Difference in Translation* (pp. 102–141). Ithaca/London: Cornell University Press.

Bastin, G.L. (1993) La notion d'adaptation en traduction. *Meta* 38 (3), 473–478.

Brisset, A. (1991) Translation and social discourse: Shakespeare, a playwright after Québec's heart. In M.L. Larson (ed.) *Translation: Theory and Practice, Tension and Independence* (pp. 120–138). Binghamton: SUNY at Binghamton.

Chan, L.T-H. (2002) Translating bilinguality: Theorizing translation in the post-Babelian era. *The Translator* 8 (1), 49–72.

Chesterman, A. and Wagner, E. (2002) *Can Theory Help Translators? A Dialogue between the Ivory Tower and the Wordface*. Manchester: St Jerome.

CNN News (2006) CNN reports: Iranian president asks end to CNN ban. 17 January 2006. On WWW at http://www.cnn.com/2006/WORLD/meast/01/16/iran.cnn/index.html. Accessed 10.11.10.

Cole, J. (2006) Informed comment, 3 May 2006. On WWW at http://www.juancole.com/2006/05/hitchens-hacker-and-hitchens.html. Accessed 10.11.10.

Davies, E.E. (2001) The translator as mitigator: 'diplomatic' translation in *Le Monde Diplomatique*. *Turjuman* 10 (2), 29–51.

Davies, E.E. (forthcoming) Translation and intercultural communication: Bridges and barriers. In C.B. Paulston, S.F. Kiesling and E.S. Rangel (eds) *Handbook of Intercultural Discourse and Communication*. New York/Oxford: Blackwell.

Davies. E.E. and Bentahila, A. (2008) Translation and code switching in the lyrics of bilingual popular songs. *The Translator* 14 (2), 247–272. Special Issue on Translation and Music, guest edited by Şebnem Susam-Sarajeva.

Delisle, J. (2005) Les nouvelles règles de traduction du Vatican. *Meta* 50 (3), 831–850.

Derrida, J. (1988) *Limited Inc*. Chicago: University of Chicago Press.

El Oifi, M. (2005) Traduction ou trahison? Désinformation à l'Israélienne. *Le Monde Diplomatique* September 2005. On WWW at http://www.monde-diplomatique.fr/2005/09/EL_OIFI/12796. Accessed 10.11.10.

Fawcett, P. (1995) Translation and power play. *The Translator* 1 (2), 177–192.

Gambier, Y. (1992) Adaptation: Une ambiguïté à interroger. *Meta* 37 (3), 421–425.

García González, M. (2005) Translation of minority languages in bilingual and multilingual communities. In A. Branchadell and L.M. West (eds) *Less Translated Languages* (pp. 105–123). Amsterdam: John Benjamins.

Godard, B. (1990) Theorizing feminist discourse/translation. In S. Bassnet and A. Lefevere (eds) *Translation, History and Culture* (pp. 87–96). London/New York: Pinter.

Greenspoon, L. (2005) Texts and contexts: perspectives on Jewish translations of the Hebrew Bible. In L. Long (ed.) *Translation and Religion: Holy Untranslatable?* (pp. 54–64). Clevedon: Multilingual Matters.

Grees, S. (2003) Translations as caricatures of the Arab world? *Al Hayat*, 4 December 2003. On WWW at http://www.qantara.de/webcom/show_article.php/_c564/_nr-11/_p-1/i.html?PHPSESSID=5. Accessed 10.11.10.

Grosholz, E.R. (2004) *Legacy of Simone de Beauvoir*. Oxford: Oxford University Press.

Gutt, E-A. (1991) *Translation and Relevance: Cognition and Context*. Oxford: Blackwell.

Helmreich, J. (2001) Journalistic license: Professional standards in the print media's coverage of Israel. *Jerusalem Letter/Viewpoints* 460, 15 August. On WWW at http://www.jcpa.org/jl/vp460.htm. Accessed 10.11.10.

Hermans, T. (1999) *Translation in Systems*. Manchester: St Jerome.
Hermans, T. (2002) Paradoxes and aporias in translation and translation studies. In A. Riccardi (ed.) *Translation Studies: Perspectives on an Emerging Discipline* (pp. 10–23). Cambridge: Cambridge University Press. On WWW at http://eprints.ucl.ac.uk/1387/1/aporia.pdf. Accessed 10.11.10.
Hjort, A.M. (1990) Translation and the consequences of scepticism. In S. Bassnet and A. Lefevere (eds) *Translation, History and Culture* (pp. 38–45). London/New York: Pinter.
Holman, M. and Boase-Beier, J. (1999) Introduction. In J. Boase-Beier and M. Holman (eds) *The Practices of Literary Translation: Constraints and Creativity* (pp. 1–17). Manchester: St Jerome.
Holmes, J.S. (1994) The state of two arts: literary translation and translation studies in the west today. In J.S. Holmes (ed.) *Translated! Papers on Literary Translation and Translation Studies* (pp. 103–111). Amsterdam: Rodopi.
Jakobson, R. (1972) On linguistic aspects of translation. In R. Jakobson, *Selected Writings* (Vol. 5) (pp. 155–75). The Hague: Mouton.
Janowitz, N. (1993) Re-creating Genesis: The metapragmatics of divine speech. In J.A. Lucy (ed.) *Reflexive Language: Reported Speech and Metapragmatics*. Cambridge: Cambridge University Press.
Jasper, D. (2005) Settling Hoti's business: The impossible necessity of Biblical translation. In L. Long (ed.) *Translation and Religion: Holy Untranslatable?* (pp. 105–114). Clevedon: Multilingual Matters.
Kidwai, A.R. (1987) Translating the untranslatable: A survey of English translations of the Quran. *The Muslim World Book Review* 7 (4), 66–71. On WWW at http://www.quranicstudies.com/articles/language-of-the-quran/translating-the-untranslatable-a-survey-of-english-translations-of-the-quran.html. Accessed 10.11.10.
Lambert, J. (2006) Literatures, translation and (de)colonization. In D. Delabastita, L. D'Hulst and R. Meylaerts (eds) *Functional Approaches to Culture and Translation: Selected Papers by José Lambert* (pp. 87–104). Amsterdam: John Benjamins.
Lefevere, A. (1990) Translation: Its genealogy in the west. In S. Bassnett and A. Lefevere (eds) *Translation, History and Culture* (pp. 14–28). London/New York: Pinter.
Levine, S.J. (1991) *The Subversive Scribe: Translating Latin American Fiction*. Minneapolis: Greywolf Press.
Levine, S.J. (1992) Translation as (sub)version: On translating Infante's *Inferno*. In L. Venuti (ed.) *Rethinking Translation: Discourse, Subjectivity, Ideology* (pp. 75–85). London: Routledge.
Lucy, J.A. (1993) Reflexive language and the human disciplines. In J.A. Lucy (ed.) *Reflexive Language: Reported Speech and Metapragmatics* (pp. 9–32). Cambridge: Cambridge University Press.
Malinowski, B. (1935) *Coral Gardens and their Magic*. London: Allen & Unwin.
Mason, I. (2002) Review of Ruth A. Roland. *Interpreters as Diplomats*. *The Translator* 8 (1), 138–142.
Mathews, J. (1966) Third thoughts on translating poetry. In R.A. Brower (ed.) *On Translation* (pp. 67–77). Oxford: Oxford University Press.
Merkle, D. (ed.) (2002) Censure et traduction dans le monde occidental. *TTR* 15 (2).
Nabokov, V. (1992) Problems of translation: *Onegin* in English. In R. Schulte and J. Biguenet (eds) *Theories of Translation: An Anthology of Essays from Dryden to Derrida* (pp. 127–143). Chicago: University of Chicago Press.

Newmark, P. (1981) *Approaches to Translation*. Oxford/New York: Pergamon.
Newmark, P. (1988) *A Textbook of Translation*. New York/London: Prentice-Hall.
Nida, E. (1988) Intelligibility and acceptability in Bible translating. *The Bible Translator* 39 (3), 301–308.
Niranjana, T. (1992) *Siting Translation: History, Post-Structuralism, and the Colonial Context*. Berkeley: University of California Press.
Norouzi, A. (2007) 'Wiped off the map': The rumor of the century. Global Research: The Mossadegh Project. On WWW at http://globalresearch.ca/index.php?context=va&aid=4527. Accessed 10.11.10.
Ó Cuilleanáin, C. (1999) Not in front of the servants: Forms of bowdlerism and censorship in translation. In J. Boase-Beier and M. Holman (eds) *The Practices of Literary Translation: Constraints and Creativity* (pp. 31–44). Manchester: St Jerome.
O'Sullivan, E. (2006) Narratology meets translation studies, or the voice of the translator in children's literature. In G. Lathey (ed.) *The Translation of Children's Literature* (pp. 98–109). Clevedon: Multilingual Matters.
Pym, A. (1992) *Translation and Text Transfer*. Frankfurt: Peter Lang.
Pym, A. (2004a) On the social and the cultural in translation Studies (Version 1.9). On WWW at http://tinet.org/~apym/on-line/research_methods/sociocultural.pdf. Accessed 10.11.10.
Pym, A. (2004b) On the pragmatics of translating multilingual texts. *JoSTrans* 1. On WWW at http://www.jostrans.org/issue01/art_pym.php. Accessed 10.11.10.
Pym, A. (2004c) *The Moving Text: Localization, Translation, and Distribution*. Amsterdam: John Benjamins.
Rabassa, G. (1989) No two snowflakes are alike: Translation as metaphor. In R. Schulte and J. Biguenet (eds) *The Craft of Translation* (pp. 1–12). Chicago: University of Chicago Press.
Reiss, K. (2000) *Translation Criticism – The Potentials and Limitations* [*Möglichkeiten und Grenzen der Übersetzungskritik* (1971)] (Erroll F. Rhodes, trans.). Manchester: St Jerome.
Robinson, D. (2003) *Performative Linguistics: Speaking and Translating as Doing Things with Words*. New York/London: Routledge.
Second Vatican Council (2001) *Liturgiam authenticam: On the Use of Vernacular Languages in the Publication of the Books of the Roman Liturgy*. On WWW at http://www.vatican.va/roman_curia/congregations/ccdds/documents/rc_con_ccdds_doc_20010507_liturgiam-authenticam_en.html. Accessed 10.11.10.
Snell-Hornby, M. (1988) *Translation Studies: An Integrated Approach*. Amsterdam: John Benjamins.
Sturrock, J. (1990) Writing between the lines: The language of translation. *New Literary History* 21 (4), 993–1013.
Tymoczko, M. (2005) Trajectories of research in translation studies. *Meta* 50 (4), 1082–1097.
Venuti, L. (1995) *The translator's invisibility*. London/New York: Routledge.
Von Flotow, L. (1997) *Translation and Gender: Translating in the 'Era of Feminism'*. Manchester: St Jerome.
Wallace, M. (2002) Writing the wrongs of literature: The figure of the feminist and post-colonialist translator. *Journal of the Midwest Modern Language Association* 35 (2), 65–74.

Weinberger, E. (2000) Anonymous sources: A talk on translators and translation. *Encuentros* 39. Washington, DC: IDB Cultural Center. On WWW at http://www.iadb.org/cultural/documents/encuentros/39.PDF. Accessed 10.11.10.

Wienold, G. (1981) Some basic aspects of text processing. *Poetics Today* 2 (4), 97–109.

Zeller, B. (2000) On translation and authorship. *Meta* 45 (1), 134–139.

Part 2
Dispositions and Enunciations of Identity

Chapter 7
A Queer Glaswegian Voice

D. KINLOCH

Tom Leonard: Class, Dialect and Translation

As a gay, middle-class teenager growing up in Glasgow in the 1970s, I found some refuge from the muffling anxieties of adolescence in books. My home was full of them; I discovered that my grandfather had been a published poet, and my parents took care to educate me at one of those peculiar establishments: a single sex Scottish public school which offered some inspirational teaching and a culture of endemic bullying. I was both extraordinarily privileged and disenfranchised in various intimate ways. Among the books I devoured were works by local and Scottish writers, one of whom would later tutor me at Glasgow University. It is their poetry, often combative and oppositional in nature, the role played in it by translation, and how this helped me towards a more authentic voice of my own that I should like to examine in this chapter.

The Scottish poet, Tom Leonard, has a concrete poem towards the end of his collection *Access to the Silence* (2004) that consists of one line: 'for those of us who have to live outside the narrative'. As an aspiring student writer at Glasgow University in 1978, I was painfully aware that I had one foot in the narrative and one foot queerly beyond it. I was a member of Leonard's execrated middle class and in a class of my own – or so I thought at the time – in silent disarray when confronted by some of the macho characteristics of Glasgow culture. Leonard's poem, of course, does not specify which narrative he is thinking of here and the humane impetus behind his work as a whole suggests a natural sympathy with those who have been denied a voice. Nevertheless it is clear where some elements at least of the 'narrative' emanate from in 'The proof of the mince pie':

> The university (and here I speak specifically about the arts faculties) is a reification of the notion that culture is synonymous with property.

> And the essentially acquisitive attitude to culture, 'education', and 'a good accent' is simply an aspect of the competitive, status-conscious class structure of the society as a whole. (Leonard, 2003a: 64)

I had a very nice accent indeed and I didn't dare open my mouth when Leonard gave a poetry reading at Glasgow University a few years after the publication of this polemical attack on higher education's reinforcement of a class-based cultural status quo. Of course I would have liked to: Leonard's poems in Glaswegian dialect are sharp and witty, and articulate the 'subordinate' cultural voice of a working-class majority. I heard versions of that voice around me as I walked about Glasgow and was attracted to it in different ways. But I was acutely conscious that it was not 'my' voice. I felt that if I were to try to write in it and express something of my then deeply buried subject matter I would be a fake. Original poetry with a gay theme written in Glaswegian dialect was definitely not on the cards in 1978, two years before homosexuality was legalized in Scotland. In any case, I was some way at this stage from understanding the extent to which all poetic 'voices' are constructed. Had I opted to write in Glaswegian there is a real sense in which I would have been writing in translation. Ironically, it is precisely this fact that would have brought me closer to the pain and energy at the heart of Leonard's work. For this is an original body of poetry that is ghosted by the figure of translation even if actual translations from foreign languages are very rare indeed in his work.

In an interview, Leonard (2003b: 10) has claimed that poetry in translation 'often didn't interest me: mainly because I couldn't hear the voice. I'd rather hear it in the original even if I couldn't understand it'. What is lost in translation for Leonard is the materiality and local specificity of the speaking human voice and, as it is the political and aesthetic reality of this fact that has constituted his life's work, it is unsurprising that he has avoided the translation of lyric poetry. Apart from his relatively recent, unpublished translation of Chekhov's *Uncle Vanya*, I have been able to find in his work just one version of a poem by Hans Arp. He has, however, given us an example of what Roman Jakobson defined as 'intralingual translation' or re-wording (Jakobson, 1959: 232): a Glaswegian adaptation of a famous poem by William Carlos Williams, which helps us to understand Leonard's position and the extent to which his dialect poetry may be read not as poetry 'in translation' but as work that figures translation as the most deeply combative element in an ongoing working-class struggle against a dominant political and aesthetic ideology enshrined by the university-educated middle classes.

Williams' 'Just To Let You Know' is one of a handful of iconic pieces which asserted the rights of a poetry made out of colloquial American speech patterns, vocabulary and subject matter. Here, plums taken from a bowl kept in the fridge are eaten and savoured. Leonard, however, considers plums too exotic to be denizens of a Glaswegian fridge – at least in the 1960s when this poem was written – and transforms them into cans of lager. This adaptation (Leonard, 2003a: 37) can stand on its own as a poem, but its real humour and poignancy are only activated if it is read as a translation of Williams' poem:

> Jist Ti Let Yi No
> (from the American of Carlos Williams)
>
> Ahv drank
> thi speshlz
> that wurrin
> thi frij
>
> n thit
> yiwurr probbli
> hodn back
> furthi pahrti
>
> Aright
> they wur great
> thaht stroang
> thaht cawld
> (Leonard, 2003a: 37)

This is a very short poem, but the range of cultural coordinates it touches on and off is considerable and this is a habitual feature of Leonard's best work. Various 'voices' are made to appear and exchange accents in this translation. Leonard's more robust cans of lager nudge Williams' red plums gently to one side, but they are hardly obscured from view, so vividly does the American poet present them to the reader in the first place. Leonard writes:

> What I like about Williams is his voice. What I like about Williams is his presentation of voice as a fact, as a fact in itself and as a factor in his relationship with the world as he heard it, listened to it, spoke it. (Leonard, 2003a: 104)

Leonard's lager cans have a physical presence, incited partly by the strength of Williams' image and partly by their iconic status in Glasgow's culture of hard drink. The translated poem also fits neatly into a long Scottish tradition of poems in which drink features prominently. But the poem does not exist simply as a homage to an influential aesthetic with which Leonard feels empathy. Leonard has always been clear that Williams' 'experiment' also had a political and ethical *raison d'être*, and his translation activates a dimension that is implicit in the original American poem. For this is a combative poem, as most of Leonard's poems tend to be. The phonetic spelling of the words at issue force an attention to the local specificity of a speaking voice that is inevitably heard against the background interference of Standard English. Reading this translation reinforces our knowledge that the true forcefulness of Williams' American ordinariness and ordinary Americanness is not wholly inscribed in a Standard English but in a form that stands at a slight tangent to the Standard. Ironically, perhaps the true foreignness of Williams' American language and something of its revolutionary dimensions can best be appreciated by non-American English language speakers, not in his original American version but in some form of local dialect translation as in the above example.

Another aspect of Williams' approach to language, however, that has been influential with Leonard is his insistence on its materiality, as a 'fact' in the world, of language 'as an object in itself' (Leonard, 2003a: 107). The phonetic spelling in Leonard's poem simultaneously signifies the linguistic specificity and rootedness of his Glaswegian speaker while – almost surreptitiously – exposing the fabricated, unnatural nature of written language itself.[1] This is a poem that becomes less jarringly artificial only when spoken aloud with a Glaswegian accent. On the page yet another act of translation takes place as we are forced to decipher perfectly 'ordinary' words and accede to the mundane reality of the referents. Again, the political implications of Leonard's strategy are clear: it does not take much – the addition or subtraction of a vowel here, a consonant there – to imply the un-naturalness of all language, imperialist Standards included. Leonard's entire career as a writer has been spent combating the pernicious assumption that language is a transparent, natural medium. His conviction is that it is a system that is constructed and learnt, an instrument open to manipulation, open to translation.

Tom Leonard's manipulations of Glaswegian dialect arise out of very real and personal experiences of class conflict. Wittily, they play notions of linguistic naturalness and artificiality off against each other and each one involves a process of translation as we are forced back and forth between dialect and standard. That process is one we speak aloud. This act of translation does not occur in silence. In a strategic move that accords well with the socialist democratic principles that underpin his poetry, Leonard moves the act of translation away from the author towards the implied reader, encouraging him or her to articulate, literally 'voice' the passage between two types of language, allowing us to hear, understand and then hopefully pass beyond the oppositional stand-off manifested by their accents.

Something of the staying power of this type of conflict, however, is suggested by the fact that, despite an evidently shared feeling that in different ways we lived 'beyond the narrative', I was unable to respond as I might have done to the full implications of his work in the late 1970s. In a poem satirizing the Glasgow 'hardman' image, Leonard offers his readers a cautionary tip:

> Geeyi a tip sun
> fyirivi stucknthi dezirt
> stuckwia Glaswwejin
> a hardman
>
> noa sumhn
> wotchyir bawz
> (Leonard, 2003a: 58)

That was both sympathetic and ambiguous advice to give a young man stuck in the Glasgow 'dezirt' of 1978 but, as I quickly came to discover in that environment, a nod is not as good as a wink and for all the intelligence of his linguistic playfulness his manner seemed to me to remain in thrall – to some extent drew inevitable sustenance from – the 'macho' image he wished in this poem to undermine.

Edwin Morgan: Rites of Passage

The late Scottish Poet Laureate or 'makar', Edwin Morgan, was my tutor at Glasgow University for a while at this time and as a young man he had exchanged the Glaswegian desert for a real one during the years of his war service. As his long poem 'The New Divan' hints (Morgan, 1990: 295–330) – and as later interviews make explicit – the desert war offered him ample opportunity to explore his homosexuality.

Christopher Whyte, in his short but astutely argued study of *Modern Scottish Poetry*, stresses the driving role of a censored sexual identity in the poet's 'fascination with codes, alien languages and forms of life, with impersonation and ventriloquism' (Whyte, 2004: 139–140). These, for Whyte, are means of 'dealing with a very specific prohibition' and he invokes Kosofsky Sedgwick's epistemology of the closet to identify the 'tension' that is 'fundamental to Morgan's poetry' (Whyte, 2004: 138). Given his constant turn to translation throughout his life, it is legitimate to ask what its role is in this pattern.

In the portion of the chapter which he devotes to Morgan, Whyte suggests that if we were to 'become skilled readers of Russian Soviet poetry' then we would 'learn constantly to be aware of the possibility of censorship and the manner in which it forms, or deforms, a specific text' (Whyte, 2004: 139). Whyte is concerned here with Morgan's original poetry of love and sexuality and we might well imagine that it was the censored nature of work by Russian and East European writers that drew Morgan to translate them. Did this embattled poet look east in the hope of finding kindred spirits?

What we discover, however – as his preface to *Sovpoems* (Morgan, 1996: 29) first published in 1961 makes clear – is that what initially gains Morgan's admiration and loyalty in his readings of Mayakovsky, Pasternak, Yevtushenko and Brecht, among others, is their commitment to different types of 'public', socially and politically committed poetry. Morgan's turn to the east is a turn outwards, not the product of an introspective drive that makes him seek out the coded worlds of sympathetic others. In general, he admires those who have worked out in their verse an enabling compromise between the needs of their own individual orientation – spiritual, cultural or sexual – and the perceived need to communicate with others who may not share that sensibility. In this sense, the critic Colin Nicholson is right to stress the way Morgan's work 'socialises by opening out homoerotic experience', preferring to site Morgan's imaginative 'dispersal' of 'centred subjectivity' in the context of the poet's 'reassembly of literary modernism against an established canon' (Nicholson, 2002: 134).

Nevertheless, the way Morgan ends his preface to the Mayakovsky translations sits slightly uneasily with this interpretation and is typical of the ambiguous and ambivalent ways in which Morgan engages through language with the world. Morgan closes by referring to verse fragments discovered at the time of Mayakovsky's death

> which movingly bring together the personal and public concerns of the poet. Usually called love poems, they are only partly that [...] they are best left to find their own way and make their own points. (Morgan, 1996: 112–113)

Morgan could have left it there, might not have translated the fragments in question or could have simply referred the reader to their location in a footnote. Not only does he choose to translate all five, but he highlights them by incorporating them within this preface. They are striking also by the contrast they make with the Scots translations, for these ones are done into English. Paradoxically, he is able to stress their significance to him by refusing any extended analysis: the gesture is one of simultaneous offering and withdrawal, engaging and disengaging, and this, I believe, is both a characteristic strategy of Morgan's poetry as whole and what helps to make it so moving. The rhetorical device that may be operating in the background here is that of 'paralipsis' where the concision or deliberately restricted nature of Morgan's treatment suggests that much of significance is being deliberately omitted or censored. The drive, the effort is that of a humane impulse to connect, to move *out*, but the acknowledgement is there that this is sometimes a complex process, complex both in terms of its motivation and in the kinds of language that best express it.

And it is certainly true that Morgan also chooses to translate conflicted figures where a certain tension may be sensed vibrating just below the surface of the poems. Take, for example, his translations of August von Platen, first published without any commentary in 1978. Reading his versions of Platen's Venetian Sonnets is akin to watching a ripple stir the surface of the lagoon: something hidden moves among familiar shapes but what exactly it might be is hard to say. A vaguely identified love affair takes place in which – as in Morgan's own original love poetry – the gender of the protagonists is not defined but the hints are there and, post-1990, offers itself for amusingly anachronistic interpretation:

> Gay all around is the dear swarm of souls
> Moving in idleness, as if freed from care;
> A queer soul can feel free here as he strolls.
> (Morgan, 1996: 320)

Such queer 'flânerie' ends with the desolate poet sighing from the Rialto:

> And in that silent space my listening ear
> Catches at times a faint cry that is blown
> Here from far canals. Ah, gondolier!
> (Morgan, 1996: 321)

This voice is just one of hundreds, translated or ventriloquized by Edwin Morgan as he moved slowly and sometimes painfully out of the space of the closet into one where a poetry of much greater sexual and autobiographical frankness could be written. Writing of Hart Crane's poem 'Passage', the theorist Thomas Yingling shows how, typically, although

> it does not explicitly examine the discursive problems of homosexuality [...] in tracing a problematic development or rite of passage into self-awareness, [it] is an instance of homosexual autobiography. (Yingling, 1990: 125)

Perhaps Morgan's decision in 1976 to entitle his most substantial book of translations *Rites of Passage* was another attempt to suggest just how far 'out' in search of the other he had to travel in the process of constructing a lyric subjectivity that would be true to the nature of the censored local space he sought to articulate. Whether one prefers to subscribe to Colin Nicholson's or Christopher Whyte's version of Morgan's poetic trajectory, it is true as Yingling says of another Crane poem that Morgan's entire oeuvre, translations included, 'is constructed in sight of the practice of homosexuality' (Yingling, 1990: 117).

MacDiarmid and the Case of the Missing Hymen[2]

Such coded gestures were beyond the ken of a first year student who really only knew Edwin Morgan in 1978 as the professor who lectured to him with moderate enthusiasm about T.S. Eliot and W.H. Auden. That year also saw the death of Scotland's greatest 20th-century poet, Hugh MacDiarmid, but at the time I could see little of personal relevance to me here either in the Scots language work of his early years or in the fiercely contested experimental work of his later period. MacDiarmid seemed to be interested primarily in national not sexual identity and when he did write about sex in his work it seemed to be of an exclusively heterosexual nature. It wasn't until I found myself in Paris ten years later and read MacDiarmid alongside the prose poetry of Rimbaud and the Portuguese poet Eugenio de Andrade that I was able to draw on him creatively and began to understand the important role played by translation in his great modernist poem, *A Drunk Man Looks at the Thistle*, first published in 1926 (1987).

Perhaps because I was living abroad and involved on a daily basis in translation activity of one kind or another, I began to notice this element in the poem more. Versions of Alexander Blok, Zinaida Hippius, Georges Ramaekers, Else Laske-Schuler and Edmond Rocher are woven into the fabric of the poem, their status as translations or adaptations highlighted by footnotes. What began to interest me now – because I was trying to write my own extended sequence of poems – was the way

MacDiarmid had positioned these adaptations within his structure and the way the reader's eye was forced via footnote and – in my modern edition – marginal comment back and forth between text and paratext, Scots and English. The English I am speaking of here is in fact the English versions or cribs MacDiarmid used, having no or very limited access to the original languages the foreign poems were written in. I began to hear and conceive of a poetic voice hovering between different but similar languages, not necessarily what MacDiarmid intended at all but something that seemed appropriate to the queer material I was working on.

Looking back on this engagement now, I see that I could have taken these intuitions much further. In particular, I could have radically revised my undergraduate opinion that this poem is not about sex when in fact one of the dominant concerns of the first thousand lines is the relationship between the sexes, the role and nature of sexual acts, how they relate to experience of the numinous or spiritual and how an understanding of all this may help to develop human potential. Had I done this, I would almost certainly have experienced a dissatisfaction with elements of the critical texts that had focused on this theme and which overlook numerous ambiguities and opacities of expression and structural positioning that make *A Drunk Man*'s exploration of sexuality much less straightforward than it has seemed. The pun is intentional.

One of the best general introductions to MacDiarmid's work remains Harvey Oxenhorn's *Elemental Things*. It is the only critical text I have come across to note that after a particular point in the poem 'there are no more translations of foreign verse' and that this coincides with various other changes in the poem including a diminution in 'the proportion of Lallans (lowland Scots) to English' (Oxenhorn, 1984: 84). These changes, according to Oxenhorn, occur from around line 1005 and are signalled by the cry 'Yank oot your orra boughs, my hert'. Oxenhorn comments: 'In the first thousand lines, everything and anything is encouraged to root and sprout; thereafter, the Drunk Man begins to prune.' While Oxenhorn's general observations here are valid, I would argue that the disappearance of translation from the text actually occurs some 400 lines earlier and that this is intimately linked to the celebrated and 'original' lyric passage known as 'O wha's the bride'. This passage is introduced by lines that contain a fragment of translated material from a poem by Edmond Rocher and no translations at all appear after the bride's poem (lines 612–635). There is, then, a sense in which the little drama enacted by the bride and her 'gudeman' or prospective husband represents a culmination of and a reply to all the translated texts that precede it, most of which offer a reflection on the relationship between the sexes or a version of the sexual act. Here is the lyric in question:

> O wha's the bride that cairries the bunch
> O thistles blinterin' white?
> Her cuckold bridegroom little dreids
> What he sall ken this nicht.
>
> For closer than gudeman can come
> And closer to'r than hersel',
> Wha didna need her maidenheid
> Has wrocht his purpose fell.
>
> O wha's been here afore me, lass,
> And hoo did he get in?
>
>> *– A man that deed or I was born*
>> *This evil thing has din.*
>
> And left, as it were on a corpse,
> Your maidenheid to me?
>
>> *– Nae lass, gudeman, sin' Time began*
>> *'S hed ony mair to gi'e.*
>
> *But I can gi'e ye kindness, lad,*
> *And a pair o willin hands,*
> *And you sall ha'e my briests like stars,*
> *My limbs like willow wands,*
>
> *And on my lips, ye'll heed nae mair,*
> *And in my hair forget,*
> *The seed o' a' the men that in*
> *My virgin womb ha'e met....*
> (MacDiarmid, 1987: 52)

It is memorable partly for the way it features the 'now-you-see-it, now-you-don't' 'maidenheid' and I am surely not the first – although I have read no published accounts of this – to see in this image a version of Derrida's 'hymen', a term he uses to figure the deferral of meaning, of presence (Derrida, 1982: 175).

The 'maidenheid' or 'hymen' is both membrane and the rupture of that membrane, implying communion and its hindrance, neither virginity nor consumation. MacDiarmid's dramatic lyric explores the undecided character of this scene. Indeed, the poem as a whole may be read as a translation of the very passage about mime by Mallarmé (1992: 237–238) on which Derrida bases his remarks about hymen and I would argue that one of the possible answers to the question the prospective husband asks the lass, 'who's been here afore me?', is simply this: 'a translator'. The husband offers the Scots bride plenitude, consummation, the full benefit of his inseminating presence only to discover that he is not the first, not an original but merely a form of re-iteration, a transposer of other men's words and actions. And they too have found themselves presumably in a similar situation 'sin time began'. Where does this leave the actual advertised translations and adaptations in *A Drunk Man*?

The flickering hymen of 'Wha's the bride' raises questions about what is original and what is secondary, about presence and its problematic assertion and insertion, questions that exist in relation to the uneasy status of the translations that precede it. Derrida eventually, playfully, directs us away from etymology, from the various meanings of the word 'hymen', suggesting that it produces its undecided effects through syntax that, as he says, 'disposes the "entre" (between) in such a way that the suspense is due only to the place and not to the content of the words' (Derrida, 1982: 249–250). And this directs us again to the issue of the placing of these translations in the overall grammar of the poem. MacDiarmid's voice slides in and out of adaptation and translation, seeking to possess a foreign tongue but the language he chooses to do this is itself a re-composition, a *sumbalein*, a throwing together of shards, fragments, membranes of various Scottish vernaculars, a tongue without origin or with a multiplicity of competing origins.

What I find most moving about 'Wha's the bride' is its dialogic, performative quality, its theatrical, possibly even its melodramatic character. Melodrama, Mallarmé once pointed out (1992: 236), is characterized by its repetitive nature, the way it produces a form of hypertheatricality, of hyperbolic gesture and expression. So the bride briefly sketches in the scene in which she has been an actor 'sin time began', one incessantly, exhaustively and exhaustingly repeated. Yet because she loves the man, or rather because MacDiarmid imagines that she may, perhaps even because she feels compassion for his delusions, she strives to give their acts the appearance of originality: here then are the traces of an orphic voice, a female Orpheus, or maybe, in the spirit of melodrama's hypertheatrical spaces, a transvestic Orpheus gathering together, half in pleasure, half in pain, the scattered fragments of a violated body: 'willin hands', 'breists', 'limbs', 'lips', 'hair', figuring the act of consummation as a repetition or imitation of the creation scene, a human translation of cosmic initiation. The beauty of this lyric is to be found not simply in the condensed sonnet-like enumeration of the beloved's charms, curious in its effects because it filters that convention through the voice of the male narrator pretending to be a woman, but in the combination of those elements with an anaphoric syntactical structure: 'And/And/And/And'. There is both the willingness characteristic of love here but also a slight desperation, a slight unease that comes partly from the strain imposed on the narrator by his act of transvestic ventriloquism, the translation of his male voice into a female one and partly – as we suspend disbelief – from the bride's feeling that her beauty may not be sufficient to distract her husband from the realisation that the creative act is a form of re-making not making, of re-composing.

The husband and bride participate, therefore, in a melodramatic performance of sexual identity formation in a manner that recalls Judith Butler's thesis in *Gender Trouble* (1990: 138): 'In imitating gender', she comments,

> drag implicitly reveals the imitative structure of gender itself – as well as its contingency. Indeed part of the pleasure, the giddiness of the performance is in the recognition of a radical contingency in the relation between sex and gender in the face of cultural configurations of casual unities that are regularly assumed to be natural and necessary. (Butler, 1990: 138)

The shifting membrane or 'maidenheid' of 'Wha's the bride' suggests that the penetrative aim of the Drunk Man's phallic thistle may be not be 'true', the implantation of an original, national, originating voice compromised from the outset by its construction as a form of translation, while the performative character of translation itself is stressed insofar as it is here figured as a form of cross-dressing. In MacDiarmid's lyric, the voice of translation sounds out playfully as a queer one indeed. And there are signs in the translated poems leading up to it that help to reinforce this interpretation.

In his reading of these translations, Oxenhorn legitimately sets them in the context of MacDiarmid's interest in Jung, arguing that

> the renderings of Blok, Hippius, and others function as [...] symbolic dreams, in which a speaker [...] encounters the libidinous unknown. These passages have been treated [...] as a supernatural counterpoint to the realist declarations. They can also be viewed as constituting a sexual counterpoint — 'female' to 'male'. (Oxenhorn, 1984: 81)

He then proceeds to read the translations and passages leading up to 'O wha's the bride' as constituting 'a protracted series of alternating "male" and "female" poems' (Oxenhorn, 1984: 82). My difficulty with this reading is that it is not entirely clear what the gender is of the character identified as a 'silken leddy' in the Blok translation. In his close analysis of MacDiarmid's reading and adaptations of Russian poets and thinkers, Peter McCarey (1987: 74) reminds us of the extent to which the poem as a whole is 'full of parody, of sacred cows'. While agreeing that the Blok translation 'introduces the visionary level of the poem', he suggests that it also

> parodies the visionary and his vision, setting the action in a pub, making him drunk and having the mysterious lady sit at a table in the pub. Furthermore, her extravagant mode of dress (silks and feathers) makes the woman extremely incongruous in a Scottish bar in the 1920s. We might suspect the poet is hallucinating. (McCarey, 1987: 74)

A remark by Catherine Kerrigan in her study of this same passage suggests how these remarks might be developed. She points out that

> the lady as an emblem of the ideal is [...] immediately questioned, because the Drunk Man goes on to suggest that what he is seeing might simply be a drunken hallucination, 'were you a vision o' mysel,/ Transmuted by the mellow liquor?'. (Kerrigan, 1983: 116–117)

Kerrigan does not dwell further on these lines but in the context of the remarks about transvestism above they repay more consideration. A queer reading might propose that while they invite us to consider that the lady is simply a vision hallucinated by the drunk man, they also leave open the possibility that she is none other than the drunk man himself reflected in the whisky glass, strangely dressed in the drag of silk and feathers. In this instance, the word 'mysel' is both the possessive pronoun 'mine' and the personal pronoun 'me'. As the drunk man explicitly admits in the following stanza: 'A man's a clean contrairy sicht/Turned this way in-outside,/ And fegs I feel like Dr Jekyll/Tak'n' guid tent o' Mr Hyde...' (MacDiarmid, 1987: 22). Is it perverse to see in the hyphenated phrase 'in-outside' a premonition of the Janus-like topography of the strange bride's hymen?

The next translation from Blok which MacDiarmid offers us just a few lines later seems to anticipate the conundrum of her predicament even more closely and it also contains its fair share of hyphenated words and dashes that seem graphically to forecast the emblem of her doing and undoing. Indeed the word 'forecast' is at the heart of MacDiarmid's translation. It is worth quoting in full:

> I ha'e forekent ye! O I ha'e forekent.
> The years forecast your face afore they went.

> A licht I canna thole is in the lift.
> I bide in silence your slow-comin' pace.
> The ends o' space are bricht: at last – oh swift!
> While terror clings to me – an unkent face!
>
> Ill-faith stirs in me as she comes at last,
> The features lang forekent ... are unforecast.
> O it gangs hard wi' me, I am forspent.
> Deid dreams ha'e beaten me and a face unkent,
> And generations that I thocht unborn
> Hail the strange Goddess frae my hert's-hert torn! ...
> (MacDiarmid, 1987: 22)

I have yet to read a sufficiently detailed account of what these stanzas actually mean, but one might argue that the narrator here finds himself in a similar situation to the bride. It is as well to remember that Eliot's *The Waste Land* is one of the poem's major intertexts: just as the bride in a Tiresias-like manner 'foresuffers all', so the narrator of the Blok translation claims knowledge of the 'Unknown Goddess' before her actual arrival, yet acknowledges that when she does arrive her face will be 'unkent', unknown. 'Strange' is the English word, MacDiarmid replaces here. Indeed, attention to the English version proposed by Deutsch and Yarmolinsky (1923: 128) – which MacDiarmid radically transforms – is instructive and helps us to understand the degree of extreme contradiction he believed to be characteristic of our experiences of both the divine and the sexual. The second line of the second stanza reads in English: 'The features long foreknown, beheld at last, will change.' MacDiarmid prefers the logical impossibility we will encounter once more in the bride's drama: 'The features lang forekent ... are unforecast.' The terms 'forekent', 'forecast', 'unkent', 'unforecast' echo and cancel each other, changing places around the hymen-like dashes and hyphens that help to signal the undecidable character of the speaker's predicament. And then, at the end of the translation, just as the gudeman in the bride's lyric discovers that he seems to have arrived too late, so the narrator queasily discovers himself present in his own future, a witness to the way offspring (his own perhaps) greet and possibly recognize the strange woman more easily than he does, despite the fact that he appears to have given birth to her too, an emanation from the very core of his body's most vital organ, the heart, emblem of both divine and human passion.

Space prevents me from attempting to tie in the following three translations to the bride's poem in as much detail. It would not be difficult, however, to relate the 'whale-white obscenity' of the 'shaggy poulp' in his version of Zinaida Hippius' poem 'The Octopus', its offering of a 'nearness I canna win awa' frae' (MacDiarmid, 1987: 30), to the invitation and repulsion inscribed within the bride's 'maidenheid'. The translation of Else Lasker-Schuler's 'Sphinx' offers what is almost a summary of the patterns I have attempted to trace: 'But ilka windin' has its coonter-pairt/— The opposite 'thoot which it couldna be—/In some wild kink or queer perversity/O' this great thistle...' (MacDiarmid, 1987: 36).

The final moment of translation in *A Drunk Man* is of the last two lines of another piece by Edmond Rocher and they lead directly into the bride's poem. In the passage which they bring to a close, the narrator hails the 'luvin' wumman' who is able to see directly into his soul. She replies in a version of Rocher's words 'Gin [if] you could pierce their blindin' licht/ You'd see a fouler sicht!...' (MacDiarmid, 1987: 50). At that, the voice of translation is silenced. Perversely it has established that one of the most effective ways of voicing the contradictions and ambiguities of the primal scene of creation is through borrowed accents. Translation can now step aside for the bride who is able, equipped to acknowledge – in verse of power and beauty – the paradoxical nature of presence and the dubious dreams of origin.

The husband in 'O wha's the bride', on the very brink of consummation, discovers that he is not original, speaks out of a lyric that redeploys the form and tropes of ballad and initiates a dialogue between tradition and the present where present speech is inevitably a form of transformation, of imitation, of translation – a process in which some of Scotland's greatest poets, including Burns, are deeply implicated, poets who were adaptors, translators, who understood writing as translation, authors of texts in which writing is conceived of as translation or where the minority discourse of translation is figured as offering a powerful performance of desire that in turn brings often painful instances of opposition such as 'major' and 'minor', 'heterosexual' and 'homosexual', 'original' and 'translation' into question and dialogue.

Each of the poets examined in this chapter contributed at different stages and to greater or lesser degrees to the forging of what I've called 'a queer Glaswegian voice'. The fearsome and fearless specificity of Leonard's work, its insistence on the accents and contestation of the inferiorities of our own local place, seems to have acted at the back of my mind as a constant goad, an insulting incitement to dig beneath my own middle-class complacencies in search of some kind of genuine passion and desire that dares to speak its name. Edwin Morgan's multifariousness, his pained and playful voicing of alien identities in original and translated poetry could never be anything other than a discreet influence during the years

I was searching for a more open, explicit voice. Paradoxically it was probably the poet who hated Glasgow most, Hugh MacDiarmid, who helped me most at the moment of greatest need. To read MacDiarmid's attempts to come to terms with his own sexual urges, however different, while simultaneously experimenting with translations into a confected vernacular which are then embedded within a larger structure sparked a moment of recognition. The sheer complexity of the imbrication of ideas and linguistic textures must have seemed like an adequate model for the kind of poetry I wished to write at the time. That I was attracted to an early 'modernist' poem rather than to his later 'postmodern' work seemed unimportant and it remains an endlessly fascinating text open to queer and other types of theorisation.

Perhaps what these examples suggest to those of us interested in forging either our own 'original' queer voices or in locating and uncovering precursors who may have gone unnoticed is simply to pay as much attention to those writers and texts that seem inimical to our concerns as to those to whom we are most naturally drawn. The point is hardly an original one and has been brilliantly theorized by Kosofsky Sedwick (1994) among others. But, as we all know, it is sometimes easy to overlook the obvious, to overlook the MacDiarmids and Leonards because they are under your nose and to prefer instead the exotic and esoteric. MacDiarmid's abiding lesson is in how to combine the local and the foreign in queerly unexpected ways.

Notes

1. This example of intralingual phonological translation may remind some readers of Catford's contested definition of 'restricted translation' (1965: 22–24; 56–63).
2. This section revises and expands an article previously published in *PN Review*, 169.

References

Butler, J. (1990) *Gender Trouble: Feminism and the Subversion of Identity*. London: Routledge.
Catford, J.C. (1965) *A Linguistic Theory of Translation*. Oxford: Oxford University Press.
Derrida, J. (1982) *Dissemination*. Chicago: University of Chicago Press.
Deutsch, B. and Yarmolinsky, A. (eds) (1923) *Modern Russian Poetry*. London: John Lane and the Bodley Head.
Jakobson, R. (1959) On linguistic aspects of translation. In R.A. Brower (ed.) *On Translation* (pp. 232–239). Cambridge, MA: Harvard University Press.

Kerrigan, C. (1983) *Whaur Extremes Meet: The Poetry of Hugh MacDiarmid 1920–1934*. Edinburgh: James Thin, The Mercat Press.
Leonard, T. (2003a) *Intimate Voices*. Buckfastleigh: Etruscan Books.
Leonard, T. (2003b) Interview with Tom Leonard by Attila Dosa. On WWW at http://www.tomleonard.co.uk/. Accessed 6.2.08
Leonard, T. (2004) *Access to the Silence*. Buckfastleigh: Etruscan Books.
MacDiarmid, H. (1987) *A Drunk Man Looks at the Thistle* (K. Buthlay, ed.). Edinburgh: Scottish Academic Press.
Mallarmé, S. (1992) *Oeuvres* (Y-A. Favre, ed.). Paris: Classiques Garnier, Bordas.
McCarey, P. (1987) *Hugh MacDiarmid and the Russians*. Edinburgh: Scottish Academic Press.
Morgan, E. (1990) *Collected Poems*. Manchester: Carcanet.
Morgan, E. (1996) *Collected Translations*. Manchester: Carcanet.
Nicholson, C. (2002) *Inventions of Modernity*. Manchester: Manchester University Press.
Oxenhorn, H. (1984) *Elemental Things: The Poetry of Hugh MacDiarmid*. Edinburgh: Edinburgh University Press.
Sedwick, K.E. (1994) *Epistemology of the Closet*. London: Penguin.
Whyte, C. (2004) *Modern Scottish Poetry*. Edinburgh: Edinburgh University Press.
Yingling, T. (1990) *Hart Crane and the Homosexual Text*. Chicago: University of Chicago Press.

Chapter 8
Translating 'the shadow class (...) condemned to movement' and the Very Otherness of the Other: Latife Tekin as Author-Translator of Swords of Ice[1]

S. PAKER

Introduction

The quotation in my title belongs to Kiran Desai in her distinctively memorable novel, *The Inheritance of Loss* (2006: 102), awarded the Booker Prize. One strand of the narrative in this novel leads Biju, a humble cook's son from a village in North West India, to New York, where he moves from one job to another, trying to survive as an illegal immigrant. That 'the shadow class was condemned to movement' happens to be a thought that crosses Biju's mind, obviously marking a moment of acute awareness as well as loneliness, a life-lesson learned in a community that can break up at any time, given their migrancy as shadows of those with 'real' and stable lives.

While reading Desai's words, I was struck by their resonance with what Latife Tekin had to say about her book *Buzdan Kılıçlar* (*Swords of Ice*, 2007)[2] soon after it was published in 1989: 'this book is not about the dispossessed or "the others"; rather, it is a story of the *shadow of others*'[3] (Tekin, 1989: 69, my emphasis). Unlike Desai's *The Inheritance of Loss*, Tekin's short novel focuses exclusively on a 'shadow' community, named generically as the 'ragged men'. Tekin's characters are not illegal immigrants in a foreign country, like Biju and his mates in the US; nonetheless, they assume a similar role as hapless players controlled by economic and social forces. For Biju's Turkish counterparts are second-generation migrants from villages who settled mainly on the fringes of the big city in their makeshift huts, *gecekondu*s, that were initially built overnight on public land. Their early years of settlement in the 1960s and 1970s are the subject of Tekin's first two best-selling novels in 1983 and 1984: *Sevgili Arsız Ölüm* (*Dear Shameless Death*, 2001[4]) and *Berji Kristin Çöp Masalları* (*Berji Kristin Tales from the Garbage Hills*, 1993[5]). These set the necessary context for an understanding of *Swords of Ice*, which represents a later stage, and an important one, in the social, economic and political evolution of *gecekondu* communities. The so-called 'ragged men' now dwell in 'houses [...] that looked like wet match-boxes' instead of the *gecekondu*s of *Berji Kristin...*; they are located outside 'the city's outermost belt [...], an electric fence that held at bay the type of neighbourhoods where they lived' (Tekin, 2007: 17, 18). Those neighbourhoods remain nameless in the book, like the city itself, Istanbul. They seem to represent a more developed, 1980s version of the shantytowns of the previous decades; the *gecekondu*s, built overnight on the garbage hills in *Berji Kristin...*, have evidently been transformed into two- or three-storey houses, presumably with more facilities, hinting at a slightly higher standard of living. In view of such differences, *Buzdan Kılıçlar* (*Swords of Ice*) seems to complete Tekin's first two books and may therefore be considered part of a trilogy. If *Buzdan Kılıçlar* has been perceived by readers as particularly challenging on its own, this may also have something to do with the fact that Tekin wrote it as a special challenge to her critics.

In this contribution, I shall discuss Tekin's original as a translation in itself, but also as one embodying a translation poetics that can be read as a manifesto of literary–political and ideological opposition and resistance, especially to the expectations of the Turkish left-wing élite. I will also argue that the 'shadow' element is to be regarded as a metonymical manifestation of her translation practice. So this chapter consists of two parts: the first describes why *Buzdan Kılıçlar* is to be considered a translation and the second analyses the reasons for this. Concluding remarks will also cover a brief discussion of the English translation, *Swords of Ice*.

Latife Tekin's 'Original' as Translation

In an interview given in 1989, the year *Buzdan Kılıçlar* was published, Tekin said:

> I choose to describe myself as a translator [...] rather than a writer. I find it more meaningful to think of myself as one who interprets, who translates the mute, 'tongueless' world of the dispossessed into the language of this world. (Tekin, 1989: 69)

This declaration actually echoes what Tekin had to say in what I call the Prologue to *Buzdan Kılıçlar*; it was made, I argue, to critique her critics, especially those who were so harsh on her previous book, *Gece Dersleri* (*Night Lessons*, 1986[6]). The ambivalence of Tekin's self-identification as 'translator' rather than 'writer' is not unproblematic. The tension or conflict that underlies her self-positioning as a 'writer of the poor' may explain the intriguing experimentations to be observed in her corpus and, at times, their estranging effects and opacity.

In his preface to *Berji Kristin...*, Tekin's second book, John Berger had noted that 'before her [Latife Tekin], no shanty-town had entered literature – had entered written narrative – as an entity in itself' as 'the centre of the world, holding the stage, addressing the sky' (Berger in Tekin, 1993: 6). Analysing the affinity of two of Berger's novels with Latife Tekin's *Berji Kristin...*, Peter Brooker observes the 'foreignness' in the latter that 'disturbs both geographical and discursive bearings' in his view: 'Just as this shanty community is estranged in its post-metropolitan niche, so Tekin's text is estranging to outside readers' (Brooker, 2002: 192, 194).[7]

In *Buzdan Kılıçlar* the main narrative is a lively one, infused with irony, humour, and a touch of melodrama about the experiences of some of the 'ragged' individuals in this community: Halilhan, who plays the lead, his two brothers, their wives and their father, Halilhan's girlfriends, his best friend Gogi, and his car the Volvo, which also serves as a mentor. At this point one may wonder how Halilhan, identified as a 'ragged man', can be in possession of a car with an expensive brand name. But 'possession' is perhaps the trickiest term in Tekin's vocabulary. Tekin introduces Halilhan as

> the first of the area's poor who had been lucky enough to transform *his sense of dispossession* into the substance of a car ... [T]he feelings this instilled in him set him visibly apart from his fellow men in the neighbourhood – that distant satellite ruled over by those fused with their possessions – [...]. (Tekin, 2007: 16, my emphasis)

But Halilhan is ambitious and convinced that his beloved Volvo, which he rescued from the scrapyard with the money swindled from his brothers, will show him the way right up to the top – to 'the men in charge of the country's economy'; this, he believes, will happen despite the efforts of 'a host of wolfish politicians' who stand watch 'in invisible towers [...] on the city's outermost belt' to keep him from reaching his goal (Tekin, 2007: 18). However, it is also important to note that the Volvo emerges as Halilhan's home, his retreat, something that he desperately wants to be at one with – a point which I shall discuss in greater detail further on.

Running occasionally parallel to the main narrative, Tekin brings into play an uncanny, other-worldly, metaphorical movement which is voiced in a poetic register, and which punctuates the apparent 'real life' movement in the story. It is this second, fragmentary narrative strand (italicized in the English translation presented below)[8] that foregrounds the sombre, 'shadow' aspect of the novel. Let me give three consecutive examples from a particular chapter.

In a drunken stupor, Halilhan, the leading character, picks up a young woman in his Volvo:

Example 8.1

[Halilhan] pressed his mouth to the woman's ear and shouted, 'Lady, would you care to accompany me to immortality?' Shocked by Halilhan's question the woman started to cry.

The ragged men had crossed the last circle around the city. Gulping up the light reflected off the snow and breathing in time together, they'd leapt lightly off into nothingness.

Halilhan could hardly bear the sight of a weeping woman because it affected his *psikoloji* so strangely ... (Tekin, 2007: 109)

Example 8.2

'Why don't you tell me your name?' [Halilhan] asked tenderly. 'I think I'll take you out for a nice meal.' He wanted her to be certain he had no dark, devious intentions but only wanted to be her friend.

With deathless looks and trembling like wind through an emptiness, they [the ragged men] *were disappearing, defying any attempt to explain their worldly existence.* 'Keriman,' murmured the woman. '*Mersi*', Halilhan replied. 'And your family name, would it by any chance be Muhammed?' (Tekin, 2007: 110)

Example 8.3

Then [Halilhan] launched into a silly song, 'Drop by drop, fly the days by... da-da, da-da, da-da. ...' He had to find a way to squeeze a little laughter out of this unlucky woman.

Their [the ragged men's] *showpiece lives, spun as they were from life's far-off reflections, were becoming veils for their vanishing.*

If only he [Halilhan] could comfort her a little ... then, tonight, in return, she might bring a tiny bit of love into their lives. (Tekin, 2007: 110)

As may be seen above, the seemingly 'real life' episode is punctuated with metaphorical descriptions of the movements of the ragged men, and pictures them 'leap[ing] lightly into nothingness', 'disappearing', 'vanishing'. At first glance, the insertions seem to function as metaphors translating the main action involving Halilhan and Keriman, which will eventually lead to a disastrous accident with the Volvo.

However, reading the text as a translation of 'the mute, 'tongueless' world of the dispossessed into the language of this world' can reverse that view. For the 'source' action of the book seems not to hinge on what appears to be 'real life' but on the other-worldly 'shadow' one; the action embracing Halilhan and Keriman translates the ragged men's ghost-like movements. The episode concerning the two individuals is metonymical, only a representative aspect of a whole, other-worldly narrative, which, as will be shown below, was Tekin's main concern.

It must be said that the interruptions of an apparently incompatible voice in the main narrative, the absence of a conventional 'plot', and the relatively loose structure do not make comfortable reading for everyone, either in Turkish or in English, but it is obvious that the book was important for Latife Tekin and that she wrote it with a special sense of purpose.

Latife Tekin comes from a socialist-activist background and began to publish in 1983 when she was 26. Her fiction, which consists of eight novels so far, still represents the boldest voice in the new Turkish novel. Her third book, *Gece Dersleri* (*Night Lessons*), came out in 1986, three years before *Swords of Ice*. This was a fictionalized account of her personal experiences as a member of a women's association of the radical left. Her criticism of the elitist and hierarchical workings of the left which (she claimed, in a later autobiographical account, Tekin, 1987; Tekin in Özer, 2005: 91–119) patronized and oppressed young activists like herself, led to harsh criticism and an outrageously unfair, *non*-literary reception of her work. What was rather shamefully overlooked or deliberately dismissed in the course of the polemics was the book's literary merit, its lyrical style in which any criticism was embedded in a dominantly metaphorical discourse. I would argue that *Buzdan Kılıçlar*, which followed three years later, is not only an important literary intervention by Tekin, but also a political/ideological response to the critics of her previous book, *Gece Dersleri*, and that the opening section or Prologue of *Buzdan Kılıçlar* reads as such a manifesto, which also interestingly explains her translation poetics.

The Prologue begins in the fairy tale mode of oral tradition, but gradually proceeds with a questioning. The narrator describes the 'ragged men' as *'those who'd so brazened it out with fate'* that nothing in the world could surprise them. *'But what can I say?'*, the narrator goes on:

> *Maybe it's true that these men inspire no more faith than the futile spells cast from the breath of a sorcerer, but their lives hold more attraction than any mysterious, gigantic magnet.*
>
> *The souls of the poor know and understand each other as no others can. To keep the reality of dispossession weighing down on them at bay — the one certainty as sharp and absolute as death —* these *'have-nots'* have been communicating in signs, silently, for hundreds of years, murmuring on in the secret language that only they can ever learn.
>
> *Take away the knowing that rises out of poverty, that impudent toad they kept in their pockets, and how could they, in full awareness of the life they've been denied, dare to tiptoe about fearfully in the cruel world of others?*
>
> *But what would you know about any of this?* (Tekin, 2007: 9, my emphases)

In no other book by Latife Tekin is there a similar, direct address to the reader. The defiant tone prevails to the end of the Prologue and in the final paragraph[9] the subject throughout is 'we'. The shift to the personal plural 'we' indicates the narrator's explicit identification with the 'ragged men', as does the final 'I'. Before the end of the Prologue, the Turkish of the original is suddenly interrupted by what sounds like gibberish: 'leri şarupdiende tisika cemi (Lerry sharupdiende tisika jemmy in the English)'. The narrator translates (into Turkish): *'This is what* we *call our belongings. Meaning, border map of the land of the have-nots'* (Tekin, 2007: 10, my emphasis). And the full blast of the narrator's protest is saved for the final paragraph which ends with 'No more! *I*'ve given enough away!' (Tekin, 2007: 10).

So, in the Prologue, the narrator actually gives an example of her translation practice, by providing the meaning of the 'original' nonsense statement *(leri şarupdiende tisika cemi)*. Given the context of the Prologue and the background to Tekin's former critical reception, the narrator of the Prologue can only be the author herself. This seems to be confirmed also by the blurb on the back cover of the first two editions of her book in Turkish, (also printed as a post scriptum in the English version): 'Writing! Faithful foe of the poor! I have used you to deepen even more the enigma of our ragged lives'.

What significance does his statement carry for Latife Tekin as writer or translator?

Latife Tekin's Poetics of Translation

In an interview published one year after the controversial *Gece Dersleri* came out, Tekin said:

> I claim poverty as my own [because] it is my history [...] I want to subvert much of what has been said about poverty by relying on my own life, on my writing and on my past as my only source of support in order to be convincing to myself and to others. (Tekin, 1987: 140)

But, if writing is the enemy of 'the poor', then could her claim to be a 'translator' be interpreted as her way out of the dilemma of being a 'writer' (Tekin, 1987: 140)? Or did she conceive of herself as something of a 'real' translator, one who was technically equipped with a source language and a specific medium of transfer to work with? Her example in the Prologue, as well as others from the rest of the book, seem to affirm my second question, in ways that will become clear in what follows. In my view the shift to 'translator' in identifying her literary profession came about over the years as much as a result of clarifying for herself the driving force of her writing as that of reacting to criticism about her self-declared ambivalence regarding her authorial status. The evidence for such an argument is to be found in an important interview (1987), held soon after she started working on *Buzdan Kılıçlar*. Aware of her paradoxical relationship with writing and poverty, Tekin explained:

> Today, like other professions, that of the writer enjoys special privileges, signifies a special seat of power. As for me, I'm still trying to identify myself with the poor. Poverty, in turn, demands of me not to have internalized either a sense of possession or a sense of power. I am ashamed of my privileged profession. Besides, in my case, there's a two-fold implication: as a writer, I claim the privilege of talking about the poor and their suffering but end up becoming a kind of authority on them. (Tekin, 1997–1998a: 129–130)

Other statements from interviews over the years provide us with clues about Tekin's 'history' and its connection with her conception of poverty. We gather from these that a persistent 'sense of lack and sorrow' ruled over her migrant's experience of Istanbul; she 'discovered that what shut [her] out was language', that power had meant language since her childhood in the city (Tekin, 1997–1998b: 128). 'All doors seemed open to her and her people "except the language of others, which filled the air with *sounds* and *sentences, words, signs* and *implications*" that kept shutting them out, shutting them up, leaving them "in a fatal struggle for breath". "That is why, when I made up my mind to write, I declared I would write in my home voice, the language we spoke at home," [Tekin] said' (Tekin 1997–1998b: 128; Paker, 2001: 11, my emphases).

The interrelationship of her conceptions of poverty and language is crucial for an understanding of why Tekin described herself in 1989 as a translator. Statements in this interview suggest that Tekin had subverted the common poor–rich binary:

> I don't think the opposite of poor (or dispossessed) is rich. I didn't feel confronted by wealth/riches, but by some massive block *giving out signals* that made me feel I was poor. I sensed that I would 'carry my existence' in this world in a different way than others. It was then that my inner world was split up into 'those like me' and 'others'. I know very well that I did not learn of poverty/dispossession from my family ... When I speak of dispossession, I'm talking about a world beyond class, about people who have no sense of possession. The dispossessed discover their position (in life, in society) from the way *they read the signs and the looks* directed at them ... (Tekin, 1989: 69, my emphases)

It was in this interview, given in the year *Buzdan Kılıçlar* was published, that Latife Tekin identified herself as a translator and redefined her literary practice:

> My position is somewhat strange [she said]. I am a *yoksul* (a have-not) who has learned to write. I don't feel like a writer [...] I choose to describe myself as a translator [...] rather than a writer. I find it more meaningful to think of myself as one who interprets, who translates the mute, 'tongueless' world of the dispossessed into the *language of this world*. (Tekin, 1989: 69, my emphasis)

In the Prologue to *Buzdan Kılıçlar* the author is more specific: 'the have-nots' are described as *'murmuring on in the secret language that only they can ever learn'* (Tekin 2007: 9).[10]

If Latife Tekin is a translator who made it her business to convey 'the mute, "tongueless" world of the dispossessed into the language of this world' of 'the others' who use that language, then what constitutes her medium of translation? The answer seems to lie in what I would describe as *shadow* words.

First let us hear how Tekin describes them. With explicit reference to *Buzdan Kılıçlar* Tekin said:

> In my novel, I tried to give an account of the world of the dispossessed (of which I am one) in the words of others, or rather, in words that we [the poor] have all *stolen* from the others ... The dispossessed do not have words of their own. Words belong to 'others'. Because they [others] are in power, they also wield power over daily life and language. In reality, such terms as 'poverty' and 'class' are words of the outsider. (Tekin, 1989: 68, emphasis added)

Such 'stolen' words abound in *Buzdan Kılıçlar*, the most conspicuous of them being the Turkish-adopted French vocabulary.

Then what kind of 'stealing' does this translation process involve? As I pointed out at the beginning, in describing her novel, Tekin claims that '*Buzdan Kılıçlar* is not the story of the dispossessed or of the others, but rather one that is of the *shadow of others*' (Tekin, 1989: 69, my emphasis). She goes on:

> When we 'the poor', are seen from the outside, it looks as if we are *imitating a life*. In my view, this is the shadow of others on 'the poor'; we dress in those shadows and when others look at us, they see us dressed in them. But the poor, though still dressed in those shadows, protect/preserve their real lives in a different place.[11] (Tekin, 1989: 69, emphasis added)

'Imitating a life [...] dressed in the shadows of others', in this context, is also a metaphor for translating a text ('life') in words ('dress') that are the *shadows* of those spoken by the others, i.e. a curious case of substituting words known but 'stolen' for words that belong, presumably, to an unspoken, unfamiliar idiom, that is at best 'murmured'. 'Stealing' in this process may be interpreted as stripping the vocabulary of 'others' of their established context and placing them in a different one. It is, in fact, a metonymical process, as I shall try to explain below.

'A basic feature of rewritings and retellings [and hence of translations, SP], is that they are metonymic,' writes Maria Tymoczko in *Translation in a Postcolonial Context* (1999: 42), her study of 19th- and 20th-century versions of medieval Irish literature. While bearing in mind Tymoczko's definition of metonymy as 'a figure of speech in which an attribute or an aspect of an entity substitutes for the whole' (Tymoczko, 1999: 42), I would, nevertheless, like to follow David Lodge's argument (1977: 75–77) based on his critical reading of Roman Jakobson's (1956) binary scheme which, as we know, significantly points to the opposing principles that govern metaphor and metonymy (and synecdoche):

> selection [metaphor, SP] is opposed to combination [metonymy, SP], and substitution is opposed to 'contexture' — the process by which 'any linguistic unit at one and the same time serves as a context for simpler units and/or finds its own context in a more complex linguistic unit'. (Lodge & Jakobson in Lodge, 1977: 76)

Lodge continues:

> But contexture is not an optional operation in quite the same way as substitution; it is rather a law of language. I suggest that the term we need is *deletion*: deletion is to combination [metonymy, SP] as substitution is to selection [metaphor, SP]. Metonymies and synecdoches are *condensations* of contexture. (Lodge & Jakobson in Lodge, 1977: 76, original emphases)

I would argue that the Volvo in *Buzdan Kılıçlar* represents such a condensation – one that functions as a fundamental metonym around which Tekin constructs her 'translation'. The Volvo, just like the French vocabulary (in Turkish transcription) in the novel, can be instantly recognized as a 'stolen word', a shadow word, a brand name but also an object that is foreign to the community of 'ragged men', one that belongs to the affluent world of 'others'. It represents no more than a *shadow*, in fact, since it signifies dispossession rather than possession for its owner, Halilhan, who, despite all the attention and decorative elements he lavishes on his car, cannot really feel at one with it. Both literally and figuratively, it has been removed from its natural habitat, so to speak; its former context has been deleted, to be replaced by a totally different one. As the car that Halilhan can never really possess, however much he wants to, the Volvo remains only a 'shadow' of wealth, a metonym, which is used to translate the presence of a 'sense of possession', in play with its absence.

But I would claim that the Volvo is also metonymic of 'home', especially in the way it functions like the *gecekondu*, the fundamental metonym, in *Berji Kristin...*, which can best be described as a micro-epic of life in the *gecekondus*, the Turkish name given to a squatter's hut; translated literally, the word means 'perched' (*kondu*) 'overnight' (*gece*). It is obviously a name given by 'the other' or outsider – not a word coined by the migrant poor themselves who built the huts overnight for a home to live in, but by the 'others' who were taken by surprise in the morning when they saw the huts that seem to have appeared out of the blue on public or private land. What this 'stolen word' signifies for Tekin is told in an interview:

> I've always felt I was from the *gecekondu*, though I never lived in one. Istanbul had crushed the memory of my birthplace and what I knew about the world. While I lived on, feeling a deep sense of want, and being scorned, I was able to revive and treasure my childhood, my peasantness, thanks to the *gecekondu*s and the *gecekondu* people. I could look back on my past with the inspiration I drew from them. One morning, when I thought my past was useless, the *gecekondu* entered my life as a possibility; it worked on the fear and on the feeling of absence that was growing in my heart. If I hadn't been spellbound by that intense vision of absence, would I have been able to build a lifestory for myself which never touched Istanbul, which began somewhere that did not exist? (Tekin, 1997–1998a: 126–127)

The 'deep sense of want' at the beginning of the excerpt above is reinforced by the 'intense vision of absence' at the end: a *deletion* of central Istanbul and its replacement with the *gecekondu* communities, a vision which not only led Latife Tekin to write but which also holds the key for an understanding of her self-perception as a writer/translator of dispossession. In Tekin's lexicon, the *gecekondu* appears as a unique site where displacement, loss of roots and dispossession overlap to generate many meanings. The *gecekondu* is used as a metonym to translate the presence of 'home' with all its connotations, a transient 'shadow' home (repeatedly demolished, as we know from *Berji Kristin*...) which, in the narrative, appears in play with the absence of the permanent home left behind in the village, thus acquiring multiple meanings by constantly deferring the permanence of that 'home'.

In *Buzdan Kılıçlar*, there is no mention of the *gecekondu*; it seems to be erased not only because it has evolved into a 'house', as I mentioned earlier on, but because it has been replaced by the Volvo. The Volvo emerges in the narrative as Halilhan's real home, where he can retreat and watch the stars in his pyjamas, where he starts his affairs with the women he picks up, where he holds his heart-to-heart talks with his buddy and listens to songs of lament, all the time wanting to unite, to become one with the car, wanting to feel that he really *possesses* it.

Conclusion

In the present analysis, Latife Tekin's intervention in contemporary Turkish fiction, conceived in the form of a 'translation' and its poetics, suggests that her literary and ideological opposition to mainstream literary politics found its strategy in the deconstruction of the dispossessed migrants' urban universe in its relation to the universe of the settled and the affluent. This fits in with her intention to 'subvert much of what has been said about poverty' (Tekin, 1987: 140).

It is possible to encounter writers who claim to be translators of an abstraction, such as dreams,[12] but what does it really mean, being the 'translator' of a concrete, so-called 'original' work produced by its author? In Latife Tekin's case, the author's translatorial claim has certainly proved to be worth taking as a point of departure in the present analysis, particularly because it has substantiated, I think, her oppositional and interventionist stance in literary and ideological terms. Tekin's paratextual discourse about *Buzdan Kılıçlar* supports as well as illuminates her authorial project of translating the abstract, of voicing the unheard tongue of 'the poor'. Text and paratext offer an ideologically oriented translation poetics that has not been commonly encountered in the literary world. Written almost 20 years ago, *Buzdan Kılıçlar* may still be regarded in its home environment as an 'odd' narrative by some, as a cherished one by others but, nonetheless, it remains a work of fiction that definitely disturbs while challenging the mainstream literary conventions' underlying ideologies.

Translating *Buzdan Kılıçlar* into the English *Swords of Ice* shares to some degree the original's challenge, in its modest attempt to unsettle the more or less established notions of what modern Turkish fiction 'is about', in terms of subject matter, style and accessibility for the contemporary English-speaking audience. First of all, the translators felt that the *shadow* aspect of the 'original translation' (as I would like to describe it), especially of the 'ragged men', should not be suppressed but highlighted in the text through the use of italics: as, for instance, in the case of the otherworldly descriptions of their movements that were inscribed by Tekin in the main narrative. Similarly, the translators italicized the Prologue, described above as the author's manifesto, disregarding once again the ordinary print form in the Turkish editions. The same principle was followed in the case of lexical items, such as the French words adopted (and transcribed phonetically in Turkish), common in Turkish parlance, but which function in the discourse of the 'ragged men' as 'stolen words'. Most of such words, assumed to be recognisable from French, the translators felt, had to be italicized and kept in Turkish instead of being represented in English translation. Such decisions were guided by an intention to foreground 'difference': that between the author's presumed 'source' (the metaphysical lives and language of the poor, according to the analysis above) and her translation into the words and actions of the named characters, which constitutes the main narrative. In more general terms, this translatorial strategy also aimed at rendering the text (paradoxically) more accessible for the target reader. The fact that the publisher's editors approved of it shows that their intercultural mediation policies could take into account a significant instance of how cultural difference or 'foreignness' may be represented in translation. But it must also be said that such otherness seems to derive from Latife Tekin's own fictional configuration of the marginal as the central which is inherent in her 'original,' in *Buzdan Kılıçlar* itself.

Notes

1. Some of the main arguments in this chapter were presented in a keynote speech, 'The metonymics of translating Turkish fiction: Latife Tekin's *Swords of Ice* and other works in English', at the 3rd International IDEA Conference, Studies in English, 16–18 April 2008, Ege University, Faculty of Letters, İzmir, Turkey.
2. Translated by Saliha Paker and Mel Kenne into English as *Swords of Ice* (2007); also excerpted in *The Warwick Review* (2007: 66–77).
3. All translations are my own unless otherwise indicated.
4. Translated into English by Saliha Paker and Mel Kenne, with an Introduction by Saliha Paker (2001).
5. Translated into English by Ruth Christie and Saliha Paker, with a Preface by John Berger and an Introduction by Saliha Paker (1993). For a review of all three novels by Latife Tekin in English translation, see Adcock (2009: 112–114).
6. Partly translated into English as *Night Lessons* by Nilüfer Yeşil and Aron Aji (1998).
7. In his sensitive analysis, Brooker also draws attention to Tekin's influence on Berger's *Lilac and Flag* (1990) and *King* (1999), discussed in Berger (1992).
8. As explained below, some parts of *Buzdan Kılıçlar* were italicized by the translators in *Swords of Ice* to raise English readers' awareness of a different strand in the narrative.
9. "Lerri sharupdiende tisika jemmy" *is what* we *call our belongings. Meaning, border map of the land of the "have-nots".*
   There's a perfectly good reason why we *preserve every moment of the life* we've *spent struggling to put food in our mouths. . . . We need to prove to ourselves that we actually live and breathe and have existed in the past. Our stage sets are a precious part of the amazing and miraculous defence system* we've *constructed to shield ourselves . . . from the aggression of your world.*
   No more! I've given enough away!' (Tekin, 2007: 10, my emphases)
10. 'Murmur' (*mırıltı* in Turkish) is a significant word in Tekin's vocabulary, to which Nurdan Gürbilek has drawn special attention in an important essay in which she analyses the shift in Tekin's discourse 'from murmur to language' (*mırıltıdan dile*) (Gürbilek, 1999: 33–58, 2011: 81–82).

11. And that 'different place' is translated to us in the Prologue, which I have already quoted above: 'leri şarupdiende tisika cemi: *This is what* we *call our belongings. Meaning, border map of the land of the "have-nots"'* (Tekin, 2007: 10).
12. See, for example, Mia Couto's speech at the WALTIC Conference 2008 (Couto, 2008) and David Brookshaw (2008) on Couto.

References

Adcock, H. (2009) Turkey. *Edinburgh Review* 125, 112–114.
Berger, J. (1990) *Lilac and Flag. Into their Labours.* London: Granta.
Berger, J. (1992) The act of approaching. Interview with Nikos Papastergiadis. *Third Text* 19, Summer, 87–95.
Berger, J. (1993) Rumour. *Berji Kristin Tales from the Garbage Hills.* London/New York: Marion Boyars.
Berger, J. (1999) *King, A Street Story.* London: Bloomsbury.
Brooker, P. (2002) *Modernity and Metropolis. Writing, Film and Urban Formations.* Basingstoke/New York: Palgrave.
Brookshaw, D. (2008) Some thoughts on translating Mia Couto. *Congress Program, WALTIC, The Value of Words* (pp. 15–17). Writers' and Literary Translators' International Congress, 29 June–2 July. Stockholm, Sweden.
Couto, M. (2008) The writer as translator. Keynote speech, Writers' and Literary Translators' International Congress (WALTIC), 29 June–2 July. Stockholm, Sweden.
Desai, K. (2006) *The Inheritance of Loss.* Harlow: Penguin International.
Gürbilek, N. (1999) Mırıltıdan dile (From murmur to language). In *Ev Ödevi (Homework)* (pp. 33–58). Istanbul: Metis.
Gürbilek, N. (2011) *The New Cultural Climate in Turkey. Living in a Shop Window* (V. Holbrook, trans.). London: Zed Books.
Jakobson, R. (1956) Two aspects of language and two types of linguistic disturbances. In R. Jakobson and M. Halle (eds) *Fundamentals of Language* (pp. 55–76). The Hague: Mouton.
Lodge, D. (1977) *The Modes of Modern Writing. Metaphor, Metonymy and the Typology of Modern Literature.* London: Edward Arnold.
Özer, P. (2005) *Latife Tekin Kitabı.* Istanbul: Everest.
Paker, S. (1993) Introduction. In L. Tekin (ed.) *Berji Kristin Tales from the Garbage Hills* (pp. 9–14). London/New York: Marion Boyars.
Paker, S. (2001) Introduction. In L. Tekin (ed.) *Dear Shameless Death* (pp. 7–17). London/New York: Marion Boyars.
Tekin, L. (1986) *Night Lessons* (*Gece Dersleri*) (N. Yeşil, trans.). On WWW at http://www.turkish-lit.boun.edu.tr/frameset2.asp?CharSet=English. Accessed 12.2.10.
Tekin, L. (1987; 1997–1998a) Yazı ve yoksulluk (Writing and poverty, interview with İskender Savaşır). *Defter*, 1. Istanbul: Metis, 133–148. Excerpted (S. Paker, trans.) in K. Brown and R. Waterhouse (eds) *Istanbul, Many Worlds/ Istanbul, un monde pluriel* (pp. 129–130). Guest eds M. Belge and I. Şimşek in the series *Mediterraneans/Méditerranéennes* 10, Winter. Paris: L'Association Méditerranéens, Maison des Sciences de l'Homme, and Istanbul: Yapı Kredi Publications.
Tekin, L. (1989) Yazar değil Çevirmenim (I'm not a writer, I'm a translator, interview). *Nokta* 12 March, 68–69.

Tekin, L. (1993) *Berji Kristin Tales from the Garbage Hills* (*Berji Kristin Çöp Masalları*, 1984) (R. Christie and S. Paker, trans.). London/New York: Marion Boyars.

Tekin, L. (1997–1998b) Istanbul is hurt about us (S. Paker, trans.). In K. Brown and R. Waterhouse (eds) *Istanbul Many Worlds/Istanbul, un monde pluriel* (pp.127–129). Guest eds M. Belge and I. Şimşek, in the series *Mediterraneans/Méditerranéennes* 10, Winter. Paris: L'Association Méditerranéens, Maison des Sciences de l'Homme, and Istanbul: Yapı Kredi Publications.

Tekin, L. (1998) *Night Lessons* (*Gece Dersleri*, 1986) (Aron R. Aji, trans.). In *Grand Street*, 66, Fall.

Tekin, L. (2001) *Dear Shameless Death* (*Sevgili Arsız Ölüm*, 1983) (S. Paker and M. Kenne, trans.). London/New York: Marion Boyars.

Tekin, L. (2007) *Swords of Ice* (*Buzdan Kılıçlar*, 1989) (S. Paker and M. Kenne, trans.). London/New York: Marion Boyars. Excerpt in *The Warwick Review* 1 (1), March 2007, 66–77.

Tymoczko, M. (1999) *Translation in a Postcolonial Context*. Manchester: St. Jerome.

Chapter 9
Translation and Opposition in Italian-Canadian Writing. Nino Ricci's Trilogy and its Italian Translation

M. BALDO

Introduction

This chapter will consider the notions of opposition and translation in Italian-Canadian writing, a body of literature produced in the last 30 years by writers of Italian background living in Canada. Specifically, I will analyse these two notions in the trilogy of novels by Nino Ricci, one of the best known Italian-Canadian novelists, and in their Italian translation.

Ricci's trilogy of novels, *Lives of the Saints* (1990), *In a Glass House* (1993) and *Where She Has Gone* (1997), deals with the experiences of an Italian family before and after they emigrated to Canada. The protagonist is Vittorio Innocente, who narrates his personal experience, from his childhood to his migration and life in Toronto, and his return back, as an adult, to his maternal village in Southern Italy. Following the literary success of the trilogy in Canada, the texts were translated into Italian in 2004 by Gabriella Iacobucci with the publishing house Fazi Editore and adapted into a TV mini-series (2004), directed by Jerry Ciccoritti and starring the Italian actresses Sophia Loren and Sabrina Ferilli. The written translation of the trilogy into Italian appears in a single book with the title *La terra del ritorno* ('The Land of Return'),[1] which reframes the novel as a homecoming of the Italian-Canadian immigrant. The translation project was conceived with the purpose of: (a) capitalizing on the launch of the TV mini-series in the same year; and (b) offering Italian readers a coherent account of the trilogy (Canton, 2002).[2]

Thus, translation is understood here not only as the material transfer operation involving texts across languages and media, but also as a metaphor strictly linked to the idea of oppositional perspectives.

Why Opposition and Translation in Italian-Canadian Writing?

Italian-Canadian writing first appeared in the mid-1970s with the work of Pier Giorgio Di Cicco, who was also one of the founders of the Association of Italian-Canadian writers in Vancouver in 1986.

The idea of translation as an abstract site of oppositions, which can be readily associated with this specific type of literature, mainly emerges out of a concrete generational gap. The majority of the writers I am referring to were either born in Canada to Italian families coming generally from rural areas of Southern Italy (as in the case of Nino Ricci), or emigrated to Canada at an early age and grew up there, and thus can be considered as second-generation immigrants. As such, they experienced a conflict between the values (such as self-promotion and individualism) conveyed in English by the school system, the media and the mainstream English-Canadian culture, and the values taught at home by their parents in an Italian dialect (such as filial obedience and patriarchal gender role division), which were often rejected (Tuzi, 1997: 14) because of the many prejudices circulating about Italians in Canada since the 1950s and 1960s (DeMaria Harney, 1998). However, the sense of guilt at attempting to break their bonds with the past provided Italian-Canadian writers with inspiration for their stories. Many narrate a journey of return to their Italian roots in their adulthood (in real and metaphorical ways) as a means of self-recognition (Pivato, 1994: 121, 163), of giving voice to a familiar past of silence.

The concept of opposition refers, therefore, to the contrast of values mentioned above and represents the driving force of Italian-Canadian writing. Writing constitutes a way of translating and negotiating cultural perspectives often in conflict with each other. As Pivato (1994: 127) has noted: 'The most important task for Italian-Canadian writers has been the uncovering and translation of their immigrant experience as an act of self-discovery'. Translation becomes a heuristic tool which enables Italian-Canadian writers to express themselves. In this Italian-Canadian writing, thus, both writing and translation meet as a practice of creation, of rewriting (Pratt, 1992), and 'writing and translating are synonyms' (Verdicchio, 1997: 110).

Heterogeneous Perspectives: Code-switching on the Page

Italian-Canadian writing is therefore born out of the need to translate a set of cultural and linguistic oppositions. The most peculiar expression of this translation is the presence of multilingualism in this literature: Italian-Canadian writing mainly appears in three or four languages, Canadian-English, French, standard Italian and a variety of Italian dialects, and often in a mixture of all these languages within the same texts. As stated by Simon (1994: 20), incorporating texts and intertexts from other languages in a given text is described as 'a poetic of translation' which characterizes borderlands where creation and translation, originality and imitation, authority and submission merge. Translation is strictly linked to multilingualism (Delabastita & Grutman, 2005: 11); this link has been analysed, for example, by authors investigating post-colonial contexts (see Bandia 1996, 2008; Bhabha, 1990, 1994; Mehrez, 1992; Tymoczko, 1999), or situations of diaspora and migration (Cronin, 2006: 45).

Since the focus of the current analysis is the constant shifts or passages from one language and cultural sphere (Italy and Canada) to another, as a way of giving expression to the many oppositions experienced by Italian-Canadian writers, I will adopt the term 'code-switching' rather than 'multilingualism'. Code-switching, a phenomenon usually observed among speakers of bilingual communities in which two or more languages are in contact, is defined in syntactic terms as:

> the alternative use by bilinguals of two or more languages in the same conversation. [...] It can occur between the turn of different speakers in conversation, sometimes even within a single utterance. (Milroy & Muysken, 1995: 7–8)

Although written and oral code-switching are not the same, the former can mimic the latter (Callahan, 2005: 100). Code-switching in literature can be considered a mimetic device used to imitate the real speech of characters in the narrative, so identifying them as members of an ethnic community (Camarca, 2005: 128). Written code-switching thus holds a sociological significance, as demonstrated by sociolinguists like Auer (1998), Gumperz (1982), Martin (2005) and Muysken (2000).[3] In the specific case of Ricci's trilogy, the use of Italian and Southern Italian dialects can serve to portray a group identity. As an example, the home language (Italian and dialect) is associated with intimacy and personal involvement (Gumperz, 1982), while the institutional language (Canadian-English) has connotations of authority and distance (Callahan, 2005: 18).

Yet, the process of indexing identity is not straightforward and rests in particular on the contrast achieved by the juxtaposition of the codes involved in the switching; this means that code-switching is partly independent from the meaning of the codes in the sociolinguistic repertoire (Gumperz, 1982: 84, 91). A concept that can clarify this aspect of code-switching is the notion of contextualization cues which are understood by Gumperz (1982: 131) as specific signposts hinting at extra textual factors whose inferential (and not referential) meaning (see Callahan, 2005: 17) speakers and listeners are forced to look at in order to contextualize a conversational activity. To Gumperz's idea of contextualization cues we can add the markedness model by Myers-Scotton (1993a: 57), which stresses further the creative role of the participants of a conversation in negotiating changes based on the type of conversation.

The complex functions of oral code-switching are further complicated in written code-switching because of the fictional nature of texts (where 'fictional' refers to the possibilities and constraints of the written medium). Written code-switching is a meta-discursive feature that, by indexing extra-textual factors, contributes to giving significance to a text (Pirazzini, 2000: 543). If the sociological characteristics of the languages involved in the switch are important, this is more so for the way these languages are embedded in the overall text and made to interact with each other (Delabastita & Grutman, 2005: 16). As an example, a writer in diasporic contexts can use code-switching to deconstruct stereotypes by putting together contrasting perceptions linked to a certain community (see also Auer, 1998). Given these considerations, a fruitful analysis of code-switching requires a detailed examination of cases of relevant shifts, as will be shown below.

Narrative and Code-switching in Ricci's Trilogy

In order to analyse the textual function of code-switching in Ricci's trilogy it is useful to borrow concepts from narratology, complementing them with insights from post-structuralism. Code-switching is a strategy that is used to construct a narrative by translating and giving voice to often conflicting perspectives. By hinting at a shift of perspectives, code-switching thus relies heavily on the concepts of *focalization* and *voice*[4] (Määttä, 2004),[5] which refer to the perspective through which we see and talk about things. Both concepts were originally referred to as *point of view* (Genette, 1980: 186), a term which conflated two different questions, namely the questions of 'who sees' and 'who speaks'. Yet it is possible to speak without having seen the events, just by reporting someone else's view or what they have seen. Speaking and seeing can therefore be attributed to two different agencies

(Bal, 1985: 143; Rimmon-Kenan, 1983: 72).[6] Seeing is what has been defined in narrative as *focalization*, which entails not only the optical but also the cognitive, emotive and ideological aspects of the perception, while speaking or narrating has been defined as *voice*. Voice can be analysed in terms of grammatical persons (Abbott, 2002: 64); these could be either first-person or third-person narratives, as explained by Genette (1980: 244–245). In a text which is narrated in the first person, like Ricci's trilogy, the narrator refers to him/herself with the pronoun 'I', and is usually also a character in the story.

The link between code-switching, focalization and voice is shown by the fact that code-switched words represent the focus of attention. This phenomenon is known in oral code-switching as *flagging* (Callahan, 2005: 9) and is signalled in written code-switching, and in the specific case of Ricci's trilogy, by the use of italics (Callahan, 2005: 9), which visually highlight the contrastive function of code-switching (Camarca, 2005: 103).

Code-switching can direct focalization and voice in a contrastive mode in different ways. This contrast might be created by switches in focalization and voice between the adult narrator and the child protagonist, for example, as in the first novel of Ricci's trilogy, which presents a character-focalized vision embedded in the developing perspective of an external focalizer; or it might be the outcome of switches between the two different selves of the adult narrator, or between the narrator and a character, or from character to character. Switches in focalization and voice also impact on the construction of the plot. A narrative plot is defined in narratology as constituted by events arranged in time sequence and causally linked to each other (Somers & Gibson, 1994: 59). In Ricci's trilogy, code-switching can stress terms related to important episodes anchored to the ideological construction of the plots and it can also anticipate events or create suspense, through the 'prolepsis' technique (Genette, 1980).

Focalization, voice and plot are thus useful fictional tools, according to which literary authors can position their readers, manipulating their understanding of narratives (Abbott, 2002: 39). This claim points towards the ideological status of narrative, the fact that narrative is one of the ways in which identity is constructed (Currie, 1998: 32), a thought that has been particularly stressed in poststructuralist narratology and social theories of narrative.[7] In the light of the above it can be argued that code-switching, by signalling changes in focalization and thus translating the cultural oppositions which characterize Italian-Canadian writing, participates in the narrative construction of an Italian-Canadian identity, and in its re-narration/translation into Italian.

Translation in this diasporic/multilingual context is thus considered not only as a tool for expanding the horizon of one language (Burns

& Polezzi, 2003: 233) and representing and constructing one's identity, but also as a strategic transfer of texts from one culture to the next, as shown by the translation of Ricci's novels into Italian. Such a translation presents a unique challenge, because it involves a re-narration of already (author-) translated oppositional perspectives in the source text (ST), including cultural stereotypes, as will be shown below.

Code-switching, Translation and Opposition in Nino Ricci's Trilogy

Code-switching in Nino Ricci's trilogy involves the **insertion** (using the definition by Muysken, 2000: 3) into a text written mainly in Canadian English of the following languages: standard Italian, *italiese* (only used sporadically), Southern Italian dialects, French and German (used very infrequently). The word *italiese* refers to a blend of *italiano* ('Italian') and *inglese* ('English') (Clivio & Danesi, 2000: 180): it consists of a mixture of Italian dialects, standard Italian (even though it is not used fluently by most speakers) (Vizmuller-Zocco, 1995: 515) and Canadian-English lexical borrowings. Along with *italiese*, the trilogy also features the use of a dialect (or a variety of dialects) from the Molise region[8] which is used in the speech of characters from the Molisan village of Valle del Sole and nearby villages, both in Italy and in Canada where these immigrants have settled.[9]

Although code-switching in *Lives of the Saints* occurs both in narration (with the presence mainly of nouns)[10] and in direct speech (with the presence of greetings, discourse openers and farewells, politeness markers, exclamations and interjections, imperatives and discourse markers), the number or frequency of switches is greater in direct speech.[11] This suggests that Nino Ricci is trying to assimilate the characteristics of orality into written language; however, this mimetic intent is constrained because of the implied Anglophone readership's limited linguistic competence in Italian or Southern Italian dialects (Camarca, 2005: 240). This stresses once more the fictional nature of written code-switching (as outlined above), which is used by an author to orient the reader towards a particular interpretation of the text that must take into account the contrastive passage from one code into another. Code-switching, both in narration and in dialogue, is mainly used to signal the following:

(a) the contradictions of the idyllic representation of the old world by first generation immigrants;
(b) the contrast of values between the old (Italy) and the new world (Canada).

With respect to the function of code-switching (point (a)), the portrayal of the contradictions of the Southern Italian world is performed through a category of nouns labelled as 'social positioning', which refer to people's status in their families (mother, father, son, etc.) and in society at large as a consequence of their jobs (doctor, teacher, etc.). The item *la maestra* ('the teacher') is often used to contrast the focalization of the child-protagonist Vittorio with the voice of his older, narrating self, as in Example 9.1 below. Here *la maestra* signals the restricted vision of the child Vittorio in the most important episode of the book, his mother's affair with a man who will consequently make her pregnant. After hearing a scream from the stable Vittorio runs to investigate and is vaguely aware of a man running away on foot, although he does not have a clear look at his face. However, upon his mother enquiring about what he has seen, he replies that he has seen nothing, justifying his answer to himself by remembering his teacher's emphasis on the need to be clear and succinct.

Example 9.1

Question and answer: that was how *la maestra* taught us our lessons at school and how Father Nicola, the village priest, taught us our catechism. (Ricci, 1990: 7)

The child's response is ironic, since it is the product of a clash between the scattered images in his mind and the manipulation of those images by the adult world. Vittorio is asked to provide a coherent account of facts, a normalization of the events in a format that can be accepted by his mother. He does so by removing from his account the blurred images of a man running away from the stable. This episode illustrates that a narrative construction, in poststructuralist terms, is always the result of an operation of selection (and thus of inclusion and exclusion) of elements of a story, which are manipulated and assembled according to the agenda of the storyteller, and the conditions under which the story is narrated.

This inability by Vittorio to reconcile contrasting perceptions of the teacher as a person with a body and sexuality and as the simple incarnation of a role[12] reminds the reader of the contradictions which characterize the moral/cultural values of Valle del Sole in relation to Cristina's affair, who will be ostracized by the villagers for her out-of-wedlock relationship. *La maestra* is also juxtaposed with Vittorio's mother, Cristina, who is dismissive of the teacher's authority, and of other authorities who try to reposition her in the traditional role of *la signora* ('the lady'), such as the village priest, the captain of the boat on which she travels to Canada and the doctor Cosabene, on duty on the same boat.

In other cases her defiance of the traditional roles is shown in conversations with the villagers with politeness markers such as *scusa* and *scusate* ('excuse me', but also 'I beg your pardon' and 'I am sorry')[13] which are marked for informality and formality respectively. In Example 9.2 the barman of the village, Antonio Di Lucci (a character in *Lives of the Saints*), drives Cristina to the hospital after a snake bit her while she was in the stable with her lover (see Example 9.1). Antonio, through his questions, pushes Cristina towards confessing a dark scandal, which is supposedly related to the snake bite in the villagers' beliefs.

Example 9.2

'Where did it bite you?'

My mother let out a sigh.

'Andò, you heard me say just a few minutes ago. On the ankle.'

'Yes, of course, on the ankle, but where were you when it bit you on the ankle?'

'Too close to a snake.'

'*Ma scusate*, Cristina, I'm asking a simple question.'

'*Scusa*, Andò, what does the doctor care where I was when the snake bit me?' my mother said, her voice tinged with irritation. (Ricci, 1990: 15)

With the directness of the informal *scusa* Cristina counteracts the formality and the indirectness of Di Lucci's formal *scusate*, breaking the reciprocity rules of the communicative speech act and foregrounding her vision of the facts. Her answer, 'too close to a snake', criticizes peasants' beliefs and superstitions behind which there is nothing but a sense of fatalism (Tuzi, 1997: 87).

With reference to the second contrastive function (point (b) above), code-switching is used on a more global level to signal clashes between the old and the new world's values, mainly through the use of discourse markers and terms (adjectives) which denote provenance (see Examples 9.3, 9.4, 9.5, 9.6 and 9.7 below). In Example 9.3, the interaction takes place at the Canadian farm in Mersea (Ontario region) where Vittorio's (the protagonist's) family has settled. The term is used by Vittorio's uncle Alfredo to address his wife Maria, who is worried about the disappearance of Mario, Vittorio's father. Alfredo firmly opposes his wife's suggestion to call the police.

Example 9.3

'Maybe you should call the police,' Tsia Maria said.

'Don't talk nonsense, what are the police going to do?'

'*Mbeh*, who knows where he's gotten to? Maybe he's lying in some ditch with his head broken.'

'*Grazie*,' Tsi Alfredo said. 'And what are you going to tell the police when they ask you why he's gone?'

'Tell them the truth, what's happened.'

'*Sì*. We might as well just publish it in the newspaper, and then everyone will know.'

'Everyone knows as it is.'

'Don't be an idiot. You know how they are here, every little thing they know about us, they make up some story. We'll take care of our own problems.' (Ricci, 1993: 27–28)

Grazie ('thank you'), used as a discourse marker rather than a politeness marker, and *sì* ('yes') foreground Alfredo's focalization of the events, his Southern Italian sarcastic distrust of social institutions and his belief that family betrayals are private and must be kept secret. He thinks that explaining (to the police) the reason for Mario's disappearance – his long-term depression caused by Cristina's betrayal – might expose the family and the whole Italian community to racism and stereotyping. *Mbeh* (well), used to foreground Alfredo's wife's different focalization of the events, shows a relationship in which the woman's opinion is not allowed to count (and in a similar way it will be used in other parts of the trilogy by Vittorio's aunt Teresa in response to her brother's violent manner). This event explains in part the development of the plot that leads to Mario's later suicide: he has been trapped by his Southern Italian sense of shame which prevented him and his family and relatives from seeking medical help for his depression from the Canadian health system.

Thus code-switching frames and transforms oppositional perspectives concerning the English/Canadian belief in institutions and the distress over the perceived old-fashioned male and female roles within the Italian-Canadian communities. By doing so, code-switching evokes the Southern Italian cultural background on which Ricci's characters draw and which they creatively challenge (see Myers-Scotton, 1993b) in view of the emerging influence of English/Canadian beliefs. This background is one of harsh life, and this is shown in the use of interjections of anger, invocation or encouragement. An example is the extensive use of *dai* ('come on!'), mostly to deal with Mario's swinging moods and negative emotions, either his anger, ruggedness, or nervousness and depression.

It is worth noticing that in Example 9.3 the item *Mbeh*, which corresponds to the Italian *embè* (a transformation of the term *be'* derived from the elision of the Italian adverb *bene*), shows the contamination of Italian words by their exposure to English-Canadian. *Mbeh* appears only in the second book of the trilogy (while *beh* appears in the other two), with characters that are all first-generation immigrants. The terms *Tsi'* (uncle) and *Tsia* (aunt) (written in capital letters) never appear in italics, probably because they are highly familiar to the protagonist of the trilogy, since he lives surrounded by his aunts and uncles. In the first novel of the trilogy the terms *Tsi'* (uncle) and *Tsia* (aunt) are spelled in standard Italian (*zia* and *zio*), while in the second novel they are spelled as they are pronounced in the Molisan dialect spoken by Nino Ricci, but at the same time contaminated by the English orthography of the phonetic cluster 'tz'. This reflects the process of change and hybridization of Italian dialects as a result of the contact with Canadian English, since for the Italian diasporic communities in Canada, Italian was not learned at school (before the Multiculturalism Act, in the years in which the novel is set), let alone spoken at home.

Another item which is inevitably connected with immigration and thus raises issues such as change and contamination among Italians living in Canada is *paesano*. According to the Italian dictionary compiled by De Mauro (1999–2007), *paesano* is the person who was born and lives in a village ('paese'). For an Italian, *paesano* is thus a person who is from the same village or small town in Italy he/she comes from. For an Italian-Canadian, *paesano* refers to Italians from the same region in Italy, while for Canadians who are not of Italian origin it can signify Italians in general and it can even include Canadians of non-Italian origin. With this meaning it is used by a German-Canadian (who owns the farm where Vittorio's father, Mario, works) to address Mario, showing spiritual kinship and goodwill (Example 9.4).

Example 9.4

'Mario,' he [the German] said. 'Mario, Mario, *como stai, paesano*?' [...]

'That was the guy I bought the farm from,' he [Mario] said. 'Those Germans – *paesano* this, *paesano* that, everyone's a *paesano*. But the old bastard just wanted to make sure I do not forget to pay him.' (Ricci, 1993: 32)

Example 9.5

'Don't think he was stupid enough to say a word about the money. You know how they are, always smiling, *amico paesano*.' (Ricci, 1993: 34)

Paesano signals the co-presence of different perceptions, the Canadian and the Italian-Canadian (Canton, 2004: 149). For the non-Italian/Canadian, *paesano* creates an emotional link with the Italian-Canadian since it suggests the idea of common aims and interests. The German-Canadian farmer's interpretation and use of *paesano*, however, is perceived as hypocritical by Mario (irony can be seen in the use of term *amico* ['friend'] as in Example 9.5), and indicates the fragility of a concept such as shared 'Canadian' identity. Code-switching thus draws our attention to contrasting perceptions of the same term (Canton, 2004: 154), on the basis of who uses it. The complex nuances of this item are also present in the following excerpt.

Example 9.6

'*Deutschman?*' he said. '*Auf wiedersehen? Nederlander? Italiano?*' '*Italiano,*' I [Vittorio] said, clutching at the familiar word. [...] *Ah Italiano!*' He thumped a hand on his chest. '*Me speak Italiano much mucho. Me paesano.*' When other boys got on the bus and came to the back, the black-haired boy said they were *paesani* as well, and each in turn smiled broadly at me and shook my hand. They tried to talk to me using their hands and their strange half-language. One of them pointed to the big silver lunchbox Tsia Teresa had packed my lunch in. '*Mucho mucho,*' he said, holding his hands wide in front of him. Then he pointed to me and brought his hands closer together. '*No mucho mucho.*' The other boys laughed. The black-haired boy took the lunchbox from me and held it before him as if to admire it. [...] '*Mu-cho mu-cho,*' he said, thrusting the sandwich away to one of the other boys and pinching his nose. [...] They began to pass the second sandwich around. I tried to leap up to pull it away but the black-haired boy's arm shot out suddenly in front of me and pinned me to the seat, and then his fist caught the side of my head hard three times in quick succession, my head pounding against the glass of the window beside me. '*No, no, paesano.*' (Ricci, 1993: 51–52)

Vittorio, the child protagonist, is questioned on the bus to school about his national origin by an older boy who bullies him, steals his sandwich and punches him. The teasing effect is reinforced by a mixture of different foreign expressions (*Deutschman, Auf wiedersehen, Nederlander, Italiano*) and in particular by producing a false German term (*Deutschman*) and by combining Spanish with English and Italian (*me speak Italiano mucho mucho*), a sort of creole language employed to produce comic effects (aided by the stress on the syllables in *mucho*). Other Canadians' ignorance of foreign languages and, more specifically, Italian language and culture, is also implied (the Italian is mistaken for Spanish) as well as their reliance on stereotypes (one of which is related to Italian food, as the lunchbox episode shows).

Paesano underlines the specificities of the Italian-Canadian immigrant's experience (Canton, 2004: 156), which is rooted in the traditional Italian concept of *paese* ('village') but which adapts this concept, utilizing but also contaminating and challenging it, in the continuous reconstruction of a sense of community abroad, by including different communities of Italians (and non-Italians) in Canada. This strong sense of community can also explain how the plot is brought forward, specifically with respect to the shame felt by Mario for his wife's betrayal which leads him to commit suicide.[14] Ricci's view is that Italians in Canada are also subjected to stereotypes which they partially believe, and therefore develop a hatred of their own pre-acquired Southern Italian values (Pivato, 1994: 180), with psychological confusion and impasse stemming from that.

This opposition between the two battling selves of the adult narrator (one more faithful to the old country, the other to the new one) is present also in *Where She Has Gone*, a novel in which the adult Vittorio returns to Italy in order to recover a past which eludes him and in place of which another narrative is invented. The code-switched expressions in this novel are few and formulaic: Vittorio does not speak much Italian and forces himself into the language, in an attempt to reclaim a culture, the Italian culture, which has become distant. In Example 9.7 he takes a taxi in Rome and is asked about his nationality by the taxi driver.

Example 9.7

'*Ah, è italiano.*' But it was clear from his forced smile that he'd in fact surmised the opposite, that I was a foreigner. [...] '*Americano?*' the cabby said. '*Sì, No.*' I had to struggle to dredge up my Italian. '*Canadese.* But born in Italy.' (Ricci, 1997: 167)

The adult protagonist struggles to define the two elements inside himself, the Canadian and the Italian. To this battle there is no resolution since in another scene Vittorio, while leaving Italy on a train to Lyons, will tell a passenger in an assertive way that he is *Canadese*, not *Italiano*. The Italian-Canadian identity, as demonstrated by Ricci's use of the item *paesano* and other adjectives of provenance, is an aggregate of diverse and potentially incompatible components (trans-national, social, psychological) which are themselves in a state of constant readjustment.

Code-switching, Translation and Opposition in the Italian Translation of Ricci's Trilogy

Before analysing the Italian translation of Ricci's trilogy, it is useful to remember that translation is not only present in the ST as a metaphor but in the form of translation techniques such as literal translation into English of the code-switched expression, paraphrase and contextual translation (see Rudin, 1996),[15] used by Ricci to facilitate the comprehension of code-switched items by the Anglophone reader. These strategies contribute to reinforcing the idea that multilingualism and translation should be considered as complementary. On the other hand, when it comes to the actual interlingual transfer of the novels into Italian, the major techniques available to the translator are either the **maintenance** or the **suppression** of italics.

Overall the source text–target text comparison shows that one of the main features of translation is the **suppression** or the diminished use of italics to reproduce code-switched items in the ST. This suppression, specifically used for items referring to cultural references and to social positioning, including *maestra* and *signora* analysed in the previous section, diminishes the visual signalling of shifts in focalization and the overall perception of opposition in the texts. The reduction of the linguistic interplay of the STs in the target texts (TTs) is a very common translation strategy for multilingual texts in general, as stated by Berman (1985), since multilingual relations depicted in the STs are deeply rooted in the ST culture and are almost impossible to reproduce in other contexts (Delabastita & Grutman, 2005: 27). In the case of Ricci's trilogy, a reduction of the effects of code-switching is partly unavoidable, given that the languages of the code-switches (Italian and Molisan dialect) are also the target language (TL) and, therefore, there is logically no need to signal a domestic term when the code-switch is no longer operative. However, given that italics are also used as an emphatic tool in general, the translator could have chosen to preserve them, or to use English to translate code-switching in the STs, as she does with the title of some English songs and with a few English terms such as 'wop'[16] that she does not translate and opts to put in italics.

This shows that the translator has a different perception of the importance of the interplay of languages in the STs; however, despite the loss of italics, she sometimes **maintains** it for *italiese* terms such as *lu boss, la ghellafriend*, or for hybrid items which are apparently in standard Italian or dialect but have been used with a different meaning as a result of immigration, like *paesano*. *Paesano* is preserved in italics (along with other code-switched terms) in the translation of Examples 9.5 and 9.6 analysed previously (and see Examples 9.8 and 9.9 below) but not in the translation of Example 9.4 (see Example 9.10 below). This different treatment is probably due to the fact that in Examples 9.8 and 9.9 the comic and derogatory effects of the interplay of foreign languages are stronger than in other parts of the novels.

Example 9.8

Tu lo sai come sono, sempre il sorriso, *amico, paesano*. (Ricci, 2004: 289)

Example 9.9

«*Deutschman?*», disse. «*Aufwiedersehen? Nederlander? Italiano?*».

«*Italiano*», dissi, aggrappandomi alla parola familiare.

«*Ah, italiano!*». Si batté una mano sul petto. «*Me speak italiano much mucho. Me paesano*». [...] «*Mucho mucho*», disse, allargando le mani davanti a sé. Poi, indicando me, le avvicinò. «No *mucho mucho*». Gli altri risero. Il ragazzo bruno mi prese il porta pranzo e lo tenne davanti a sé come per ammirarlo. Poi lo aprì e scartò uno dei panini, ne annusò il contenuto. Storse la faccia.

«*Mu-cho, mu-cho*», disse, passandolo a un altro e chiudendosi il naso con le dita. (Ricci, 2004: 306–307)

Example 9.10

«Mario», disse. «Mario, Mario, **come stai**, paesano?». [...] «Quello era l'uomo dal quale ho comprato la fattoria», disse. «Questi tedeschi ... paesano qua, paesano là, tutti sono paesani. Ma quel vecchio **figlio di puttana** è venuto solo a vedere se mi sono dimenticato di pagarlo». (Ricci, 2004: 287)

In Example 9.10 the loss of italics is **compensated for** by the use of a very informal/derogatory expression, *figlio di puttana*, to translate the term 'bastard', which emphasizes Mario's anger and sarcasm.

Along with the maintenance and the suppression of italics, three **compensation** techniques are employed: they range from changing the register of a sentence to paraphrasing and glossing linguistic material around code-switching (also used in the case of the item *scusa/scusate*, analysed in Example 9.3) in order to convey some of the pragmatic force of the ST's code-switches. In Example 9.11 below (which corresponds to ST Example 9.2), the Italian translation emphasizes the formality and indirectness of Di Lucci's speech by using the second-person plural of the personal pronouns you, *vi* and *voi* and of the verb 'to stay' (*stavate*), and stresses the directness of Cristina's speech by using the second-person singular of the verb 'to hear' (*hai sentito*). These strategies cannot be used in English, which does not distinguish morphologically between 'you singular' and 'you plural' in verbs and pronouns.

Example 9.11

«Dove **vi** ha morso?».

Mia madre si lasciò sfuggire un sospiro.

«Andò, **l'hai sentito** giusto un momento fa. Alla caviglia».

«Sì, va bene, alla caviglia, ma dove **stavate voi** quando **vi** ha morso alla caviglia?».

«Troppo vicino ad una serpe».

«Scusate, Cristina, sto solo facendo una domanda». (Ricci, 2004: 26)

Along with compensation, we have in Ricci the **transformation** of the code-switched item in the following ways: (a) when dialect is substituted with standard Italian and vice versa; (b) when the spelling of the Italian words are changed in order to reproduce the Italian graphic representation of terms; and (c) when an item is translated with a standard term or an expression more specific to the target culture.

In Example 9.10 above, the mispronounced and hybrid greeting (a mixture of Italian and Spanish) *como stai* in the ST is transformed in the TT into the standard Italian *come stai*. This happens also for the colourful discourse marker *mbeh* transformed into the standard Italian *be'*, or the item *Tsi'/Tsia* translated into the dialect term *zi'* (and not into the standard Italian *zio/zia*) (see Example 9.12 below). Here the translator corrects the spelling of these items, to make them sound either more Italian or dialect (Molisan dialect).

Example 9.12

«Forse devi chiamare la polizia», disse zia Maria.

«Non dire fesserie, che deve fare la polizia?».

«**Be'**, chi lo sa dov' è andato? Magari sta in fondo a un fosso con la testa rotta».

«**Grazie**», disse **zi'** Alfredo. «E che dici alla polizia quando ti chiede perché è andato via?». (Ricci, 2004: 282)

The use of more specific terms and the change of spelling may be meant to facilitate the Italian reader's encounter with the text, 'aligning it more closely with domestic conventions' (Woodham, 2007: 78). This suggests a different perception by the translator of the implied readership, a perception that seems to be shared by Italian publishing houses in general which seem to avoid non-standard Italian linguistic forms, and what they see as grammatical and spelling mistakes, even though these textual elements might carry an important meaning.

Conclusion

The analysis of some examples of written code-switching in Ricci's trilogy has revealed that the narrator is able to move beyond a simple stereotypical portrayal of Italianness and Italian-Canadianness; he does so by juxtaposing the focalization of minority subjects (see Fisher, 2002: 50) such as the child Vittorio and Cristina, with that of the authority, or by showing the opposition and the need for integration of old and new modes of existence for the Italian immigrants in Canada. This need will lead the protagonist back to his maternal village in Italy in search of a home that will never be found and has, instead, to be re-invented. In Ricci's trilogy, therefore, the constant shifting of perspective through code-switching creates a narrative identity which is in constant flux and which challenges nationalist diasporic narratives centred on the myth of return, on the nostalgic portrayal of the old country and on women's morality. Such a narrative can be compared to a journey made of constant new departures and arrivals, and can be defined as transcultural (Pan, 2004: 10), one that is always projected outside itself, and because of this yearns for further translations and journeys. One of these journeys is the return to Italy. Gabriella Iacobucci translated the trilogy into Italian with the clear intention of returning Nino Ricci home. However, the analysis of the translation, where the translation pays little attention to the hybridity of the texts and to the ironic and contrastive aspect of code-switching, shows that this type of return is an illusion, since it appears as though the Italian-Canadian migrant has never migrated.

This chapter elaborates on the general notion of opposition by focusing on the identity construction of Italian-Canadianness. Previous work on

Italian-Canadian writing has almost totally focused on thematic aspects of relevant literary works, ignoring the analysis of multilingualism and translation. This article represents the first investigation of Ricci's trilogy and contributes to the enrichment of an understanding of written code-switching[17] and translation (an area also neglected by narratological theories). The model of analysis suggested here can give a better understanding of (post)-migrant writing in general, by strictly linking micro-analysis with macro-analysis. At the micro-level, code-switching, a common feature of (post)-migrant writing, explains that the construction of a narrative is a sort of metaphorical translation because the text constantly refers to something else within itself. At the macro-level, this otherness within the text itself might tell us why works like those of Ricci, which involve the translation of terms which have already migrated, long to return to the place of departure through canonical translation, and how such a return/translation happens in practice. Linguistic analysis can thus clarify the narrative assumptions that make possible such translations, since the mechanisms of the text construction mirror those of the narratives circulating in society.

It would be highly interesting and methodologically productive to test this model on other (post)-migrant works in order to expand and enrich it, for example by seeing how code-switching can be linked to other textual devices or by identifying other textual elements which can be pivotal in the construction of the narrative text as well as for the need for translation.

Notes

1. Iacobucci (personal correspondence between September and November 2008).
2. Iacobucci (personal correspondence between September and November 2008).
3. My choice of the term 'code-switching' is in line with the practice of scholars such as Bandia (1996, 2008), who employs the notion in analysing situations of multilingualism and power in post-colonial settings, along with the notion of translation, and the work of other scholars, Bandia (1996, 2008) included, who apply the term to written texts (Callahan, 2005; Camarca, 2005; Martin, 2005; Vizcaino, 2005; Woodham, 2007; Zabus, 1991).
4. The concept of 'voice' is also important because Italian-Canadian writing's main purpose was to give voice to a voiceless familial past (Pivato, 1994).
5. This issue has received some attention in two studies, one by Tuzi (1997: 77–78) and one by Baena (2000), who have analysed the double perspective in Ricci's *Lives of the Saints*. Voice and perspective have also been investigated recently by scholars in Translation Studies, who have attempted to define the translator's voice or the translation point of view (Bosseaux, 2004; Hermans, 1996).

6. 'Point of view' is an older general term which in English and North American criticism (see Booth, 1961; Stanzel, 1955) often includes the concept of 'voice' (Abbott, 2002: 190).
7. This view is dominant in scholars such as Currie (1998), Gibson (1996) and Somers and Gibson (1994).
8. It is important to note that the Italian dialects spoken abroad do not undergo the diachronic change that characterizes dialects in Italy (Vizmuller-Zocco, 1995: 514), and that a degree of dialect levelling occurred in Canada among speakers of different dialects as a result of immigration (Tosi, 1991: 407).
9. Nino Ricci (personal communication, June–October 2008) stated that the dialect used in the trilogy is the transcription, based on personal memories, of the dialect of his parents, who are from two villages in the province of Isernia, and of his relatives from the same or nearby villages.
10. Researchers in conversational code-switching have found that nouns are the most readily borrowed parts of discourse (Van Hout & Muysken, 1994: 39).
11. According to Camarca (2005: 230), 126 of the total of 337 instances of code-switching in Ricci's trilogy are in direct speech.
12. This contrast is accentuated by the fact that the teacher narrates to her pupils the stories of the lives of the saints (from which the title of the first novel is taken), in a way that makes religious concepts become more familiar but at the same time more disturbing because she often invokes the carnality of the body and the idea of nakedness as sinful thoughts.
13. *Scusa* and *scusate* can perform both the speech act of apologizing and the action of attracting the attention of the interlocutor, and thus function also as discourse markers (Collins English Dictionary, 2005).
14. To Mario, his wife's betrayal implies his inadequacy as a man, since he has not been able to take revenge by killing his wife's lover and punish her. However, in Canada he has to cope with the pressure of a different value-system, which gives vengeance no legitimacy or approval.
15. 'Contextual translation' is a translation in which the meaning of code-switching is inferred from the context, when, for example, a question is inferred from its answer (see also Bandia, 1996: 141–142).
16. 'Wop' is a derogatory term, sometimes used playfully to refer to people of Italian origin in Canada.
17. Written code-switching has been much less analysed than oral code-switching.

References

Abbott, H.P. (2002) *The Cambridge Introduction to Narrative*. Cambridge: Cambridge University Press.
AICW (Association of Italian-Canadian Writers) website (2009) On WWW at http://www.aicw.ca/. Accessed 16.4.09.
Auer, P. (1998) Bilingual conversation revisited. In P. Auer (ed.) *Code-switching in Conversation: Language, Interaction and Identity* (pp. 1–24). London/New York: Routledge.
Baena, R. (2000) Italian-Canadian double perspective in a childhood narrative. Nino Ricci's *Lives of The Saints*. In R.G. Davis and R. Baena (eds) *Tricks with a Glass: Writing Ethnicity in Canada* (pp. 93–109). Amsterdam: Rodopi.

Bal, M. (1985) *Narratology: Introduction to the Theory of Narrative*. Toronto: University of Toronto Press.
Bandia, P. (1996) Code-switching and code-mixing in African creative writing: Some insights for translation studies. *TTR* 9 (1), 139–154.
Bandia, P. (2008) *Translation as Reparation. Writing and Translation in Postcolonial Africa*. Manchester: St. Jerome.
Berman, A. (1985) La traduction comme épreuve de l'étranger [Translation and the trials of the foreign]. *Texte* 4: 67–81. In L. Venuti (ed.) (2004) *The Translation Studies Reader* (pp. 276–289). New York/London: Routledge.
Bhabha, H.K. (1990) *Nation and Narration*. London/New York: Routledge.
Bhabha, H.K. (1994) *The Location of Culture*. London/New York: Routledge.
Booth, W. (1961) *The Rhetoric of Fiction*. Chicago: University of Chicago Press.
Bosseaux, C. (2004) A study of the translator's voice and style in the French translations of Virginia Woolf's *The Waves*. PhD thesis, University of Manchester.
Burns, J. and Polezzi, L. (2003) Migrazioni tra Sconfini e Sconfinamenti [Migrations between trespassings and borders]. In J. Burns and L. Polezzi (eds) *Borderlines: Migrazioni e identita? nel novecento* [*Borderlines: Migrant identities in the 20th century*] (pp. 13–21). Isernia: Cosmo Iannone editore.
Callahan, L. (2005) *Spanish–English Code-switching in a Written Corpus*. Amsterdam/Philadelphia: John Benjamins.
Camarca, S. (2005) Code-switching and textual strategies in Nino Ricci's Trilogy. *Semiotica* 154 (1/4), 225–241.
Canton, L. (2004) The clash of languages in the Italian-Canadian Novel. In L. Canton, L. Moyes and D. A. Beneventi (eds) *Adjacencies* (pp. 143–156). Toronto: Guernica.
Clivio, G. and Danesi, M. (2000) *The Sounds, Forms, and Uses of Italian: An Introduction to Italian linguistics*. Toronto/Buffalo/London: University of Toronto Press.
Collins English Dictionary (2005) London: Collins.
Cronin, M. (2006) *Translation and Identity*. New York/London: Routledge.
Currie, M. (1998) *Post-modern Narrative Theory*. New York: St. Martin's Press.
De Mauro, T. (1999–2007) *Il dizionario della lingua italiana*. Salerno: Paravia.
Delabastita, D. and Grutman, R. (eds) (2005) Fictional representations of multilingualism and translation. *Linguistica Antverpiensia New Series* 4, 11–35.
DeMaria Harney, N. (1998) *Being Italian in Toronto*. Toronto: University of Toronto Press.
Di Cicco, P.G. (1978) *Roman Candles: An Anthology of Poems by Seventeen Italo-Canadian Poets*. Toronto: Hounslow Press.
Fisher, L.W. (2002) Focalising the unfamiliar: Laurence Yep's child in a strange land. *Journal of Ethnic Studies* 45 (2), 48–65.
Genette, G. (1980) *Narrative Discourse* (A. Sheridan, trans.). New York: Columbia University Press.
Gibson, A. (1996) *Towards a Post-modern Theory of Narrative*. Edinburgh: Edinburgh University Press.
Gumperz, J. (1982) *Discourse Strategies*. Cambridge: Cambridge University Press.
Hermans, T. (1996) The translator's voice in translated narrative. *Target* 8 (1), 23–48.
Määttä, S.K. (2004) Dialect and point of view: The ideology of translation. *Target* 16 (2), 319–339.

Martin, H.E. (2005) Code-switching in US ethnic literature: Multiple perspectives presented through multiple languages. *Changing English* 12 (3), 403–415.
Mehrez, S. (1992) Translation and the postcolonial experience: The Francophone North African text. In L. Venuti (ed.) *Rethinking Translation* (pp. 120–138). London/New York: Routledge.
Milroy, L. and Muysken, P. (1995) Introduction: Code-switching and bilingualism research. In L. Milroy and P. Muysken (eds) *One Speaker, Two Languages: Cross-disciplinary Perspectives on Code-switching* (pp. 1–14). Cambridge: Cambridge University Press.
Muysken, P. (2000) *Bilingual Speech. A Typology of Code-mixing*. Cambridge: Cambridge University Press.
Myers-Scotton, C. (1993a) *Social Motivations for Code-switching, Evidence from Africa*. New York: Oxford University Press.
Myers-Scotton, C. (1993b) *Duelling Languages. Grammatical Structure in Code-switching*. Oxford: Clarendon Press.
Pan, D. (2004) J.G. Herder, the origin of language, and the possibility of transcultural narratives. *Language and Intercultural Communication* 4 (1/2), 10–20.
Pirazzini, D. (2000) Plurilinguismo letterario come procedimento citazionale: *Sostiene Pereira* ... – Sosteneva Ingravallo ... [Literary plurilingualism as a quoting procedure: Pereira claims ... – Ingravallo claimed ...]. In F. Brugnolo and V. Orioles (eds) *Eteroglossia e plurilinguismo letterario. II. Plurilinguismo e letteratura* [*Heteroglossia and Literary Multilingualism. II. Multilingualism and Literature*] (pp. 541–569). Roma: Il Calamo.
Pivato, J. (1994) *Echo: Essays on Other Literatures*. Toronto: Guernica.
Pratt, L. (1992) *Imperial Eyes: Studies in Travel Writing and Transculturation*. New York/London: Routledge.
Rimmon-Kenan, S. (1983) *Narrative Fiction: Contemporary Poetics*. London: Methuen.
Rudin, E. (1996) *Tender Accents of Sound: Spanish in the Chicano Novel in English*. Tempe, AZ: Bilingual Press/Editorial Bilingue.
Simon, S. (1994) *Le traffic des langues: Traduction et culture dans la littérature québécoise* [*The Traffic of Languages: Translation and Culture in the Literature of Quebec*]. Montreal: Boreal.
Somers, M.R. and Gibson, G.D. (1994) Reclaiming the epistemological "Other": Narrative and the social constitution of identity. In C. Calhoun (ed.) *Social Theory and the Politics of Identity* (pp. 37–99). Oxford/Cambridge, MA: Blackwell.
Stanzel, F. (1955) *Narrative Situations in the Novel: Tom Jones, Moby-Dick, The Ambassadors, Ulysses* (J.P. Pusack, trans. [1971]). Bloomington: Indiana University Press.
Tosi, A. (1991) *L'italiano d'oltremare. La lingua delle comunità italiane nei paesi anglofoni* [*Overseas Italian. The Language of the Italian Communities in the English-speaking Countries*]. Firenze: Giunti.
Tuzi, M. (1997) *The Power of Allegiances. Identity, Culture and Representational Strategies*. Toronto: Guernica.
Tymoczko, M. (1999) Post-colonial writing and literary translation. In S. Bassnett and H. Trivedi (eds) *Post-Colonial Translation: Theory and Practice* (pp. 19–40). London/New York: Routledge.

Van Hout, R. and Muysken, P. (1994) Modeling lexical borrowability. *Language Variation and Change* 6, 39–62.
Verdicchio, P. (1997) *Devils in Paradise: Writings on Post-emigrant Cultures.* Toronto: Guernica.
Vizcaino, M.J.G. (2005) Translating code-switching in Chicano fiction. *Translation Studies in the New Millennium*, 111–121.
Vizmuller-Zocco, J. (1995) The languages of Italian-Canadians. *Italica* 72 (4), 512–529.
Woodham, K. (2007) Translating linguistic innovation in Francophone African novels. PhD thesis, University of Nottingham.
Zabus, C. (1991) *The African Palimpsest: Indigenization of Language in the West African Europhone Novel.* Amsterdam/Atlanta: Rodopi.

Primary sources

Canton, L. (2002) Translating Italian-Canadian writers. Un' intervista con Gabriella Iacobucci [An interview with Gabriella Iacobucci]. In L. Canton (ed.) *The Dynamics of Cultural Exchange: Creative and Critical Works* (pp. 225–231). Montreal: Cusmano.
Fazi editore website. At http://www.fazieditore.it/. Accessed 16.3.09.
Nino Ricci's official website. At http://www.ninoricci.com/. Accessed 28.3.09.
Ricci, N. (1990) *Lives of the Saints.* Dunvegan: Cormorant Press.
Ricci, N. (1993) *In a Glass House.* New York: Picador USA.
Ricci, N. (1994) *Vite dei santi* [*Lives of the Saints*] (G. Iacobucci, trans.). Vibo Valentia: Monteleone Editore.
Ricci, N. (1997) *Where She Has Gone.* Toronto: McClelland & Stewart.
Ricci, N. (2000) *Il fratello italiano* [*The Italian Brother*] (G. Iacobucci, trans.). Roma: Fazi editore.
Ricci, N. (2004) *La terra del ritorno* [*The Land of Return*] (G. Iacobucci, trans.). Roma: Fazi Editore.

Chapter 10
Croker versus Montalembert on the Political Future of England: Towards a Theory of Antipathetic Translation

C.O'SULLIVAN

Introduction: Sympathy in Translation

Received wisdom in translation has, since the 17th century at least (Venuti, 1995: 274), advocated that the translator should feel a special bond with the author they translate. Translation critics have taken it as read that to translate is to agree with the author of the text one is translating, or at least to achieve agreement by subsuming one's identity within that of the source text (ST) author: 'No longer his Interpreter, but He', as the Earl of Roscommon puts it (as cited in Venuti, 1995: 274). Fuelled by the equation of authorship with individual inspiration which is the legacy of the Romantics, this idea has been remarkably tenacious in the discourse of translation criticism. An 1863 review of two recent translations of Horace in *Blackwood's Edinburgh Magazine* is characteristic. In poetry, we are told,

> [...] where the manner of the language, and the spirit that underlies it, are infinitely more significant [than in prose], the necessity of a penetrating sympathy with the mind of the original writer becomes far more apparent. The translator must, for the time being, actually see with the eyes, and hear with the ears, and feel with the heart, of another man [sic]. (Anonymous, 1863: 184)

Not only is a feeling of oneness with the author a prerequisite for successful translation, but it can even render the buttress of translation theory superfluous:

> The nearer he attains, for the purposes of composition, to this transfusion of moral and intellectual identity, the more habitual and unconscious will be his observance of all true law, and the less will he

need support from any elaborately constructed theory. (Anonymous, 1863: 184)

Justin O'Brien restates the position in his essay in Reuben Brower's influential 1959 volume *On Translation*:

> [...] one should *never translate anything one does not admire*. If possible, a natural affinity should exist between translator and translated. When Rainer Maria Rilke, who was to re-create in German some of Paul Valéry's most beautiful poems, first read the French poet, he wrote to a friend that he had discovered an *alter ego*. Of course we cannot all hope to bring to our French poet what Rilke brought to the interpretation of Valéry, but we can at least choose a subject, or victim, who is greatly congenial to us. (O'Brien, 1959: 85, emphasis in original)

The need for sympathy in translation may conversely impose an ethical requirement on the literary translator in the choice of authors to translate. In 1930 the Russian translation theorist Chukovsky advised: 'A translator should avoid authors whose temperament or literary bent he finds alien or hostile. A translator partial to Hugo should not be translating Zola: he would be doomed to failure' (1930, quoted in Friedberg, 1997: 73).

Lawrence Venuti has dubbed this ideal identification of translator with author, still current in the discourse of translation reviewers and critics, 'simpatico' (Venuti, 1995: 273–306) and has shown how it reflects assumptions about the transparency of translation. Translation is always an act of interpretation, but the agency that this interpretation invests in the figure of the translator is a source of anxiety in translation end users. Discourses of 'simpatico' act as a check on interpretation and a buttress to the presumption of sameness or equivalence in translation.

In the professional sphere translation is regulated, at least to some degree, by associations whose codes of conduct set limits on the degree of intervention possible in the text. The standard contract used by the Literary Translators' Association of Canada (LTAC) stipulates that

> The Translator will translate the Underlying Work accurately, without omissions, additions or other changes except as necessary to produce a translation that is idiomatic and faithful to the Underlying Work in spirit and content. (Literary Translators' Association of Canada, 2007)

The code of practice of the French Literary Translators' Association (ATLF) is even more emphatic on the point:

> Le traducteur s'interdit d'apporter au texte toute modification ou déformation de nature à altérer la pensée ou le style de l'auteur. Il ne

pourra effectuer les coupures ou remaniements du texte qu'avec l'assentiment ou la volonté clairement exprimée de l'auteur. Si l'œuvre appartient au domaine public, il devra, dans la mesure du possible, signaler au lecteur les coupures qu'il aura été amené à faire. (Association des Traducteurs Littéraires de France [n.d.])

[The translator abstains from making any modification to or deformation of the text which would change the ideas or the style of the author. He [sic] may not cut or manipulate the text unless with the agreement or the clearly expressed will of the author. If the work is in the public domain, he must, in so far as it is possible, flag to the reader any cuts that he may have made.]

Of course gestalt in translation is not possible to achieve – a fact recognized by Borges's Pierre Menard who, after years of attempting to achieve cognitive identity with Cervantes, and despite generating a translation which coincided word for word with its original, produced a text which differed fundamentally from itself. The experience of the translator within a given translation project can vary from total immersion to utter alienation (cf. e.g. Macey, 2000: 4). In translation theory since the 1970s, theories of equivalence have given way to the awareness of the linguistic, aesthetic and ideological gaps and shifts which characterize all translation. As Gentzler and Tymoczko have put it in their collection *Translation and Power*, translation is a 'deliberate and conscious act of selection, assemblage, structuration and fabrication' (Gentzler & Tymoczko, 2002: xxi).

Although these acts of selection and structuring may not be deliberate, or conscious, they take place regardless of the translator's position in relation to the ST. The problem, of course, lies in that space hinted at in the LTAC contract, which requires translators to abstain from 'omissions, additions or other changes *except as necessary*' (my italics). Here the contract, which rests on a fundamental concept of possible equivalence in translation, acknowledges the fragility of equivalence in the face of interlinguistic and intercultural difference. Even where the alignment of a translator with the producer of the ST approaches the ideal, the translator will nevertheless have to interpret and compromise in the process of making the text available to the target language (TL) readership. This opens up a space for negotiation and agency which invites some searching questions when we consider translations where the translator has taken a consciously oppositional stance to the text.

Theo Hermans has recently theorized translation as a form of 'ironic discourse' or 'echoic utterance' whereby translation can be read as

> direct speech contaminated by indirect speech, an impure mix of direct and indirect discourse in which several simultaneous voices have a stake. The margin between frame and enactment contains the potential for dissonance as well as consonance. (Hermans, 2007: 76)

Hermans' discussion of translation as quotation and as irony includes many examples of translations produced at a time when elements of their content were inimical to target culture norms. Such texts are seen effectively on a cline where the translators can distance themselves from a text as a whole, as in the case of the team-translation of *Mein Kampf* published in the US in 1939 (Hermans, 2007: 53–58), or where they can distance themselves from part of the text only, as in the case of some passages in Boccaccio's *Decameron* (Hermans, 2007: 60–62).

This distinction between wholesale and partial opposition to a text merits further attention. While expurgated translations may employ bowdlerism and paraphrase, deletion of textual material, displacement into footnotes, inclusion in the source language or even in a third language (Ó Cuilleanáin, 1999; O'Sullivan, 2008), Hermans argues that philological exactness is a feature of the Ripperger *et al. Mein Kampf* because the anti-Nazi agenda 'requires a full, unexpurgated, scrupulously accurate rendering of Hitler's words, so as to expose them for what they are – to the extent, of course, that translation is able to show them for what they are' (Hermans, 2007: 56). This position is echoed by Francis Jones who, when called upon to translate a poem by Radovan Karadžić 'in order to understand what sort of a poet could order the burning of libraries' (Jones, 2004: 720), observes that

> [...] one might ask whether verse of [poor] quality in support of a destructive ideology or by an evil poet should be *down*graded in translation. Such a descent, however – from promotion to smearing – would have been an ethical step too far. Moreover, the only reason I had for translating such work was to inform about 'the other side.' Thus [...] I translated exactly what I saw. (Jones, 2004: 720)

There is a suggestion here that extreme cases of translator dissociation may trigger treatments of the text which contrast with those adopted by translators taking a more concessionary approach to their source material. The object of the present chapter is to explore to what extent such distinctions can be productive in translation criticism. It should be noted that the conclusions of the chapter are hypotheses, to be supported or disproved by further research. These are certainly not watertight categories; nevertheless it seems desirable to explore whether this is a category for which more texts or translation types exist, and whether antipathetic insights can be brought fruitfully to bear on the question of dissociative translation.

Antipatico in Translation: Croker and Montalembert

Let us begin by exploring a translation where there is substantial evidence documenting the translator's hostility to the ST. Such a position might be termed 'antipatico'. An examination of a sample text will allow us to ask what theoretical usefulness such a critical concept might have, and whether it can be considered as distinct from the textual filtering which is potentially activated in all acts of translation.

The text I will take as my potential example of antipathetic translation is *De l'avenir politique de L'Angleterre* (*The Political Future of England*) by the Comte Charles Forbes de Montalembert.[1] *De l'avenir politique de L'Angleterre*, published in two parts in the journal *Le Correspondant* in late 1855 and shortly thereafter published as a single volume by Didier of Paris, is a political tract praising English culture and the liberalism of English political institutions and suggesting that further democratic reform and the re-adoption of Roman Catholicism are alone wanting for England to achieve political utopia. While the work can be situated within a tradition of favourable French commentary on English politics (see Zeldin, 1959), its subtext clearly concerns the political and press repression obtaining under the rule of Louis Napoléon.

A translation of the text was published in the UK by John Murray in March of 1856 (TT1), immediately suppressed, and republished by the same publisher with the translator's notes and introduction removed (TT2). The translation was unattributed, and there is some confusion surrounding its precise authorship, but there is no doubt as to who its instigator and prime mover was. The Irish lawyer John Wilson Croker (1780–1857) was a well-known Tory politician and essayist of conservative views and a long-standing contributor to the *Quarterly Review*, also published by John Murray (Fetter, 1958). It was Croker who pitched the book to Murray and who superintended its translation and revision. By 1856 Croker was an elderly man in indifferent health, but his reputation for pith and vinegar was still, as we will see, still very much deserved.

The story of the translation may best be approached achronologically. It came to public attention through a bitter exchange of letters in *The Times* between Croker and another occasional contributor to the *Quarterly*

Review, Abraham Hayward (1805–1884), also a translator and a commentator well known for his acid pen. The correspondence began on 2 April 1856 with the appearance of a letter from Hayward, representing the interests of Montalembert and enclosing a note from the latter. Montalembert's note refers to a recent positive review of the book and complains that

> I must declare that I cannot acknowledge this translation as a true and faithful reproduction of my essay. There is hardly a page in which the meaning of the original is not weakened by useless expletives, or altered by unaccountable suppressions, or misrepresented by downright errors. (Hayward, 1856)

This letter was followed by a brief but energetic correspondence in which Croker and one 'H.B.', claiming to be the translator, repudiated Hayward's criticisms, while making it clear that Croker was far from being in sympathy with the ideas expressed in the text. Hayward fiercely maintained the bad faith of the translation and of the translator and editor, whose identities were hotly debated. The correspondence in *The Times* came to an end with a final broadside by Croker on 8 April, but by this time it had also been taken up in the major periodicals, and the debate continued for some months.

Ironically, in the light of what was to come, Croker had initially been very enthusiastic about Montalembert's work, as his unpublished correspondence with John Murray reveals.[2] On 17 January 1856, having read the first section of the work in *Le Correspondant*, Croker wrote to Murray to advocate the translation of 'the ablest and most interesting thing that I have read for a long long time – perhaps I might say since Burke'. He went on to say that 'there are many small errors of detail but the substance & general line of argument & illustration are admirable' (Croker, unpublished letter to Murray, 17 January 1856).[3]

By the next morning, however, he was already suggesting 'a few lines of introduction and half a dozen notes both absolutely necessary for the English public' (Croker, unpublished letter to Murray, 18 January 1856). Having agreed that Croker's secretary, one Mademoiselle Boislève,[4] would translate the work under Croker's superintendence and that Croker would act as editor of the volume, Croker's letters to Murray over the following weeks as the project progressed give evidence of increasing hostility to Montalembert's essay, particularly on the discovery that much of the second part of the work, which Croker received in the meanwhile, was taken up with advocacy of Roman Catholicism and criticism of the behaviour of Anglican clergy. On 24 February Croker wrote to Murray to complain of 'the cloven foot [Montalembert's advocacy of Roman Catholicism] that became so obtrusive in the sequel' and to repeat that 'it is really <u>necessary</u> that so insidious a work should be exposed' (emphasis in original).

The translation was swiftly completed in the space of a few weeks. Miss Boislève also seems to have found herself in fundamental disagreement with the text. On 7 March 1856, acknowledging receipt of the payment for the translation, Croker writes that Boislève, a Protestant, 'stopp'd short at the chapter on Anglicanism & would not have gone on, I believe, if it was not for the hope of the notes which she hoped would remedy the mischief'. He goes on to discuss a proposed additional review of the book in the *Quarterly Review*:

> My intention would be to go no further than an exposure & refutation of Montalembert & no more of politics than my notes contain – I think the <u>Review</u> necessary for your sake & mine, as I shall be known to have recommended it. I really do not think we should be justified either in reputation or conscience to have sent forth the book without a protest [...][5] (emphasis in original)

Croker's position in relation to the work is made abundantly clear in the introduction and footnotes to the book's first edition (TT1). The paratextual apparatus constitutes a sustained attack on Montalembert's political and religious views. The introduction questions Montalembert's political integrity, derides his faith and casts aspersions on his associations with prominent Roman Catholic thinkers such as Lamennais and de Maistre. Croker amends 17 of the ST's 54 footnotes and adds another 183, giving the lie to his declaration at the end of the Introduction that '[h]aving called the reader's attention to some prominent points, we leave the rest to his own awakened judgement' (Croker, 1856a: xviii–xix). On the contrary, the inclusion of footnotes on almost every page of the book suggests that Croker felt the reader's awakened judgement needed robust and ongoing support.

Some of the footnotes provide material correction of facts. Others counter some of Montalembert's less flattering comments about England, such as his strictures on the army (TT1: 17–21). Some highlight alleged inconsistencies in the text:

> Here is another of the inconsistencies of the Author's arguments. Catholic emancipation was conceded in 1829; the disfranchisement of the close boroughs was in 1830; and the repeal of the corn laws was in 1845. [...] to give anything like consistency to his arguments, he should

have considered these events to be, *as they really were*, symptoms, if not products, of the revolutionary spirit which he everywhere so eloquently deplores. – Ed. (TT1: 45, emphasis in original)

The footnotes also serve the important function of linking Montalembert's remarks with France rather than with England:

The reader will no doubt see in this obscure and (to the translator at least) scarcely intelligible phrase a sign of the coercion under which the French press is placed. – Ed. (TT1: 13)

It is obvious that much of this fine passage is a bitter allusion to the existing Government of France. – Ed. (TT1: 27)

Montalembert's strongly pro-Catholic political and religious views incur particular derision on Croker's part:

Monomania! The frequent obtrusion of these sneers at *'Protestantism'* will provoke from ordinary English readers only a smile of wonder, but with those who, like ourselves, really feel interested in the better parts of M. de Montalembert's work, they excite regret and pity at such wanton aberrations from good taste and good sense. (TTI: 143)

Sarcasm is perhaps the overarching feature of the footnotes:

The possible improvement thus hinted at would be, as we judge from the sequel, a return to Popery, with perhaps a democracy. *Grand merci!* – Ed. (TT1: 33)

This phrase, which we translate with more of sorrow than surprise, [...] (TT1: 63)

The whole of this chapter [Catholicism in England] would afford ample room for criticism; we content ourselves with a protestation against most of its statements and almost all its inductions. – Ed. (TT1: 216)

This is all very complimentary, but it might be wished that it were a little less of what is expressively called *twaddle.* (TT1: 260)

Nor does Montalembert's style escape censure:

An attentive reader will be at no loss to account for the author's approbation of 'l'usage illimité de la plus éclatante inconsequence.' No one that we know has more largely availed himself of it. – Ed. (TT1: 61)

Even Croker's compliments have stings in the tail:

> Very just and true; but we shall see by and by but too many instances in which the author sacrifices this justice and truth to fits of his monomania. – Ed. (TT1: 167)

> [...] With this explanation, the reader will overlook the technical errors and misnomers which the author falls into with respect to English wills and entails. His general argument is clear and just – Ed. (TT1: 110)

The most striking feature of the footnotes is, however, their simple recurrence. The cumulative nature of the footnotes, and the range of features of the ST with which they take issue (consistency, coherence, accuracy, dogma, style, argumentation) have the ultimate aim of discrediting the text in both the broad sweep of its ideas, the progression of its argument and the local specificity of its descriptions of English life and politics.

The pepperiness, not to speak of the *ad hominem* attacks, is certainly one of the factors which led John Murray, under pressure from Abraham Hayward (who had seen an advance copy of the introduction and, having done so, demanded to see the notes as well), to suppress this first edition of the translation immediately (Brightfield, 1940: 295). The suppressed edition was immediately replaced by a new edition without the preface or Croker's added notes, but instead with a short 'Notice' inserted before the title-page as follows:

> The Translator thinks it necessary to state that he was induced to undertake the task not from any confidence or concurrence in the Author's political or religious views, but because the work has made a considerable sensation abroad, and may afford some useful warnings, if not lessons, to ourselves at home. (Croker, 1856c)

Hayward's protests continued unabated. When the revised edition appeared, to positive reviews, he launched the correspondence in *The Times*, which was enthusiastically seconded by a rather hasty review in the May 1856 edition of *Fraser's Magazine*. Other periodicals followed suit, and over the next couple of months the affair was much talked of in the press and in the monthly magazines, the more so because the book's ideas had caused a stir both in France and in Britain.[6] Most periodicals took a moderate position, agreeing that the translation was faulty but not to the degree maintained by Hayward, and that the vexed question of the translator's identity was a red herring, in that Croker's editorial intervention was clearly so substantial as to make him to all intents and purposes the translator, even if he did not make the first draft.

Animus in the Translation: Textual Analysis

The suppression of the first edition of Croker's and Boislève's translation and the republication of the translation with minimal paratextual apparatus pose an interesting critical and methodological question for the translation scholar. Without the rhetorical battering provided by Croker's footnotes and introduction, to what extent does his open animus towards Montalembert and his text actually manifest itself in the translation? Croker's avowed purpose in bringing out the translation of a work with which he emphatically disagreed was to frame it in a way which would make it less persuasive to English readers. Are there elements in the text itself which also fulfil this purpose? And how might the effect of any such elements be gauged?

A conventional transtextual reading reveals some minor points of interest. Religion is, predictably, a stumbling block. Speaking of the mass emigration from Ireland in the 1840s as a result of the Famine, Montalembert observes that the emigrating Irish population took their religion with them:

Example 10.1

ST	Literal translation	TT
Une immense émigration, qui porte partout avec elle **la foi catholique et des mœurs chrétiennes**, a été organisée. (ST: 226–227)	An immense emigration, which brings with it everywhere **the Catholic faith and Christian morals**, was organized.	An immense emigration, carrying with it everywhere **the Catholic faith**, was organized. (TT2: 186)

Montalembert conflates Roman Catholicism with Christian values; the translator's omission of 'des mœurs chrétiennes' indicates an unwillingness to group Catholicism and Christian values together, thus emphasizing the denominational divide. Personal and political animus is also occasionally visible in Croker's translation, as when a complimentary remark about the Irish politician Daniel O'Connell, an ally of the Whigs, whom Croker cordially detested, is removed in the translation:

Example 10.2

| En restant sur le terrain où **le génie d'O'Connell** a planté leur drapeau, ils demeurent inattaquables, et peuvent être sûrs de marcher en avant. (ST: 224) | In staying on the ground where **the genius of O'Connell** planted their flag, they remain unassailable and can be sure to advance. | In maintaining the ground where **O'Connell** planted their flag, they are unattackable and are sure to advance. (TT2: 185) |

A slightly unflattering comparison of the relative English and French appeal to colonial subject nations is not permitted to stand:

Example 10.3

| Peut-être les manies bureaucratiques de notre administration auraient-elles retardé ou compliqué l'œuvre de la colonization: mais en revanche **la nature beaucoup plus sympathique du caractère français** eût plus facilement gagné le cœur des populations indigènes [...] (ST: 272) | Perhaps the bureaucratic manias of our administration might have delayed or complicated the work of colonization: but **the much more sympathetic French character** would more easily have won the hearts of the indigenous population [...] | Perhaps the foolish officialities of our administration might have deferred or complicated the work of colonization; but, on the other hand, the **sympathetic nature of the French character** would have more easily won the heart of the natives [...] (TT2: 223) |

These apparently overt signals of translatorial deletion are, however, not representative of the text as a whole. A previous reference to O'Connell uniting 100,000 Irishmen 'frémissant sous sa main' (ST: 32) is translated with no sign of animus as 'thrilling under his master hand' (TT2: 29). On the contrary, 'his hand' in the ST has become 'his master hand' in TT2. A contrastive reading of the two texts reveals few examples of simple deletion, even at points where we know from the paratext that Croker emphatically disagreed with his ST.

The tendency which does, on the other hand, come across strongly from a parallel reading of ST and TT2 is the tendency towards explicitation, which Blum-Kulka has hypothesized as a translation universal (1986/2004). The translation has sought to clarify a number of points and in many places the cohesion and coherence of the text are greatly increased. Explicitation at the grammatical level (e.g. pronouns) is accompanied by explicitation for collocational purposes (the creation of phrases with the correct rhetorical 'weight' in English which also happen to reinforce key ideological messages in the text). These additions in many places go beyond Blum-Kulka's own concept of explicitation which is a specifically grammatical one. What is of interest for this study is the way that Croker justifies shifts which take place in the translation as merely bringing out what is inherent in the text itself (see Example 10.9 below) – a statement which we should treat with due caution, and yet a statement which textual analysis frequently supports. For reasons of space, a few of the most illustrative examples must suffice:

Example 10.4

Mais en dehors des **préoccupations de la politique contemporaine** ou du patriotisme alarmé, et pour **le petit nombre de ceux qui professent encore le culte de la liberté et de la dignité humaine**, il n'y a pas, à l'heure qu'il est, de problème **plus vital** que celui des destinées prochaines de l'Angleterre. (ST: 1)	But apart from the preoccupations of contemporary politics or of alarmed patriotism, and for the small number of those who still profess the cult of liberty and human dignity, there is, at the present moment, no more vital problem than that of the near future of England.	But apart from either the **speculations of rivalry** or the apprehensions of patriotism, **there is a third class of observers with whom the question is of still higher and more universal interest**. With every one (too few, alas! in number) who still professes any respect for the liberties of mankind and the dignity of human nature, there cannot be a subject of **more anxious, more vital** solicitude, than the future fate of England, **hitherto the greatest example and guarantee of both**. (TT2: 1)

The interpretive shift from 'préoccupations de la politique contemporaine' to 'speculations of rivalry' can be traced back to Croker's acute awareness of the binary structure of British party politics, an awareness evidenced elsewhere in Croker's translation too. The other changes in the passage can, however, be categorized under the heading of explicitation. The 'third class of observers with whom the question is of still higher and more universal interest' are distinguished from the alarmed patriots and the dedicated party politicians, and identified with the 'petit nombre de ceux qui ...'. Abstract nouns, always more acceptable in French than in English, are concretized, with 'liberty and human dignity' becoming 'the liberties of mankind and the dignity of human nature'. The 'alas!' has its genesis in the ST's obvious approval of those who worship freedom and human dignity. 'Plus vital' is rhetorically doubled to become 'more anxious, more vital' (rhetorical manipulation is again a common feature of the translation).

The most conspicuous addition to the passage is of course the final phrase, not present in the ST, 'hitherto the greatest example and guarantee of both'. It is an aggrandizement of England, but is characteristic of

Montalembert's overall discourse which is highly laudatory of English culture and institutions. The translation makes explicit what is already implied in the link between the interest in freedom and dignity and the interest in the future of England.

Example 10.5

| Depuis **l'avortement ou l'abdication du libéralisme continental,** elle est désormais seule au monde. Partout s'exhale la secrète impatience de ceux qui disent: Quand donc le monde sera-t-il débarrassé de ce cauchemar? Qui nous délivrera de ce nid d'aristocrates opiniâtres et de **libéraux attardés?** Quand brisera-t-**on** l'orgueil de ce peuple qui brave **les lois de la logique,** qui a l'audace de croire en même temps à la tradition et au progrès, de maintenir la royauté et de **pratiquer la liberté,** de repousser la révolution et **d'échapper au despotisme?** (ST: 3–4) | Since the abortion or the abdication of continental liberalism, she [England] is now alone in the world. Everywhere breathes the secret impatience of those who say: 'When will the world be freed of this nightmare? Who will deliver us from this nest of stubborn aristocrats and old-fashioned liberals? When will the pride be broken of this people which braves the laws of logic, which dares to believe at the same time in tradition and in progress, in keeping royalty and practising liberty, in repelling revolution and escaping despotism?' | Since the **failure of the ultra-liberal or revolutionary experiments on the Continent**, England stands alone in the world **as an example of rational Liberty**, and is the object of the secret envy of all its enemies. 'When,' they say to themselves, 'when shall the world get rid of this nightmare? Who will deliver us from this nest of obstinate aristocrats and of **hypocritical reformers**? When shall **we** break down the pride of this **obstinate** people, who, defying **the laws of revolutionary logic**, have the audacity to believe at once in tradition and in progress – who maintain royalty while they **pretend to practise liberty**, and escape from revolution **without submitting to despotism**?' TT2: 3–4 |

Explicitation of elements already arguably present in the text can be seen in the addition of 'As an example of rational Liberty' and in the transformation of 'Ceux qui disent' into 'enemies'.

We also have ample evidence in this passage of Croker's own political position. A fervent opponent of the Reform Act of 1832, which extended voting rights and abolished the rotten boroughs, Croker is very distrustful of Montalembert's advocacy of democratic reform. For Montalembert, revolution on the continent constituted the failure of the more gradual aristocrat-led reforms which were his ideal. Continental liberalism has been 'aborted' or 'abdicated' and replaced by a destructive absolutism. For Croker, on the other hand, democratic reform is of itself an evil and he makes no distinction between Montalembert's longed-for aristocratic reform and the violent upheavals seen in France and elsewhere. 'Continental liberalism' in the ST is thus deliberately misunderstood as 'ultra-liberal or revolutionary experiments'. Abstractions in the ST tend to be concretized in the TT. 'Liberals' become 'reformers' – and not 'attardés', which has the force here of 'holdovers from a previous age', but 'hypocritical'. Instead of 'practising liberty' Croker has Montalembert say that England 'pretends to practise liberty', an extrapolation which has much less basis in the ST than many of his other extrapolations from context.

Example 10.6

| La vie publique et privée de ce grand homme de bien offre un modèle tellement accompli de ferveur, de charité et d'humilité chrétienne qu'on a peine à s'expliquer comment tant de vertus ont pu exister hors de la vérité suprême. (ST: 241) | The public and private life of this great man offers such an accomplished model of fervour, of charity and of Christian humility that one has difficulty in explaining how so many virtues could exist outside the supreme truth. | The public and private life of this great man [William Wilberforce] offers such a perfect pattern of fervour, of charity, of Christian humility, that **I** find it difficult to understand how so many virtues could exist beyond the bosom of supreme truth – **the Catholic Church.** (TT2: 196) |

Here Croker glosses Montalembert's 'supreme truth' as 'the Catholic Church'. This is undoubtedly what Montalembert is implying – Wilberforce's moral greatness is such that Montalembert is astonished that he was an Anglican – but the explicitation allows Croker to keep Montalembert's reprehensible religious 'monomania' yet again before the reader's eye.

The translation into English of impersonal constructions is often difficult, and is likely to result in shifts of agency. Here one can at least say that linguistic demands to explicate the subject of 'avoir a peine à s'expliquer' (the impersonal 'on' becomes 'I') coincide with Croker's own interest in underlining Montalembert's religious beliefs wherever possible. It must be admitted, however, that on many of these occasions Croker's reading is the likely one, as in the following passage:

Example 10.7

| Il va sans dire que **nous ne regardons pas comme un mal ce que certains apôtres et certains ennemis de la démocratie révolutionnaire confondent trop souvent avec elle, savoir: le progrès du droit, de l'égalité devant la loi, du bien-être et de l'instruction du peuple, l'émancipation des consciences de tout joug séculier.** (ST: 45) | It goes without saying that we do not see as an evil that which certain apostles and certain enemies of revolutionary democracy too often confuse with it, namely: the progress of rights, of equality before the law, of the wellbeing and the education of the people, the emancipation of consciences from all secular yoke. | I need not repeat, that **I** do not consider as an evil that which many, both advocates and adversaries, of revolutionary democracy too often confound with it: **I** mean that progress of the natural rights of the people, their equality before the law, their well-being and instruction, and the emancipation for all **religious consciences from all *secular* restraint** (TT2: 39, emphasis in original) |

Here the expansion of 'consciences' to 'all religious consciences' in contrast to the notion of secular restraint undoubtedly reflects Montalembert's only possible implication (though it is of course in Croker's interest again to keep the religious aspect of Montalembert's argumentation as visible as possible). The 'nous' in the ST is clearly a rhetorical device referring to the writer himself, but again, it is in the translator's interest to enhance Montalembert's visibility within the text, which is achieved by the replacement of **nous** with no less than three repetitions of the first person singular.

Example 10.8

| Certains esprits impatients appellent à grands cris la **chute** de l'Eglise anglicane, et y voient d'avance le triomphe du catholicisme en Angleterre (ST: 245). | Some impatient spirits call loudly for the fall of the Anglican church, and foresee in it the triumph of Catholicism in England. | Some impatient spirits **amongst us** call loudly for the **overthrow** of the Anglican Church, and in that fall they anticipate the triumph of Catholicism in England (TT2: 200) |

Here the 'fall' of the Anglican church becomes its 'overthrow'. This is a substantial distinction between the collapse of an institution because of internal weaknesses (Montalembert's position) and its demolition by outside agency. Croker's imputation is supported by the addition of 'amongst us', casting Montalembert as one of a group threatening the stability of Anglicanism, whereas Montalembert's text suggests that he does *not* belong to the 'esprits impatients', much though he believes it would be to England's benefit to exchange Anglicanism for Roman Catholicism (Montalembert, 1856b: 165–190; 1856c/1860: 235–250).

Our final example is one of the passages most contested by Hayward and other commentators:

Example 10.9

| Contenir et régler la démocratie sans l'avilir, l'**organiser** en monarchie tempérée ou en république conservatrice, tel est le problème de notre siècle: mais ce problème n'a encore été résolu nulle part. (ST: 42) | To contain and regulate democracy without debasing it, to organize it into a liberal monarchy or a conservative republic, such is the problem of our century: but this problem has not yet been resolved anywhere. | To restrain and guide democracy without debasing it, to **regulate and reconcile** it with a liberal monarchy or a conservative republic – such is the problem of our age; but it is a problem which has been as yet nowhere solved, **except in England**. (TT2: 37) |

Note the increase in tension between 'organiser' and 'reconcile'. The great change, however, is the addition of 'except in England', apparently a gratuitous addition with no basis in the ST. It is defended by Croker in a letter of 12 May 1856 to Murray on the grounds that:

> I really forget whether she [H.B.] or I added these words – but they are absolutely necessary to make sense of the rest of the book, which proceeds altogether on the assumption that England has had the good luck of combining a wise democracy with a constitutional monarchy – that is the main scope of Montalembert's argument & without the words '<u>except in England</u>' be understood, the whole is nonsense & this is so obvious that I think every one who had read the passage without them would have thought it was a mere slip of the author's pen to have omitted them. (emphasis in original)

In fact, Montalembert does go on in the rest of the passage to argue that England alone shows the potential for combining democracy with aristocracy in appropriate and stable proportions, avoiding the polar evils of anarchy and despotism (Montalembert, 1856b: 37–38; 1856c/1860: 42–43).

But Montalembert also makes clear that he does not believe that the problem has been entirely resolved in England, however likely its resolution appears. Croker's interpolation may be attributed to a subtle combination of the will to explication and the nationalist chauvinism which leads him to aggrandize descriptions of England at several points in the text.

For reasons of space, the many other examples which might have been discussed must be put aside, but what our necessarily brief and symptomatic analysis of ST and TT2 has sought to indicate are some of the potential complexities of the relationship between text and paratext in antipathetic translation. As Puurtinen (2003: 59) recognizes, 'even minor, seemingly superficial changes can have unintended consequences for the translated text as a whole'. The translator's own ideological positioning is clearly fundamental to the translation choices made. Nevertheless, many of the changes may be attributed to contrastive linguistic and cross-cultural rhetorical differences as well as to animus. Cohesion is one of the areas in which translation shifts are inevitable. A more systematic corpus analysis of the texts, perhaps along the lines suggested by Munday (2002), might yield interesting results in looking at characteristic patterns of translation shifts. A comparison with previous translations by Croker might also illuminate the discussion by offering further data about Croker's own translation style.

Paratextually, Croker's translation of Montalembert appears admirably to fulfil the criteria for an antipathetic translation. Textually, on the other hand, it seems much less crudely interventionist than many censored or expurgated translations of the 19th century. Previous research on translations of classical texts by Catullus or Apuleius (O'Sullivan, 2008) shows substantial textual intervention in the form of omission or bowdlerism which might or might not be flagged in the paratext. Another way of eliminating problem content was to excerpt, and cheap popular classic series such as Routledge's Universal Library were able to include authors such as Rabelais or Boccaccio by simply omitting episodes which might be thought to adversely affect the moral tone of readers. Readers might also be protected by leaving certain passages in Latin, French or Italian in the translation. Much of the criticism of Croker's translation, fanned by the hostile article in *Fraser's Magazine*, was due to an erroneous assumption in *Fraser's* that Croker had omitted an entire chapter on Daniel O'Connell from Montalembert's book, when in fact that chapter had been added in a later French edition and had never been seen by Croker and H.B. Overall, their translation is very complete, though, as we have seen, it exhibits textual features which can plausibly be linked with the translator's political and religious beliefs.

A distinction must of course be made between the reasons for republishing (and censoring) a classic author such as Boccaccio, Rabelais or Catullus and the reasons for publishing a text of contemporary relevance. In the case of Catullus, for instance, the Bohn Classical Library edition of 1854 observes that

> [...] some of his poems are hideous from the traces of a turpitude to which we cannot without a painful effort make even a passing allusion. But so are portions of almost every Roman poet; and amidst our natural disgust at these abominations, and at the filthy ribaldry of many of the short pieces of Catullus, it is right to remember that these things were the vices of the age rather than of the individual. (Kelly, 1854: 2–3)

These 'vices of the age rather than of the individual' are counterbalanced by Catullus's 'extraordinary versatility', 'consummate skill', 'graceful turns of thought' and 'exquisite happiness of expression' in which he has 'never been surpassed' (Kelly, 1854: 3). Similarly, the introduction to an 1884 edition of the *Decameron* in the Routledge's Universal Library series, which retailed to a mass market at one shilling and which reproduced only 40 of the 100 stories in the text, declares that 'the novels of "The Decameron" illustrate in their own way the saying, drawn from Hesiod, that sometimes the half is greater than the whole' (Morley, 1884: 8). The literary quality of the work justifies publication and republication, and the retranslation takes place *in spite of* problem elements in the text, which can be dealt with locally. Croker's translation of Montalembert, on the other hand, is undertaken not *despite* certain elements in the text, but precisely *because of* those elements. Since a translation of the work was inevitable,[7] undertaking the translation himself and framing it for the target readership was Croker's only weapon against the dangerous reformist ideas it contained. Croker's ultimate aim in bringing out the translation is a prophylactic one. As he says in his suppressed introduction, 'the discussion raised by M. de Montalembert may be of great use by reviving public attention to the indefatigable and encroaching spirit of Romanism amongst us' (Croker, 1856a: xiv).

Croker's strategy is thus much closer to the approach taken to the translation of *Mein Kampf* discussed by Hermans, where only full rendition of the ideas contained within the text could achieve the skopos of the translation, which was to put readers on their guard against a dangerous text. If anything, Montalembert's ideas are, as we have seen, intensified by the increased coherence and cohesion of the translation.

Hermans' notion of irony in translation amply accounts for these different approaches; nevertheless, a qualitative distinction may still be worth making between 'concessionary' translations of valued literary texts and what we might call 'preventive' or 'prophylactic' translations. The concessionary translation presents a work which is on the whole valued by the receiving culture, and removes those elements not valued by the receiving culture, usually by some form of under-translation. The prophylactic translation seeks to forestall the potential harm done by a potentially threatening text by presenting it in a form which will neutralize any negative consequences, which may, as in the case of Montalembert, involve over-translation. The proposed category of prophylactic translation might also include forensic translations in law. When the bookseller and pornographer George Cannon was prosecuted in 1831 for supplying a copy in French of Sade's *Juliette*, prosecutors presented as evidence in court a literal translation of part of the contentious text (see Kearney, 1982: 104). A juryman questioned the motives and choices of the Society's translator, suggesting that the translation might not be a faithful rendering of the ST, given the purpose of the translation. However, on being shown the French text and the English translation together the juror acknowledged that 'it is a most literal translation indeed. So much so, that it is *worse* than the book itself' (Anonymous, 1831, emphasis in original).

Another text to come under the heading of prophylactic translation would be Rudolf Hoess's *Commandant of Auschwitz*, translated by Constantine FitzGibbon with an introduction by Primo Levi (1995/2001). Here we are reminded of Croker's strictures on Montalembert's style. The book 'has no literary quality, and reading it is agony' but 'it is one of the most instructive books ever published' (Levi, 1959/2001: 19). Ultimately, the book warns against 'the ultimate consequences of blindly accepted Duty' (1959/2001: 25).

To recap, the concessionary translation is likely to be valued as a text in itself, with the exception of certain problematic elements (moral, religious). It may be a classic work. It may take considerable liberties with the text. Omissions and expurgations may be required to allow the text entry to what Lefevere has called the 'margin', a zone of compromise which may facilitate a text's circulation even if it violates target culture norms (see O'Sullivan, 2009).

The prophylactic translation, on the other hand, is likely to have a contemporary relevance, if only because it is perceived as a threat to potential readers. It may be published not in the margin, but at the centre (major publishers, official or public entities), as representing a consensus opinion on the ST. Such a text is likely not to be valued as a text in itself but, on the contrary, heavily criticized for style as well as content (see also Jones, 2004). (Having said that, we must bear in mind that some of these criticisms may be based on discomfort with the likely or proven rhetorical effectiveness of the text.) Prophylactic translations may be literal or at least completist in approach.

The notion of 'antipathy' in translation is a strong one, and I have argued here that it should be linked more with preventive approaches to translation rather than concessionary ones. Such a binary model is, of course, by definition suspect, and one might imagine translations of this type as existing on a cline rather than in distinct categories. Other scholars might well introduce translations which trouble simplistic distinctions, and I would be very interested to hear from readers who have come across other examples of potentially 'antipathetic' translations, with a view to developing and if necessary nuancing a model which seems, at least in the light of the examples studied here, potentially productive.

Notes

1. The Comte de Montalembert (1810–1870) was a French Catholic politician, brought up in England where his father had fled at the time of the Revolution. Montalembert retained close ties with England but was most active as a political figure under successive administrations of the Restoration and afterwards of the Second Empire under Louis Napoléon.
2. Many of Croker's letters to Murray have been preserved in the Murray Archive at the Scottish National Library. For the correspondence regarding *De l'avenir politique de l'Angleterre* see Ms. 42142 (435C). I am grateful to the librarians for their support and advice during my visit to the Archive in October 2008.
3. Except where otherwise stipulated, references to the correspondence between Croker and Murray are from the unpublished letters in Ms. 42142 (435C) in the John Murray Archive at the Scottish National Library.
4. The identity of 'H.B.' was hotly debated, with Abraham and others accusing Croker of inventing a translator under a *nom de plume*. *Fraser's Magazine* was particularly sceptical, in the light of the fact that H.B.'s correspondence address was also Croker's own. The Croker correspondence at the Murray archive confirms that 'H.B.' was Croker's secretary Miss Boislève, and that she was responsible at least for drafting the translation. It also seems likely that the translation was thoroughly reviewed by Croker before submission.
5. Croker's review appeared in the *Quarterly Review* of March (Croker 1856b).
6. The book was a key reference point for both sides in a debate in the House of Commons on 24 April on the reform of civil service entrance examinations (*The Times*, 25 April 1856, pp. 6–7).
7. Indeed a translation had previously been commissioned by Abraham Hayward (*The Times*, 7 April 1856, p. 12).

References

Anonymous (1831) The King, on the prosecution of the Society for the Suppression of Vice, vs. George Cannon. *Morning Chronicle*, 11 February 1831.
Anonymous (1856a) M. Montalembert and John Wilson Croker; or, Traduttore Traditore. *Fraser's Magazine*, May 1856, 563–583.
Anonymous (1856b) Review of *De l'Avenir Politique de l'Angleterre* in both its French editions, and of *The Political Future of England*. The Dublin Review 40 (80), 441–454.
Anonymous (1863) Translations of Horace. *Blackwood's Edinburgh Magazine* 574 (August), 184–198.
Association des Traducteurs Littéraires de France (n.d.) *Code de Déontologie du Traducteur Littéraire*. On WWW at http://www.atlf.org/Code-de-Deontologie-du-Traducteur.html. Accessed 30.12.10.
Blum-Kulka, S. (1986/2004) Shifts of cohesion and coherence in translation. In L. Venuti (ed.) *The Translation Studies Reader* (pp. 290–305). New York/London: Routledge.
Brightfield, M. (ed.) (1940) *John Wilson Croker*. Berkeley, CA: University of California Press.
Croker, J.W. (1856a) Introduction. In Montalembert, *The Political Future of England* [suppressed edn] (pp. v–xix). London: John Murray.
Croker, J.W. (1856b) Review of *The Political Future of England* by the Count de Montalembert, of the French Academy. *Quarterly Review* CXCVI (March), 534–572.
Croker, J.W. (1856c) Notice. In Montalembert (ed.) *The Political Future of England*. London: John Murray.
Fetter, F.W. (1958) The economic articles in the *Quarterly Review* and their authors, 1809–52. *Journal of Political Economy* 66 (1), 47–64.
Friedberg, M. (1997) *Literary Translation in Russia: A Cultural History*. University Park, PA: University of Pennsylvania Press.
Gentzler, E. and Tymoczko, M. (eds) (2002) *Translation and Power*. Amherst: University of Massachusetts Press.
Hayward, A. (1856) Letter. *The Times* 2 April 1856, 12.
Hermans, T. (2007) *The Conference of the Tongues*. Manchester: St. Jerome.
Hoess, R. (1959/2001) *Commandant of Auschwitz* (C. Fitzgibbon, trans.). London: Phoenix.
Jones, F.R. (2004) Ethics, aesthetics and décision: Literary translating in the Wars of the Yugoslav Succession. *Meta* 49 (4), 711–728.
Kearney, P. (1982) *A History of Erotic Literature*. Hong Kong: Parragon.
Kelly, W.K. (1854) *Poems of Catullus and Tibullus, and, The Vigil of Venus*. A literal prose translation with notes, by Walter K. Kelly. To which are added the metrical versions of Lamb and Grainger, and a selection of versions by other writers. London: George Bell & Sons.
Lefevere, A. (1992) *Translation, Rewriting, and the Manipulation of Literary Fame*. London/New York: Routledge.
Levi, P. (1995/2001) Introduction (J. Neugroschel, trans.). In R. Hoess (2001) *Commandant of Auschwitz* (C. Fitzgibbon, trans.) (pp. 19–25). London: Phoenix.
Literary Translators' Association of Canada (2007) Trade book model contract for translation. On WWW at http://attlc-ltac.org/?q=node/74. Accessed 30.12.10.

Macey, D. (2000) Beginning the translation. *Parallax* 6 (1), 2–12.
Montalembert, Le Comte de (1856a) *The Political Future of England*. London: John Murray [suppressed edn].
Montalembert, Le Comte de (1856b) *The Political Future of England*. London: John Murray.
Montalembert, Le Comte de (1856c/1860) *De l'avenir politique de l'Angleterre*. Paris: Didier.
Morley, H. (1884) Introduction. In *The Decameron of Giovanni Boccaccio including Forty of its Hundred Novels* (pp. 5–8). London: George Routledge and Sons.
Munday, J. (2002) Systems in translation: A systemic model for descriptive translation studies. In T. Hermans (ed.) *Crosscultural Transgressions. Research Models in Translation Studies II: Historical and Ideological Issues* (pp. 76–92). Manchester: St Jerome.
O'Brien, J. (1959) From French to English. In R. Brower (ed.) *On Translation* (pp. 78–92). Cambridge, MA: Harvard University Press.
Ó Cuilleanáin, C. (1999) Not in front of the servants: Forms of bowdlerism and censorship in translation. In M. Holman and J. Boase-Beier (eds) *The Practices of Literary Translation: Constraints and Creativity* (pp. 31–44). Manchester: St. Jerome.
O'Sullivan, C. (2008) Censoring these 'racy morsels of the vernacular': loss and gain in translations of Apuleius and Catullus. In E. ní Chuilleanáin, C.Ó Cuilleanáin and D. Parris (eds). *Translation and Censorship: Patterns of Communication and Interference* (pp. 76–92). Dublin: Four Courts.
O'Sullivan, C. (2009) Translation within the margin: The 'libraries' of Henry Bohn. In J. Milton and P. Bandia (eds) *Agents of Translation* (pp. 107–129). Amsterdam: John Benjamins.
Puurtinen, T. (2003) Explicitating and implicitating source text ideology. *Across Languages and Cultures* 4 (1), 53–62.
Venuti, L. (1995) *The Translator's Invisibility: A History of Translation*. London/New York: Routledge.
Zeldin, T. (1959) English ideals in French politics during the nineteenth century. *The Historical Journal* 2 (1), 40–58.

Chapter 11
Translation as a Means of Ideological Struggle

C. DELISTATHI

Introduction

This chapter explores the relationship between the translation of the *Communist Manifesto* into Greek issued by the Communist Party of Greece in 1933, and its contemporary political context. More specifically, it investigates two issues: firstly, the ways in which ideological struggles between counter-hegemonic forces for the 'ownership' of Marxism conditioned paratextual features and translational decisions in the target text (TT); and, secondly, how the (para)textual specificities, in conjunction with translation criticism, aimed to influence the reception of the TT with a view to establishing a particular translation of the *Communist Manifesto* as the only correct one. Recent research in Translation Studies concerned with the 'institutional translation' (Kang, 2008) of political texts has focused mainly on practices, processes and products within the EU (Koskinen, 2000, 2001; Schäffner, 1997, 2004a, 2004b). Whereas the focus of such research has been on translations issued by an institution that is part of the hegemonic apparatus, this chapter studies institutional translation carried out by a political party with counter-hegemonic political ideas, thus broadening our understanding of the role of translation in institutional settings.

In the writings of the Italian Marxist Antonio Gramsci (1971/1978), the term 'hegemony' acquires different meanings. The best summary definition for the purposes of this essay is provided by Raymond Williams. In its simplest sense, hegemony refers to relations of political predominance between social classes; such predominance encompasses a way of seeing the world (Williams, 1976/1986: 145).[1] Although Gramsci employed the term 'hegemony' to discuss relations of power and domination between social classes, it is now used in social sciences in a variety of contexts. For Gramsci, the contradictions of capitalism itself create the potential for the spontaneous emergence of alternative ideas and practices, so hegemonic ideas always exist on the fault line with 'counter-hegemonic' ones. In this chapter, Marxism is considered a counter-hegemonic political ideology whose interpretation was contested by different political organizations.

The *Communist Manifesto*, written in German in 1848 by Karl Marx and Friedrich Engels, is one of the most important political texts ever written. Linking theory to political activity, it summarized the principles of a group of revolutionaries who called themselves communists and articulated a radical analysis and critique of contemporary capitalism. The text, which was published during a period of revolutionary upheaval in Europe, became the most important founding statement of those who considered (and still consider) themselves communists or socialists and has been so widely translated that scholars are in no position to provide a definitive number of its translations. The *Communist Manifesto* has been influential to entire generations of left-wing political activists all over the world and it is a text with enormous symbolic as well as educational significance. The followers of its ideas have transformed world politics.

Within the Greek context, the *Communist Manifesto* played a significant role in ideological struggles which have shaped political forces and ideological developments in Greek society for many decades. The term 'ideology' is used here in a narrow sense to denote a coherent set of political ideas, whereas the term 'ideological struggle' will refer to the battle of ideas between political forces. The discussion will focus mostly on the early 1930s and the translation published by the Communist Party of Greece [Κομμουνιστικό Κόμμα Ελλάδας, henceforth KKE] in 1933. This is because, around the time of the publication of this translation, the KKE was engaged in an ideological struggle on two fronts: firstly, against the hegemonic ideas of the ruling class; and secondly, against the party's rivals on the left for the establishment of the KKE's own interpretation of Marxism as the only correct one (see section on translation criticism, below). In this context, the term 'counter-hegemonic' encompasses a heterogeneous entity. Thus, power struggles can take place not only between hegemonic and counter-hegemonic forces but also between counter-hegemonic forces.

In late 1920s and early 1930s Greece, the ideological struggle between Marxist-oriented political organizations for the control of Marxism was at its peak. The significantly different interpretations of Marxism that these organizations presented led to alternative and competing strategies for bringing about social change. The outcome of the ideological struggle within the left determined which organizational model and vision for the future was proposed to those striving for social change and affected subsequent political trends and social movements. To understand the role of the *Communist Manifesto* in these struggles within Greek society, it is necessary to outline the reasons for its retranslations and to explain the context of the ideological struggles around the time of the publication of the 1933 translation.

Retranslations: A Brief History of the *Communist Manifesto* into Greek

The *Communist Manifesto* was introduced in Greece relatively late, in 1908; this coincided with the first efforts to establish socialist and trade union organizations in the country. The chronology and configuration of subsequent translations is shown in Table 11.1.

As shown in Table 11.1, within the space of 25 years, four new translations and two revised editions of the text were issued. The reasons for the

Table 11.1 Retranslations of the *Communist Manifesto* into Greek until 1933

Year of publication	Commissioner	Editor/ translator	Completeness of translation	Format of publication
1908		Kostas Chatzopoulos (translator)	Incomplete, missing section III	Serialized in the newspaper *The Worker*
1913		Kostas Chatzopoulos (translator)	Revised 1908 translation; incomplete, missing section III	Brochure
1919 (revised and reprinted in 1921)	SEKE (forerunner of the KKE)	A. Sideris (editor); A. Doumas (translator)	Complete	Brochure
1927		G. Kordatos (translator)	Complete	Brochure
1933	KKE	I. Iordanides (translator)	Complete	Brochure

frequent retranslation of the text concern the quest for a good quality translation that would guarantee the correct rendering of such an important text in the target language (TL). However, as will be discussed, they also relate to ideological concerns. The first translation was carried out by Kostas Chatzopoulos, a prominent literary author and, at the time, a socialist. Chatzopoulos's unsuitable linguistic choices which 'complicated, in many places, the pleasant reading' of the text (Sideris, 1919: ε´) and the fact that his translation was incomplete, were not the only reasons why this translation failed to satisfy the needs of the SEKE [Socialist Labour Party of Greece], the forerunner of the Communist Party of Greece. In 1917, Chatzopoulos headed the government's censorship committee (Noutsos, 1991: 414) and had become an anti-communist.[2] In essence, he had sided with the party's political opponents and this was another reason that made his translation unusable and necessitated the issue of a new one by the SEKE.

The translator of the 1919 translation by the SEKE was Antonis Doumas, a member who later left the party. The editor was the socialist MP Aristotelis Sideris, who was also a member of the SEKE. Later, he also left the SEKE and joined a rival political organization. Questioning again the quality of all previous translations, Giannis Kordatos published his own translation in 1927. Giannis Kordatos was the KKE's former General Secretary who had been expelled shortly before the publication of his translation. He identified himself as a Trotskyist[3] at the time, but was not aligned with any Trotskyist organization. However, all these translations were dismissed by the KKE on the basis that their poor quality distorted Marxism (see section on translation criticism, below). This assertion is especially pronounced in 1933 at a time of intense ideological struggle for the ownership of Marxism. In response to these concerns, the KKE published yet another new translation in 1933.

Ideological Struggle: 'The Monopoly of Marxist Theory'

In the period leading up to World War II, very important and complex social, political and ideological developments took place in Greek society. Here I will only outline those most relevant to this discussion. In 1924 the KKE became a full member of the Comintern (i.e. the Communist International organization) and its subsequent political profile was affected by the events that took place in the USSR and in the Comintern itself. In the late 1920s, the KKE went through a period of crisis which resulted in the expulsion of several of its members, such as Kordatos, the translator of the 1927 translation.

In the 1920s, after Stalin had become the leader of the USSR, the parties affiliated to the Comintern underwent fundamental changes which have been described by scholars as 'Stalinism' or 'Stalinization' (Alexatos, 1997: 180–182; Cliff, 1970; Paloukis, 2003: 227; Reiman, 1987). These changes concerned major theoretical and organizational transformations within the Communist parties. Leon Trotsky, leader of the Red Army during the Russian revolution, led the faction Left Opposition (1923–1927) in the Bolshevik party and fought against Stalinism. The International Left Opposition was formed in 1930 as a faction group within the Comintern and had supporters in several countries, including Greece. From the late 1920s, within the USSR, members and supporters of the Left Opposition faced persecution and Trotsky was murdered in 1940 while in exile in Mexico. Outside the USSR, Communist parties were very hostile to Trotskyist groups in their countries. The most significant organizations supporting the International Left Opposition in Greece were the organizations *Archive of Marxism* [Αρχείο του Μαρξισμού] and *Spartakos* [Σπάρτακος], the Archive being the larger of the two.

From the late 1920s, the KKE's objective on the ideological front was the appropriation of Marxism from its rivals within the left. The aim to establish the monopoly of representation of Marxism in Greece was an endeavour that continued after the 1930s, but from the late 1920s to the mid-1930s efforts were particularly intense. The party's Central Committee in its 1927 'Decision on the activity of the propaganda section' stated:

> The monopoly of theory. Our Party ought to aim at the monopoly of representing the Marxist–Leninist theory. This is also one of the numerous criteria of the theoretical and political maturity of the Party. It must also seek, through the operation of extensive propaganda, to promote the dissemination of Marxist and Leninist literature.
>
> Securing the monopoly on Marxist and Leninist theory strengthens the Party against hostile organizations, reactionary at heart, which are hidden behind the mask of communism and communist teaching. (*Rizospastis*, 16 April 1927: 1)[4]

This statement expresses the conscious decision by the KKE to appropriate Marxism. Establishing the monopoly entailed, on the one hand, the marginalization of the KKE's political opponents on the left, both Trotskyists and reformists, by exposing them as agents of the bourgeoisie and, on the other hand, the KKE's own launch as the only true representative of Marxism in Greece. But, since Marxist and Leninist theoretical texts were mainly written in German, English and Russian, the monopoly of Marxism in Greece involved first of all control of the translations of Marxist texts. Such control could be attained through their retranslation with the purpose of establishing them as the only accurate interpretations of the originals. Retranslating works by Marx, Engels and Lenin was particularly important because, until then, rival organizations had issued most of the translations of Marx's, Engels's and Lenin's works. Petranos, who reviewed the previous translations of the *Communist Manifesto* in the KKE's theoretical journal *Komep*, wrote shortly before the publication of the KKE's 1933 translation:

> ... one of the main duties for safeguarding our ideological line would be, apart from all other things, to inspect all the translations of Marx-Engels-Lenin-Stalin's writings that we have in Greek and to reveal or correct the mistakes and the distortions which are found in them. (Petranos, 1933b: 22)

A corollary of this is that the monopoly of the Marxist theory also necessitated the development of specific strategies to dominate its interpretation. However, the KKE was in no position to prevent other political organizations or individuals from translating Marxist texts. What it was able to do was to appraise previous translations and translators and implicitly promote its own translations as the only accurate ones. To this end translation criticism aimed to demonstrate that the translations issued by other political forces were inaccurate and, more importantly, that inaccuracies were deliberate mistranslations motivated by the translators' political beliefs. The increased translation activity carried out by the KKE particularly from 1927 onwards (further facilitated by the ascent to power of a less oppressive regime after the fall of the Pangalos dictatorship) and the retranslation of the *Communist Manifesto* in 1933 have to be seen not only as a way of addressing a general need for more and better translations of Marxist works (which, as Elefantis [1976: 137f] notes, were indeed few), but also as a valuable means of ideological struggle against its opponents on the Left. The control of translation did not decide the outcome of these ideological struggles, but it played a significant role in them.

The ideological struggle between the KKE and the Trotskyist organizations involved the interpretation of Marxism mainly in relation to the prospects of revolution in Greece and of the defeat of fascism. The KKE saw the necessity for a democratic bourgeois revolution before a proletarian one, whereas the Trotskyists advocated a socialist proletarian revolution without the intermediate stage of a bourgeois intervention.

These differences impacted on the organizational models which these parties adopted and necessitated alliances with diverse social and political forces. The Trotskyists used the *Communist Manifesto* to legitimize their critique of the KKE's (and the Comintern's) political line of 'socialism through stages'. For example, Pantelis Pouliopoulos, the leader of the Trotskyist organization Spartakos, in order to support his critique of the KKE's line that the proletarian revolution would proceed in stages, urged his readers to study the *Communist Manifesto* (Pouliopoulos, 1934/1980: 120f). The KKE's fierce opposition to Trotskyism was prompted firstly by the growth of Trotskyist forces which challenged the dominance of the KKE within the left. Indeed, between 1926 and 1928 the membership of the Archive of Marxism was larger than the KKE's (Kardasis, 2002). Secondly, in the KKE's view (which was also Stalin's view) the Trotskyists represented a bourgeois, anti-working-class trend which disguised itself as Marxist.

On the other hand, the ideological struggle between the KKE and the social reformists concentrated mainly on the means of achieving social change: social reformists advocated the impossibility of a socialist revolution in Greece and posed the alternative of gradual change through state reforms. To a greater or lesser extent they referred to Marxism for their analysis of Greek society. Sideris, who edited the 1919 translation by the SEKE, had by then become an exponent of this strategy and he was criticized by the KKE as a 'social-fascist'. The term 'social-fascist' was used by Communist parties in the 1930s to describe individuals and organizations that supported social-democracy, that is, reformism. It derived from the Comintern's analysis that social-democracy was a form of fascism. Soon the KKE would adopt the term when referring to its opponents in the Left, particularly at the peak of the ideological (and political) struggle of the early 1930s. With this in mind, the following excerpt from the KKE's daily newspaper provides a glimpse of the relationship between the *Communist Manifesto* and its contemporary political situation. It refers to the new translation of the text.

> Its study is a colossal theoretical boost for everyone and it gives new strength in the struggle against capitalism and its agents the social-fascists, Trotskyists and other leaders. (*Rizospastis*, 12 March 1933: 4)[5]

In this excerpt, readers are encouraged to read the new translation with explicit objectives in mind: to use it as an asset in the struggle against the KKE's political adversaries who were viewed as sinister agents of the bourgeoisie. This contextualization of the reading of the *Communist Manifesto* smoothed the process of claiming authority over its interpretation.

The *Communist Manifesto* has a dual significance for the Left: as an educational means, explaining the principles of Marxism, and as the 'emblematic' text of communism and of all communists. The term 'emblematic texts' is used here to signify a category of texts which are representative and evocative of a whole community. They form the basis for evaluations (including who belongs to the community and who does not), interpretations, judgments and actions; they are the source of other texts and metatexts. Texts that have acquired such social significance include religious ones, such as the Bible or the Qur'ân, or political texts in the wider sense, such as the Universal Declaration of Human Rights. Translation has made these texts available to linguistically diverse groups which, in turn, have formed distinct communities, such as Christians, communists, etc. The concept foregrounds the social value of texts at a particular historical time and relates aspects of the social context to textual choices. Because the Communist Manifesto is the emblematic text of communism, the question of whose translation (and thus interpretation) of the text would be established as the most reliable one was very important, particularly in the late 1920s and mid-1930s, a period when 'ownership' of the Marxist theory was at stake. Efforts to establish the KKE's interpretation as correct are traceable in textual and pictorial elements of the covers of the publication, in textual choices in the TT and in translation criticism.

Establishing Lineage

The covers of a publication, described by Genette (1997: 1) as a type of 'paratexts', present the text and can affect its reception. Moreover, according to Harvey (2003: 68),[6] they function as sites for the representation of ideological positions. Thus, their investigation can foreground the publisher's assumptions about the text and how it should be read. The publication of the 1933 translation of the *Communist Manifesto* was institutionalized, that is, it was issued by the People's Bookshop [Λαϊκό Βιβλιοπωλείο] whose publishing activities were under the control of the KKE's Central Committee (Elefantis, 1976: 142). Consequently, the analysis of its covers (Figure 11.1) can reveal the KKE's own evaluation of the text and its suggested reading. It will be argued that both their textual and pictorial elements evoked a particular relationship between the text and the KKE which facilitated the party's claims on the monopoly of Marxist theory. The 1933 translation was published in the form of a pocket-size brochure denoting the popular orientation of the publication.

Figure 11.1 The 1933 edition of the *Communist Manifesto* by the KKE: front cover. *Source*: Αρχεία Σύγχρονης Κοινωνικής Ιστορίας (ΑΣΚΙ) Digital Archive with kind permission.

The project to establish the monopoly of Marxist theory was a venture concerning, among other things, the monopoly of all the symbols and references which had come to be associated with Marxism and this was manifested in the design of the covers. The red colour used for the title is an immediate and recognisable sign related to communism, dominates the front cover. The surnames of the authors printed at the top are followed by the title of the publication, *The Communist Manifesto* [Το Κομμουνιστικό Μανιφέστο]. Alternating between upper- and lower-case letters, the font is striking, modernist and, to my knowledge, unique to this publication. The effort made and the care shown in its design demonstrate the importance of the publication to the KKE. To the left of Marx and Engels's portraits is the inscription-tribute (cf. Genette, 1997: 118) 'for the 50 years since Marx's death', which announces the commemorative character of the publication. Honouring the anniversary was a symbolic action by which the KKE asserted its descent from Marx and promoted itself as the natural inheritor of his thought. The placing of the inscription on the front cover suggests the significance that the KKE attached to this assertion of ancestry. On the otherwise plain white back cover, there is an inscription: the publication was 'issued after the decision by the Politburo of the KKE's Central Committee for the 50 years since Marx's death'. Therefore, the publication as a whole was authorized and approved by the party which was responsible for its issue and which endorsed the interpretation of Marxism presented in the translation as the official interpretation of the party.

The suggested direct relationship between the KKE, the text and the authors makes the cover comparable to an *enthymeme*. An enthymeme is a form of syllogism with a suppressed premise, which can only be supposed if it is deducible from common experience, knowledge or belief (Voloshinov, 1987: 100f). For example, the argument, 'Socrates is a man, therefore he is mortal' contains the suppressed premise that all men are mortal (Voloshinov, 1987: 100f). However, an enthymeme is a reminder of a special kind as it also conveys social evaluation which is presupposed and which organizes behaviour and actions (Voloshinov, 1987: 100–101). Voloshinov uses the term with reference to verbal signs and for recalling already acquired knowledge and evaluative attitudes. Its use here can be extended firstly by encompassing pictorial as well as verbal elements. Secondly, the enthymeme here does not remind the reader of a generally accepted premise (as noted above, not everyone accepted that the KKE was the natural heir of the Marxist theory). Instead, it seeks to establish this by utilizing already accepted cues of social evaluation which promote the assessment of the translation (and the publication) as authoritative and the relationship between the text and the KKE as a historical continuum. The cover as an enthymeme promotes a particular evaluation of the text as naturally and therefore legitimately owned by the KKE. It is an example of how conscious struggles in the politico-ideological domain can mark discursive products such as translations.

Establishing Textual Reliability

Venuti rightly argues regarding retranslation that

> [c]laims of greater adequacy, completeness, or accuracy should be viewed critically, […], because they always depend on another category, usually an implicit basis of comparison between the foreign text

and the translation which establishes the insufficiency and therefore serves as a standard of judgment. This standard is a competing interpretation. (Venuti, 2004: 26)

In its struggle to reclaim Marxism from rival interpretations it was essential for the KKE to promote its own translations, in Nida's terminology as the only 'textually reliable' ones (Nida, 2001: 25). In the 1933 translation, German words are inserted in brackets in the TT after their Greek equivalents. These words referred to concepts for which formal equivalence was difficult to establish or did not exist in the TL. In section 1 of the TT there are five such instances of SL words in brackets.

To demonstrate the quality of its translation, the KKE claimed firstly, that this translation was textually reliable and, secondly, that this was the *only* textually reliable one. As regards the first issue, the examples below show how earlier translators dealt with challenging terms. The term *Stände* [orders][7] refers to pre-capitalist social stratification for which, due to its historical specificity, there was no formal equivalent in the TL. It was rendered as shown in Table 11.2.

The concept of class is central to Marxism; what constitutes a social class and who belongs to it has been a controversial issue as it affects the understanding of a society's organization and, consequently, the prospects for social transformation. *Stände* [orders] relates to the feudal structure of society: 'more exactly, [they are] a social stratum organized in a juridical relationship fixed by the state or tradition, not simply by economics' (Draper, 1994/2004: 210). A wrong or simplified translation of *Stände* [orders] could create misconceptions regarding the stratification of earlier societies. In 1933, in order to demonstrate that his translation was textually reliable and of superior quality to all previous ones, the translator did three things in an attempt to translate *'Stände'* [orders] accurately: he put his translation in inverted commas to signify that the meaning was something like that within the inverted commas, provided the SL term in brackets, and added an explanatory footnote with the following definition: 'Stände (singular *Stand*, French *état*). Social classes each [having] a specific legal situation (with specific privileges or with specific legal

Table 11.2 Translation of the SL term *Stände* [orders] in different TTs

1919 TT	1927 TT	1933 TT	SL term
κοινωνικές τάξεις [social classes]	κοινωνικές τάξεις [social classes]	'τάξεις' (Stände) ['classes' (Stände)]	Stände [orders]

disadvantages)'. Although this definition contextualizes the term, it also contradicts the problematized translation in the main text and asserts that *Stände* means, in fact, classes. On the basis of this definition, the translations of the term across translations do not differ significantly.

Of course, the practice of including foreign or SL words in a text was neither unique to this translation nor to texts in general. For example, Pantelis Pouliopoulos (leader of the Trotskyist organization Spartakos) occasionally used foreign words without translation in his book *Democratic or Socialist Revolution in Greece?* (Pouliopoulos, 1934/1980).[8] Kordatos in his 1927 translation included foreign words in brackets on two occasions in section 1. Therefore, the translator in 1933 did not employ an unusual or new method to highlight the perceived lack of formal equivalence in the TL. The practice underscored the translational difficulties faced by translators and concerned terms evaluated as important enough to be included in the text in the SL. The effect of this decision on the 1933 TT readers, particularly on those who could read German, was to show that the translator stayed close to the source text (ST) and the assumption was encouraged that the translation was faithful to the original. On this basis, its evaluation by the readers as a textually reliable translation was also promoted.

Another example of SL words in the TT concerns the terms *Pauper* [pauper] and *Pauperismus* [pauperism].[9] It is worth noting that Kordatos in his 1927 TT 'considered the French translation' (1927: 5), so 'pauperisme' in brackets (see example below) might refer to that translation.

Example 11.1

1919: Ο εργάτης μεταβάλλεται σε φτωχό, και η φτώχεια μεγαλώνει πειό γλήγορα ακόμα από τον πληθυσμό και τον πλούτο. (1919: 42)

The worker becomes poor and poverty increases even more quickly than the population and wealth [do].

1927 (Kordatos's non-KKE translation): Ο εργαζόμενος πέφτει στη φτώχεια και η φτωχολογιά (pauperisme) μεγαλώνει γρηγορότερα από τον πληθυσμό και τον πλούτο. (1927: 51)

The working person falls into poverty and the poor people (pauperisme) increase more than the population and the wealth.

1933: Ο εργάτης καταντά θεόφτωχος (Pauper), και η αδιάκοπη αύξηση της μαζικής φτώχειας (Pauperismus) αναπτύσσεται γληγορότερα παρά ο πληθυσμός και τα πλούτη. (1933: 40)

The worker ends up extremely poor (Pauper) and the uninterrupted growth of mass poverty (Pauperismus) develops faster than the population and wealth.

ST: Der Arbeiter wird zum Pauper, und der Pauperismus entwickelt sich noch schneller als Bevölkerung und Reichtum.[10]

The worker becomes a pauper, and pauperism develops even more quickly than population and wealth.

The word *Pauper* (Latin: poor person) had been used since the middle ages to describe people who were in receipt of welfare money by church parishes. The term *Pauperismus* is the term historically used to describe the phenomenon of mass poverty in the first half of the 19th century caused by the liberalization of the rural economy, early industrialization and rising unemployment (Conze 1989: 217–218). In this sense, the terms *Pauper* and *Pauperismus* are 'technical terms' describing a particular kind of poverty, at a certain historical time and as a result of specific social conditions, namely, the restructuring of the economy along capitalist lines. They revealed the workers' prospects in capitalism, but they had no major theoretical implications; the different translators did not diverge considerably in their interpretation of the terms. Nevertheless, their translation became, in the KKE's view, proof of the distortion of Marxism by previous translators.

Translation Criticism: The Reliability of Interpretation

For the KKE, the ideological struggle for establishing itself as the only correct interpreter of Marxism went hand-in-hand with the 'unmasking' of other current interpretations of Marxism as reactionary (as seen in the Central Committee's statement earlier). During the 1920s, the Trotskyist organization Archive of Marxism had carried out most of the translations of Marxist texts (Elefantis, 1976: 137f). In 1933, Petranos, writing for the KKE's journal *Komep* on the translations of Marxist texts, opined that if the KKE had revealed to the masses the distortions in the translations carried out by the Archive of Marxism, this would have assisted in the decline of 'Archive-fascism' because it would have exposed the organization as 'a ghastly distorter of Marxism' and an 'agent of the objectives of the bourgeoisie' (Petranos, 1933a: 14). Thus, for the KKE there was a correlation between translational choices and political beliefs.

Petranos averred that previous translations carried out by individuals associated with reformist socialism (Chatzopoulos and Sideris) or with

Trotskyism (Kordatos) (that is, precisely the type of political ideas that the Comintern viewed as hostile), falsified Marxism and that this was a conscious decision on their behalf in order to find justification for their political positions (Petranos, 1933a: 15). In contrast, it was implied that the KKE did not need to resort to manipulating Marxism because it was in possession of its correct interpretation. In his review of the previous translations of the *Communist Manifesto* into Greek, Petranos provided an inventory of translational errors that he had identified in previous translations of the text, such as the rendering of '*Pauperismus*':

> [when the translators] translate the word *Pauperisme*, which means 'extremely bad economic situation' [εξαθλίωση] they render it as 'poverty' [φτώχια] (Kordatos, Sideris) and as 'poor people' [φτωχολογιά] (Hatzopoulos). There is no bigger blindness or worse distortion of Marx's notion. (Petranos, 1933a: 17)[11]

Interestingly, as shown in Example 11.1, in the 1933 translation which was authorized by the party, *Pauperismus* was translated as 'mass poverty' [μαζική φτώχεια], which was not Petranos's suggested translation and does not differ substantially from the previous translations. This shows that the debate on translation quality was ideologically motivated.

Petranos also criticized the editor of the 1919 translation, Aristotelis Sideris:

> But Sideris, defending the betrayals of international social-democracy, tries so shamefully to excuse the crimes of imperialism in 1914 and to help the preparation of new imperialist wars and the invasion of the USSR by conning the masses with distortions in his translations. (Petranos, 1933a: 18)

It should be noted that Kordatos, in the introduction to his 1927 translation, also censured the quality of the 1919 translation which he judged to be 'neither satisfactory nor completely faithful and without errors' (Kordatos, 1927: 3–4). Nonetheless, he did not accuse the previous translator of manipulation. It is this relationship between translation quality and the translators' political trajectories introduced in KKE publications that is of interest here, because it connects translation and translating with the struggle for the appropriation of a political theory. It should also be stated that scholars such as Paloukis (2003: 214) and Elefantis (1976: 137f) agree that in this period there was a genuine case for criticizing the quality of translations of Marxist texts independently of ideological purposes as, they argue, these translations were of poor to medium quality by today's standards. Nevertheless, Paloukis rightly adds that these translations were an important achievement at the time (Paloukis, 2003: 214). Furthermore, when assessing those translations one should consider that neither professional training nor a variety of reference materials were available at the time, with obvious consequences for the translator's work.

After his departure from the party, Sideris assisted in the formation of the 'Workers Socialist Union of Greece' [Εργατική Σοσιαλιστική Ενωση Ελλάδος] and in 1932 became Finance Secretary in a reformist government headed by Prime Minister Papanastasiou (Noutsos, 1992/1994: 46–47). Branding Sideris as disreputable and a falsifier was an attack on his integrity, but also on the political forces he aligned himself with. Similarly, the condemnation of Kordatos was also a condemnation of the Trotskyists. For the KKE, both Sideris and Kordatos were manipulative translators, but their motives were far more sinister: the poor quality of their translations was part of a wider objective of the political forces they subscribed to, to distort Marxism and mislead the working class. To establish itself as the sole true representative of Marxism meant for the KKE, as regards translation, to reveal the alleged distortions and true identity of the translators and, consequently, of their organizations, and to produce, as the party saw it, its own good quality translations which channelled the correct interpretation of Marxism.

Theofylaktos Papakonstantinou, a critical reviewer from a non-party-affiliated, left-wing publication, challenged the KKE's premise of deliberate translational errors. Commenting on Petranos's review (which reproached the previous translators of the *Communist Manifesto* as manipulators), Papakonstantinou stated that 'there is nothing more natural than translational errors' and rebuked the KKE for attaching ideological importance to those errors (Papakonstantinou, 1934: 326). Papakonstantinou also accused the translator of the 1933 translation of repeating errors that the KKE had previously branded as ideologically motivated distortions (Papakonstantinou, 1934: 326) and he argued that the KKE's criticism was ideologically motivated by the party's effort to 'clear the ideological front' and by KKE members who were only concerned with furthering their careers (Papakonstantinou, 1934: 325). The debate on translation quality aimed to regulate the reception of the KKE's translation and interpretation and it reveals how a translator's political identity and trajectory can affect the reception of their translation.

Conclusion

This chapter set out to examine the role of translation in ideological struggle and investigated the manifestations of that struggle at the discursive level in the translation of the *Communist Manifesto* published in 1933. Firstly, the front cover of the publication evoked a direct relationship of lineage between the authors and the KKE and, thus, encouraged the evaluation of the translation as an authoritative one. Secondly, there is an attempt to establish the textual reliability of the KKE's translation both intratextually and intertextually. The preservation of challenging SL lexical items in the TT highlighted the translator's concern to translate accurately and to make this visible to the reader. Intertextually, these efforts were underpinned by translation criticism which censured the quality of previous translations and the motives and integrity of their translators. The intended effect was to guide the reader towards a favourable reception of the KKE's translations against translations issued by the party's rivals.

In the 1930s, the debate on translation quality masked the real debate which concerned different interpretations of Marxism and their ensuing varying propositions of political action. Translation criticism is not usually (directly) associated with politico-ideological struggles, and its use in this context reveals the breadth of means by which ideological battles are often fought and the complex situations in which translation criticism can take place. It also demonstrates the role of the translator as an agent in the battle of ideas which is rarely mentioned by historiographers and sociologists; an investigation along these lines broadens our understanding of the relationship between political institutions, ideological struggles and discursive practices.

Notes

1. More specifically, according to Williams, hegemony 'is not limited to matters of direct political control but seeks to describe a more general predominance which includes, as one of its key features, a particular way of seeing the world and human nature and relationships. It is different in this sense from the notion of 'world-view', in that the ways of seeing the world and ourselves and others are not just intellectual but political facts, expressed over a range from institutions to relationships and consciousness' (Williams, 1973/1986: 145).
2. See Chatzopoulos's personal correspondence in 'Fifty unpublished letters of K. Chatzopoulos to the socialist N. Yiannios and his wife Athina Gaitanou-Yianniou', *Nea Estia*, 1958, 63 (732), 30–31.
3. That is, a supporter of Leon Trotsky's ideas; see next section for a more detailed explanation. A letter written by the socialist Nikos Yiannios responding to an earlier letter by Kordatos expresses Yiannios' delight with Kodatos' description of himself as Trotskyist (Noutsos, 1993: 639).
4. All references to Rizospastis are from the electronic database of the National Library of Greece. All translations from Greek are mine. 'The decisions of our 3rd Party Conference; the decision on the activity of the propaganda section',

on WWW at http://www.nlg.gr/digitalnewspapers/ns/pdfwin_ftr.asp?c = 65&pageid=-1&id=40011&s=0&STEMTYPE=0&STEM_WORD_PHONETIC_IDS=&CropPDF=0.
5. 'We must disseminate the Communist Manifesto broadly', on WWW at http://www.nlg.gr/digitalnewspapers/ns/pdfwin_ftr.asp?c = 65&pageid = -1&id = 16125&s = 0&STEMTYPE = 0&STEM_WORD_PHONETIC_IDS = &CropPDF = 0. All translations from Greek are my translations.
6. The discussion on the pragmatic functions of the cover's verbo-pictorial elements (format, font, inscription, portraits) is based on Genette (1997). The present study owes its general position, that covers are sites of traceable ideological standpoints, to Harvey (2003) and shares his semiotic analysis of textual and pictorial elements of the covers.
7. The term is used in the ST to describe social gradation in pro-capitalist societies, from ancient Rome to the feudalist societies. I have used the translation *order* here, as this is the equivalent of *Stände* in the 1888 English translation of the *Communist Manifesto*.
8. See, for example, Pouliopoulos (1934/1980: 40, 67).
9. For more examples see Delistathi (in preparation).
10. Karl Marx/Friedrich Engels, *Manifest der Kommunistischen Partei*, on WWW at http://www.mlwerke.de/me/me04/me04_459.htm – T30.
11. Please note that Petranos uses 'Pauperisme' instead of the German word 'Pauperismus'. He also attributes to Kordatos the translation of the word as 'poverty' [φτώχια] whereas Kordatos rendered it as 'poor people' [φτωχολογιά].

References

Primary sources
Marx, K. and Engels, F. (1919) *The Communist Manifesto* (A. Doumas, trans., A. Sideris, ed.) [Τὸ Κομμουνιστικό Μανιφέστο, μετάφραση Α. Δούμας, επιμέλεια Α. Σίδερις, Αθήνα: Σοσιαλιστικό Εργατικό Κόμμα της Ελλάδος]. Athens: SEKE.
Marx, K. and Engels, F. (1927) *The Communist Manifesto* (G. Kordatos, trans.) [Τὸ Κομμουνιστικό Μανιφέστο, μετάφραση Γ. Κορδάτος, Αθήνα: Ακαδημαϊκόν]. Athens: Akadimaikon.
Marx, K. and Engels, F. (1933) *The Communist Manifesto*. (I. Iordanidis, trans.) [Τὸ Κομμουνιστικό Μανιφέστο, μετάφραση Ι. Ιορδανίδης, Αθήνα]. Athens: Laiko Vivliopoleio/Λαϊκό Βιβλιοπωλείο.

References from literature in English and German
Cliff, T. (1970) *Russia: A Marxist Analysis*. London: Pluto Press.
Conze, Werner (1989) "Pauperismus" in J. Ritter & Karlfried Gründer (eds) Historisches Wörterbuch der Philosophie, Band 7: P-Q, Darmstadt: Wissenschaftliche Buchgesellschaft, pp. 217–218.
Delistathi, C. (in preparation) Translation and ideological struggle; a case study of the translations of the Communist Manifesto into Greek, 1919–1951. PhD thesis, Middlesex University.

Draper, H. (1994/2004) *The Adventures of the Communist Manifesto*. Alameda: Centre for Socialist History.
Genette, G. (1997) *Paratexts: Thresholds of Interpretation*. Cambridge: Cambridge University Press.
Gramsci, A. (1971/1978) *Selections from the Prison Notebooks* (Q. Hoare and G. Nowell Smith, ed. and trans.). London: Lawrence and Wishart.
Harvey, K. (2003) 'Events' and 'horizons' – reading ideology in the 'bindings' of translations. In M. Calzada Pérez (ed.) *Apropos of Ideology* (pp. 43–69). Manchester: St Jerome.
Kang, J-H. (2008) Institutional translation. In M. Baker and G. Saldanha (eds) *Encyclopedia of Translation Studies* (pp. 141–145). London/New York: Routledge.
Koskinen, K. (2000) Institutional illusions: Translating in the EU Commission. *The Translator* 6 (1), 49–65.
Koskinen, K. (2001) How to research EU translation? *Perspectives: Studies in Translatology* 9 (4), 293–300.
Nida, E. (2001) Bible translation. In M. Baker (ed.) *Routledge Encyclopaedia of Translation Studies* (pp. 22–28). London/New York: Routledge.
Reiman, M. (1987) *The Birth of Stalinism: The USSR on the Eve of the 'Second Revolution'* (G. Saunders, trans.). Bloomington, IN: Indiana University Press.
Ritter, J. and Gründer, K. (1989) *Historisches Wörterbuch der Philosophie, Band 7: P–Q*. Darmstadt: Wissenschaftliche Buchgesellschaft.
Schäffner, C. (1997) Strategies of translating political texts. In A. Trosborg (ed.) *Text Typology and Translation* (pp. 119–143). Amsterdam/Philadelphia: John Benjamins.
Schäffner, C. (2004a) Political discourse analysis from the point of view of translation studies. *Journal of Language and Politics* 3 (1), 117–150.
Schäffner, C. (2004b) Metaphor and translation: some implications of a cognitive approach. *Journal of Pragmatics* 36 (7), 1253–1296.
Venuti, L. (2004) Retranslations: The creation of value. In K. Faull (ed.) *Translation and Culture* (pp. 25–38). Lewisburg, PA: Bucknell University Press.
Voloshinov, V. (1987) *Freudianism: A Critical Sketch*. Bloomington/Indianapolis, IN: Indiana University Press.
Williams, R. (1976/1986) *Keywords – A Vocabulary of Culture and Society*. London: Fontana Press.

References from literature in Greek

Alexatos, G. (1997) Η Εργατική Τάξη στην Ελλάδα: Από την Πρώτη Συγκρότηση στους Ταξικούς Αγώνες του Μεσοπολέμου, Αθήνα: Ρωγμή [*The Working Class in Greece: From the First Composition to the Class Struggles of the Interwar Years*. Athens: Rogmi].
Elefantis, A. (1976) Η Επαγγελία της Αδύνατης Επανάστασης – ΚΚΕ και Αστισμός στο Μεσοπόλεμο. Αθήνα: Ολκός. [*The Announcement of the Impossible Revolution – KKE and Bourgeoisie in the Inter-war Years*. Athens: Olkos].
Kardasis, V. (2002) «Η Περιπέτεια του Ελληνικού Τροτσκισμού», Ελευθεροτυπία 26/7/2002 στο. http://archive.enet.gr/online/ss3?q=%D4%F1%EF%F4%F3%EA %E9%F3%EC%FC%F2&a=&pb=0&dt1=&dt2=&r=5&p=0&id=48394416. [The adventure of Greek Trotskyism. *Eleftherotypia* 26 July 2002]. Accessed 18.9.06.

Kordatos, G. (1927) «Εισαγωγή», στο Το Κομμουνιστικό Μανιφέστο, Αθήνα: Ακαδημαϊκόν Βιβλιοπωλείο, σσ 3–16. [Introduction. *The Communist Manifesto* (pp. 3–16). Athens: Akadimaikon Vivliopoleion].
Noutsos, P. (1991) Η Σοσιαλιστική Σκέψη στην Ελλάδα από το 1875 έως το 1974, τόμος Β' (Α'), Αθήνα: Γνώση [*The Socialist Thought in Greece from 1875 to 1974* (Vol. IIA). Athens: Gnosi].
Noutsos, P. (1993) Η Σοσιαλιστική Σκέψη στην Ελλάδα από το 1875 έως το 1974, τ. Γ', Αθήνα: Γνώση [*The Socialist Thought in Greece from 1875 to 1974* (Vol. III). Athens: Gnosi].
Noutsos, P. (1992/1994) Η Σοσιαλιστική Σκέψη στην Ελλάδα από το 1875 έως το 1974, τ. Β' (Β') [*The Socialist Thought in Greece from 1875 to 1974* (Vol. IIB). Athens: Gnosi].
Paloukis, K. (2003) 'Η «Αριστερή Αντιπολίτευση» στο ΚΚΕ', χρήστου χατζηιωσήφ (επιμ.) (2003) Ιστορία της Ελλάδας του 20ου αιώνα, Β (2): 203–243, Αθήνα: Βιβλιόραμα. [The 'Left Opposition' in the KKE. In H. Hatziiosif (ed.) *History of Greece in the 20th century* B(2): 203–243. Athens: Vivliorama].
Papakonstantinou, Th. (1934) «Μαρξ-Ένγκελς, Το Κομμουνιστικό Μανιφέστο» στη Νέα Επιθεώρηση, περίοδος Β' 10(25), χωρίς εκδότη, σ.325–329. [Marx-Engels, The Communist Manifesto. *Nea Epitheorisi*, 2nd period 10 (25), 325–329].
Petranos Orf. (1933a) 'Το Κομμουνιστικό Μανιφέστο με το Φακό του Ελληνικού Οππορτουνισμού, Ι', Κομέπ 8, 15/4/1933. ΚΚΕ. σ.13–19. [The Communist Manifesto through the lens of the Greek opportunism, I. *Komep* 8, 15/4/1933. KKE, 13–19].
Petranos Orf. (1933b) 'Το Κομμουνιστικό Μανιφέστο με το Φακό του Ελληνικού Οππορτουνισμού, ΙΙΙ', Κομέπ 11, 1/6/1933. ΚΚΕ. σ.16–22. [The Communist Manifesto through the lens of the Greek opportunism, III, in *Komep* 11, 1/6/1933. KKE, 16–22].
Pouliopoulos, P. (1934/1980) Δημοκρατική ή Σοσιαλιστική Επανάσταση στην Ελλάδα; Αθήνα: Πρωτοποριακή Βιβλιοθήκη [*Democratic or Socialist Revolution in Greece?* Athens: Protoporiaki Vivliothiki].
Sideris, A. (1919) «Εισαγωγή», Το Κομμουνιστικό Μανιφέστο, Αθήνα: ΣΕΚΕ, σ.ε'-ιβ'. http://archive.enet.gr/online/ss3?q=%D4%F1%EF%F4%F3%EA%E9%F3%EC%FC%F2&a=&pb=0&dt1=&dt2=&r=5&p=0&id=48394416 [Introduction. *The Communist Manifesto* (pp. ε'-ιβ'). Athens: SEKE].

Chapter 12
'You say nothing; I will interpret': Interpreting in the Auschwitz-Birkenau Concentration Camp

M. TRYUK

Introduction

Community interpreting is the type of interpreting which occurs in the public service sphere to facilitate communication between officials and lay people: at the police station, immigration departments, refugee and social welfare centres, medical and mental health offices, schools and other institutions of this kind. This type of interpreting is bi-directional and carried out consecutively. It covers interpreting in face-to-face situations and is probably the oldest and most common type of interpreting in the world. Sometimes it is performed by volunteers, untrained bilinguals, friends or relatives, even by children.

The role of an interpreter is as vital to successful communication in community interpreting as it is in any other type of interpretation. Involvement in face-to-face interaction emphasizes the interpreter's role as both language and social mediator. Nowadays the interpreter also plays a crucial and complex role in the process of integration in society, often playing the role of a coordinator, a cultural mediator or even a censor.

The fact that interpreting takes places in different institutional contexts, involving various aspects such as empowerment, equity and access to social capital, makes it necessary also to examine interpretation from a historical perspective.

Accounts of the work of interpreters in extreme situations – critical situations which are important and difficult in their human aspect for all the main participants (i.e. the involved parties and the interpreter her/himself) – have been presented on numerous occasions in the writings on interpreting, both those of an empirical, observational and interactive character and those more analytical and theoretical in nature. These accounts include reports on interpreting at the trials of the Nazi war criminals in Nuremberg (Bowen & Bowen, 1985; Gaiba, 1998) or Eichmann's trial in Jerusalem (Morris, 1998); as well as more recent reports on the role of interpreters at the hearings conducted by the Commission of Truth and Reconciliation in South Africa (Wiegand, 2000), at the UNO peace missions in Lebanon and the countries of the former Yugoslavia (Thomas, 1997), and the humanitarian missions of NGOs in Iraq or Afghanistan (Szymczukiewicz, 2005). Equally extensive has been the treatment of interpreting by public prosecutors' offices and at all stages of court hearings and interrogations. Researchers of both empirical and theoretical aspects of court-based community interpreting have tried to reveal the ethical norms which are binding on an interpreter in her/his work (Tryuk, 2004, 2006). These norms are deontological, *sui generis*, and include: reliability, morals beyond reproach, linguistic competence and expertise, faithfulness in interpreting, impartiality and neutrality, acting in an unassuming way, awareness of social and cultural peculiarities, high resistance to stress, and observance of the rules of professional ethics. Among all the norms described, impartiality and/or neutrality are usually assigned primary importance; most studies emphasize that, above all, a court interpreter is expected to be accurate and impartial. This means the interpreters are expected to be neutral with regard to the people and discourse they interpret.

In all the studies on community interpreters, there has so far been no research into the work of the interpreters in the concentration camps and at Gestapo interrogations during World War II. Interpreters were needed in those extreme conditions, as is evidenced in the diaries, memoirs and records of the former concentration camp inmates. These might have been *ex officio* interpreters who over-zealously joined these functions with other police-like duties or, not infrequently, prisoners themselves like the camp *Schreiber/in* ('registrar') or *Läufer/in* ('messenger').

The goal of the present research is to study the records of the Auschwitz-Birkenau concentration camp former prisoners in order to trace the recollections of and about camp interpreters, their work and their attempts to ease the hardships of other prisoners, often risking their own lives in the process. It is also my intention to show that the generally accepted norms applicable to interpretation in courts, police stations, jails and holding cells were not applicable to concentration camps, and that different norms were adopted which were highly justified by the circumstances.

This work is based on the experiences and recollections of former concentration camp inmates collected in the Auschwitz-Birkenau Memorial and Museum Archives. The collection includes 134 volumes of recorded statements (3000 separate incidences), 200 volumes of recollections (1000 reports) and 76 volumes of the trial of the General Commandant of the Camp, Rudolf Höss. This material is a unique example of the ontological narratives referred to by Baker (2005). It relates the experiences of the victims of the Nazi regime and presents an account of their arrest, their life in the camps, their relationships with other prisoners and their expressions of fear of the SS men and other camp officials. An important strand which is evident to the careful reader is that the accounts point to 'the good chap' who would help one survive, who would be willing to share his meagre rations as well as any information he had obtained. The good chap could also be the interpreter. Despite the massive amount of material, it should be noted that references to interpretation are rather scant, and when they do occur they tend to be random, brief and laconic, usually consisting of dry facts. In addition, inmates often offer differing versions of the same event. For the above reasons obtaining an objective, empirical account of events is virtually impossible. This chapter focuses mainly on the profiles of the camp interpreters, the *Lagerdolmetscher*.[1]

Why Were Interpreters Needed in the Concentration Camps?

In each Nazi concentration camp the inmates represented 35–40 different national or ethnic groups, each having their own language. All the inmates lived in extreme conditions, with the German language ever present. The communication, if any, with the German *Kapo* had to be in German and if any postal services were allowed at all, all the paperwork had to be in German. In the barracks and work blocks all rules, orders and directions were delivered in German. In *Konzentrationslager* (KL) Auschwitz the use of Polish, Russian or Italian was forbidden (Gunia, 2006: 51). The General Commandant of the Camp, Rudolf Höss, issued an order on 30 July 1940 forbidding the camp staff to use any foreign language they might know, in particular forbidding their use of Polish or Czech. This order was directed to the Silesians and *Volksdeutsche* ('ethnic Germans') who performed various function in the camps. In addition, every inmate was required to memorize some basic phrases in German: their concentration camp number, their barrack number, and the texts of songs they were required to sing for the amusement of their guards. Only in a few instances were certain signs posted in both German and Polish, for example: 'Halt! Stój!'. Concentration camp German was, however, of a specific nature. Cronin defines it as follows: 'German, in this instance, is a language not of requests but of orders' (Cronin, 2006: 77). Survival in the concentration camp without some knowledge of German was practically impossible. Primo Levi notes that:

> The inmates who didn't know any German, a group including nearly all the Italians, usually died within ten or fifteen days after arrival. On the surface they died from starvation, cold, exhaustion or illness, but in fact they died from lack of information. Had they been in a position to talk with the older inmates they might have been able to manage – they would have learned how to obtain clothes and shoes, how to obtain food illegally, how to avoid overwork, how to overcome camp illnesses, and especially how to avoid contact, often fatal, with the SS men. I do not mean to suggest that they would have survived their experience, but they certainly would have survived longer and had a greater chance of getting on their feet in concentration camp life. (Levi, 2007: 113)

Further on, Levi notes that:

> The French (from Alsace or else Jewish, hence knowing either German or Yiddish) became our natural interpreters, in particular translating for us the commands given daily in German and the day's orders: 'Rise', 'Line-up', 'Get in line for bread', 'Gather in pairs, or groups of five' and other daily commands. (Levi, 2007: 117)

In essence, however, two languages were used in the camps: German and the 'unofficial' language, that is Polish or its sociolectal variety, the so-called *Lagersprache* (Gunia, 2006). Polish was used owing to the dominating number of Polish inmates. *Lagersprache* was created out of Polish, Yiddish, Silesian dialects and Hungarian. It was a camp slang – a way for the inmates to communicate among themselves in the camp, although it also happened that some German functionaries and even SS troops took some expressions from *Lagersprache*. It is noteworthy that there were two varieties of this sociolect: a different *Lagersprache* was in use in the men's camps and in the women's camps. As regards the role of Polish for inmates coming from other countries and nationalities, Levi writes that:

> Even today I can remember how our camp prison numbers were called out in Polish, which was placed above my name on the list of prisoners in one of the barracks [...] because the inmates in this barrack were mostly Polish and it was them who parcelled out the soup rations. Polish there took on the role of a kind of official language, and when someone's number was called out they were to take their place in line with their soup bowl extended in their hands so as not to lose

> their place in line. Thus in order not to be surprised it was best to move toward the soup kettle when you heard the number of the prisoner whose name was just above you on the list. (Levi, 2007: 114)

Levi also notes that another 'language' was frequently used in the camp: '... beatings were commonplace. ... they were the only language used by the [*Kapo*]. ... In this Tower of Babel, beating was the one language understood by all' (Levi, 2007: 87). In addition Shelley (1986: 363), in presenting the profile of Karl Roch, the sadistic *Unterscharführer* from the *Politische Abteilung* ('Political Section') in the Auschwitz-Birkenau camp, recalls that he had a 'saying' that *Die Peitsche ist der beste Dolmetscher, sie spricht alle Sprachen* ('the best interpreter is the whip; it speaks all languages'). The camp inmates' first contact with an interpreter occurred during their interrogation by the Gestapo. As J. Karwacki recalls:[2]

> Here I have to explain that the way of interpreting the message didn't really reflect the form in which we prisoners were addressed. I came to understand it much later, when there were no interpreters and we were addressed directly in German. We were always addressed by *Sie*. It was equally true of common talk, orders, commands, abuse or ridicule. Always *Sie* was used. It was a dismal farce. You were civilly addressed with *Sie*. You were selected to be transported to the gas chamber with *Sie*, you were abused and punished with *Sie*. You were downtrodden in what remained of your human dignity, so stubbornly defended, with *Sie*. Everything with *Sie*.
>
> I think that inherent in it was an additional perfidy of making the victim break down psychologically. Due to this *Sie*, every utterance involved a hidden sneer: sneer at a Sir in rags and in total degradation, the state to which anyone can be brought as a result of undernourishment, overwork and life in permanent fear of what other kind of anguish is to follow.
>
> Interpreters for the Gestapo did not understand the full significance of the sneer involved in this form of address and translated it as 'you'. This gave them the delusive feeling of superiority over the prisoner. (Karwacki, 1981/1982: 15)

An equally dramatic picture of the interpreter during the Gestapo interrogation is given by Mostowski as detailed in the memoirs stored in the Auschwitz-Birkenau Memorial and Museum Archives:

> I asked for an interpreter, since I wasn't confident in my knowledge of German. I only knew some German from my school lessons, and knew

that I was bound to encounter expressions which were completely foreign to me. But when I finished the session with my interpreter – of Silesian origin – I felt as though I'd gotten less than nothing from him. I was not beaten by the German officer conducting the interrogation and asking the questions; nor was I beaten by the officer taking down the protocol; but this greasy and obese interpreter went out of his way to insult and humiliate me ... (APMA-B vol. 20: 11–14)

Just like in any other multilingual social situation, interpreters were needed in the concentration camps. Auschwitz-Birkenau was no different. Upon arrival in the camp a number of inmates listed their profession as *Dolmetscher*. These declarations can be found in the registration documents of new arrivals to the death camps. In the majority of cases, persons declaring themselves to be interpreters were Jews born in Poland or Russia, often transported to the camps from France or Belgium. Very few of them survived.

Who Were the Interpreters?

It is not easy to present a profile of those chosen to act as interpreters in the concentration camps. From the memoirs stored in the Auschwitz-Birkenau Memorial and Museum Archives, it follows that they belonged to a very specific type with multilingual competencies but with German as the dominant language. In the Auschwitz-Birkenau camp three groups of persons acting as interpreters can be differentiated.

The first group consisted of the SS men from the *Politische Abteilung* ('Political Section'), often *Volksdeutsche* or Silesians fluent in Polish and employing Polish during the initial interrogation. Shelley (1986) names the following SS members: Klaus Dylewski, Gerard Lachman, who most likely joined the Foreign Legion after the war, Johann Schindler from Łódź, Joseph Stetnik, a Pole from Silesia, Karl Broch, Alois Lorenczyk, a *Volksdeutscher* from Rybnik, Joseph Pach from Silesia, as well as the *Volksdeutsche* Witold Witkowsky and Georg Woznitza. The SS guard Lachman also assumed the function of *Lagerdolmetscher* (see the statement of Pilecki, APMA-B vol. 97: 19).

A second group consisted of female prison inmates working in the *Politische Abteilung*. These were mostly Slovakian or Hungarian Jews, *Schreiberinnen* ('registrars') or *Läuferinnen*, ('messengers') such as, for example, Mala Zimetbaum, working in the following sections:

- *Registratur* ('Registry, Document section'). Among the persons working in this section was one Hella Cougno, a Greek from Thessaloniki,

who later described her arrival at the camp as follows: 'My mother's number was 38911, mine 38912 – and work began. We were assigned as interpreters'. When the transport of inmates from Greece ceased, Ms. Cougno writes that: 'My mother and I were no longer needed as interpreters. We were therefore dispatched back to Auschwitz, to the *Politische Abteilung*' (Shelley, 1986: 47).
- *Schreibstube* ('Secretariat'). Shelley worked here (Shelley, 1986: 97); she wrote: 'I also served as secretary for out-of-town Gestapo officials who came to interrogate camp prisoners. [...] Frequently, one of the girls of my commando served as interpreter for Polish, Ukrainian or Russian prisoners'.
- *Vernehmungsabteilung* ('Interrogation section')
- *Standesamt* ('Civil section')
- *Rechtsabteilung* ('Legal section')
- *Aufnahmeabteilung* ('Reception')
- *Erkennungsdienst* ('Photographic section')

The third group of interpreters that can be differentiated were those prisoners who declared that they knew German (or another language necessary in the camp). They were singled out as camp interpreters, that is *Lagerdolmetscher*. The rest of the present chapter is entirely devoted to this group of inmate interpreters.

Stanisław Skibicki (APMA-B vol. 149: 99) writes that: 'The camp commanders communicated with us using interpreters as intermediaries.' The interpreters often had to perform this function in addition to the other murderous work activities forced upon them like all the other inmates. Their interpretation work did not guarantee them any privileges in terms of how they were treated; for example, they received no additional rations. Nor did it guarantee them survival. Their knowledge of German did, however, give them access to information and enabled them to communicate better with other inmate functionaries, and in addition simply allowed them to help others.

Camp interpreters wore an arm-band on their striped prison uniforms like the other functionaries in the camp. Jerzy Poźmiński (APMA-B vol. 82: 2) recalls it as a white arm-band with black letters reading 'Dolmetscher'. Tadeusz Paczuła (APMA-B vol. 111: 155), however, writes that the 'Lagerdolmetscher wore a black arm-band'.

The role of the camp interpreter was fulfilled by the following persons:
- Władysław Baworowski
- Leonard Belewski
- Franciszek Galus/Kalus

- Józef Baltaziński/Baltasiński
- Kurt Machula
- Egbert Skowron
- Eugen/Łukasz Łukawiecki, who was the last interpreter in Auschwitz-Birkenau left until the final evacuation of the camp.

Władysław Baworowski

Władysław Baworowski (Figure 12.1) was assigned concentration camp number 863. He was born on 10 August 1910 in Germankówka and was among those transported to Auschwitz from Kraków and Tarnów on 20 June 1940; he died from exhaustion and hunger on 1 June 1942. Former Auschwitz camp inmates remember Baworowski as one of the first camp interpreters. Stanisław Skibicki writes:

> As I remember the camp interpreter was Franciszek Kalus, who arrived with the first Silesian transport (nr 1000), because Baworowski – who also should be mentioned – was then only an assistant interpreter. Kalus was really a nerd, but I have to admit that he was useful, wrote different letters and petitions for the inmates and was always willing to help. (APMA-B vol. 149: 99)

Zając Kazimierz notes:

> I was taken to what was then block no. 5, where Józef Baltaziński was designated as the barrack interpreter. He was a bad man. He

Figure 12.1 Władysław Baworowski. By courtesy of the Auschwitz-Birkenau Memorial Museum Archives in Oświęcim

was very afraid of the Germans and carried out all their orders with zeal. On more than one occasion I was abused by him. He came from the same area where I was born, from Jasień near Brzesk. [...] He spoke very good German and immediately had a better position than others in the camp. Together with Baworowski he became first interpreter, and later advanced to barrack interpreter. (APMA-B vol. 136: 192)

In the recollections of the former inmates, Władysław Baworowski usually interpreted the 'welcoming' speech given to the inmates by the Camp Commandant Rudolf Höss or his assistants. Czesław Rychlik writes:

> First there was a speech by the Commandant of the camp. His speech was translated by Baworowski. Pointing to the crematorium chimney, he explained to us that that was the only way out of the camp. Whether we lived longer or shorter depended on how hard we worked and our strict obedience to camp regulations. (APMA-B vol. 26a: 97)

Baworowski was present and interpreted a number of punishments and sentences handed out to the inmates. Zdzisław Wiesiołek recalls:

> After two months, during evening roll call, eleven of us were escorted to the front of the roll call area. In the presence of the other inmates gathered there Fritzsch [the *Lagerführer*] read out our death sentence. His sentence was translated from German by the inmate Baworowski, who explained to us that Fritzsch, in the exercise of his pardon powers, was reducing our sentence to five years of hard labour in the stone quarries and 25 lashes. (APMA-B vol. 33: p. 29)

Henryk Król writes:

> Following the escape of a prisoner, the interpreter – Baworowski – translated to us the punishment announced by the Camp Commandant: 'You will remain standing for three days and three nights – without food or water.' (APMA-B vol. 76: 199)

Władysław Baworowski was treated even worse than others by the SS men, on account of his origins and his German pronunciation using the characteristic French 'r'. As Alojzy Drzazga recalls:

> During the installation of the inmates in the barracks, the most beaten inmate was Baworowski, later a camp interpreter, who was initially beaten on every occasion, accompanied by shouts of *Graf* ['Count']. (APMA-B vol. 33: 47)

This same inmate writes about the first night in the camp, in a stuffy room without a bunk:

> The person who suffered most at the time was the *Lagerdolmetscher* Count Baworowski, against whom the SS guards had the greatest resentment. (APMA-B vol. 86: 71)

Jan Zdebik notes:

> Those persons in charge of supervising us, either SS guards or German criminal inmates, were characterized by a high degree of sadism. All their sadistic acts seemed to give them great pleasure. In particular they singled out Count Baworowski. He had a strange pronunciation and his lifestyle was also different from the other inmates. Generally speaking he was a quite fine man. He didn't survive the camp. (APMA-B vol. 139: 90)

The most dramatic recollection of Baworowski's suffering is given by Henryk Król (APMA-B vol. 76: 199), who describes how the SS made him eat faeces. This incident also shows up in a number of statements by other former inmates. The humiliation of this individual greatly moved the other inmates and gave them an indication as to what might await them at the camp.

Among others, Janusz Walter writes of Baworowski's death:

> I also recall the matter of Count Baworowski, who before the war was a person with a title and fortune and had great influence in various governing circles. During his early days at the Auschwitz Camp he carried out the function of interpreter [*Lagerdolmetscher*] and enjoyed the respect of the SS authorities. It is even said that he once ate supper with the Commandant of the camp. Over time however he sunk to a lower and lower rung in terms of his standing at the camp, sinking to a point where the German inmates made him sit up like a dog begging for food in order to obtain his bread ration. And he agreed. Baworowski was waiting for a release from the camp, and had swelled up like a Muselman [...] and then died. Shortly afterward his release papers came through. (APMA-B vol. 74: 133)

Bronisław Cynka (APMA-B vol. 75: 87–88, 95) writes:

> None of the inmates were ever certain of surviving the day, or even the hour. Some died from stupidity or lack of will power. For example Baworowski, upon being dismissed as a camp interpreter, deteriorated to such an extent that he went rooting through the garbage in search of food scraps.

Józef Baltaziński/Baltasiński

Concentration camp number 749, later released from the camp, Baltaziński/Baltasiński performed various functions, for example, block interpreter and block supervisor. He zealously carried out all the orders of the Germans. His inhumane treatment of young inmates, beating them and kicking them out in the snow, is recalled by Stanisław Hantz (APMA-B vol. 88: 163–165), Andrzej Rablin (APMA-B vol. 50: 6), Kazimierz Brzeski (APMA-B vol. 35: 38) and Kazimierz Zając (APMA-B vol. 136: 189). As Baworowski had done, Baltaziński also interpreted the 'prison welcoming ceremonies'. Włodzimierz Borkowski writes:

> These ceremonies were very disorganized and inefficient, for many in the audience didn't understand the commands. It wasn't until Józef Baltaziński approached individual columns and started giving the commands in Polish – *Baczność! W prawo – zwrot! Naprzód – marsz!* ['Attention! Right-turn! Forward march!'] – that the columns began to move in an orderly fashion. (APMA-B vol. 115: 5)

Kurt Machula

Concentration camp number 12355, born on 1 May 1913 in Katowice, transported to Auschwitz on 17 April 1941 from Katowice, Kurt Machula fulfilled the function of camp registrar and interpreter. He was released in 1944. As far as possible, he tried to help the inmates. Adam Cyra writes that:

> [...] My father, rest his soul, was also fortunate thanks to the intervention of one of his acquaintances, from the days prior to his capture, from Katowice, a man who ran an optician's shop on Świętego Jana Street, who remembered my father from times when he changed camera film for him, and was known in the camp as an 'old inmate' and worked in the canteen as Kurt Machula [...], who became a *Lagerdolmetscher*. When we were 'received' into barrack building no. 23 he wrote down the number of my father and tried to obtain work for him in *DAW – Deutsche Ausrüstungswerke Holzbüro*, and my father worked as a *Schreiber* until that memorable day on 28.10.1942. It makes one think – just how much good one can do in order to help another. (APMA-B vol. 133: 228)

Roman Nawrot notes, however:

> Unfortunately there were also some of us who helped others in the hope of securing a debt of gratitude in the future. One such man was

> the inmate Kurt Machula from Bytom, an optician by trade. Supposedly he belonged to an SS formation and in September entered Silesia together with Hitler's army. His homosexual inclinations (so it is said) landed him in the concentration camp, from which he was released in 1944. I don't know his post-war history. In any case this Machula, when helping other inmates, scrupulously recorded their personal data, counting on future rewards after the end of the war. (APMA-B vol. 80: 107–108)

The same author also writes:

> In 1942 I became ill with spotted typhus and was taken to the hospital. I managed to get out early and escaped the gas chamber. I learned about my fate from Kurt Machula – a camp interpreter. (APMA-B vol. 65: 137)

The function of an *ad hoc* interpreter was fulfilled by many inmates, but only those referred to in the present chapter wore the 'Lagerdolmestcher' arm-band, hence it seems appropriate to refer to them as 'official' interpreters.

How Were the Interpreters Recruited for the Job?

Camp interpreters were either assigned *ex officio*, or selected from the groups of prisoners. We have little hard evidence of the process for choosing camp interpreters, only individual recollections, such as the following by József Kret:

> I remember during my stay in the Auschwitz camp that in the early days of October there was an announcement during roll call for all inmates knowing Russian and German to gather in front of barrack building no. 25 following the roll call. About 100 inmates showed up and were organized into a line, after which they were led in, several at a time, to one of the rooms in the building. There they were examined in German and Russian by a committee, consisting of the *Lagerdolmetscher*, two inmates and one SS officer.

> When the exam was over the results were announced and 25 inmates, including me, were deemed to have 'passed'. We were told to remain in the camp. During this time I heard that we were to join the transport of Russian prisoners of war and act as interpreters. (APMA-B vol. 4: 431–433)

What Were the Language Combinations?

In the camp there were primarily German–Polish interpreters and a group of young multilingual Jewish girls (in the *Politische Abteilung*) who interpreted during the interrogations of Polish, Slovakian and Hungarian inmates, Russian and Ukrainian prisoners of war, and so on. Inasmuch as the predominant numbers of inmates were Polish, the primary need was for interpreters working from German into Polish. Nevertheless, a review of the recollections contained in the documentation also contains references to other language combinations, for example, from German into French. Lagus writes:

> A large number of French worked in the *Weberei*. I should point out that they were not French Jews, but *maquis*, many of whom were well-educated. Because I had a good knowledge of French (having studied in France before the war) I spoke with these French inmates. The *Unterkapo* Bogdan – I can't recall his last name – who was from Czechoslovakia noticed this and informed the *Oberkapo*. Thanks to this coincidence the *Oberkapo* assigned me to the French as an interpreter – hence I was given a relatively easy job. (APMA-B vol. 78: 171–172)

There was also a need for interpretation from German into Czech. Karel Stransky recalls:

> During our stay in barrack no 11 a transport of criminal prisoners from Czechoslovakia arrived. The group, about 200 to 300 men, had previously been interned in Prague's Pankrac prison. During their intake registration the Germans were unable to communicate with them, hence they used me as an 'interpreter', since as a long-time worker in Czech I knew their jargon. As a sign of recognition of my services the barrack supervisor gave me a piece of bread and sausage. (APMA-B vol. 84: 54)

Owing to the large number of Russian prisoners of war there was a need for interpreters from German into Russian. Jakub Jan Szegidewicz/Jakub Sehyd remembers:

> As soon as the Russian prisoners of war arrived in the camp I was sent to barrack building no 22a as a German interpreter. I carried out this task until the liquidation of the prisoner of war camp in Auschwitz. (APMA-B vol. 45: 37–42)

Service as a camp interpreter as well as knowledge of the functioning of the camp was sometimes useful following liberation:

> On May 4, 1945 the Red Army took control of the area where I hid out. I came out of the woods, and owing to my looks the Russians took me for a spy and wanted to shoot me. However, one of the Russian soldiers who had been a prisoner of war in the Auschwitz camp during the time I served as interpreter intervened to save my life. (APMA-B vol. 45: 41)

Ludwik Kończal notes:

> A month later I returned to barracks building no. 5 as a registrar and Russian interpreter, as there were then Russian prisoners of war in the barracks. This was just two weeks after they gassed the first transport of prisoners of war from barrack no 13. (APMA-B vol. 75: 76)

What Were the Duties of the Interpreters?

As indicated earlier, the interpreters' duties included assisting at the hearings, acting as camp *Schreiber* or *Läufer* and some other duties. Above all the interpreters were required to be active during the arrival at the camp of new prisoners, at times when punishment was inflicted and during the 'management' of inmates. Jan Janicki writes:

> I remember that during my first days of imprisonment at the KL Auschwitz all the prisoners were escorted onto the roll call area to watch a public hanging of an entire family: father, mother and daughter, as punishment for the escape of their son from KL Auschwitz (as explained to us by the interpreter). (APMA-B vol. 94: 162)

Nikodem Pieszczoch recalls:

> They were brought to Blockführerstube, where the interpreter, Count Baworowski, dictated to the candidates for the orchestra a letter they were to send to their families with a request for musical instruments. (APMA-B vol. 72: 14)

Orlik (APMA-B vol. 94: 179) writes:

> The head of the camp, SS-Obersturmführer Karl Fritzsch, screamed at the stuttering prisoners: 'Why are you bandits, you Polish dogs, barking and bothering us?!' The interpreter was Count Baworowski from the Poznań lands. He read out all the names on the transport list and

acquainted us with the rules of the camp. The violation of any regulation was punishable by death. No complaints or appeals were allowed to be addressed to the SS authorities.

The SS troops needed interpreters during their interrogations. Maria Karawacka remembers:

> That same day the messengers from *Schreibstube* came with the order that the following day we were to report to the *Politische Abteilung*. [...] My trance of fear was broken by the call of my number. I entered the chamber. They told me to approach the desk. The initial questions concerned my personal data. I answered them only after the questions were translated from German into Polish by a female inmate. I addressed my answers to her rather than to the camp official seated behind the desk. An SS guard stood beside me. He appeared upset that I had directed my answers to the interpreter. He hit me, and as a result I didn't hear the next question and thus didn't know how to answer. He then beat me repeatedly. I lost consciousness and awoke in the corridor, completely covered in blood, with my blood smeared clothes sticking to my body. (APMA-B vol. 46: 92)

Wanda Sawkiewicz writes:

> [...] Mandel [the head of the female camp in Birkenau] led me to one of the buildings where the functionaries were German women; both the barrack supervisor as well as four *Kapo*. The only inmate whose name was uttered, Hania Łukasiewicz, was the acting interpreter. [...] After Mandel left, the barrack supervisor called me over to her and asked me who I was, how old I was, and what I was arrested for [...] Our talk was interpreted by Hania Łukasiewicz. [...] Later I met once again with Hania Łukasiewicz in barrack no. 11 [the death barrack], where she gave me her sweater. (APMA-B vol. 88: 145)

Józef Kret notes:

> Along the entire length of the loading ramp stood a long train with boxcars. The boxcar doors were closed. It was explained to us that the boxcars contained Russian prisoners of war and that we were to translate into Russian the orders given by the SS troops. [...] An SS guard told us as interpreters to organize them into lines of 100 persons. ... The next day we went to the first floor of building no. 24, where our *Schreibstube* was – there we sat at tables and registered the prisoners of war who were gathered in lines in front of us. (APMA-B vol. 4: 431–433)

Interpreters were also engaged in other 'tasks'. Stanisław Cienciała writes:

> An alarm sounded [following the escape of a prisoner], we stood and waited until our work crew returned. *Lagerältester* Franz immediately pulled us out of line. He knew our numbers. It appears that he was the new interpreter, the one who replaced Baworowski. We stood in front of the *Lagerführer*, a man with a pockmarked face who stood in front of us with his crooked legs spread and his hands on his hips. The inmates singled out stood around him, and the columns returned to barracks. The question arose: Why didn't you escape? Quite surprising! The interpreter wanted to interpret (Idzikowski and I had earlier agreed that I would do the speaking) when I said, in German: 'I don't need an interpreter!' Knowing the mentality of the SS, I hollered out like I was in a platoon, more or less as follows: 'We live in the third barracks. We didn't know Kutscher. He lived in the Kutchers' barracks.' I tried to speak in a soldier-like voice; loud, quick and decisive. [...] Fritzsch [the *Lagerführer*] answered with a hand signal: to the left, that meant to our barracks, to the right, that meant to barrack no 11 [the death barrack]. He signalled to the left. (APMA-B vol. 87: 37)

Girls from the *Politische Abteilung* also took part in the interrogations as interpreters. Hermine (Herma) Markovits (née Hirschler) writes:

> Erber employed me frequently as an interpreter for the Polish and Czech prisoners, although he himself, being a Czech citizen, probably understood just as much of what they said as I did. On these occasions I tried to frame the answer to favour the defendants. 'Is your translation accurate?' Erber once suddenly asked me.

> 'As far as I understand Polish it is. I am Czech, not Polish', I answered. He looked at me, frowning. 'Your translation is incorrect. So shut your mouth.' (see Shelley, 1986: 120)

Further on, she writes:

> In the *Politische Abteilung* one could help only in the way I did, by making intentional typographical errors or interpretations in favour of the accused. With Brose this was not necessary. He himself changed the interrogations to the advantage of the inmates as much as possible. (Shelley, 1986: 125)

These examples show how the camp interpreters not only fulfilled the normal roles of an interpreter but also tried to divert the fate of their fellow inmates.

How Did They Perform their Duties, *What* Strategies and Techniques Did They Employ and *What* Were the Roles of Interpreters?

In light of the sparse data available, we know little about the techniques employed by the interpreters. K. Hałgas writes:

> *Lagerführer* Fritzsch spoke to us from the steps of our barracks. His words were translated word for word by Count Baworowski. (APMA-B vol. 89: 174)

None of the accounts explain precisely what is meant by the phrase 'translated word for word'. Most likely this referred to the sentence by sentence translation of military-like orders, which were short and to the point. Primo Levi (1958: 21, quoted in Cronin, 2006: 77) recalls his arrival at the camp. An inmate by the name of Flesch steps forward and announces he will be interpreting the SS guards' 'welcome' into Italian. Cronin comments on Levi's recollections:

> The Italian writer is struck by the physical toll of the interpretation task on the interpreter. Flesch is used as an instrument, a mouthpiece, but the mouth that utters the words also expresses its revulsion, the expressive and alimentary functions of the same organ combining to articulate the distress of the interpreter who becomes a hostage of his own skills. (Cronin, 2006: 77–78)

Sometimes it happened in the camp that the interpreter's help was invaluable, even to the point of saving other inmates' lives. Alfred Wilk writes:

> The day after Christmas Eve (or maybe it was another day) an inmate appeared at the gate, wishing to speak with the *Lagerführer*. The interpreter who was present, the inmate Baworowski – quickly realized that the matter was of great importance. He tried to get the inmate to explain to him why he so badly wished to see the *Lagerführer*. The inmate did not want to reveal his reasons; he even became threatening. I don't know what arguments Baworowski used, but in the end he learned the truth of the matter. The inmate was wandering around near the kitchen on Christmas Eve and heard other inmates singing

the Polish national anthem – and this is what he wanted to tell the *Lagerführer*. He was counting on a favour in return. When Baworowski learned the truth, he told the appropriate person and the denunciator was finished off during the night by Brodniewicz (the *Lagerältester*) or the *Kapo* Arno. It was a very sad incident, and if Baworowski had not intervened, many inmates would have lost their lives, not excluding such prominent camp functionaries such as Brodniewicz and the *Kapos* Arno and Diego. (APMA-B vol. 78: 1078)

Zygmunt Kędziora remembers:

> When I appeared in front of the *Lagerführer*, the interpreter present, an inmate with fair hair whose name I cannot remember, told me: 'You say nothing, and I'll interpret.' I knew a bit of German, but I understood from his offer that he wanted to help me. The interpreter, turning to Aumeier [the *Lagerführer*] said that my matter was one of the 'radio matters'. He added that one of the participants in that matter had been released from the SK [*Strafkompanie*, i.e. 'punishment corps'] several days earlier. The interpreter handled the entire conversation with great skill and presented the matter such that the *'Herr Lagerführer'* understood everything completely and considered it obvious that I should also be released from the punishment corps. (APMA-B vol. 83: 263)

Zygmunt Jankowski remembers:

> For some period of time a certain Olpiński – a camp squealer and traitor – worked in DAW. I knew him from the pre-war period. [...] In the camp he told the inmates that he was arrested because he refused to agree to serve as Prime Minister in the Nazi puppet Quisling government. In this way he earned the trust of the inmates. We later learned from Ms Dąbrowska, who was an interpreter in the *Politische Abteilung*, that he passed all his information along to the SS. [...] That's why we had to get rid of him. We gave him a beautiful English sweater with lice infected with typhus. When he became infected, no one in the camp hospital took care of him and he died. (APMA-B vol. 65: 174)

Concluding Remarks

An interpreter in the Nazi concentration camp was not simply 'a disembodied container of others' messages' (Wadensjö, 1998: 279), as we can see. The recollections of the former inmates illustrate the complex role a camp interpreter had to assume, faced with tasks which went far beyond the neutral transfer of information. The picture of the interpreter presented above also illustrates the role of ethical norms in interpretation. In court/police interpreting, the prevailing norms have been described in detail. The ideal picture of interpreters is that they do not demand any space of their own, but function as unobtrusive recorders or translation machines from one language into the other, conveying messages between speakers. A commonly held belief is that the interpreters are only conduits of information and as such have little impact on the communicative situation. Several studies have demonstrated that this ideal does not hold up when confronted with real-life interpreting interactions between human beings in various institutional settings. The interpreter's role is certainly not that of a passive conduit, but active, governed by their social and linguistic knowledge of the entire communicative situation, including not only competence in the appropriate ways of speaking, but also in the management of the intercultural interpreting event.

Particularly in extreme situations, such as interpreting during an interrogation, the role of an interpreter may be compared to that of a facilitator, an assistant to one of the parties, life-saver, informer, and so on. (Tryuk, 2004). It is through the interpreters that, often for the first time, those who until that moment have not had the opportunity to present their opinions and talk about their suffering, tortures and persecutions are finally given a voice, a rare occurrence in a concentration camp. The numerous examples quoted here show how the interpreters tried to divert the tragic lives of other inmates. Basing his observations on Levi's recollections of interpretation in the camps, Cronin describes the role of the *Lagerdolmetscher* as follows:

> The fact of Flesch [an interpreter] having a body situated in place and time not only means that his body will give expression, voluntarily or involuntarily, to his world-view. His embodied agency also means that he is immediately aware of the consequences of his interpreting activity. Not only as a speaking body is he affecting the bodies of the other deportees but as an embodied agent he is uniquely vulnerable to torture and worse should he fail to discharge his duties to the satisfaction of his superiors. (Cronin, 2006: 78)

The *Lagerdolmetscher* found himself at the heart of the crisis, in the centre of the interaction which likely changed his life as well as that of his fellow prisoners. What he needed to translate impacted on his life, as has been illustrated by the history of Władysław Baworowski as well as by other personal narratives quoted in this chapter. Camp interpreters were not, and could not, remain unbiased, neutral observers of the reality which they were required to interpret. In no other situation has an interpreter played such a deeply human role. By reflecting on their works, the complexities of interpreting and the dilemmas the interpreters may have faced can be seen in a new light.

Acknowledgments

I would like to express my deep thanks to Dr Piotr Setkiewicz, the head of the Auschwitz-Birkenau Memorial and Museum Archives in Oświęcim, for making available to me the materials kept in the Museum, that is the statements and recollections of the former inmates as well as photographs, including that of Władysław Baworowski. It would not have been possible to write this article without his invaluable and kind assistance.

Notes

1. An in-depth study of the work of all the interpreters in the Auschwitz-Birkenau concentration camp will appear in the next work of this author, currently in progress (Tryuk, in preparation).
2. All quotations from the narratives are my own translation.

References

APMA-B. Auschwitz-Birkenau Memorial Museum Archives. *Statements*. Vols 4, 8a, 9, 20, 21, 26b, 29, 33, 35, 36, 39, 45, 46, 47, 50, 61, 64, 65, 66, 67, 72, 73, 74, 75, 76, 77, 78, 79, 80, 82, 83, 84, 86, 87, 88c, 89, 89b, 91, 94, 96, 97, 100, 101, 111, 114, 115, 122, 124.
APMA-B. Auschwitz-Birkenau Memorial Museum Archives. *Recollections*. Vols 131, 133, 136, 139, 145, 148, 149, 154, 167.
APMA-B. Auschwitz-Birkenau Memorial Museum Archives. *The Trial Record of Rudolf Höss*.
Baker, M. (2005) Narratives to and of translation. *Skase Journal of Translation and Interpretation* 1 (1), 4–13.
Bowen, D. and Bowen, M. (1985) The Nuremberg Trials (Communication through Translation). *Meta* 30 (1), 74–77.
Cronin, M. (2006) *Translation and Identity*. London/New York: Routledge.
Gaiba, F. (1998) *The Origins of Simultaneous Interpretation: The Nuremberg Trial*. Ottawa: University of Ottawa Press.
Gunia, A. (2006) Język obozów koncentracyjnych [The language of the concentration camps]. *Języki Specjalistyczne* 6, 50–60.
Karwacki, J. (1981/1982) *Życie wśród śmierci* [*Life among Death*]. Warszawa: Serwis multimedialny Sp. z o.o.
Levi, P. (2007) *Pogrążeni i ocaleni* [*The Drowned and the Saved*] (S. Kasprzysiak, trans.). Kraków: Wyd. Literackie.
Morris, R. (1998) Justice in Jerusalem – interpreting in Israeli legal proceedings. *Meta* 43 (1), 110–118.

Shelley, L. (1986) *Secretaries of Death. Accounts by Former Prisoners who Worked in the Gestapo of Auschwitz*. New York: Shengold Publishers.
Szymczukiewicz, M. (2005) L'interprétation communautaire dans l'armée. Etude de cas: missions polonaises de paix. Unpublished MA thesis, University of Warsaw.
Thomas, R. (1997) United Nations Military Observer Interpreting in a community setting. In S.E. Carr, R. Roberts, A. Dufour and D. Steyn (eds) *The Critical Link: Interpreters in the Community* (pp. 249–257). Amsterdam/Philadelphia: John Benjamins.
Tryuk, M. (2004) *L'interprétation communautaire. Des normes et des rôles dans l'interprétation*. Warszawa: Wyd. TEPIS.
Tryuk, M. (2006) *Przekład ustny środowiskowy* [*Community Interpreting*]. Warszawa: PWN.
Tryuk, M. (in preparation) *Interpreters in Nazi Concentration Camp. Auschwitz–Birkenau–Dachau–Buchenwald*.
Wadensjö, C. (1998) *Interpreting as Interaction*. London/New York: Longman.
Wiegand, C. (2000) Role of the interpreter in the healing of a nation: an emotional view. In S.E. Carr, R. Roberts, A. Dufour and D. Steyn (eds) *The Critical Link 2: Interpreters in the Community* (pp. 207–218). Amsterdam/Philadelphia: John Benjamins.

Part 3
Socio-cultural Gates and Gate-keeping

Chapter 13
Dialectics of Opposition and Construction: Translation in the Basque Country[1]

I. URIBARRI ZENEKORTA

Introduction

The word for a Basque person in Basque is *euskaldun*, 'the person who speaks Basque', which suggests that language is strongly connected to the identity of the Basques. Indeed, the link between the communicative/instrumental and the ideological functions of the Basque language is perceived to be a very strong one. The goal of this chapter is to describe the reality and functions of translation into/from Basque. More specifically, the chapter deals with the changing context of the Basque language and culture and the role of translation in their evolution. Translation into/from Basque has been and is still located in a context of conflicting powers, where social identities find themselves in perpetual flux and reconstruction. Translation into Basque has fulfilled an oppositional role favouring diversity, as well as a constructive role, working towards homogeneity.

Translation into/from Basque involves on the one hand all the problems related to less diffused languages, with the ensuing problems of productive weaknesses and diglossia. On the other hand, translation takes place in a bilingual (or even multilingual) social context, in which Basque has only recently acquired an official status. Basque has always had a small number of speakers and a weak tradition of written literature. The language almost reached the point of no return at the end of the 19th century, due to emigration, lack of political support and decreasing cultural prestige. A period of recovery followed in the first decades of the 20th century, with an increase of prestige and more widespread use. The situation rapidly deteriorated after the Spanish Civil War (1936–1939) and, as a consequence, there was almost no printed literature in Basque in the 1940s. In 1949–1950 books started to be published in Basque in the Spanish Basque Country yet the output remained meagre for some more years (Torrealdai, 1979: 572–574). From about 1960, and especially since Spain's return to democratic rule in 1975, the recovery has been steady.

In the last 30 years there has been an intense normalization effort in defining a unified standard form of Basque and in modernizing the language, as well as in extending its use from everyday affairs to high culture and science. Yet Basque remains a less spoken language in a diglossic situation, with all the limitations this entails. Basque is currently spoken by some 800,000 people divided in three administrative structures: two autonomous communities within Spain (the Basque Country and Navarre) and the three provinces (Labourd, Basse Navarre and Soule) located within the French Pyrénées Atlantiques department.[2]

Historic Evolution

The Basque Country has never had a unified political identity in modern times, and this political fragmentation is reflected in linguistic fragmentation: several dialects and sub-dialects are spoken, and there was no standard Basque until well into the 20th century. For centuries, Basques developed an interesting oral literature in their mother tongue, but the same was not the case for written literature. The language of education and high culture was either Spanish or French. As a consequence, fewer than 200 books were written in Basque from the early 16th century until 1879; half of these were translations.

Translation has had a variable presence at different moments of the evolution of Basque culture. From the first Basque publication (Etxepare's inaugural book written in 1545 bears the fitting title *Linguae vasconum primitiae* [*First Fruits of Basque Language*]) until the end of the 17th century, translation constituted 16.6% of the overall literary production; from 1700 to 1875, the presence of translation increased to 35.2%, only to drop to a plateau of 13.3% between 1876 and 1935. After the Spanish Civil War, Basque literature started to recover, especially from the 1960s onwards, and translation constituted 22.3% of the total literary output. With the end of the Franco regime, Basque literature and translation started to thrive, translation reaching a peak of 43.6% of the overall book production in 1993. Translation continued to grow afterwards, but its percentage has been reduced to 30.8% as a result of the growing numbers in original Basque production. If we compare these data with norms observed in other countries (see Venuti, 1995 for an analysis of the 'Anglo-American' context and Casanova, 1999 for an international/comparative study), it is clear that Basque literature is far more open to imports in comparison with more dominant cultures; yet the data related to Basque do not differ considerably from those of Italy, Greece or Sweden and are similar in general to other less diffused languages (Torrealdai, 1997, 2005).

What may historically distinguish the Basque system as unique, however, may be the fact that many publications are firmly rooted in contexts where converging and oppositional forces are intertwined. For example, early Basque works were published in the French Basque Country in the 16th century, in the context of religious competition between Catholicism and Protestantism.[3] Jeanne d'Albret, Queen of French Navarre and mother of Henri IV, later king of France, entrusted the translation into Basque of the *New Testament* and some Calvinist writings to Joannes Leizarraga, and they were published in 1571. Leizarraga had no linguistic models for his translation task and had to work *ex nihilo*. He took one of the northern dialects as the basis and enriched it with morphological and lexical forms of other northern dialects. This could be characterized as the first step towards a standard Basque, but the effort was not consequential, because Protestantism failed to prevail in the French Basque Country and most copies of the translations disappeared. Thus, lacking any political support, these initial efforts to create a literary tradition were not successful, which explains the small number of publications in Basque appearing erratically in the following decades.

During the 17th and 18th centuries it was mostly religious Catholic works that were written in Basque, such as the classic *Gero* (*Later*) by Pedro Axular in 1643. Several books were also translated into Basque, but the numbers were small and the language remained fragmented. No unified standard form of Basque language was available and this may explain the occurrence of interesting interdialectal translations, that is, translations of the same text into two (or more) different Basque dialects. The few translations available were characterized by their formal, if not frozen, style (House, 1997: 41–42) and the very frequent use of Latinisms; such stylistic idiosyncrasies can be attributed to the religious character of the texts and the lack of expertise of the translators.

During the 18th century there was a clear shift of the centre of literary production from the French to the Spanish Basque Country. By the 18th century, Basque had been weakened considerably in France, especially as a result of strong centralist policies adopted by the post-revolutionary governments. South of the Pyrenees the Enlightenment had some impact: the Royal Basque Society and the Royal Seminary of Bergara were founded in 1765 and acted as liberal and progressive institutions. In this context a new literary genre had some success: moral fables. Félix María Samaniego, inspired by Aesop and La Fontaine, wrote *Fábulas morales* in Spanish. Following the new enlightened spirit, the educated middle classes used literature as a pedagogical tool to debate moral issues independently from religious precepts.

The use of Basque remained limited. The Basque elites mostly used Spanish, and popular culture in Basque was transmitted orally. The beginning of the 19th century was the time of the so-called 'apologists' like Larramendi; the apologists were individuals who extolled Basque for its ancient origin and purity. They wrote in favour of the Basque language and stated, for example, that Basque was the prebabelic language of paradise. They also defended the special legal status of the Basque Provinces within Spain, but they did it mainly in Spanish. Some authors did use Basque, however. Juan Antonio Mogel wrote a famous dialogue in Basque, *Peru Abarka* (1802), as well as several fables and a translation of the *Pensées* ('Thoughts') by Pascal. Moreover, his niece Bizenta Mogel translated a collection of fables by Aesop from Latin into Basque, *Ipui onac* ('Good tales') (1804). Other compilations of fables were also published, one in the Biscayan dialect, and La Fontaine was translated into Basque in France. These were important milestones in the development of Basque identity through cultural production, but the most influential translation effort of the 19th century was made under the leadership of the French Prince Bonaparte. He developed an interest in the Basque language, particularly in the different dialects of Basque. He asked some representative writers to translate parts of the Bible into their dialects. Jean Pierre Duvoisin, for example, translated the complete Bible, *Bible Saindua edo Testament Zahar eta Berria* (*The Holy Bible, or the Old and New Testaments*). These translations provided the basis for drawing up a map of the Basque dialects.

It must be noted that during the 19th century the Basque Country was involved in two civil wars, the Carlist Wars.[4] The chief outcome of the wars was the abolition, after the second Carlist war (1873–1876), of the *foruak*, which were the special legislative privileges that had constituted the basis for Basque self-rule. The shock and the sense of loss were enormous and triggered a drive for the promotion of Basque literature; such development can also be seen against the backdrop of the Romantic movement that was spreading in Europe, following the shock waves of the so-called 'effet Herder' (Casanova, 1999: 113–118).

Other significant oppositional forces were also at play in the 19th century. An oppositional discourse supporting Basque cultural and political interests soon developed as a reaction to the homogenizing discourse which sought to create a modern, centralized Spanish state by marginalizing and excluding anything that was peripheral and heterogeneous. A good example is the work of Sabino Arana, the main proponent of modern Basque nationalism, who imagined and articulated an alternative political discourse: the old and pure lineage of the Basques had to be recovered and brought together in a new Basque state unifying all seven Spanish and French provinces. His agenda was based on Romantic, antimodern ideas, which were in vogue in other parts of Europe too. Racial arguments were used in the beginning, but were later replaced by linguistic ones. The Basque language was an obvious pillar in the building process of the new national identity. The recovery of the language was based on purist ideas, which tried to keep the language clear from Latin and Greek influences and to invent new Basque words by resorting to its etymological pool. Literary production, of course, played an important counter-discursive role in this context of competing narratives. Since Basque prose fiction was almost non-existent, turning to translation proved to be a productive move – a trend that can perhaps be considered as a norm in cases of less widespread languages and especially systems which are in their 'formative stages'.[5]

Karmelo Etxegarai (1865–1925) took Flemish culture as a model for the revival of Basque culture, and translated Hendrik Conscience's *De Maegd van Vlaenderen* ('The Virgin of Flanders') (1858) into Basque, using the French version as the source text. Etxegarai's translation swerved away considerably from the French. Etxegarai translated this piece in 1891 with the aim of defining a new national discourse. The original story consists of a premonition in which Flemish people sleep, unaware of the looming risk: the coming of the oppressors and, with them, destruction. Then the people wake up and sing patriotic songs, and the story ends with a prediction of a glorious future for Flanders. Etxegarai substituted all Flemish references (the names, the patriotic songs) with references to the Basque Country; the title was also changed to *Euskal-Erria* ('Basque Country'). As a result, the translator maintained the pragmatic and ideological function of the Flemish source text in a new *national* context (Verbeke, 2006).

From the end of 19th century, translation work increased in parallel with original production in Basque. The first decades of the 20th century just before the Spanish Civil War were very productive in cultural terms. Prose fiction took its first steps in the works of Txomin Agirre, who foregrounded a bucolic reality full of traditional values, obscuring the rapid industrialization that the Basque Country was experiencing at the time. During these years, prose translations had different functions. Literature for children and young adults, for example, was vital for the creation and maintenance of linguistic and cultural traditions; it served both as a literacy boosting device and as a way of introducing a nation-building agenda through domesticating translations. Important translation milestones include compilations of the tales by the Grimm brothers and other collections of tales. Other translations constituted vehicles of importing modern and prestigious European prose into the young literary field: prime examples include an anthology of short stories by Oscar Wilde (translated in 1927) and Dickens' *A Christmas Carol* (translated in 1931).

Poetry, however, was more open to contemporary trends and ideas. In 1927 Joseba Arregi published a collection of poems by Heine, *Heine'ren olerkiak* ('Poems by Heine'). This rather comprehensive compilation constituted a representative sample of Heine as the earlier Romantic, but also the (later) sharp thinker. Plays were also very important at that time as a vehicle for creating a self-image of urban Basque speakers. Original production was high, and many literature prizes contests were instituted. As for translations, classics entered the Basque dramatic field: *Macbeth* was translated in 1926, *Antigone* by Sophocles in 1933, and *Wilhelm Tell* by Schiller in 1934–1935. *Antigone* could be seen as an expression of the difficulties encountered by many Basques to reconcile Catholicism with a nationalistic political stance that distinguished them from their Catholic 'neighbours' (a 'transfigured' opposition between Antigone's values and Creon's code of behaviour). *Wilhelm Tell* was clearly selected to foreground the thematics of the birth of a nation after suffering foreign oppression. It is noteworthy that in all these translations of drama, the dominant norm in terms of translation strategy was one of cultural adaptation: the dramatic setting was invariably brought closer to the Basque-speaking audience.

A similar target orientation can be observed in views voiced about translation and instances of (self-)censorship. A prime example of this practice is Nikolas Ormaetxea (1888–1961), known as 'Orixe', who was probably the most influential writer of this period. Ormaetxea was a prolific translator of literary and religious books. He won a translation prize in Pamplona in 1928 for a translation of the ninth chapter of *El Quijote*. Also in 1928 he wrote an article in favour of translation and against what he called 'literary xenophobia'. In 1929, he published the translation of the Spanish classic *El lazarillo de Tormes* (*Tormes'ko itsu-mutilla*) ('The Life of Lazarillo de Tormes'), in a bilingual edition. In this piece of work, he modified anything erotically charged or 'immoral', anything that went against his Catholic beliefs. The ending, too, was totally transformed into an edifying happy end. Since it was a bilingual text, he had no choice but to change the original text too, so that it would tally with his translation. Ormaetxea produced another interesting translation in 1930: *Mireio*, written by the epic national Provencal poet Frédéric Mistral. This translation must have motivated Ormaetxea to 'refract' Mistral's work the following year in an original epic poem of his own with Basque thematics; the poem was entitled *Euskaldunak* ('The Basques') (1931). After surviving the Civil War,[6] he avoided politically charged writings and turned to translations of religious texts.

In the years after the Spanish Civil War, the importation of foreign culture through translation was accepted by Basque nationalists, but the negative effects of the 'impure' act of translation, in both political and religious senses, were countered by resorting to purist linguistic choices. The new Basque identity created with the aid of translations was not an act of novelty, but a re-creation of what the original core of that identity was perceived to be. Even the Basque word for translation, 'itzuli', signals 're-turning' and 'conversion'. Translation, therefore, was metaphorically construed as an (ideological) act of returning to the blemished original and repairing it. Thus translation was used as a vehicle of new patriotic narratives and the recurrent translation strategy was cultural adaptation. In many cases, place names, personal names, even musical instruments were replaced by local references: for example, while translating Grimm's Fairy Tales, *Bremer Stadtsmusikanten* ('The City Musicians of Bremen') is replaced by *Durango'ko erri-abeslariak* ('The folk singers from Durango'), and *Hänsel und Gretel* is rendered as *Yulitxo eta Libetxo*, using two names with a characteristic Basque diminutive ending. On a paratextual level, drawings accompanying the text show Basque farmers in traditional outfits, and the seven dwarves wear Basque berets. More intrusive changes take place on the plane of the universe of discourse of each work: kings and queens become lords and ladies, while kingdoms are 'edited out' in order to avoid possible connections with Spain. These translations create narratives for a nation without a state and without its own crown.

Although the first decades of the 20th century were a golden period in Basque literature, no lasting reward remained after the Civil War. The cultural consequences of the war were disastrous: some cultural agents were executed; many others had to go into exile; and the Francoist repression was especially harsh with the 'traitor provinces', Gipuzkoa and Bizkaia, as they were named by officials of the regime following the Francoist decree 247 (enacted on the 23 June 1937 and derogated in 1976). All areas of culture, administration and social life fell under the shadow of the censorship imposed by Franco's regime, which wanted a 'unified, big and free' Spain (*Una, grande y libre*). After the Civil War, Basque language and culture were excluded from public life and actively banned in the educational system. Cultural life in Basque only started to recover slowly in the 1950s and 1960s, first in contexts of exiled communities and later within the remit of the Basque Country, as the regime underwent a limited liberalization process. Some translators continued to work in exile in Latin America along the pre-war lines. This was the time when Jokin Zaitegi and other well-known intellectuals translated Greek and Latin literature: Homer, Sophocles, Euripides, Aeschylus, Plato, Virgil, Ovid, Horace, Pliny and Cicero. They also translated other classics like Dante's *Divine Comedy* and most of Shakespeare's plays. The translators who remained in the Basque Country, mostly religious men, also worked with the classics. This trend dominated the scene up to 1960, with a few exceptions. Those translators working in exile and also later in the Basque Country wanted to enrich the language and raise its cultural level through these translations. These sorts of translations were also more readily acceptable to the censors, because the symbolic capital attached to them convinced them of their edifying/non-threatening role. The overall linguistic strategy for these translations was still influenced by purist views; yet gradual change was already to be seen, with the introduction of more flexible attitudes towards lexical imports and new syntactic structures.

Meanwhile, the Basque Country regained its privileged position as an industrial powerhouse, which brought massive immigration of non-Basque speakers and changed the linguistic situation in the Basque Country. More importantly, new cultural and philosophical trends were introduced, mainly through France. As a consequence, cultural and political activism gained strength in the 1960s. Thus the first steps towards a standard Basque were taken. At the same time, Marxist-minded young nationalists organized themselves against the regime, moving away from the mere cultural activism that older generations favoured and opting for a more proactive political activism, including actions of armed resistance. A new generation of young writers and translators who had grown up after the war was much more open to new subjects and new genres; they wanted to reflect contemporary realities using contemporary means. It was the generation that sought to define themselves both against the realities of Francoist oppression and censorship and against the establishment of an older and still influential generation in their own socio-political constituency. The ensuing generation clash saw the 1960s generation prevail. This was the decade when innovative literature and other art forms emerged, when a new translation reality took shape, a period of great productivity for Basque language and culture.

The new generation used translation extensively to import new literary forms and new ideas, a trend that continued into the 1970s, and which was strengthened by the fact that original production remained meagre.

Translation filled the void, playing a decisive role in the effort to expand the Basque literary repertoire. The new generation broke with some of the basic approaches of the past, such as religiosity, Greco–Latin classicism and the tendency to introduce Basque neologisms. The linguistic strategy changed radically from purism towards a more functional outlook. Translation (*itzulpena*) was no longer nostalgic for a lost origin; it was reconciled with the innovative aspect of culture. The new goal was to connect Basque culture with modern European culture, to broaden the range of imported literature, and also to reach beyond literature and to create adequate translations of scientific and 'pragmatic' texts.[7]

Translations had a clear oppositional, even subversive, role at that time in two senses. They helped to resist the cultural homogenization practised by the Spanish establishment, according to which Spain was a culturally and linguistically homogenous country, where other peripheral realities were branded as backward, marginal realities, if not cultural relics. At the same time, translation served to construct a new modern Basque nationalism, in conflict with old forms of conservative nationalism. A prime example of this state of affairs is the poetry and prose translations by Paris-born Jon Mirande; these translations were aimed at fighting the traditional connection between Basque nationalism and religion (most notably by translating Nietzsche, among other authors). Mirande's frank way of dealing with sexuality was also highly innovative. In a similar vein, Antonio Maria Labaien made a point of using his translations of Brecht, Frisch and Dürrenmatt in order to modernize Basque theatre. His efforts attracted criticism from the older generation, for whom the new subjects and forms were alien and 'inappropriate'. In the early 1970s, some translations of Marx, Engels and other socialist authors were produced, in the context of the construction of a progressive Basque nationalism. The younger generation born just after the Civil War was disenchanted with the old Christian and conservative Basque nationalism that was basically backward-looking, nostalgic for the old and pure Basque Country. The younger writers, musicians and cultural activists were open to new influences and they were forward-looking in political and aesthetic terms; they wanted to create a new Basque Country.[8] These texts were already available in Spanish, but some were banned in Basque translation. The censors were well aware of the symbolic value of language.

The Contemporary Situation

With the arrival of democracy in Spain in 1975, a far-reaching change took place in the Basque Country. Devolution started in 1979, and the hegemony of Basque nationalism in regional politics brought official status to the Basque language in 1982. This had multiple consequences for translation. Regional and local authorities were almost immediately affected, since they had to produce all official documents in both Basque and Spanish. This triggered an enormous translation activity of legal and administrative documents, mostly in the Spanish-to-Basque direction. Basque was also introduced in the education system on a massive scale, and reached higher education a few years later; such developments triggered a great amount of translations. Publishing houses working mainly in Basque flourished at that time, and many of them had a section dedicated to translations. The use of Basque also reached the papers, with a Basque-only national newspaper and many local ones; some radio stations worked also partially or totally in Basque. A Basque-only TV station was even created and it consistently geared much of its (translation) effort towards the educational needs of children.

However, the academic response to all this translation activity was very slow. For some years since 1979, only a private translation school ('Martuteneko Itzultzaile Eskola') existed, and it was only in September 2000 that a four-year degree in Translation Studies was launched at the University of the Basque Country. The work of some other institutions was also essential. Euskaltzaindia, the Academy of Basque Language, increased the visibility of language work by launching a normative grammar and dictionary, the first of their kind for standard Basque. In addition, the Basque Writers' Association was created (EIE, 'Euskal Idazleen Elkartea'). Some 300 writers publish in Basque these days, and around 1500 titles are published each year in the Basque language, with two-thirds being new titles and the other third translations. The Association of Translators, Revisers and Interpreters of Basque Language (EIZIE) was also created. As a result of all of these developments, the visibility of Basque increased dramatically.

Yet many problems remain. Some are *normal* consequences of the diglossic situation of a not fully standardized language spoken by fewer than a million people. Other problems have to do with legal constraints which block the use of the language in some areas (the judicial system, for example) or with the conflictive political situation: *Egunkaria*, the only daily paper written in Basque, was closed after allegations of connivance with ETA (several years have passed since the initial allegations and no trial has been heard yet).

It must be said that the symbolic value of language remains all-important. Basque is the native language for part of the population and they demand the right to use it in as many domains as possible. This right is limited by the sociolinguistic reality of the Basque Country, where most people are monolingual Spanish or French speakers. The long-term changes needed to meet this demand and to reach a situation of real bilingualism, including positive discrimination in favour of the weaker language, are considered to be unfair by the part of the population not interested in Basque and willing to use Spanish.

Let us now examine the link between political empowerment and translation activity into Basque. The political majority agenda of recovering the language in the Basque Country is the force behind much of the translation activity nowadays, under the direct or indirect patronage of the regional government. Some translation programmes were also created or backed by the regional government and other institutions in order to translate world literature and thought into Basque.

Literatura unibertsala ('World literature') constitutes the single major project which has sought to translate the classics of world literature into Basque. It started in 1989 with the sponsorship of the culture department of the regional government and is managed by EIZIE. The translations are assigned every year through an anonymous contest among a closed list of works selected by a committee formed by members of the Association and the editors. The original goal was to reach 100 titles in 10 years but the collection continued and is now about to reach 150. Similar projects have been undertaken by non-profit foundations supported by both the public and the private sector; *Pentsamenduaren klasikoak* ('Classical works of philosophy') was launched in 1991 and was sponsored by a major Basque financial institution and local universities. The goal of this project was to translate 100 classic humanities texts, covering works in the areas of philosophy, economy, psychology, linguistics, anthropology and history by well-known authors, ranging from Plato to Foucault.

These translations provide models of standard Basque and models of quality translations. They establish a link between Basque and world literatures and thought. The aim is the reconstruction of the Basque language as a modern communicative and creative tool. This is possible thanks to these new aesthetic models, new genres and new authors, all of which help to further develop literature and argumentative texts in Basque. The central and long-term goal of this activity, then, is to bring new life to the language by establishing a basic corpus that will enable it to thrive in contemporary society.

It must also be noted that translations have played a central role in the long journey from dialectal fragmentation towards a standard form of Basque. This process has not been a smooth one, since the central and widely spoken dialect was taken as a basis, which triggered a negative reaction from other peripheral dialects. While translation has had a strong constructive role in the formation of a badly needed standard form of the language, it has also had a negative role, since it has sidelined the use of some dialects. In the initial stages of the process many speakers were led to feel that their spoken dialect was *bad* Basque and that everyone had to use standard Basque in any situation. Now the situation has stabilized, and a revival of different dialects can be observed; the standard variety and peripheral dialects are both used, albeit in different situations.

Translation work related to Basque is carried out in a bilingual and diglossic environment. As a consequence, interferences from the much more diffused languages (Spanish and French) into Basque are inevitable. This is an issue which has been closely monitored in discussions about the standardization process of Basque. A second interesting consequence of the bilingual and diglossic situation is that many authors are, at the same time, translators, mostly from Spanish or related languages. These translations are routinely used to introduce new authors/models into Basque literature. For example, the very well-known authors Gabriel Aresti, Jon Juaristi and Joseba Sarrionandia collected their translations of T.S. Eliot in one book (*Eliot euskaraz* ['Eliot in Basque'], 1983). Many other writers currently continue this tradition. Apart from translating into Basque, they also write their own original works in Basque and then self-translate their work into Spanish/French, a phenomenon that remains under-researched. This practice was negligible until 1980. The few translations from Basque before the end of the Franco regime were self-translations almost exclusively into Spanish. Since the early 1980s, many writers in Basque adopted this technique, as it constituted the easiest and cheapest way to spread their work into the Spanish market. A secondary motivation, of course, may have been the need to improve communication between the linguistic communities in the Basque Country: Spanish speakers in the Basque Country would also have access to the same material. Self-translation has also become a creative tool, since most self-translations into Spanish are 'rewriting exercises' (Lefevere, 1992: 110), second creative moments, as many Basque writers who translate their own work have acknowledged.[9]

Translations from Basque quickly secured public sponsorship (some literary prizes included extra funds for the specific purpose of a translation). The driving force of those translations, therefore, is often not the needs of the target culture market, but forms of patronage in the source culture (Lefevere, 1992: 15), which seek to make the language and the culture more visible, and to gain some cultural prestige in the process, nationally or internationally (Casanova, 1999: 374). It is also important to consider that the target audience of most translations from Basque is the Spanish-speaking part of the same community and thus planned, 'strategic' translation activity of this sort can help boost the cohesion of this community. This would contradict or at least enrich Toury's (1995) standard methodology of observing translation as a 'target culture' phenomenon, especially in cases such as these where financial gain or functionality is complemented (if not superseded) by cultural and ideological arguments.

Concerning translations from Basque into languages other than Spanish/French, the Spanish version rather than the Basque original serves as the source text. The status of Basque as a minority language may also mean a shortage of translators who work with Basque in 'less conventional' combinations. Some years ago, an attempt was made to sponsor direct translations from Basque, but the project was hastily planned, proved to be unproductive and was discontinued. However, there have been some direct translations from Basque into German, with the aid of associations like Euskalema. Currently, such exceptions do not constitute a paradigm shift; indirect translations will continue to be the norm, but at least direct translation projects do redress the balance somehow and possibly serve as models for future work.

The use of pivot languages and its consequences are now the object of study (Manterola, 2007). For example, *Behi euskaldun baten memoriak* ('Memories of a Basque cow') by Bernardo Atxaga, the best known writer in Basque, was transformed into *Memorias de una vaca* ('Memories of a cow') in its Spanish translation: since the majority of the 12 translations available in other languages used Spanish as a pivot language, almost none of them refer to the Basqueness of the cow in the title.[10] Indeed, indirect translation in many cases results in (sometimes significant) divergence from the Basque source text. For example, the source language and culture are completely opaque in *Memories of a Cow* in the English and German translations.

Similarly ambivalent realities can be found in the translation of children's literature. In a short period of time, the education system changed from zero Basque presence to the increasing prominence of the Basque language in various domains. From the early 1980s, the school system required many Basque texts, but the limited local production could not meet the demand for children's and young adults' literature. This made it necessary to import translated texts. Translation, therefore, acquired a central role in this weak and young literary (sub)system. Only 25 out of the 256 books for adults published in 2000 were translations. By contrast, in the field of children's and young adults' literature, the ratio was 204 translations out of the 371 titles. According to a study carried out by Lopez

Gaseni (2000), children's literature in the 1980s and 1990s covered about 72% of all the literature translated into Basque.

In the beginning many of these translations were produced by educators with little experience in translation: translations were done quickly; quality control was non-existent; and aiming for acceptability was the norm. Most translations were also made indirectly, using Spanish as a pivot language. As a result, the common translation techniques employed were omissions and simplifications in structure and rhetorical organization. The number of translations, and the poor quality of some of them, gave rise to negative comments from local literary critics who pointed to the risk of excessive exocentrism, of becoming too dependent on cultural imports. At the same time, the positive influence of those translations cannot be denied. Translation was the channel of importing formal innovations, diversity, new topics and richer narratives, and helped consolidate new forms in original writing too. For example, through a more prominent presence of translations, Basque children's literature is more representative of international literary trends than the area of literature for adults (Lopez Gaseni, 2002).

In light of the above, it can be said that the Basque literary (sub)system is not homogeneous at all. It sometimes functions as a weak and *dependent* subsystem of the Spanish literary system, with subsystems within it being open to massive translation imports. Yet the same literary context can be seen from the angle of a newly formed system that is 'under construction', a state of affairs that encourages creativity and independent development.

Concluding Remarks

Translation in the Basque Country is a rich and rapidly evolving reality. In a bilingual society that is trying to recover and re-construct its language while coexisting with Spanish/French, translation is an everyday situation. Translation and translators have played a significant role in the contemporary social and ideological debates. Translation is also a fragile reality, because its social and political basis is not stable enough: it depends on the commitment of a majority of citizens to a more complex and more expensive alternative than Spanish/French monolingualism, since linguistic and cultural diversity is more difficult to manage than linguistic and cultural homogeneity. Diversity brings translation, but then translation and diversity can be seen as problematic in contexts of (desired) monolingual uniformity.

The first widespread use of translation in the Basque Country was made reluctantly: resorting to translations in order to bring new life to the language was in opposition to the main goal of keeping the original purity of the Basque language and culture. Later, this rather incongruous stance was replaced by a more dialectical one, where old and new discourses, and standard and peripheral dialects, clashed and interacted: the overall aim was to introduce innovative forms of representation as a basis for a new definition of Basqueness. Translation should be a way to feed language and culture with productive difference, which should help us to define a rich evolving identity, not a monolithic one based in static oppositions (see Bhabha, 1994). In a situation where most Basque speakers are bilingual, the way forward does not seem to lie in vindicating a return to the *original* Basque monolingualism that would avoid the need to translate. It would not be legal and, most importantly, it is not socially supported.

Yet in the Basque diglossic bilingual situation, intercommunity communication is not balanced. Legal constraints, the sociolinguistic reality and the market favour the stronger language. When the political power has favoured homogeneity (Franco's dictatorship, for instance) and Basque speakers have suffered symbolic and physical violence, translation was condemned to insignificance. Thus its occurrence was automatically linked with cultural and political opposition. On the contrary, when the political power has acted as a patron of the language, as the different Basque governments have done since 1980, translation has played an important role in the rapid normalization of the linguistic situation, so that Basque now has a chance to survive in a contemporary globalized world. The difference with the French Basque Country is very telling: Basque does not have any public support there and the language is vanishing. This political patronage has been vital in widening the once small public space of Basque in Spain and giving it due visibility, since the cultural market alone would not have had the same diversity-friendly consequences. For instance, publicly funded translations have had an important role in bringing canonical Western literary and philosophical works into Basque. Indeed, the constructive role of translation has been instrumental in the modernization process of the Basque language.

On an academic level, the new degree in Translation initiated in Vitoria-Gasteiz in 2000 should be an effective tool for providing a solid base for the constructive role of translation in the Basque Country. Basque is now for the first time part of the curriculum as a target language, and researchers are already working on some aspects of translation in the Basque Country. All these efforts will help to better reflect the rapidly changing situation of translation in the Basque Country. Further analysis of the complex translation reality in the Basque literary system could certainly provide new insights into translation as a linguistic, communicative, social and cultural activity.

Translations also have had political significance by helping regain some communicative balance within the Basque society between bilingual Basques and monolingual Spanish/French speakers. However, the situation remains problematic; the way things are translated may have wide symbolic and political consequences. As the referendum for the new Spanish Constitution was looming in 1978, the text approved by the Spanish Parliament was translated into Basque, and a bilingual booklet was circulated (Anonymous, 1978). The penultimate derogatory disposition stated: 'Asimismo quedan derogadas cuantas disposiciones se opongan a lo establecido en esta Constitución' ('With the coming into effect of this *Constitution* all previous rules contrary to it are hereby revoked'). However, the Basque version said: 'Era berean derogaturik geratzen dira Konstituzio hontan ezartzen diren disposapen guztiak' ('With the coming into effect of this *Constitution* all rules included in it are hereby revoked'). The fact is that the new constitution was approved in a referendum everywhere in Spain apart from the Basque Country. The translation *error* was *corrected* later, but the political conflict remains. Translation could play a part in improving communication between the different communities and bridging their differences. I cannot end the chapter without mentioning that, while this chapter was being written, a former local councillor, Isaías Carrasco, who belonged to the ruling Spanish socialist party, was murdered by members of ETA. This way of dealing with otherness, translating the other into nothing, does not seem to be a communicative, creative or productive use of translation in any sense.

Notes

1. This chapter is a result of the research project 'Literatura alemana en euskara. Aspectos lingüísticos y culturales de la traducción' (EHU 06/114) funded by the University of the Basque Country, and the consolidated research group IT518-10 (TRALIMA), Department of Education, Universities and Research, Basque Government.
2. The French Senate has approved twice in the last few months the inclusion of the regional languages as a 'valuable cultural heritage' in the French Constitution. The *Académie française* reacted to this with an outcry, denouncing it as a measure that would 'injure the national identity'. As a consequence, the French Congress has quashed this constitutional change. France, on the other hand, has not ratified the European Charter for Regional or Minority Languages (1992). A similar issue of 'visibility' of the Basque language can be seen in the specialized narratives of academic works where the issue of linguistic and literary systems is discussed. For example, Casanova mentions 'L'international des petits nations' (Casanova, 1999: 339–345), where she speaks about Norway, Belgium and Ireland (she also mentions Catalonia, a nation without state,

in another part of her work). However, she does not mention Basque or the Basque Country, despite the fact that there are French writers living in France and publishing their work in Basque.
3. It is necessary to dwell on historical specificities here, because this greater context of cultural production remains largely unknown. Academics tend to study very complex areas but to treat them as relatively uniform. For example, most works on translation in Spain only consider Spanish as a source and target language. Antony Pym (2000), for example, shows some interest in the situation in Catalonia, but he does not mention Basque, despite the fact that the main issues of his book concern changing frontiers and intercultures.
4. The Carlist Wars were fought between 1833 and 1876 between the followers of Carlos V and the followers of Queen Isabel II. They were not in fact a feud for the throne between the reigning monarch and the contender, but a wider conflict between traditionalists and liberals, between regional minorities and centralist forces.
5. See, for example, the discussion of Shakespearean sonnets in the Hebrew literary polysystem (Toury, 1995) or the genesis of the theatre field and drama translation in Egypt (Hanna, 2005).
6. Other prominent Basque poets, such as Esteban Urkiaga 'Lauaxeta', were executed by Francoists.
7. This is not a concern that is exclusive to the Basque context. One need only have a look at similar contexts such as Ireland to observe similar issues of culture-formation; as Cronin observes: 'The absence of a wider range of prose translation has attracted criticism [. . .]. The failure to translate more works of philosophy, science, psychology means that there is greater difficulty in developing an autonomous intellectual life and community in Irish' (Cronin, 1996: 189).
8. This clearly contradicts the dichotomy proposed by Casanova between conservative national writers and progressive international ones (Casanova, 1999: 379).
9. The most widely translated Basque writer, Bernardo Atxaga, takes a postmodern stand towards authorship, claiming that he wants his works translated, whatever the outcome. Other well-known authors like Anjel Lertxundi have a more modern approach; they claim that the author's own voice should be maintained through the translation process.
10. The German and Esperanto versions are exceptions, probably because they were done directly from the Basque.

References

Anonymous (1978) *La constitución española/Espainiako konstituzioa* (*Spanish Constitution*).
Bhabha, H. (1994) *The Location of Culture*. London: Routledge.
Casanova, P. (1999) *La république mondiale des lettres* (*The World Republic of Letters*). Paris: Seuil.
Cronin, M. (1996) *Translating Ireland*. Cork: Cork University Press.
Gentzler, E. (2002) Translation, poststructuralism, and power. In M. Tymoczko and E. Gentzler (eds) *Translation and Power* (pp. 195–218). Amherst: University of Massachusetts Press.

Hanna, S.F. (2005) Hamlet lives happily ever after in Arabic: The genesis of the field of drama translation in Egypt. *The Translator* 11 (2), 167–192.

House, J. (1997) *Translation Quality Assessment. A Model Revisited*. Tübingen: Gunter Narr.

Lefevere, A. (1992) *Translation, Rewriting, and the Manipulation of Literary Fame*. London: Routledge.

López Gaseni, M. (2000) *Euskarara itzulitako haur eta gazte literatura: funtzioak, eraginak eta itzulpen-estrategiak* (*Children's Literature Translated into Basque: Functions, Consequences and Translation Strategies*). Bilbao: Universidad del País Vasco.

Lopez Gaseni, M. (2002) An analysis of children's and young people's literature translated into Basque: Functions, influences, and strategies. *Senez* 24. On WWW at http://www.eizie.org/en/Argitalpenak/Senez/20021001/Lopez. Accessed 12.4.08.

Manterola, E. (2007) Euskal literatura beste hizkuntzetara itzulia (Basque literature translated). *Senez* 32. On WWW at http://www.eizie.org/Argitalpenak/Senez/20080201/manterola. Accessed 14.4.08.

Pym, A. (2000) *Negotiating the Frontier: Translators and Intercultures in Hispanic History*. Manchester: St. Jerome.

Torrealdai, J.M. (1979) *Euskal idazleak gaur* (*Basque Writers Today*). Donostia: Jakin.

Torrealdai, J.M. (1997) *Euskal kultura gaur* (*Basque Culture Today*). Donostia: Jakin-Elkarlanean Fundazioa.

Torrealdai, J.M. (2005) Euskal liburugintza 2003 (Basque publications 2003). *Jakin* 146–147, 11–161.

Toury, G. (1995) *Descriptive Translation Studies and Beyond*. Amsterdam/Philadelphia: John Benjamins.

Venuti, L. (1995) *The Translator's Invisibility*. London: Routledge.

Verbeke, F. (2006) The Basque Country and Flanders: intercultural transfers between multilingual and peripheral societies. In I. Uribarri (ed.) *Estudios sobre interculturalidad en literatura y traduccion* (*Essays on Interculturality in Literature and Translation*) (pp. 101–114). Leioa: Universidad del País Vasco.

Chapter 14
The Translation of Sexually Explicit Language: Almudena Grandes' Las edades de Lulú *(1989)* in English[1]

J. SANTAEMILIA

Introduction

Las edades de Lulú [*The Ages of Lulu*] was Almudena Grandes's first novel, published in 1989. For the last two decades this novel has been a constant source of polemical reactions and has been a privileged testing ground to rethink some of the limits affecting contemporary Spanish literature in a variety of dimensions – as art, business or moral spectacle. The novel has been the subject of an extensive debate which, to name just a few issues, ranges from the difference between *canonical* and *marginal* literature to the gap between the erotic and pornographic novel; it also cast in sharp relief issues such as the existence, or not, of a tradition of *feminine* erotic writing and the legitimacy, or not, of using shocking sexual incidents as a way to achieve commercial success and/or to have access to the Spanish literary establishment.

These and other issues help to justify the immense appeal this novel retains even today, in terms of sales figures, the critical debate and perceptions of the erotic aura the work still has. In this chapter I will focus on the treatment of sexually explicit language in the 1993 English-language translation.

Eroticism versus Pornography: A Site of Moral Ambivalence

Before entering the world of *Las edades de Lulú*, I wish to emphasize how difficult it is to define those texts which revolve around sexuality and which contain sexually explicit language, as well as explicit descriptions of sexual organs and acts. Sexually explicit material has been deemed pornography in certain periods and 'great literature' in others. Different historical periods have reacted differently. For example, sexuality permeates *The Arabian Nights*, whose universe of discourse is replete with wives, concubines and the charged atmosphere of harems; in a way, this picture has shaped the ancient Arab world in contemporary minds. In ancient Greece, a rhetoric of frank sexuality was acceptable, so long as it did not endanger the class system. Since the 18th century, pornography was the Western response to the destabilizing effects of sexuality (see Hunt, 1993). Twentieth-century Nazi and Fascist dictatorships responded to sex-related material with state censorship. In the USA and the UK, books such as *Fanny Hill* or *Lady Chatterley's Lover* remained outlawed until the 1960s, on the grounds of obscenity (see Rabadán, 2000; Seruya & Lin Moniz, 2008).

The recent history of Western censorship has been marked by three main concepts: *pornography*, *obscenity* and *eroticism*. The source of the term 'pornography' seems to lie in the Greek roots *porne* (whore) and *graphein* or *graphos* (writing); that is, they refer to the written depiction of whores or of prostitution. The term 'obscenity' has an unclear etymology – either *obscenus* (what remains outside the scene) or *ob-caenum* (filth, dirtiness). The third term, 'eroticism', constitutes an artistic or representational category and derives from *Eros*, the Greek god of love and sexual desire. Though it would seem that these three terms are clearly distinguishable, whenever attempts are made to identify them in a specific text or artistic representation disagreement ensues. In theoretical terms we could say that, on the one hand, an *erotic* text depicts sexuality artistically and that, on the other hand, a *pornographic* text is obscene and attacks decency and propriety. But in practice definitions and criteria are highly problematic.[2] Is *Fanny Hill* erotic or pornographic? And how does it compare to the *Genesis* or *Las edades de Lulú*? Can this definition be given irrespective of the actual texts depicting love, sexual desire and passion? The weight of tradition or prejudices, religion or social class, make such terms extraordinarily ambiguous (or rich). Bermúdez (1996: 170), for example, points out the fuzzy boundaries between the erotic and the pornographic in *Las edades de Lulú*. The erotic, for Maginn, 'has never belonged to any stable or consistently defined category because its classification has always depended upon social mores influenced by religious beliefs and moralistic convictions' (Maginn, 2002).

The indeterminacy of definitions along the erotic/pornographic continuum may clash with the readiness of relevant reactions, ranging from praise, tolerance and veiled sneer to harsh moral judgement, censorship and severe punishment. The only common denominator seems to be the presence of sex-related language or behaviour. Yet the debate continues with respect to definition, status and effects of pornography, or on the new (technological) varieties adopted for contemporary sexual representations. Besides, contemporary life has brought about a certain blurring of categories:

> The lines drawn between porn and other forms of sexual representation also seem much less clear than they did in the past; mainstream representation has become more explicit and 'perverse' and imagery and language, which would have been classed as pornographic not very long ago, have become part and parcel of popular culture. (Atwood, 2002: 94)

Pornography, in particular, has provoked deeply felt reactions in women. Pornography and other forms of representations are deeply enmeshed in the history of prejudices against women, as they depict the sexually explicit subordination of women. For many women, pornography signals degradation, violence and sexual objectification. 'More than any other type of sexual representation, pornography has frequently focused deep-seated cultural anxieties about the (de)generating pleasures that arise from the conflicted libido' (Bristow, 1997: 147). There is a tradition of conflicting feminist approaches to pornography. In particular, late 20th-century woman-authored Spanish erotic novels 'implicitly dismantle the inherited models both of eroticism and of literature' (Ríos-Font, 1998: 362). Young novelists like Almudena Grandes, Lucía Etxebarria, Mercedes Abad and María Jaén, among others, have chosen to describe in graphic detail the desires and sexual practices of their female protagonists. As is likely to happen with all the literary representations of sexuality, these erotic/pornographic novels written by women have as many defenders as they have detractors.

This definitional ambivalence is likely to continue. Erotica or pornography or obscenity are highly relative notions which are constantly negotiated in space and time. Further attempts at definition will only enact this negotiation process. Whatever the label used, one of the outstanding features of pornography is the presence of explicit sexual language and situations. Of course, sex-related language is not the same as sex or sexuality; yet language is

> arguably the most powerful definitional/representational medium available to humans, [it] shapes our understanding of what we are doing (and of what we should be doing) when we do sex or sexuality.

The language we have access to in a particular time and place for representing sex and sexuality exerts a significant influence on what we take to be possible, what we take to be 'normal' and what we take to be 'desirable'. (Cameron & Kulick, 2003: 11–12)

Sexuality is natural, but it has become an ideological and moral construct throughout history and culture. Moral positions notwithstanding, pornography, eroticism or obscenity have made an important contribution to culture. Moreover, in analysing the discourse of sex it is equally important what is said and what remains unsaid (see Sauntson, 2005). As Bourdieu has aptly put it, every expression

> is an accommodation between an *expressive interest* and a *censorship* instituted by the field in which that expression is offered; and this accommodation is the product of a process of euphemization which may even result in silence, the extreme case of censored discourse. (Bourdieu, 1993: 90, original emphases)

Las edades de Lulú

Las edades de Lulú can be seen as a key text that marks the period of transition from Franco's dictatorship to democratic rule. It constitutes a new literary voice in a period of reappraising artistic, communicative and sexual canons. The novel belongs to a genre – the erotic or pornographic novel – which tradition had labelled as masculine, both in its language as well as in the sexual stereotypes depicted.

Las edades de Lulú is a compelling story of love, hate and sex between Lulú, a middle-class young woman, and Pablo, a close family friend who tempts her into the forbidden territories of sexuality. Through their turbulent relationship, Lulú discovers love, titillation, sex and degradation. She enters 'the world of erotic cravings and sexual experimentation in her path toward womanhood' (Bermúdez, 1996: 168). The novel has elicited different, sometimes opposing, interpretations: for some it is a heavy, excessive fairy tale or *Bildungsroman* (Bermúdez, 1996, 2002; Mayock, 2004); for others, a sadist, misogynistic text which reflects 'the illusion of female liberation in the post-Franco era' (Robbins, 2003: 161); and for some it constitutes a subversion of the masculine pornographic model (Maginn, 2002). For most, the novel remains controversial and plurivalent in nature. Ríos-Font (1998: 368) has described it as a 'disturbing text' from a 'traditional feminist point of view'.

Stylistically, *Las edades de Lulú* is furnished with a transgressive force of sexual lexicon, an underexplored terrain in literary criticism. The novel can be seen as a repository of taboos inherited from eras of repression: a literary taboo (a *marginal* novel with the potential of becoming a standard *commercial* bestseller); a linguistic taboo (the heavy use of sexually explicit language, which goes against the traditional sociolinguistic stereotype associating women with prestige forms); a gender taboo (gender identities are explored in the novel, through Lulú's endless transgressive sexual experimentation, the performative effects of the stylized repetitions of feminine ideals); and a sexual taboo (the exploration of erotic combinations that goes far beyond socially accepted behaviours). Lulú, certainly, represents 'the incarnation of the performativeness of gender and desire' (Ríos-Font, 1998: 369) and her narrative is a 'journey toward sexual self-knowledge' (Bermúdez, 1996: 167).

The above-mentioned taboos become conventions that point to a powerful female figure, in a country that was desperately trying to regain its position within Europe and to overcome 50 years of isolation. The novel can be seen in the context of a textual tradition that foregrounds women's darkest and most repressed desires. Indeed, during the 1980s and 1990s a surge of women authors began to publish in Spain; most of them explored women's sexual experiences and language and participated actively in a wide-ranging 'talking about sex and sexuality' (Bermúdez, 2002: 223) which, among other things, characterized the post-Franco period.[3]

A further taboo can be added here – an editorial taboo, which was linked to an ever-present commercial strategy. In 1977 the publishing house Tusquets Editores created the new collection *La Sonrisa Vertical* [*The Vertical Smile*], in an attempt to cash in on the newly regained freedom after Franco's death, and to expand the sexual and literary horizons of Spanish readers. Quality erotica was the genre chosen by Tusquets to take advantage of the sexual permisiveness of the 'transition' period (1975 onwards) and to create a new literary market for a new generation. The *Sonrisa Vertical* Prize was a risky literary award instituted in 1978 to recognize each year's best erotic novel.[4] This constituted an act of legitimizing and bringing to the fore a previously 'marginal' genre which was intended for wider circulation. Thus, what was initially the by-product of an economic strategy (the commodification of literature), ended up generating a series of debates over canonical versus non-canonical literary forms, over women's presence in the Spanish literary world, and over 'feminine literature' itself (and its commodification).

Almudena Grandes is seen today as the originator of the boom in erotic literature. *Las edades de Lulú* focuses on the position of women within the literary market and on the extent to which women (be they authors, narrators or characters) are allowed to have a say in sexual matters. Over the last decades, literature has undergone a double process of institutionalization and of commodification, which in essence occasioned such shifts as the transformation of 'margins' into 'canons' and canons into full commercial products. In an ironic twist, *Las edades de Lulú* was published in 2004 in an author-revised edition, thus abandoning the *Sonrisa Vertical* series for the *Andanzas* series, a black-covered, serious-looking collection which houses best-selling authors such as John Connolly, Henning Mankell, Ernst Jünger, John Updike, Marguerite Duras and so on. Almudena Grandes herself has 'corrected' the original version, eliminating short passages and removing 'a number of pretentious and affected excesses' (Grandes, 2004: 17). She has not eliminated the sexual passages. On the whole, Grandes's introduction shows her immense gratitude to a novel she considers a radical and exasperated 'sentimental chronicle' (Grandes, 2004: 20) of a certain historical period. It is highly significant, however, that a novel which was considered immoral by many was assimilated by the publishing industry and the book market and transformed into a canonical, cult novel, an object of art in itself, worthy of critical and stylistic revision. In this way, through the combined efforts of the whole literary industry, *Las edades de Lulú* has entered the circuit of academic books, for university study and research. Indeed it was a brave book breaking new ground against the literary and gender hierarchies at the time it was published. Yet now, 15 years later, it has undergone a process of academic and publishing legitimation, acquiring 'symbolic capital', to use Bourdieu's term (1992: 166–167).

The Ages of Lulu

The Ages of Lulu was published in 1993, four years after the original novel in Spanish. It was a translation by Sonia Soto – who has also translated a number of works of contemporary Spanish authors such as Antonio Muñoz Molina, José Carlos Somoza and Arturo Pérez Reverte – for a regular 'non-erotic' collection. The aim of this section is to show how the English translation relays the socio-political specificities of the source text (ST), as the latter are encoded in the abundant use of sexually explicit language in *Las edades de Lulú*.

We know that sexual language poses a serious challenge to translators, both on a personal and a professional level; transgression, self-discovery, shame, social taboos and manipulation are all implicated (see Santaemilia, 2005). In a similar vein, von Flotow considers sexual language as a 'field that is notoriously difficult to translate for reasons of cultural and generational differences – a *cas limite* that in some ways serves as a test of translation' (von Flotow, 2000: 16).

I do subscribe to von Flotow's view when she accepts the fact that 'every translation must change a text' (von Flotow, 2000: 14). This is what she considers an unavoidable 'translation effect'. Translations are (re)written messages that travel from language to language, thus becoming new texts and producing new contexts. Sexually explicit language also travels in time and space. Erotic or pornographic literature has unpalatable edges that may threaten the moral ecology of a new literary environment. But contemporary publishing machineries swallow up all literary texts and turn them into cultural commodities. If the original text goes through processes of legitimation, translation can be seen along the same lines of legitimation in a different context. For this particular genre, we must emphasize the fact that translation was done into English, a dominant lingua franca used in countries with elaborate and 'clearly' defined literary systems. A book such as *The Ages of Lulu* was no doubt accepted into British and American systems because it is 'acceptable to the various ideologies and poetics' (Lefevere, 1992: 21) that currently dominate those systems. In other words, translation is

> part of a process of creating meaning, the circulation of meaning within a contingent network of texts and social discourses. If this is so, then, the cultural and ideological contexts in which a translation is produced and marketed will have an effect on the way a text is prepared, consciously, for the new audience. (von Flotow, 2000: 15)

To elaborate on this point, there are various factors which help to shape an acceptable product in the target culture; in this instance there is a prestigious and experienced translator (Sonia Soto), who is bound to adhere to very high professional standards, and a prestigious collection launched by a respected publishing house. Indeed, professionals, patronage and the dominant poetics (Lefevere, 1992: 5) may be factors that can directly impinge on the language of a novel, serving as 'filters' of transgressive literary material. In a pornographic work marketed by the publisher *as* pornographic literature, one would expect a certain 'excess', a series of 'dirty' words possibly signalling erroneous or word-for-word translations; such 'oversexualizations', as it were, can reinforce the offensiveness of the original text. By contrast, in a piece of quality erotica by a reputable Spanish author who has gained the right to be translated into English, the translator would presumably tend to couch his/her version in the most elegant, objective and detached language, thus aligning the ST with the dominant ideological and aesthetic values of the target culture. Explicit sexual language, of course, does entail paradoxes. In the case of Grandes's novel, the central element is sexually explicit language, which is not easily tolerated in the Spanish literary system, but eventually gained status. Such systems of oppositions, paradoxes and expectations are bound to be mirrored in the target literary system, and this is the issue that will be elaborated in the next sections.

The Translation of Sexual Vulgarity

To fully comprehend the sexual atmosphere in Grandes's novel, we can observe the extremely colloquial expressions used about the characters' sexual behaviour. *Las edades de Lulú* boldly explores the most explicitly sexual language and actions in Spanish literature. We can see that very little escapes an intense sexualization. The novel's characters have the most intense and varied sexual lives. In one of the initial perverse triangles, Pablo is speaking on the phone with Marcelo while at the same time he is arousing Lulú sexually; in this part Pablo tells Marcelo that he is not doing anything wrong with his sister, who, however, is [1] 'old enough to be wanking her eyes out' (p. 33),[5] as the target text (TT) goes. Lulú, shortly after her first sexual lesson with Pablo, runs to her friend Chelo and tells her all about it – they are on a night out and try to [2] 'pick up some guys, in some trendy club, just for a laugh, like two old tarts, and tomorrow would be another day' (p. 53). Further down, when Lulú is separated from Pablo, she meets Ely, her transsexual friend, who asks her about her 'husband'. Lulú responds that they are no longer together and that [3] 'he's involved with a girl, a redhead, now' (p. 58).

The relationship between Lulú and Pablo, with its ups and downs, its separations and reconciliations, is literally fraught with sexually explicit erotic experiments. In this sense, the sexual is presented in a straightforward, graphic way, within the erotic genre expectations. It is true, however, that the array of sexual positions and partner combinations are alarmingly limited – as George Steiner (1967: 69) comments, '[t]he mathematics of sex stop somewhere in the region of *soixante-neuf*'. In the novel, Lulú tries to give Pablo [4] 'a brilliant blow job' (p. 86). In a conversation with Ely, Lulú boasts that she [5] 'fucked my eyes out' (p. 90). While in prison, Marcelo and Pablo are given 'ten blow jobs' (p. 98) with the money she has sent to them. This is just one of the many love/sex triangles to be encountered in the novel. Mayock (2004: 241) affirms that 'Lulú, Marcelo, and Pablo are inextricably linked emotionally throughout the narration, a link which terminates with a dramatic physical union of the three inside Lulú's body.' Still, while in prison, Pablo even thought of having sexual relations with 'the Portuguese guy', as [6] 'it couldn't be all that different from buggering a woman' (p. 99). At the risk of oversimplification, examples [1]–[6] are significant instances of a linguistic and rhetorical norm: when trying to relay the sexual vulgarity present in the Spanish text, English proves less physical, less colloquial. *The Ages of Lulu* deletes crude references to body parts, to sexual acts and to the frenzy Grandes's female characters experience in wild sexual activity.

Apart from such cases where sexually explicit langauge is relayed in a straightforward way, there are references that are irretrievably lost in the English translation. A good example is the instance when Lulú refers to Luis, an old school partner, who at the moment is experiencing [7] 'a bad case of post-traumatic stress syndrome after the break-up of a romantic relationship' (p. 169) [Sp. '... con **cuernos** dolorosos ...' (p. 233)]. Spanish *cuernos* ['horns'][6] is a symbol and emblem of the cuckold, and is one of the most idiosyncratic cultural references to be found both in Spanish literary tradition and in daily conversations. Deleting it in the English translation is tantamount to losing the figurative and colloquial character of the original text. If *cuernos* is part and parcel of the Spanish-language tradition to define illegal sex, the word *corrida* is a dirty, vulgar word for (usually male) orgasm. Encarna, an old friend of Lulú's who used to own a boarding house for bullfighters, has now changed business and started to [8] 'rent out rooms for another type of **corrida**' (p. 194) [Sp. '... otro tipo de **corridas**' (p. 269)], meaning male orgasm. This solution is disconcerting. The English translation has either missed the point completely or resorts to a certain exoticization process whereby a stereotypical image of Spain as an unchangeable land of bullfighters is perpetuated. The two solutions given to the two central concepts here (as conveyed through *cuernos* and *corrida*) dramatically desexualize the original text, which is highly erotic and profoundly ironic.

One of the most characteristic expressions in Spanish denoting bravery is expressed by the narrator Lulú, when she affirms that Mario, one of the gay men she is in touch with, [15] 'had a really **gutsy** approach to life' (p. 145) [Sp. 'Le echaba unos **huevos** tremendos a la vida' (p. 199)]. The reference to *huevos* [Eng. 'balls'] constitutes a very common trend of construing courage and moral superiority in terms of the male genitalia in Spanish. It constitutes an unabashed celebration of male sexual attributes which is encoded in language.

The characters in *Las edades de Lulú* boldly verbalize their sexual urges, which unmistakably identifies them with erotic literature and with an extremely colloquial register. Typical instances are bold statements by or about female characters along the lines of [9] 'I was **hot, turned on** in the true sense of the word' (p. 36) [Sp. *'caliente, cachonda* ...' (p. 54)] or [10] 'She was very **aroused**' (p. 111) [Sp. '... *muy salida*' (p. 154)]. Both [9] and [10] seem reasonable options for the Spanish sexually explicit terms. There are other examples, however, which would seem to indicate that there are terms or turns of phrase which are either untranslatable or at least highly idiomatic. When in prison, 'the Portuguese guy', a sort of girlfriend to all the prisoners in a period of political unrest [11], 'was quite **taken with** Marcelo' (p. 99) [Sp. '*encoñado*' (p. 138)]. *Encoñarse*[7] or *encoñado*[8] are extremely sensitive terms to translate: firstly, because they are derived from the female pudenda (*coño*, Eng. 'cunt'), most probably the strongest taboo word in the Spanish language; secondly, because they point to an unconscious association between the sex of women and passing, capricious infatuation; and thirdly, because they refer to a (gay) man. These examples seem to confirm the trend of women-related terms undergoing a process of semantic derogation (see Schultz, 1975) and acquiring overtly sexist overtones. A woman's body and sexuality is one of the main sources of verbal hostility and abuse. All this is markedly lost in Sonia Soto's translation.

Sex-related language is also used figuratively to evaluate other characters' morality. Lulú's mother, for instance, is ashamed of Marcelo's behaviour, for she considers him a communist, and also [12] 'a lout, stays out till all hours, a real **troublemaker**...' (p. 108) [Sp. '*golfo*' (p. 151)]. She is also ashamed of the way Isabel, another daughter of hers, is behaving lately; Isabel [13] 'used to be such a **good girl**, and now she's getting into more and more trouble...' (p. 108) [Sp. '*tan formalita*' (p. 151)]. Lulú herself, when referring to Susana's sexual life, concludes that [14] 'Susana's become a little **goody-goody** recently' (p. 126) [Sp. '*formalita*' (p. 174)]. The terms *golfo*[9] [12] and *formalita*[10] [13, 14] refer not only to boldness or sensibility, but especially to people who ignore [e.g. *golfo*] or respect [e.g. *formalita*] the norms imposed by social morality. Both terms have clear sexual connotations which are conspicuously absent from dictionaries and – maybe as a consequence – absent from the English translation.

We could add further examples of sexual vulgarity present in *Las edades de Lulú* and its English translation. Most of the translations are rather accurate, more often than not showing great skill and providing effective alternatives. But something does get lost in translation: Spanish is a more earthly, physical and immediate language. The TT, either because it is *into* English or a *translation*, tends to be desexualized, lacking crude references, or not featuring the most direct or idiomatic phrases. On the whole, the TT shies away from the more direct relationship between language and sexuality, bodily phenomena, sex organs and so on.

The Translation of Emphatic Intensifiers and of Swear Words

A fundamental discursive dimension in any erotic or pornographic text is the recurring use of sex-related language for (emotional) emphasis.

The Spanish language (over)exploits body parts, sexual organs or erotic activities to convey a wide range of emphatic meanings or euphonic associations, of spontaneous and colloquial reactions, all of them indicative of a highly informal, oral register.

An example of this technique can be seen at the point when Lulú is 16 and a powerful family triangle system 'solidly entrenches itself as Pablo has sex with the virginal Lulú simultaneously speaking with Marcelo on the phone' (Mayock, 2004: 244). In this scene, Pablo's cynicism is foregrounded as he is having sex with Lulú and simultaneously denies it emphatically on the phone. He informs Marcelo that this evening Lulú [16] 'had a **fucking brilliant** time' (p. 31) [Sp. *'de puta madre'* (p. 47)] while caressing her nipples; the expression *de puta madre* [impossible to convey literally, as it would be something like an adjective meaning 'whore mother's'] links two of the strongest socio-sexual taboos (prostitution and motherhood) in one single expression of abuse, and that seems impossible to convey in English (see Santaemilia, 2008a: 17). In the same scene, in order to add an element of truth to his denial, he says to Lulú's brother: [17] '**Fuck off**, Marcelo! How should I know...' (p. 31) [Sp. *'¡No me jodas ...!'* (p. 48)], while caressing her thighs this time. *Joder* [Eng. 'to fuck'] is an oft-repeated sex-related word which is used in non-sexual, emphatic contexts. It is a vulgar term whose lexical meaning is 'to copulate' (derived from Latin *futuere*) but which is especially used in countless idiom-like phrases to convey (with pragmatic force) emotional reactions (protest or surprise) as well as semantic meaning ('to ruin', 'to mess up'). Nearly at the end of the novel, when Lulú is going through her maddening exploration of sexual perversions, an old partner from university who had a bar warns her to do things more discreetly, protesting: [18] 'don't do it here **for fuck's sake**' (p. 163) [Sp. *'joder'* (p. 225)]. In [17] and [18] we can see similar solutions in the ST and TT. Semantic meaning is also quite common. Lulú, now in her thirties, is reminiscent of the times when Marcelo and Pablo were young idealists, fighting against rules and impositions, and showing their rebellion in attitudes like shortening their surnames: Marcelo truncates his aristocratic surnames (Ruiz-Poveda y García de la Casa) into plain 'Ruiz García' [19] 'just to **piss** the family **off**' (p. 168) [Sp. *'por joder'* (p. 232)]. It is interesting here to note the addition of the phrase 'the family' in the English translation, which clarifies the (implicit) meaning of the Spanish original, and turns a vague, irreverent action into a clearly defined objective. In another scene, in the period in which Lulú becomes addicted to male prostitutes, she loses all control over her sexual experimentations and finds herself in a dangerous situation in Encarna's flat. Before being saved by Pablo, Lulú is only able to think: [20] 'Poor

Encarna, I thought. They're really **buggering up** your place' (p. 200) [Sp. *'jodiendo la casa'* (p. 277)]. In this last example, both ST and TT show a similar use of sex-related terms for emphatic effect.

Another favourite emphatic intensifier in the novel is *coño* [Eng. 'cunt'], in stereotypical retorts like [21] 'And **what the fuck** do you care?' (p. 93) [Sp. *'qué coño'* (p. 131)]. There is indeed a systematic overexploitation of female genitals to articulate anger or contempt in colloquial conversation (see Santaemilia, 2008b). Fixed expressions like *¿qué coño ...', ¿dónde coño ...?* or *¿cómo coño ...?* [Eng. lit. 'what the cunt', 'where the cunt' and 'how the cunt'] are heard everywhere in Peninsular Spanish. In some cases there is a certain accummulation of sex-related emphatic resources. In the scene mentioned above, in which Pablo is speaking to Marcelo on the phone while simultaneously having sex with Lulú, Pablo dismisses his friend's fears by sounding offended: [22] '**What the fuck** does Lulu care if **I'm cheating** on my girlfriend?' (p. 33) [Sp. *'¿Qué coño ... le ponga los cuernos ...?'* (p. 49)]. In this sentence, the emphatic values of *coño* are reinforced through alliteration and the cultural cliché of *cuernos* ('horns' – see example [7]). The examples are explicit and emotionally charged but surely, for many readers, this excessive repetition is likely to deprive sex-related terms of some of their force, leading even to a certain desensitization.

In *The Ages of Lulu*, there is an almost systematic use of 'fuck' as an equivalent of practically all the Spanish sex-related emphatic intensifiers. Excerpts [16], [17], [18], [21] and [22] are prime examples. McEnery and Xiao (2004) have found the word 'fuck' to be one of the most versatile in the English language, as it is variously used as a general expletive, a personal insult, an emphatic intensifier, an idiom or a metalinguistic device. In their study of the BNC (*British National Corpus*), it is shown that it is primarily used as an 'emphatic intensifier' (55.85% of occurrences) – that is, its main aim is to add emotional values to the words or phrases it accompanies. The most striking aspect, however, is that the denotative sexual meaning of 'fuck' ('to copulate') is rarely used (7.16% of cases, as opposed to 92.84% of non-sexual usages). This points to a process of de-semanticization of the lexeme 'fuck' in English across settings and genres, and a marked preference for emotive and emphatic values. In spite of this overwhelming preference for non-sexual usages, we cannot help perceiving that a term like 'fuck' *sexualises* the communicative events in which it is used (see Santaemilia, 2008b).

Even more remarkable is perhaps the presence of sex-related insults and swear words. Body parts, sexual deviation as opposed to accepted behaviours, sexual organs, illegitimacy, and so on, are unlimited sources of insult, derision and moral condemnation. Among the basic aesthetic codes of erotic literature we can mention a very colloquial register and the use of swear words. Constant repetition brings together rhythm/sound and sexual pleasures. There is a time-old tradition in Spanish literature – Francisco de Quevedo or Camilo José Cela, and more recently Almudena Grandes or Lucía Etxebarria, to name but a few – of a liberal use of sex-related swear words: *hijo de puta* [Eng. 'son of a bitch'], *cabrón* [Eng. 'bastard'], *maricón/marica* [Eng. 'queer'], *puta* [Eng. 'whore'], *zorra* [Eng. 'slut'] or *gilipollas* [Eng. 'jerk'] are only a few of the terms which appear again and again on every page.

The phrase *hijo de puta* [Eng. 'son of a bitch'] is one of the building blocks of colloquial or vulgar texts. When Lulú, accompanied by Ely, orders a white batiste blouse to please Pablo, the woman who takes the order is frightened and asks: [23] 'You haven't brought me a bloody copper, have you, you **bastard**?' (p. 62) [Sp. *'hijo de puta'* (p. 90)]. One night, when Pablo and Lulú are driving through the red light district, a man punches Pablo in the face. Lulú, a contradictory character and narrator, is at times overly dominating and at times submissive and powerless. In this incident, Lulú reacts in a stereotypically 'male' fashion, shouting and being verbally violent: [24] 'Come back here, you **bastard**, let's see if you dare.' (p. 76) [Sp. *'hijo de puta'* (p. 108)] and the tragicomic [25] 'You **bloody bastard**, how dare you hit my boyfriend!' (p. 76) [Sp. *'hijo de la gran puta'* (p. 109)]. While the ST and TT are similar in terms of lexical meaning, they may not be so in terms of pragmatic force. Many Spanish-speaking readers or speakers would feel greatly offended by examples [23]–[25], which, for them, are situated far beyond the line of decency in Spanish culture, as they include a reference both to the illegitimate child and to his/her mother. In highly colloquial contexts there is some ambiguity as to whether these terms are used as (strong) insults or to add extra emotional emphasis, or both.

Other swear words which are used in *Las edades de Lulú* are *cabrón* [Eng. 'bastard'] or *maricón* [Eng. 'queer'], which will be considered below. When the young Marcelo is sent to prison, his father scorns and criticizes him and considers that this will serve him right: [26] 'They'll straighten him out in that prison, the **little bastard**' (p. 96) [Sp. *'cabrón'* (p. 135)]. Encarna is a friend of Lulú's who owned a boarding house which used to be surrounded by bullfighters and banderilleros, and her opinion about them is that [27] 'they were all bastards who left without paying half the time' (p. 194) [Sp. *'cabrones'* (p. 269)]. Lulú, in the incident in which she defends her 'boyfriend', gives way to intense verbal aggression: [28] 'I'll kill you, you pig, I'll get you, coward, you **queer**, I'll kill you!' (p. 76) [Sp. *'maricón'* (p. 108)]. In her foolish search for pleasure, Lulú is desperate to [29] 'go to bed with a couple of **queers**, or three, or four' (p. 163) [Sp. *'maricones'* (p. 224)]. The main difference between these two terms is that *cabrón* is used emphatically, while *maricón* is used derogatorily.

As can be seen in these examples, most of the swear words used revolve around men's sexual adequacy, or lack thereof. According to Fernández Dobao (2006: 230), in colloquial Spanish 'men are most intensively insulted through their women', that is, by questioning the loyalty of their wives (*cabrón*), the morality of their mothers (*hijo de puta*) or their perceived gender inadequacy (*maricón*). These men-related terms reveal intense linguistic violence and social transgression. Besides, they are profoundly sexist, especially offensive with regard to women and female sexuality. In examples [23]–[29] the English translation resorts only to the terms *bastard* and *queer*, thus showing less variety than the Spanish.

Conclusion

The translation of sexually explicit language is an area of personal struggle, of ethical or moral conflicts, of ideological controversies, even of (self-)censorship. When translating sexual vulgarity or sex-related swear words, we are not dealing with lexical accuracy. Besides the actual meaning of the terms and expressions involved, there are aesthetic, cultural and ideological components. This chapter illustrates this point by focusing on sexually explicit material in *The Ages of Lulu*, the 1993 English-language translation of Almudena Grandes's *Las edades de Lulú* (1989), one of the key texts marking the period of transition from Franco's dictatorship to democratic rule in Spain. This novel is part of a widespread movement of young women novelists who started to write in the late 1980s and who chose to describe in very explicit sexual terms the sexual lives and attitudes of their female protagonists.

The Ages of Lulu seems to be a professionally executed translation, which is on the whole accurate from a linguistic point of view; yet the translator seems to be fully aware of the fact that *Las edades de Lulú* is a highly sensitive text, replete with sexually explicit language. The solutions offered in the TT are less evocative than the ST material, possibly influenced by such variables as respect for Almudena Grandes, today an acclaimed (and canonical) author of 'serious' literature, as well as respect for a powerful sexually explicit language that is constantly endangering the (canonical) status of the book. Indeed, the translator can be seen as striking a balance between two opposing views: on the one hand, social norms dictating that sexual language is suspect, deviant and loathsome; and, on the other hand, norms requiring the elimination of desire, amorality, alterity, sex(uality) and the sense of one's body. The translator seems to advocate a delicate middle ground. The 'translation effect' (von Flotow, 2000) here seems to drive the TT version of Grandes's novel into somewhat desexualized territory, where issues of restraint and propriety (together with the usual, matter-of-fact sexually explicit terms) are more important than the subtleties and transgressions which make *Las edades de Lulú* stand way above other erotic novels. Thus Maginn's comment seems to be highly relevant: '[t]he study of literary sub-genres can shed a great deal of light on the workings and drives of a society, especially a changing society such as the Postfrancoist Spain' (Maginn, 2002).

Further research is needed into sexually explicit language in various authors and literary periods. This will allow us to gain rich insights into the periods under study, in terms of cultural dynamics, ideological struggles or ethical attitudes. We need combined analyses of the macro-context (the socio-cultural background of publishers, translators, writers, etc.) and of the micro-level textual data to get a fuller picture of the complex operations involved in translation. Not many studies have so far sought to analyse or describe the discrepancies between ST and TT when it comes to the expression of sexually explicit language, but recent and ongoing research looks promising. Simms (1997) edited a book on the translation of sensitive texts, which includes an analysis on the translation of Henry Miller into Spanish; von Flotow (2000) details the process of severe desexualization of Simone de Beauvoir's novels *L'invitée* (1943) or *Les mandarins* (1954) in their English translations; Bush (2003) analyses his own translation of Juan Goytisolo's *A Cock-eyed Comedy*, where sexuality is a key element. Santaemilia (2005, 2008b) has dealt with the intricacies of both the sex of translation and the translation of sex, focusing on the danger of self-censorship(s). Billiani (2007) and Seruya and Lin Moniz (2008) offer stimulating editions on translation and censorship. A conference held at Concordia University in April 2009 addressed the translation of erotica. Sexually explicit language is, undoubtedly, a privileged area to study the cultures we translate into – it is a site where 'issues of cultural sensitivity are encumbered by issues of gender stereotyping and cliché' (von Flotow, 2000: 31), where each culture places its moral or ethical limits, where we encounter its taboos and historical dilemmas.

Notes

1. This chapter was partly funded by the Spanish *Ministerio de Ciencia e Innovación* (Research Project FFI2008-04534/FILO).
2. See Santaemilia and Pruñonosa (2000) or Toledano (2003). Also, as D.H. Lawrence (1928: 64) wrote, 'What is pornography to one man is the laughter of genius to another'.

3. 'Interestingly enough, this talking about sex and sexuality has already been taking place in Spain since the early seventies as part of the emergent literary, critical, and theoretical practices that were to flourish in the twilight years of Francoism, and that were somehow further unveiled by the destape years of the transición (transition)' (Bermúdez, 2002: 223).
4. Also in 1977, Bruguera Editorial inaugurated a *Clásicos del Erotismo* series, whose objective was to popularize foreign-language erotic works in Spanish translation. All in all, it was a parallel strategy to that of Tusquets Editores; both, however, were attempts at satisfying the demand for sexually explicit texts in a period of sex-related artistic frenzy.
5. In the following pages, the original Spanish quotes will only be offered alongside the English translations for comparison purposes. Each example is assigned a number in brackets for ease of reference.
6. In William Wycherley's *The Country Wife* (1675), one of the main characters (Horner) retains in his name this metaphorical association between 'horns' and 'cuckoldry'. See Santaemilia, 2000.
7. '**Encoñar** (*vulg*) **A** *tr* **1** Dominar o someter [una mujer a un hombre] con el sexo. [...] **B** *intr pr* **2** Encapricharse u obsesionarse sexualmente [un hombre con una mujer]. [...] **b)** Enamorarse o sentirse muy atraído sexualmente [por alguien (*compl* de)]' (Seco *et al.*, 1999: 1798).
8. '**Encoñado, da** adj. Muy enamorado o atraído sexualmente. // Encaprichado' (León, 1984: 70).
9. '**Golfo –fa I** *adj* (*col*) **1** [Muchacho] que vaga por las calles, al margen de las normas sociales de comportamiento. [...] **b)** [Muchacho] descarado y desvergonzado. [...] **2** [Pers.] viciosa o de mal vivir. [...] **3** [Pers.] sinvergüenza, o que actúa sin escrúpulos morales' (Seco *et al.*, 1999: 2353).
10. '**Formal** *adj* [...] **3** [Pers.] juiciosa en su comportamiento. [...] **b)** [Pers.] que cumple sus compromisos' (Seco *et al.*, 1999: 2214–2215).

References

Atwood, M. (2002) Reading porn: The paradigm shift in pornography research. *Sexualities* 5 (1), 91–105.

Bermúdez, S. (1996) Sexing the Bildungsroman: *Las edades de Lulú*, pornography, and the pleasure principle. In D. Foster and R. Reis (eds) *Bodies and Biases. Sexualities in Hispanic Cultures and Literature* (pp. 165–183). Minneapolis: University of Minnesota Press.

Bermúdez, S. (2002) Let's talk about sex? From Almudena Grandes to Lucía Etxebarria, the volative values of the Spanish literary market. In O. Ferrán and K.M. Glenn (eds) *Women's Narrative and Film in Twentieth-century Spain: A World of Differences* (pp. 223–237). New York: Routledge.

Billiani, F. (ed.) (2007) *Modes of Censorship and Translation. National Contexts and Diverse Media.* Manchester: St. Jerome.

Bourdieu, P. (1992) *The Rules of Art: Genesis and Structure of the Literary Field* (S. Emanuel, trans.). Stanford: Stanford University Press.

Bourdieu, P. (1993) *Sociology in Question.* London: Sage.

Bristow, J. (1997) *Sexuality.* London: Routledge.

Bush, P. (2003) The act of translation: The case of Juan Goytisolo's *A Cock-Eyed Comedy. Quaderns. Revista de traducció* 10, 121–134.

Cameron, D. and Kulick, D. (2003) *Language and Sexuality*. Cambridge: Cambridge University Press.
Fernández Dobao, A.M. (2006) Linguistic and cultural aspects of the translation of swearing: The Spanish version of *Pulp Fiction*. *Babel* 52 (3), 222–242.
Grandes, A. (1989) *Las edades de Lulú*. Barcelona: Círculo de Lectores.
Grandes, A. (1993/2001) *The Ages of Lulu* (S. Soto, trans.). London: Abacus.
Grandes, A. (2004) *Las edades de Lulú* (revised edn). Barcelona: Tusquets Editores. Colección Andanzas.
Hunt, L. (ed.) (1993) *The Invention of Pornograghy: Obscenity and the Origins of Modernity, 1500–1800*. New York: Zone Books.
Lawrence, D.H. (1928) Pornography and obscenity. In H.T. Moore (ed.) *Sex, Literature and Censorship* (pp. 64–81). New York: The Viking Press.
Lefevere, A. (1992) *Translation, Rewriting, and the Manipulation of Literary Fame*. London/New York: Routledge.
León, V. (1984) *Diccionario de argot español* (4th edn). Madrid: Alianza Editorial.
Maginn, A. (2002) Female erotica in post-Franco Spain: The will-to-disturb. *Ciberletras* 8. On WWW at http://www.lehman.cuny.edu/ciberletras/v08/maginn.html. Accessed 24.7.2007.
Mayock, E. (2004) Family systems theory and Almudena Grandes's *Las edades de Lulú*. *Anales de la Literatura Española Contemporánea* 29 (1), 235–256.
McEnery, T. and Xiao, Z. (2004) Swearing in modern British English: the case of *fuck* in the BNC. *Language and Literature* 13 (3), 235–268.
Rabadán, R. (ed.) (2000) *Traducción y censura inglés-español 1939–1985: Estudio preliminar*. León: Universidad de León.
Ríos-Font, W. (1998) To hold and behold: Eroticism and canonicity at the Spanish fines de siglo. *Anales de la Literatura Española Contemporánea* 23 (1), 355–378.
Robbins, J. (2003) The discipline of the Spanish subject: *Las edades de Lulú* (Female liberation as portrayed in novel by autor Almudena Grandes). *Anales de la Literatura Española Contemporánea* 28 (1), 161–182.
Santaemilia, J. (2000) *Género como conflicto discursivo*. Valencia: Universitat de València.
Santaemilia, J. (2005) The translation of sex/The sex of translation: *Fanny Hill* in Spanish. In J. Santaemilia (ed.) *Gender, Sex and Translation: The Manipulation of Identities* (pp. 117–136). Manchester: St. Jerome.
Santaemilia, J. (2008a) Gender, sex, and language in Valencia: Attitudes toward sex-related language among Spanish and Catalan speakers. *International Journal of the Sociology of Language* 190, 5–26.
Santaemilia, J. (2008b) The danger(s) of self-censorship(s): The translation of '*fuck*' into Spanish and Catalan. In T. Seruya and M. Lin Moniz (eds) *Translation and Censorship in Different Times and Landscapes* (pp. 163–173). Newcastle: Cambridge Scholars Publishing.
Santaemilia, J. and Pruñonosa, J. (eds and transl.) (2000) *John Cleland – Fanny Hill: Memorias de una mujer de placer*. Madrid: Cátedra.
Sauntson, H. (2005) Saying and not saying: Gender, sexuality and discourse analysis. In J. Santaemilia (ed.) *The Language of Sex: Saying & Not Saying* (pp. 25–44). Valencia: Universitat de València.
Schultz, M.R. (1975) The semantic derogation of women. In B. Thorne and N. Henley (eds) *Language and Sex: Difference and Dominance* (pp. 64–75). Rowley, MA: Newbury House.

Seco, M., Andrés, O. and Ramos, G. (1999) *Diccionario del español actual* (2 vols). Madrid: Aguilar.

Seruya, T. and Lin Moniz, M. (eds) (2008) *Translation and Censorship in Different Times and Landscapes*. Newcastle: Cambridge Scholars Publishing.

Simms, K. (ed.) (1997) *Translating Sensitive Texts: Linguistic Aspects*. Amsterdam/Atlanta: Rodopi.

Steiner, G. (1967) 'Night words' (high pornography & human privacy). *Language and Silence* (pp. 68–77). New York: Atheneum.

Toledano, C. (2003) *La traducción de la obscenidad*. Santa Cruz de Tenerife: La Página Ediciones.

Von Flotow, L. (2000) Translation effects: How Beauvoir talks sex in English. In M. Hawthorne (ed.) *Contingent Loves. Simone de Beauvoir and Sexuality* (pp. 13–33). Richmond, VA: University Press Virginia.

Chapter 15
Serbo-Croatian: Translating the Non-identical Twins

T.Z. LONGINOVIĆ

Language Falls Apart

The language I still can't help but call Serbo-Croatian, despite political changes and violent national identity shifts within my destroyed homeland, acquired its latest avatar in 2007. After Montenegro's separation from Serbia, the newly independent parliament voted to introduce Montenegrin as the official language of the new sovereign state, adding a fourth version of the formerly common language to the collection of new-yet-old idioms. The first three, Bosnian, Croatian and Serbian, have been given their present name by the pragmatic translators of the International War Crimes Tribunal in The Hague, creating the virally echoing BCS acronym to name the former lingua franca of the region. Interestingly, the judicial origin of the name immediately invokes the prosecution of war crimes on the territory of the former Yugoslavia, positioning the new-yet-old idiom as part of the palliative political and military apparatus that was to decide on the readiness of the former warring parties to enter the European Union. This article merges my own experience as a person trying to come to terms with the linguistic divisions imposed as a result of Yugoslavia's violent dismemberment with my scholarly interest in understanding translation as a cultural practice promoting communication and understanding. In fact, the conclusions drawn from the post-Yugoslav case will prove that translation can be effectively used as a political tool for the construction of differences and the tearing down of cultural bridges that might promote understanding.

The recognition of linguistic particularities was especially necessary to support the painful birth of Bosnia–Herzegovina as a separate political entity after 1992, inspired by the notion that an independent state needs a language that bears its name as well. For those of us teaching this language to foreign students at university level, the dilemma of the language's name will become even more complex with the introduction of 'M' into the BCS formula, especially if we take into account the fact that these four incarnations of former Serbo-Croatian are mutually intelligible on the level of everyday communication for the vast majority of its speakers.

In fact, the case of Serbo-Croatian is a painful reminder of a cultural reality whose language is the marker of collective identity and the extension of national territory. Structured by extra-linguistic forces tied to the power of social elites and their projected political aims, language performs the most basic interpellation of those subjected to the national imaginary. Discussing quite a different relationship between Québécois and French, Annie Brisset comes to a conclusion that also rings true in the case of Serbo-Croatian:

> [t]ranslation becomes an act of reclaiming, of re-centering of the identity, a re-territorializing operation. It does not create a new language, but it elevates a dialect to the status of a national and cultural language. (Brisset, 2000: 346)

The literal reclaiming of national territories through the violent break-up of the common South Slavic state during the Wars of Yugoslav Succession (1991–1995) and in their aftermath (Montenegro, 2006; Kosovo 2008) has witnessed at least seven 're-centring' operations of the kind outlined by Brisset, performed through different operations of linguistic cleansing accompanying the ethnic ones. Each of the seven post-Yugoslav political entities (Bosnia–Herzegovina, Croatia, Macedonia, Montenegro, Kosovo, Serbia and Slovenia) has retaliated against the former lingua franca of the common state in a cultural mode reflecting its new identity, by creating different visions of their national territory by linguistic means. I will limit myself to discussing Serbia and Croatia, although it is possible to imagine a book-length study mapping this type of opposition to a common code of communication. The production and exaggeration of linguistic difference required by the new becoming of each of these political entities raises the issue of translation between them. This issue is particularly problematic since many of the emergent cultures do not require translation to come to terms with meanings articulated by the other one.

The very beginning of this translation conundrum was engendered during the war between the two largest of the post-Yugoslav nations, Serbia and Croatia, bringing to the foreground the issue of cultural relations between the two 'non-identical twins' joined in their linguistic identity through the name of the dominant language of their former common state: Serbo-Croatian. By symbolically removing the hyphen between them, ethnic conflict created the need for translation as a cultural practice that would confirm and amplify differences between the two warring parties. In fact, some of the differences were already there, but they were more on the level of dialect, word choice and orthography within a single linguistic continuum, rather than on a level of insurmountable semantic difference necessary for a language to declare its independence on scientific grounds and to require translation.

It is commonly held that that there is about a 20% difference in vocabulary items between Eastern and Western versions of Serbo-Croatian; Western ones largely use the Latin script, while Eastern versions use both Cyrillic and Latin scripts. The complexity of Bosnian identity is in fact the main problem in simply naming the Western variant of Serbo-Croatian 'Croatian' and the Eastern one 'Serbian', especially after the break-up of the common Yugoslav cultural continuum. For example, the Serbs of Bosnia speak a dialect of Serbo-Croatian closer to Croatian, but would never agree to call their language 'Croatian'. They will insist that they speak 'Serbian'. They are also reluctant to call their language 'Bosnian', since that would conflate their national identity with that of Bosniaks, that is the Bosnian Moslems, the only group that wholeheartedly accepts the new name of the language. The Croats of Bosnia have the same issue with 'Bosnian', since they call their language 'Croatian' despite the fact that they live within the political confines of the territory of Bosnia–Herzegovina. The case of Montenegro reproduces the same sort of linguistic issue, since approximately half of the population opposing national independence call the language 'Serbian', while the other half, favouring the new state entity, insists on 'Montenegrin' as the name of the language they speak. In the case of this new independent state, both of these names refer to an absolutely identical linguistic code shared by its speakers.

Translating the Nation

The effect of translation as a cultural instrument of sovereignty and a vehicle for national re-invention shows up both the obvious absurdity of an attempt to discard similarity and the legacy of identity based on the common *štokavian* dialect chosen by the South Slavic enlighteners Vuk Karadžić and Ljudevit Gaj. The 1850 Vienna agreement to champion a common tongue serving as a platform for the political unification of Serbs-under-Turks and Croats-under-Hungarians envisioned a unified philological territory that was to serve as a cultural weapon in their struggle against the imperial rule of the Ottomans and the Habsburgs.

This anti-imperial move of the non-identical linguistic twins was based on the idea of a common Slavic *ethnos* that would use the kinship based on their shared language to develop a nation. Besides this historical decision by Vuk and Gaj, other dialects within the Croat national domain (*čakavski* and *kajkavski*) were quite dissimilar from the *štokavski*, so linguistic standardization based on the idiom shared with the Serbs also made sense even from the point of view of narrowly conceived Croat nationalist politics. It was the majority dialect and the alliance with the Serbs could be used tactically, especially since the latter led the anti-imperial struggle in the Balkans since the first 1804 uprisings. Siding with the stronger Slavic brother, who was supposed to embody rebellion against foreign rule, could only be a tactical move, at least until the right to full independence could be realized under the banner of Croatia as a sovereign state entity.

After the 1991 declarations of independence from the common South Slavic state, Croatia was the first to invent and emphasize their existing minor linguistic differences in order to justify the discourse of ethnic particularism, despite the fact that *štokavski* speakers from Serbia and Croatia could understand each other much better than speakers of *kajkavski* and *štokavski* dialects within Croatia itself. The latest political platform of ethnic particularism required an emphasis on the insurmountable distinctiveness of the constituent peoples, based on pseudo-clerical interpretations of differences between the cultures of Christian Orthodoxy and Catholicism. In the case of Bosnia, Islam would be used with a similar purpose, attempting to define culture as a prosthesis of religion and not of language. In fact, the failure of the Yugoslav state confirmed that the Romantic notion of the nation-state, imagined as a territory based on common linguistic heritage and a shared folklore, had been radically shaken, as the historically residual cultural formation based on religious affiliation and identification with the former imperial master suddenly became dominant during the 1990s in the public discourse of emergent nations in the Western Balkans. There was a palpable shift in the definition of the imaginary foundations of culture, as an uncanny return of old imperial alliances began its haunting yet again.

Thus, the birth of post-Yugoslav nations was accompanied by the reinforcement of a fantasy resting on the twin pillars of monolingualism and freedom. 'To acquire a native language is to be reborn in a free country, to have a country entirely to oneself' (Brisset, 2000: 353). The monolingual fantasy of the pure native realm, not shared with any other nation or language, intentionally mistakes any mode of cultural sharing as domination, intent on placing full faith in the operative force of what Freud labelled 'narcissism of minor differences', to account for the discourse of

Eurocentric nationalism of his day (Freud, 1930: XXI, 114). By creating a gap between those who are in possession of the national prerogative (derived from religious affiliation this time) and those sudden aliens not sharing the strictly policed symbolic order deriving from Roman Catholicism, the Croat elites intentionally fostered the separation of the languages spoken by the non-identical Yugoslav twins to destroy the notion of the nation based on a common Slavic origin. The rebirth of Croatian as a separate language required translation as the distancing practice that would preclude sharing the language with the Serbs, both as the conquering external other and the insidious alien within the country that could not be imagined as free and pure, unless this residual element of exaggerated difference was expelled from the realm of shared signification and renounced as incomprehensible.

This type of separatist political practice sets itself against what is commonly assumed about translation as a *par excellence* activity, devoted to the bridging of cultural gaps and palliating misunderstandings after Babelic punishment, to provide humanity with the potential of overcoming legacies of conflict, war and trauma. A community engaged in this kind of translational nationalism struggles to discover and invent differences that would anchor it in the territory belonging to a single country, an imaginary monoculture that would not compromise its sovereign and independent status even at the price of a superfluous translation whose unstated political aim is the separation from a cultural location shared with its previous linguistic twin-turned-adversary.

Hyphenated Difference

'The miracle of translation does not take place every day; there is, at times a desert without a desert crossing,' writes Jacques Derrida, while addressing the growing issue of 'unreadability' haunting the extended public space created by globalization (Derrida, 1998: 72). The issue of the former Serbo-Croatian is therefore even more puzzling, since desert crossings were available on many different levels between the two warring states, yet the choice of the nationalist elites was to lose oneself in the desert sands of one's own particularity and to make sure that paths disappear in the violent hurricanes of nationalist becoming.

One of the most bizarre episodes in the history of unnecessary translation took place in Zagreb, Croatia, on the occasion of the first Serbian film premiere after the end of the Serbo-Croatian war. The film was *Wounds* (*Rane*) by Srđan Dragojević, a surreal story reflecting on the violence and life of Belgrade youth during the worst years of the Slobodan Milošević regime. Although the idioms used by the youth of both cultures are almost equivalent and mutually highly intelligible, the movie distributers in Croatia decided the film ought to be subtitled. This is how the journalist of the *Feral Tribune*, the voice of anti-nationalist Croatian intellectuals, described the atmosphere in the cinema:

> First the original title shows up on the screen in Latin script *Beograd, jesen 1991*, and then right below it the subtitle in Latin script explains, *Beograd, jesen 1991*[...] Pandemonium erupts in the movie theater. Laughter, tears, and enthusiastic knee slapping, although we're only two minutes into the film. There's no doubt, this is perhaps the most insane film event in the history of cinema, comparable maybe only to the premieres of American silent comedies. (Jurak, 1999: 32, my translation)

Reminiscent of the poetic device employed in Borges' story *Pierre Menard, autor del Quijote*, where the translation of Cervantes' masterpiece is really a non-translation by Pierre Menard a few centuries later, the reality of this event points to the cultural mechanism involved in the production of difference at any price (Borges, 1944: 54–64). The reaction of the Croatian audience is symptomatic of the division between the official cultural dictates of a new nation-state in the making and the general public that sees through transparent attempts to exaggerate differences and separate one cultural space from another, however absurd that may appear in the virtually identical languages of the Croats, Serbs, Bosnians, Montenegrins, and so on. Since the film itself uses the highly localized speech patterns of Belgrade urban youth, redolent with obscenities familiar in both Serbian and Croatian versions of the language, the task of the translator becomes even more complicated and bizarre as s/he is interpellated by the national demand to create difference where there is none to be found.

One of the most difficult problems that arose was in the translation of the vulgar signifier for the female sexual organ, often used to denote a person bearing moral qualities of spinelessness, cowardice and a lack of masculine power: *pička*. One of the characters, a young thug from the urban wasteland of New Belgrade, demonstrates his masculinity by declaring he will not run away from any sort of confrontation as if he were a coward: '*Neću da bežim k'o pička!*' The subtitler uses a synonymous word for the female sexual organ, *pizda*, claiming it for Croatian as a *differentia specifica* of the new national identity: '*Neću bježati kao pizda!*' In American English, it would be roughly translated as: 'I won't run off like a pussy'. Besides pointing to the most frequent syntactic difference (*da bežim/bježati*, or *da* + verb in the present tense as Serbian preference or using the infinitive as a Croatian one), the use of the *pička/pizda* for the female sexual organ is absolutely exchangeable across the BCSM territories. Miljenko Jergović, one of the most popular post-Yugoslav writers to emerge on the Croatian literary scene, specifically questions this inability of the subtitler to produce differences when translating dialogue saturated with obscenities.

> Namely, our language makers have invented no less than three words for helicopter (*uvrtnjak, vrtolet* and *zrakomlat*), but have not until the present day reported what's the score in the sexual acts and organs game, which are, perhaps by pure accident, most common in the creation of curses both among Serbs and Croats. (Jergović, 1999: 46, my translation)

His irony is poignant and recalls the relationship between the two nations and their widely shared arsenal of obscenities to demonstrate how similar the two non-identical twins of Yugoslavia are when it comes to the most profane level of speech culture, which remains out of step with the high literary standards that nationalist language creators try to impose on the general population. It is at this most colloquial level of language that the translation between the two former warring sides proves to be unnecessary, if not ridiculous, giving rise to the direct opposition of viewing audiences to artificially imposed official standards of linguistic (non-)difference.

There were no polemical articles in the Croatian press attempting to argue for the new cultural policy of translating from Serbian, since the linguistic facts about such practice were obviously very difficult to come by. Returning to Derrida's desert metaphor for untranslatability, one could say that the crossings were created to get to an already familiar place, one that the translator had set out from even before the winds had begun to obliterate the paths between the two non-identical cultural twins. Although German is used as the name of the language spoken in Switzerland, Austria and Germany, and English as the name of the language spoken in the United States and Australia, former Serbo-Croatian has been sentenced to the removal of its hyphen and subjected to nationalist cultural cloning, striving to produce linguistic difference as a metaphor for political and national sovereignty.

Fiction after Yugoslavia

Croatian author Borivoj Radaković uses the term *politolect* to describe the creation of what can be seen as a 'field-specific sociolect' (Hatim & Mason,

1990: 46) used by a closed circle of political functionaries and bureaucrats intent on promoting a monocultural vision of the country, in its struggle to gain the status of absolute semantic and linguistic difference (Kostić, 1999). The collective identity based on this principle is similar to that of other closed in-groups (prisoners, criminals, soldiers, sports fans, etc.) who create their particular idioms out of the need to prevent understanding by other social groups sharing the same 'national' language. One of the features of the *politolect* invoked by Radaković is its distinction from other types of jargon: its obvious intent is to come up with terms and usages that would require translation even from the perfectly comprehensible 'brotherly' idiom. The fact that the creation of the new *politolect* is based on the intentional invention of a language that would serve the dual purpose of instituting the necessity of translation on the one hand, and excluding ethnically opposing forces from the public sphere of the nation on the other, was the most conspicuous cultural effect of the Yugoslav break-up.

The 1997 statement by the leading Croatian literary critic Stanko Lasić that, as far as he is concerned, 'Serbian literature now occupies the same status as the Bulgarian one' has galvanized discussions about the issue of translation and contact between the two formerly related literary traditions, providing a new impetus for translation between the two non-identical cultural twins (Brešić, 2006: 122, my translation). Bulgarian is definitely a Slavic language different from both Serbian and Croatian, whose similarity is much greater than its difference. Lasić's statement is performative within the context of a dissolving country since it employs the notion of differentiation between Orthodox- (Bulgarian and Serbian) and Catholic- (Croatian) based cultures to reinforce the political sense of separation. Choices made in the translation of literary works since the secession of Croatia from Yugoslavia in 1991 are in themselves quite symptomatic of this cultural trend. Kostić writes about the first translation of the novel *Gifts of Time* (*Darovi vremena*) by Zoran Živković from Serbian into Croatian. The examples he provides parallel those discussed above in the translation of captions for the film *Rane*; some sentences are never translated, while those that are translated are so minimally different from the original that the act of translation just shows up the absurdity of this cultural practice in the context of former Serbo-Croatian. An apt example of this practice can be seen in an excerpt quoted by Kostić (1999: 32). The 'original' Serbian by Zoran Živković reads as follows:

> Prešao je pogledom po zidu naspram prozora. Nije mogao dobro da vidi u polumraku, ali to nije ni bilo potrebno. Znao je šta se tamo nalazi.

The translator of the novel, Stanislav Vidmar, rendered this very same sentence as follows:

> Prošao je pogledom po zidu nasuprot prozora. Nije mogao dobro vidjeti u polumraku, ali to nije ni bilo potrebno. Znao je što se tamo nalazi.
>
> [His gaze moved along the wall across from the window. He was not able to see well in the semi-darkness, but that proved unnecessary. He knew what was there.]

Differences between the two versions are mostly dialectal and often present former Serbo-Croatian synonyms as terms embodying the national *differentia specifica* between the formerly related Serb and Croat cultures (e.g. *naspram/nasuprot* [Eng. *across*] are synonyms). This trait of translation as the agent of literary difference offers a glimpse into the processes of nation-building that have been regulating the standardization of modern European languages ever since the end of the 18th century. As the evolution of Italian or German after the 1870s testifies, the process of national self-identification relied on the literary canon to imagine the new national territory and to establish laws that would regulate proper linguistic usage at the expense of a former heteroglossia of territories inhabited by a variety of ethnic subjects. The dominance of one dialect over another, such as the suppression of Southern Italian dialects at the expense of Northern ones during the formation of standard Italian, would have been similar, except for the fact that a certain standardization of usage had already occurred in Serbo-Croatian during half a century of the common Yugoslav state. The use of the *šta/što* pronoun from the last sentence of the quote is indeed so fluid and undecidable between different speakers of Serbian/Croatian/Bosnian/Montenegrin that its minimal vocalic a/o alternation is probably the most vivid linguistic manifestation of the absurd nature of this conflict between separate political entities whose languages are commonly intelligible to each of their respective subjects.

Some of the responses to this kind of absurdity were themselves quite ingenious – the Croatian anti-war magazine *Arkzin* established a literary prize evocatively named *Bvulgarica* (Latin for Bulgarian, adj.). This act of framing a public narrative of division by 'labelling' (see Baker, 2006: 122) was done in order to respond to the already mentioned statement by Stanko Lasić about Serbian literature slipping further Eastward into the Bulgarian cultural zone for Croat readers. This 'Orientalization' of Serbian is in tune with the overall political struggle to assert sovereignty by claiming incompatibility between the two formerly fraternal cultures. After all the barbarity exhibited by the 'other side', by the Serb twin one loves to hate, translation is now considered a necessity despite their mutual sense of understanding. The two South Slavic twins cannot speak the same language, since the Serbs are labelled/framed as genocidal *guslars* whose culture could only serve as an instrument of oppression if the tiniest sign of understanding is shown to them. Therefore, translation has to be instituted, even when it brings with it the a/o divide in *šta/što* to emphasize the difference which has a hard time being a difference at all. The common idiom of Serbo-Croatian is simultaneously recognized as a trace of that abject and scorned Other and the glorious illusion of a proper national identity born in the struggle with that demonic Other. The similarity of myself to that demonic Other has to be denied in every aspect of culture, especially in language shared for more than a century and a half. Some scholarly responses from translators working in the former Yugoslavia have tried to come to terms with this issue from the perspective of the cultural outsider forced to take sides in the conflict and to fit themselves into the liberal paradigm used to explain the conflict to Western observers. A notable example is the writing of Francis Jones, who embraces the Bosniak narrative in order to distance himself from the Serbs and to some extent the Croats as well (Jones, 2004). Although he translates into English and his work is therefore only tangentially relevant to this article devoted to mutual Serbo-Croat translation, it is symptomatic of a trend created by Western intellectuals to assuage their consciences and divide their loyalties between the warring parties.

Can opposition to translation, which paradoxically promotes cultural understanding between Serbs and Croats and resists the monolingualist fantasy of pure difference in the guise of an official national tongue, be understood as a force of an old nostalgia for Yugoslavia? If nostalgia rests on the rational demand to preserve what is common in the service of understanding, then the resistance to translation between the non-identical twins could be construed as a preservation of common Slavic roots as a linguistic legacy, apart from the nationalist call for misunderstanding and hatred. The imaginary economy of borderline tendencies dominant in the psychic life of small nations whose identity is reinforced by the fallacy of monolingualist hallucinations yields separatist political outcomes, the cultivation of state *politolects* as tools of ethnic separation from the evil twin, and enforces the vision of a pure beauty of the native landscape belonging to a single national configuration. It is more likely that the impulse to choose non-translation in the case of non-identical twins comes from the everyday life of subjects engaged with otherness as a part of a new global call for understanding despite hostility. While the common south Slavic standard will not be required under those circumstances, translation between the formerly fraternal nations will not be required either.

The translation practices outlined in this article have been instituted during a particularly volatile post-conflict period in the former Yugoslavia and reflect the desire of the new nationalist elites to establish political sovereignty by cultural means. It is also true that this practice has been largely abandoned in Croatian cultural activities after the defeat of the right-wing Tuđman government. Translation between the cultures of the non-identical Serbian and Croatian twins still persists within the legal system that now certifies official translators for administrative documents originating in Serbia. This soft return of the hyphen in Serbo-Croatian is proof that cultural bonds between the two Slavic cultures are definitely stronger than the over-political agendas of nationalist leaders poised to strengthen their power through the production of difference at the expense of bridging the gaps between the sides involved in the conflict. The case of post-Yugoslav translation during the 1990s will serve as an example for scholars who tend to take translation as an exemplary vehicle for intercultural understanding, by demonstrating that misunderstanding can be manufactured within contexts in which understanding already exists as a cultural given.

References

Baker, M. (2006) *Translation and Conflict: A Narrative Account*. London/New York: Routledge.
Borges, J.L. (1944) *Pierre Menard, autor del Quijote*. In *Ficciones*. Buenos Aires: Editorial Sur.
Brešić, V. (2006) Lasić i njegovi sugovornici [Lasić and his interlocutors]. *Zarez* 183, 29 June, 55–57.
Brissett, A. (2000) Translation and cultural identity. In L. Venuti (ed.) *The Translation Studies Reader* (pp. 337–368). London: Routledge.
Derrida, J. (1998) *Monolingualism of the Other or The Prosthesis of Origin* (Patrick Mensah, trans.). Stanford: Stanford University Press.
Freud, S. (1930) *The Standard Edition of the Complete Psychological Works* (James Strachey, trans.). London: The Hogarth Press.
Hatim, B. and Mason, I. (1990) *Discourse and the Translator*. London/New York: Longman.
Jergović, M. (1999) Marš u sporni organ [Back to the wrong organ]. *Feral Tribune* 707, 5 April, 23.

Jones, F. (2004) Ethics, aesthetics and decision: Literary translating in the wars of the Yugoslav succession. *Meta* 49 (4), 711–728.
Jurak, D. (1999) Rane na hrvatskom [Wounds in Croatian]. *Feral Tribune* 707, 5 April, 34.
Kostić, S. (1999) Prvi prevod srpskog romana na hrvatski jezik [The first translation of the Serbian novel into Croatian]. *Vreme* 456, 2 October, 17–18.
Lasić, S. (1997) Letter to Rafo Bogišić. *Vijenac* 99, 32–35.

Chapter 16
Translation as a Threat to Fascism

C. RUNDLE

Introduction

In my research on translation in Fascist Italy (Rundle, 1999, 2000, 2004, 2010) I have been struck by one feature which I think is worth reflecting on and which, perhaps, goes counter to normal expectations concerning the role of translation and translators within a dictatorship or totalitarian system. This is that the regime's main concern was not the impact of individual texts that may have slipped through the censor's net, nor the potentially seditious effect of politically unreliable translators; rather it was concerned with the symbolic, and therefore political, value of translation as an overall phenomenon. In this chapter I shall describe the two significant stages in the evolution of the regime that directly affected its perception of translation. Firstly, translation as a form of cultural exchange came into conflict with Fascist imperialist ambitions, calling into question the cultural hegemony of the regime and its ability to expand abroad. Secondly, with the introduction of racist legislation, translation came to be seen as a form of cultural miscegenation, a practice that, if allowed to continue uncontrolled, could threaten the cultural purity of the nation. In both these instances it was the symbolic, propaganda value of translation that was the focus of the regime's attention. They did not fear the translators or publishers, over whom they had quite sufficient control; they did not see translation as an act of opposition in itself, given that this form of cultural exchange could fairly easily be accommodated within a Fascist rhetoric of cultural renewal. Instead, the regime reacted against the phenomenon when it could no longer avoid perceiving translation as a threatening sign of its own weakness, a sign of the failure of its cultural project. It was for this specific reason, I shall argue, that the regime intervened when it did against translation.

Fascist Imperialism and Translation

In October 1935 Italy invaded Ethiopia and by May 1936 it was officially annexed and became *l'Africa Orientale Italiana* (Italian East Africa). The decision to embark on a process of imperial conquest was one which Mussolini had been preparing for some time. He felt that the transformation of the Italian people which he had started at home needed to be completed through the tempering experience of war and conquest abroad. Furthermore, he wanted to impress upon the world the new vigour and power of the Italian nation and take what he felt to be his rightful place among the world's superpowers.[1]

The colonial enterprise brought about some profound changes in the cultural climate in Italy. The imposition of sanctions on Italy by the British-led League of Nations provoked a furious reaction on the part of the Italians. There was an upsurge of national pride and xenophobia, which took the official shape of a policy of economic autarky, a policy which then continued even after the sanctions ended. This climate of resentment against foreign influence and intervention soon encouraged those who disapproved of translation to intervene, in particular the Authors and Writers Union, led by the futurist poet F.T. Marinetti. They had long felt that the new market for translations of popular fiction was spoiling the Italian readership by creating a taste for low-quality literature published in cheap editions. With some justification, it must be said, they saw their own more elitist province of literary aesthetics being eroded by the sheer volume of pulp literature that was being imported, and rapidly sold.[2]

Much political significance was also being attributed at the time to recent statistics showing that Italy published more translations than any other country in the world. This was already an unpalatable fact in itself, that Italy should be so *receptive* to foreign influence, but what made it more galling was the fact that only a very small number of Italian texts were being translated into other languages. In other words, there was a *translation deficit* which undermined any confidence in the success of Italian culture abroad.[3] Clearly, translations were being seen as an indicator of the cultural health of the nation, a sign of the corrupting influence of the publishers in the eyes of writers like Marinetti, but also the source of much needed cultural stimulus in the eyes of those who sought to encourage the development of Fascist culture. Comparisons were drawn with Germany, which also published a high number of translations, but whose translation trade balance was comfortably in surplus with a very high number of titles being translated out of German (though the Germans themselves where by no means so confident of the successful expansion of their culture).⁴ In a rather martial vision of cultural exchange, translations out of Italian were potentially a very Fascist 'instrument of penetration', allowing Italian culture to vigorously reach out and force its way into other cultures like some sort of literary sword. But, by the same token, the success of translations at home were a sign of weakness on the part of the Italian people, showing how far they still were from achieving a strong national and Fascist culture.⁵

Mussolini's campaign for economic autarky provided Marinetti and the Authors and Writers Union with the opportunity they sought to try and encourage some form of official intervention against translation. They argued, in public conferences and in the press, that autarky should also be imposed on the cultural sphere and that translations should be subject to some form of quality control, as well as being governed by a principle of reciprocity – that is the number of translations published from a particular language should be proportional to the number of Italian works translated into that same language. They called for the institution of an official register of translators and for a ministerial Translations Commission to be formed to monitor the situation; both were suggestions intended to undermine the independence of the publishers whom they accused of unpatriotically favouring their own profit over the interests of the nation – damaging accusations which the publishers vehemently refuted.

While no concrete barriers were set up in response to this campaign, the regime did begin to take an increasing interest in the question of translation in the wake of the Ethiopian war, showing a new determination to exert control over the literary life of the nation that the rise to the status of imperial power brought with it. The years following the establishment of the empire in 1936, up until the introduction of racist legislation in late 1938, were years of increasing pressure in which, for the first time, the regime began to take a specific interest in translation. The first significant step was to require publishers and printers to inform the Ministry for Popular Culture (*Ministero della Cultura Popolare*), the state censor, *beforehand* when they intended to publish a translation – to my knowledge the first official instruction to target translation specifically rather than the more general dispositions concerning literature that we find before this date.⁶ This was then followed by the launching of a detailed survey of all translations that had been published so far since World War I and all those that were intended to be published in the future. Finally, in March 1938, just two months after the launch of the survey, new instructions made it obligatory for publishers to obtain *prior authorization* from the Ministry before publishing a translation.⁷

So how are we to understand the significance of these measures? On the one hand these new instructions did not greatly alter procedures for the publishing of translations; in theory all publications needed prior authorization (from the police authorities) before being distributed. However, these measures did ensure that the Ministry would have access to updated information on the translations being published and they also ensured that the publishers were aware that translations were now an issue in which the Ministry was increasingly taking an interest. It is my belief that this increased interest was not the result of a concern for the artistic and commercial interests of the authors but was instead the natural consequence of a cultural policy that was slowly adjusting itself to the ideological implications of imperial conquest. The first implication was that a nation of the status that Italy was now supposed to have acquired ought to be a nation that was culturally dominant, as well as politically so. The second implication was that, as the nation came into closer contact with new races that it was supposed to rule over, and in the face of which it was supposed to show a natural superiority, then it became imperative that that nation's culture also show a natural superiority on an international level. Clearly, the reality portrayed in the figures on translation, of Italy's limited cultural influence and especially the ease with which it was being influenced from outside, was very different from such ideal objectives. What we see here, then, are the first signs of the regime taking stock of the situation and beginning to act, and translations became a focal point for all that was considered wrong with the current situation and that needed to be addressed/corrected. That the regime did not react more aggressively can be attributed to a number of factors. Firstly, despite the accusations levelled at them by Marinetti and the Authors and Writers Union, the Publishers Federation was in fact quite loyal to the regime and, on the whole, enjoyed a cordial and collaborative relationship with the Ministry, especially with the division responsible for books. In its capacity as censor, the Ministry probably felt little inclination, therefore, to damage the publishers by introducing severely restrictive measures against translations – at this stage at least. Another probable reason for initial tolerance shown towards translations is that a growing market for popular mass culture was not in itself an unfascist phenomenon. On the contrary, cheap popular fiction created on an industrial scale using new production and distribution methods might help to dismantle the ivory tower into which intellectuals had, according to the Fascist view, always withdrawn; this was quite in tune with the more anti-bourgeois, anti-establishment, spirit of Fascism.

Fascist Racism and Translation

We have seen how, between an initial period when the Fascist regime had no specific policy concerning translation, and the period we are about to describe when racist legislation was introduced in Italy, there was an interim period during which an increasing interest in (and potential hostility towards) translation was one of the consequences of a campaign of imperial conquest. The particularity of these years, 1935–1938, is that translation was discussed in terms which were dominated by notions of cultural conquest and cultural trade wars, but where explicit racism and anti-Semitism were still absent from the discourse. The seed was being sown as the regime came to realize that it was being culturally penetrated but had not, as yet, openly blossomed into a desire to purge the national culture of all that was simply foreign.

The introduction of racist legislation in 1938 was to have an enormous impact on the cultural life of the regime and, indirectly, on the translation industry. We left the Italian Ministry for Popular Culture in March 1938 requiring that prior authorization be requested for all new translations. In the autumn of that same year, the Minister of Education (*Ministro dell'educazione nazionale*), Giuseppe Bottai, anticipating the racial laws that he knew would shortly be introduced, informed schools – as the school year was about to begin – that all text books by Jewish authors would have to be replaced. This caused the schools, and the publishers who were supposed to supply them, considerable problems, not least because it was by no means clear who would classify as a 'Jewish' author under the new legislation. A practical solution was found thanks to the collaborative spirit of the Publishers Federation which drew up its own list of Jewish authors whose text books should be removed from distribution.[8]

This event was important because it marked a watershed in the publishers' relations with the regime: for the first time since its consolidation in the mid-1920s, the regime was imposing its political priorities on the publishers in a way that left no room for manoeuvre or negotiation in favour of their commercial interests; and furthermore, the publishers reacted to this change by actually helping to tie the noose that would be used to hang them in a rather undignified effort to limit the damage by making sure no non-Jewish authors were accidentally included in the ban. From this time onwards, the publishers would find themselves continually on the defensive as their relative independence and freedom of manoeuvre would gradually be eroded by a series of restrictive measures.

At the same time as they were having to deal with the new regulations imposed by the Education Minister, the publishers also had a new threat to face from the Ministry of Popular Culture in the form of the notorious Commission for the Purging of Books (*Comissione per la bonifica libraria*). The commission had two main objectives: to apply the new 'racial directives' (which officially became law in November 1938) and to deal with the question of translations. In the words of the Minister, Dino Alfieri:

> The task of the commission is to draw up precise criteria and identify the quickest and most suitable means to achieve a complete review of book production in Italy and of foreign works translated into Italian. The need for this review is all the more imperative in relation to the racial directives imparted from above.[9]

Once the commission began to operate, however, it seems that its first priority was to carry out its racist purge and the question of translations took second place, with little reference being made in surviving documents to foreign books, either in the original or in translation. The publishers were allowed to attend the meetings of the commission but they were not given a role in the selection of the texts that were to be purged. This exclusion from the selection process contrasts noticeably with the way the Education Minister had just entrusted the publishers with the task of eliminating textbooks by Jewish authors – in effect a form of self-regulation – and would seem to imply a greater hostility and mistrust on the part of the Culture Minister, more in line with the suspicion felt by the Authors and Writers Union.[10] Feeling the snub, the Publishers Federation tried to take back the initiative by pre-empting the decisions that the commission would make by removing from circulation those texts which they expected to be purged.

It is worth reflecting for a moment on the source of this mistrust. While the publishers could, on the whole, be trusted not to publish seditious or immoral literature, the Culture Ministry clearly did not feel that they could be entrusted with the task of imposing a degree of self-regulation and restraint on themselves when it came to the profitable question of translation – a question which was becoming politically sensitive in the new climate of imperial Italy but which was not, strictly speaking, a censorship problem. It was a question of image, of what was considered suitable, a question which relied on a political understanding of Italy's position and which could not easily be set in the balance against the inevitable losses that the publishers would sustain in the event of any restrictions. The campaign for 'cultural autarky' led by the Authors and Writers Union had succeeded in highlighting the anomaly that translations represented. Publishing high numbers of translations was becoming a political liability – something the publishers had feared since they were first the target of hostile campaigns in the press in 1934–1936 but which had never fully materialized until now.

In February 1939, then, roughly six months after its first meeting, the commission met in a plenary session to approve the lists of banned works that had been prepared. The president of the Publishers Federation was also present and he announced that the publishers had tried to facilitate the work of the commission by voluntarily removing 900 books from circulation – to the satisfaction of the Minister.[11] The publishers had bowed to the inevitable and given proof of their reliability, probably in the hope of earning a bit of leniency when it came to the question of translations.

Another issue on which the publishers gave way without question was that of children's literature, when a conference was held on the subject in Bologna in November 1938. This was an issue where no distinction of any kind was made between an anti-Semitic purge and a purge of translations; all outside influence was considered potentially pernicious and had to be removed. Representatives of the Publishers Federation were present and the conference was presided over by their great antagonist Marinetti. The concluding document voted by the conference expressed two objectives where children's literature was concerned: to exclude all foreign imports, and to insist on a clearly Fascist spirit in all that was published.[12] This was a second significant watershed, in that here the publishers publicly stood by a decision to ban all foreign, or foreign-inspired, works – the sort of measure they had always resisted and fought against. It would appear that, as with the question of racial purity, the appeal for vigilance over the purity of Italian youth was so imperative that it was politically impossible to put forward any objections.

By April 1940 the work of the commission was almost complete: over 1400 works had been withdrawn from circulation. Satisfied with the progress made in removing all Jewish literature from circulation, the new Culture Minister, Alessandro Pavolini, now turned his attention more closely to the question of translation which, though it was not as politically sensitive, was clearly bound up in his mind with the need to maintain the status of Italian culture and to purify it of all unsuitable elements. Pavolini was quite explicit in his disapproval of the invasion of translations that Italy had seen during the 1930s. He felt that it was the 'eternal task' of Fascist Italy to 'irradiate' rather than receive.[13] Furthermore, he felt that it was racially inappropriate for Italian culture to be so open to foreign influence and talked of translations being 'a disorganized and poisonous importation of doctrines' that had clouded the edges of 'that great and pure current which is the Italian tradition' with 'art and life that are entirely alien to the style and genius of our race'.[14] Within the Minister's ideology of racism and its rhetoric, then, translation had now become a cultural pollutant, as well as a symptom of the failure of Fascist cultural expansion.

Although he would tackle the translation problem with much more determination than that shown, in the end, by his predecessor Alfieri, Pavolini was probably more sympathetic to the publishers and their interests, adopting a method of consultation and persuasion rather than blank imposition, and choosing not to use the commission – which was in effect a kind of jury of peers inflicted on the publishers.[15] Nevertheless, for the next two years he began a slow process of clamping down on the translation market.

In October 1940 Pavolini informed publishers, to their dismay, that he was planning to impose a quota of 10% on translations, though this did not take immediate effect. Then in March 1941 the Ministry ruled that all fiction sold in periodical (or magazine) format must also have prior authorization, thereby closing a loophole that a number of publishers had been exploiting to publish cheap, popular, translated fiction. Shortly afterwards, in July 1941, the Ministry banned all crime fiction in periodical format. This was aimed at reducing the market for such literature (which was dominated by translations) by removing low-cost editions and allowing only expensive hardback editions to circulate, here too with prior authorization. In fact, just a year later, all crime fiction would be banned by Pavolini's successor. The final act in Pavolini's own campaign against translations took place in January 1942, when he imposed a quota of 25% – that is translations could make up no more than 25% of each publisher's overall production. This much less severe quota was negotiated and agreed with the publishers.[16] Aside from its actual impact, which is hard to gauge given the paper shortages and other difficulties that were increasingly hindering publication during the war, this quota has an important symbolic value. It marks the end of a long and gradual process of closure towards translation (by which I mean translations in book form) – a restriction which is, perhaps, more remarkable for the fact that it came so late, than for the fact that it was imposed at all.

Conclusion

In this chapter we have seen, then, how the Fascist regime's attitude towards translation was conditioned by two important political events: the establishment of the empire and the introduction of racist legislation. The first event created a political climate in which those members of the cultural establishment who felt threatened by translations felt authorized to attack them. And while the regime did not respond with any direct measures, there is clear evidence that it too began to view translation with increasing hostility – a hostility due principally to the sheer extent of the phenomenon, rather than due to what was actually being published. The second event brought with it such drastic policies of intervention in the cultural life of the country that the relationship between the regime and the publishers was irrevocably changed. The publishers were put on the defensive and although they continued to strive for more favourable conditions, they were unable to reverse the ideological shift which had now been consolidated, where an unhindered flow of translation was no longer tolerated by the regime but was seen as part of a wider threat of cultural pollution from which the nation needed to be defended. When translation was either part of a reciprocal cultural exchange, or when it was the expression of Italian cultural dominance, it met with Fascist approval. But when it was a form of cultural miscegenation, an unhealthy fascination for the exotic, an unrestrained intermingling with all that was most decadent in foreign culture, it was a phenomenon that, to the Fascist mind, was full of dangers.

Notes

1. Mussolini's desire for international influence also led him to send troops to Spain to fight alongside Franco – to the dismay of many on the left wing of the Fascist party, who could not understand how Mussolini could align himself with the forces of ecclesiastical reaction against the forces of republican revolution.
2. For a more detailed account of the history of translation in Fascist Italy during the 1930s, see Rundle (2010). For more details specifically on the period after the war in Ethiopia, see Rundle (2004).
3. See Rundle (2010: chap. 2).
4. The Nazis complained that too many of the texts that were being translated out of German were by Jews or political exiles and that they were creating a distorted image of the German *Volk* abroad. See Sturge (2004: chap. 3, especially pp. 92, 99).
5. See Santoro (2003) on Fascist attempts at cultural penetration abroad, especially in Eastern Europe.
6. Some limitations on the serialization of translated fiction in the daily press had, however, already been introduced, a fact which is in line with the generally much more severe censorship policy that was applied to periodical publications as opposed to books. See Fabre (2007: 28).
7. Rundle (2010: chap. 4). For more details on Fascist censorship of translation, see Bonsaver (2007: 221–236), Fabre (1998, 2007), Dunnett (2002) and Rundle (1999, 2000).
8. See Fabre (1998: 114, 121) and Rundle (2010: chap. 5).
9. From a note to Mussolini written on 12 September 1938, the day before the first meeting of the commission. The original can be found in Archivio Centrale

dello Stato (Rome), Ministero della Cultura Popolare, b.59, 'Produzione libraria italiana e straniera tradotta in italiano. Revisione totale'.
10. Cf. Fabre (1998: 74) on Alfieri's probable hostility towards the publishers.
11. The meeting and Alfieri's response are reported in *Giornale della libreria* LII-6, 11 February 1939: p. 42.
12. See Rundle (2010: chap. 5). The conference was reported in the *Giornale della libreria* LI–47, 19 November 1938: 325–327.
13. The importance that Pavolini attributed to this vision of an expansionist Fascist culture is confirmed by the fact the he was chairman of the National Institute for Cultural Relations Abroad (*Istituto nazionale per le relazioni culturali con l'estero*, IRCE), which was founded in 1938 with the task of '[promoting] scientific, artistic and social relations between Italy and foreign countries as a means of spreading Italian culture' (Santoro, 2003: 55).
14. The quotes are from a speech given by Pavolini at the annual inauguration of the Italo-Germanic Association [n.d.]. Archivio Centrale dello Stato (Rome), Ministero della Cultura Popolare, b.103, f. 'Discorsi ed articoli del Ministro Pavolini'.
15. What Bonsaver (2007: chap. 8) has called 'weak autarky'.
16. See Rundle (2010: chap. 5).

References

Bonsaver, G. (2007) *Censorship and Literature in Fascist Italy*. Toronto: University of Toronto Press.
Dunnett, J. (2002) Foreign literature in Fascist Italy: Circulation and censorship. *TTR: Traduction, terminologie, rédaction* 15 (2), 97–123.
Fabre, G. (1998) *L'Elenco. Censura fascista, editoria e autori ebrei*. Torino: Silvano Zamorani editore.
Fabre, G. (2007) Fascism, censorship and translation. In F. Billiani (ed.) *Modes of Censorship and Translation* (pp. 27–59). Manchester: St Jerome.
Rundle, C. (1999) Publishing translations in Mussolini's Italy: A case study of Arnoldo Mondadori. *Textus* XII (2), 427–442.
Rundle, C. (2000) The censorship of translation in Fascist Italy. *The Translator* 6 (1), 67–86.
Rundle, C. (2004) Resisting foreign penetration: The anti-translation campaign in Italy in the wake of the Ethiopian war. In F. Brizio-Skov (ed.) *Reconstructing Societies in the Aftermath of War: Memory, Identity and Reconciliation* (pp. 292–307). Boca Raton, FL: Bordighera Press.
Rundle, C. (2010) *Publishing Translations in Fascist Italy*. Oxford: Peter Lang.
Santoro, S. (2003) The cultural penetration of Fascist Italy abroad and in eastern Europe. *Journal of Modern Italian Studies* 8 (1), 36–66.
Sturge, K. (2004) *'The Alien Within': Translation into German During the Nazi Regime*. Munich: iudicium.

Chapter 17
Censors and Censorship Boards in Franco's Spain (1950s-1960s): An Overview Based on the TRACE Cinema Catalogue

C. GUTIÉRREZ LANZA

Introduction

This contribution, which is part of the work undertaken by the TRACE project,[1] sets out to provide an account of the tensions that arose as a result of censorship policies and activities in relation to foreign cinema in Spain during the 1950s and 1960s. During this significant period within Franco's regime (1939–1975), the views of successive government ministers changed from conservative to more liberal. As a part of this liberalization process, in contrast to previous decades, the 1960s witnessed a political *apertura* ('opening up') from within, and a series of institutional readjustments which caused numerous changes in the way the censorship system worked. Official decisions at the *Ministerio de Información y Turismo* ('Ministry of Information and Tourism'[2]; hereafter 'MIT') under Minister Manuel Fraga Iribarne were generally assumed to be more permissive and tolerant than under his predecessors.

A very important role in this process of *apertura* was played by translated – both dubbed and subtitled – cinema. A new, more liberal *Junta de Clasificación y Censura de Películas Cinematográficas* ('Cinema Classification and Censorship Board'), created in 1962, raised the level of tolerance and approved for the commercial circuits many dubbed films which had been banned by the previous *Junta* on the grounds of poor moral standards. This way, some morally controversial topics such as infidelity, adultery and broken marriages, characteristic of many foreign melodramas, made their way onto Spanish screens. Besides, from 1967 Spanish audiences were allowed to watch many foreign films which were not considered suitable for the commercial circuits, by patronising the so-called *Salas Especiales* (those special cinemas of no more than 500 seats in cities with populations of over 50,000 or in specific tourist resorts, exclusively intended to show foreign films in their original or subtitled versions or Spanish 'films of special interest' in a proportion of 3:1 respectively) or *Salas de Arte y Ensayo* (those *Salas Especiales* destined to show selected 'quality films').

However, this new, more open attitude resulted in opposition from pro-regime extreme groups on the one hand, especially from the most conservative members of the Catholic Church, who could not accept the growing distance between the Church and the State, and resistance from anti-regime groups on the other hand, suspicious of a more lenient approach to the control of cultural products. A fierce attack from some members of the Catholic Church on the new, more progressive ministerial decisions of the Fraga Iribarne period resulted in an extensive official *Informe* (an unpublished report) issued in 1963, which not only tried to defend and justify those new liberalizing decisions, but also provided a detailed account of the profiles of the new censors and a list of the films and plays approved or banned by this new team.

This *Informe*, and the change of course in the Ministry reflected by it, together with the official ministerial decisions (*Órdenes* and *Decretos*) on censorship published at the time in the periodical *Boletín Oficial del Estado* ('Official State Bulletin'; hereafter '*BOE*'), will be used as our main sources; examples from the handwritten and signed reports issued by cinema censors will also be used. Such reports are part of the documentation TRACE researchers have consulted in the AGA (*Archivo General de la Administración*, 'General Administration Archive') when investigating the English–Spanish translation and censorship of foreign cinema productions. They have also been integrated in the TRACE cinema catalogue of English–Spanish translated censored films that have been compiled and analysed in the framework of the TRACE project. These documents will be used to provide empirical evidence of the internal procedures of censorship under Franco in relation to translated films (dubbed for the commercial circuits and subtitled for *Salas Especiales* and *Salas de Arte y Ensayo*).

Censors and Censorship Boards in Spain (1950s–1960s): A Brief Historical Account

Background

In 1942 the *Comisión Nacional de Censura Cinematográfica*, whose work was overseen by the *Junta Nacional Superior de Censura Cinematográfica*, took over responsibility for cinema censorship (*BOE* 26 November 1942). From then on the presence of the representative of the *autoridad eclesiástica* ('ecclesiastical authority') was compulsory in any of the sessions of the *Comisión Nacional*.[3] This increasing control of the official censorship bodies by the Catholic Church, particularly characteristic of the 1940s, confirms its privileged position with respect to other social groups at the time. It reached its peak in 1946, the year when the Spanish regime was condemned and sanctioned by the United Nations and when the *Junta Superior de Orientación Cinematográfica* was created (*Orden Ministerio de Educación Nacional* 28 June 1946; *BOE* 19 July 1946) in an attempt to simplify procedures and apply unified criteria to all decisions. As stated in article 4 of this *Orden*, the presence of the ecclesiastical representative, considered an expert in moral and religious issues, remained compulsory. Moreover, from then on the Church representative was the only member of the board to enjoy the power of veto, which preserved his own independence from the rest of the members of the board. This privilege was also emphasized in article 13 of the *Orden* of 7 October 1947 (*BOE* 11 October 1947), which contained the internal guidelines of the *Junta Superior*.

The conservative years (1950s): The need for international recognition of the regime

A politician with traditionalist views, Gabriel Arias Salgado, was in charge of the Ministry of Information and Tourism in the 1950s – from 18 July 1951 until 10 July 1962. During this decade, the conservative views of the Ministers and their wish to preserve the nature of the Spanish regime contrasted with the need for acceptance abroad, which included the establishment of political agreements with other countries. After very complex negotiations, Spain signed the *Concordato* ('Concordat') with the Vatican in 1953 under Pius XII which, among other things, allowed Franco to control the selection of new bishops, something which many members of the Spanish Church had not easily accepted. Spain was also finally admitted as a member of the United Nations in 1955 (Lleonart Amsélem, 1995: 101). These events heralded on the one hand the awaited international recognition of the Spanish regime and on the other hand the start of the growing distance between the Spanish Catholic Church and the Spanish State. This emergent decline in the relationship between the Catholic Church and the State was made evident in the regulations of the *Junta de Clasificación y Censura*, created in 1952 (*Decreto* of the *Presidencia del Gobierno* 21 March 1952; *BOE* 31 March 1952). As part of this *Junta*, in the Censorship Branch there was an *Ordinario Diocesano*,[4] who was in charge of the preservation of moral standards, but he was prevented from using the power of veto, which was finally abolished by ministerial law issued by the MIT on 20 February 1964 (*BOE* 14 March 1964).

Directions on film censorship had originally been given by Pius XI in his Encyclical Letter 'Vigilanti Cura' (Pius XI, 1936), later repeated by Pius XII in his Encyclical Letter 'Miranda Prorsus' on motion pictures, radio and television (Pius XII, 1957). On 17 February 1950, the Spanish ecclesiastical authorities approved the *Instrucciones y normas para la censura moral de espectáculos* ('Instructions and Standards Regarding Moral Censorship of Public Performances'). It was a written code of censorship norms which coexisted with the official, political censorship system and provided a unified moral guide for public performances aimed at critics, priests and audiences by means of the following film classification, published in the same year in the periodical *Ecclesia* (for further discussion, see Martínez Bretón, 1988):

(1) *Todos, incluso niños* ('all audiences, including children');
(2) *Jóvenes* ('young viewers from 14 to 21 years of age');
(3) *Mayores* ('adults 21 years and older');
(3R) *Mayores, con reparos* ('adults 21 years and older, with reservations regarding moral grounds');
(4) *Gravemente peligrosa (léase rechazable)* ('seriously dangerous [the film should be banned]').

Although this code was systematically used to classify every film that was shown on Spanish cinema screens, only the official boards of censorship had the power to issue the final verdict. According to the TRACE cinema catalogue, out of a total of 1321 films authorized by the *Junta de Clasificación y Censura*, dubbed from English into Spanish and shown in Spanish cinemas during the Arias Salgado period, only 13 (0.98%; 13/1321) were classified as '4' by the religious censors. The relatively small percentage of so-called 'seriously dangerous' films authorized by the *Junta* for showing demonstrates that the *Junta* was very much in favour of preserving the moral doctrine of the Church at that time. The 13 foreign films which were actually approved for showing are shown in Table 17.1, by date of release in Spain.

The political *apertura* (1960s): Opposition and resistance

During the 1960s there was a desire for a new spirit of cultural liberalization in Spain. The new Minister of Information and Tourism, Manuel Fraga Iribarne (10 July 1962–29 October 1969), initiated a period of 'moderate

Table 17.1 Foreign films dubbed into Spanish from English, classified as '4' by religious censors, approved by civil boards and shown in Spanish cinemas during the Arias Salgado period (18 July 1951–10 July 1962)

Original title (director and year)	Translated title	Release in Spain
Rio (Brahm 1939)	Noches en Río	22/10/1951
The Lady Gambles (Gordon 1949)	Dirección prohibida	26/11/1951
Rope of Sand (Dieterle 1949)	Soga de arena	31/12/1951
Duel in the Sun (Vidor 1946)	Duelo al sol	12/10/1953
My Forbidden Past (Stevenson 1951)	Odio y orgullo	01/02/1954
Gone to Earth (Powell & Pressburger 1950)	Corazón salvaje	28/09/1954
Kiss Tomorrow Goodbye (Douglas 1950)	Corazón de hielo	27/09/1955
Love in the Afternoon (Wilder 1957)	Ariane	14/10/1957
Cat on a Hot Tin Roof (Brooks 1958)	La gata sobre el tejado de zinc	01/02/1960
Portrait in Black (Gordon 1960)	Retrato en negro	02/04/1961
That Kind of Woman (Lumet 1959)	Esa clase de mujer	28/08/1961
Go Naked in the World (MacDougall 1961)	Desnuda frente al mundo	06/11/1961
Butterfield 8 (Mann 1960)	Una mujer marcada	23/11/1961

Source: TRACE cinema catalogue.

tolerance' (Gutiérrez Lanza, 2002: 152), which included the reappointment of José María García Escudero as the new *Director General de Cinematografía y Teatro*. Previously appointed to the post in 1951, García Escudero had resigned prematurely in 1952, mainly because of his liberal approach and his willingness to promote certain films that included social criticism.

García Escudero was quite an influential figure during and after the Francoist period. As the author of several books and articles, the organizer of conferences and the subject of many interviews, his works and public appearances allowed him to express not only his liberal views on the cinema in general, but also his critical opinions about the Spanish political, social, religious and cultural situation. Of especially notorious importance were his opposition to the kind of puritanical censorship practised by the Spanish Catholic Church and his defence of an 'intelligent censorship', quoted many times later on, which was the topic of his conference on Censorship and Freedom at the *Universidad Pontificia de Salamanca* on 16 December 1951:

> Los beneficios de la censura – dije – se perciben en seguida y sus perjuicios sólo a la larga; con la libertad sucede al revés: produce muchos males inmediatos, que el tiempo transforma en buena medida en bienes. (García Escudero, 1995: 228)

> [The benefits of censorship – I said – are perceived immediately and its drawbacks only in the long run; with freedom it is the opposite: it causes a lot of immediate harm, which to a large extent time turns into good.]

García Escudero was in favour of a radical change in the way moral issues were traditionally addressed, by promoting the type of education which would allow the viewers to judge cinematic events from a critical distance, thus making censorship unnecessary:

> Esa educación moral tiene un presupuesto, que es la educación cinematográfica. [...] Pues bien, se trata de enseñar a dominar la película en vez de ser dominado por ella. (García Escudero, 1970: 44)

> [This moral education comes with the assumption of education about the cinema. [...] Therefore, it is about teaching [the audience] to control the film instead of being controlled by it.]

Within this context, the new period opened up with the reorganization of the *Junta de Clasificación y Censura de Películas Cinematográficas* by *Decreto* of the MIT dated 20 September 1962 (*BOE* 28 September 1962); the internal guidelines ruling the Censorship Branch of the new *Junta* were issued by the MIT on 20 February 1964 (*BOE* 14 March 1964). After the selection of candidates, the new *Junta* was constituted and the names of the new members belonging to the Board of Directors and to the cinema Censorship and Classification Branches were made official and public (*Orden* MIT 3 December 1962; *BOE* 11 December 1962).[5] The Board of Directors was headed by the *Director General de Cinematografía y Teatro*, José María García Escudero; this, together with the personal and professional profiles of the other members of the *Junta*, marked the start of a period of change moving towards a more lenient attitude to censorship on the part of the authorities, which not only had an impact on the public showing of films in cinemas but on other types of cultural events as well.[6] Suffice it to say that, according to the TRACE cinema catalogue, out of a total of 1017 films translated from English (all of them dubbed into Spanish, except for the ones shown in special cinemas), approved by the new *Junta* and shown in Spanish cinemas during the Fraga Iribarne period, 67 films (6.59%; 67/1017) were classified as '4' ('seriously dangerous') by religious censors. The fact that nearly 7% of films officially approved for showing had been classified as 'seriously dangerous' by the Church censors, compared to circa 1% between 1951 and 1962, demonstrates that a poor moral classification of a film no longer necessarily prevented it from being approved. Table 17.2 shows a sample of eight of those films, by date of release in Spain (our selection includes one film per year of release, from 1962 until 1969).

During this period, the long-awaited code governing civil censorship boards was approved on 9 February 1963 and finally published in 1963 both in the *BOE* (8 March 1963) and in the periodicals *Revista internacional del cine* and *Film ideal*. Although the Christian basis of this code was still apparent, its publication not only silenced the general demand for a specification of what was and was not permissible, but also caused different reactions and comments, for example, in the form of a 194-page volume of articles, interviews, editorials and opinion polls, entitled *La censura de cine*

Table 17.2 A sample of eight foreign films dubbed from English into Spanish, classified as '4' by religious censors, approved by the new *Junta de Clasificación y Censura de Películas Cinematográficas* and shown in Spanish cinemas during the Fraga Iribarne period (10 July 1962–29 October 1969)

Original title (director and year)	*Translated title*	*Release in Spain*
Bonjour Tristesse (Preminger 1958)	Buenos días, tristeza	18/10/1962
Sweet Bird of Youth (Brooks 1962)	Dulce pájaro de juventud	18/03/1963
The Night of the Iguana (Huston 1964)	La noche de la iguana	07/11/1964
Where Love Has Gone (Dmytryk 1964)	Adonde fue el amor	13/05/1965
The Idol (Petrie 1966)	Falso ídolo	05/12/1966
This Property Is Condemned (Pollack 1966)	Propiedad condenada	15/05/1967
Point Blank (Boorman 1967)	A quemarropa	26/08/1968
Alfie (Gilbert 1966)	Alfie	22/08/1969

Source: TRACE cinema catalogue.

en España, edited in 1963 by Pascual Cebollada, one of the members of the new *Junta*. After the publication of the code, for many the situation remained more or less the same (further details may be found in various sources: e.g. the periodical *Dirigido por...*, 1974: 30; Pérez Merinero & Pérez Merinero, 1975: 97). As pointed out by Gutiérrez Lanza, some people thought that:

> [...] the code was too general, too ambiguous, and too open to interpretation; thus it did not help script writers and translators anticipate the censors' final verdict. Moreover, the most intolerant critics maintained that extensive foreign cultural material was representative of Protestant cultures, whose society allowed both divorce and adultery, and whose cinema was flooded with marriages heading for disaster and other depictions of sin. [...] By contrast, enemies of censorship did not believe that the atmosphere was sufficiently liberal and still argued for more tolerant attitudes. (Gutiérrez Lanza, 2002: 154)

Another influential measure that was taken following García Escudero's reappointment was the raising of the age limit for adult audiences (2 March 1963; *BOE* 9 March 1963) from 16 to 18. This measure allowed many controversial topics such as the ones banned by Norm 8.4 of the 1963 code (adultery, abortion, prostitution, the use of contraceptive devices, suicide, etc.) to be considered suitable for an audience over the age of 18, as long as specific 'harmful' words and expressions were not explicitly mentioned.

A few years later on 12 January 1967 a new guideline was issued (*Orden* MIT, *BOE* 20 January 1967), stating the need to start showing films of special interest in the *Salas Especiales* and the *Salas de Arte y Ensayo*. The very existence of these *Salas* was in itself a sign of liberalization. Although they did not completely escape the effects of censorship and were not part of the commercial circuit – thus reaching relatively small audiences – thanks to them, many foreign 'quality films' were seen by Spanish viewers, which greatly contributed to improving the image of Spain abroad. For example, according to the periodical *Cine Asesor* (1967), among the first set of films distributed exclusively for *Salas de Arte y Ensayo* from October to December 1967 were the foreign films listed in Table 17.3, all of them shown in their original versions with Spanish subtitles.

Meanwhile, in response to the harsh criticism from certain ecclesiastical circles against what they considered to be the excessive permissiveness of the official censorship, in 1963 the *Dirección General de Cinematografía y Teatro* issued a private unpublished report, the *Informe sobre la Censura Cinematográfica y Teatral*,[7] which specifically aimed at defending three factors: the personal profiles of the members of the new *Junta*, stressing

Table 17.3 Foreign films exclusively distributed for *Salas de Arte y Ensayo* from October to December 1967

Original title (director and year)	Translated title
Mamma Roma (Pasolini 1962)	*Mamma Roma*
Repulsion (Polanski 1965)	*Repulsión*
Ensayo de un crimen (Buñuel 1955)	*Ensayo de un crimen*
Beata (Sokolowska 1965)	*Beatriz*
The Servant (Losey 1963)	*El sirviente*
Akahige (Kurosawa 1964)	*Barbarroja*
Hiroshima, mon amour (Resnais 1959)	*Hiroshima, mon amour*
Saturday Night and Sunday Morning (Reisz 1961)	*Sábado noche, domingo mañana*

Source: Anonymous (1967).

those aspects which would bring them near ecclesiastical doctrine; the procedures followed during the design of the censorship norms of 1963; and the controversial decisions taken by the new *Junta*, that is to say, the approval for an audience over the age of 18 of many 'problematic' foreign films previously classified as 'seriously dangerous' by the Catholic Church. Each of these points is discussed briefly below.

Personal profiles of the Junta

The *Informe* pointed out that two of the official Church members had been appointed by both the Archbishop of Pamplona and the Patriarch of Madrid-Alcalá, while the appointment by the MIT of the rest of the ecclesiastical members had been confirmed by the corresponding ecclesiastical authorities. According to the *Informe*, the non-Church members of the *Junta* were doctors, lawyers, public servants, writers and critics: *seglares de plena confianza, caballeros cristianos cien por cien, hombres de alta cultura y de carrera* ('secular men completely trustworthy, Christian gentlemen a hundred per cent, erudite men of high culture') (MIT, 1963: 30).

Procedures followed by the Junta

Still trying to defend and justify the new 'permissiveness', in relation to the code of censorship norms approved on 9 February 1963, the *Informe* points out that, imprecise though these may seem, their detailed description allows them to work as a guide not only for those in charge of their application but also for authors, directors, producers, distributors and exhibitors.

Approving 'seriously dangerous' foreign films: The Junta's defence

In relation to the approval for an audience over the age of 18 of many so-called problematic films, the *Informe* claimed that the decisions taken by the new *Junta* could not possibly damage the attitudes of young people. Another argument which they used to defend themselves against the Church's objections was that decisions had been straightforwardly accepted by the cinema industry. In fact, even in the case of those films criticized as harmful by the Church and approved by the new *Junta* for an audience over the age of 16, the film producers voluntarily accepted at a later point the suggestion made by the *Dirección General*, raising the age of attendance to the new limit of 18. Table 17.4 shows those films which, according to the *Informe*, were approved by the new *Junta* and were later affected by this shift in age of 16 to 18 as the dividing line for young people and adults; i.e. they could no longer be shown to young people of 16 and 17 years of age. All of the films – cited here in the order in which they appear in the *Informe* – were foreign in origin.

Other films approved by the new *Junta* were also believed to be appropriate for an audience over the age of 18 on three grounds: firstly, that individual and subjective judgement makes differences of opinion unavoidable; secondly, that many of the critical comments show confusion between 'strong' and 'immoral' (a film can be both strong and highly moral as long as, according to Pius XII, evil deeds are presented in such a way that they deserve to be damned); and thirdly, that civil censorship cannot be as strict as religious censorship, devoted to educating people's

Table 17.4 Films approved by the new *Junta* and later affected by the shift in age from 16 to 18 (young people/adult borderline)

Original title (director and year)	Translated title
Bonjour Tristesse (Preminger 1958)	Buenos días, tristeza
Splendour in the Grass (Kazan 1961)	Esplendor en la yerba [sic]
Eclisse, L' (Antonioni 1962)	El eclipse
Phaedra (Dassin 1962)	Fedra
Walk on the Wild Side (Dmytryk 1962)	La gata negra
Sweet Bird of Youth (Brooks 1962)	Dulce pájaro de juventud
The Best of Everything (Negulesco 1959)	Mujeres frente al amor
Isola di Arturo, L' (Damiani 1962)	La Isla de Arturo
Sanctuary (Richardson 1961)	Réquiem para una mujer

Source: *Informe sobre la Censura Cinematográfica y Teatral* (1963).

consciences. For all these reasons, since civil and religious censorship serve different purposes, the *Dirección General* believed that there was no obstacle to the *Junta*'s approval of at least some of those films that had previously been classified by the Church as 'seriously dangerous': '4. *Gravemente peligrosa (léase rechazable)*'.

Case Study: *The Best of Everything* (Negulesco, 1959): *Mujeres frente al amor*

The censorship documents associated with the film *The Best of Everything* (Negulesco, 1959) (translated into Spanish as *Mujeres frente al amor*), kept in file number 20.996, clearly exemplify the kind of negotiations that were taking place at the start of the 1960s both between the censors and the distributors and among the censors themselves. This morally controversial film, classified as 'seriously dangerous' by religious censors and included in the group of films approved by the new *Junta* and later affected by the shift in age from 16 to 18 (see Table 17.4), was finally given official approval following a number of changes to the film dialogue in the Spring of 1963. The film had originally been banned by the *Junta de Clasificación y Censura* on 14 September 1960, and again by the *Comisión Superior* on 10 October 1960 with the Spanish title *Mujeres en busca de amor* ('Women in search of love') in spite of some initial changes in the dialogue which:

> aunque no son sustanciales, sin embargo adaptan mejor el clima moral de la película a las condiciones sociales de la nación. (Letter from A.S. Films S.A. addressed to the *Comisión Superior de Censura*, 10 October 1960)

> [although not substantial, however, they adapt the moral climate of the film to the social circumstances of the nation.]

One of the censors of the *Comisión* leaves no room for doubt in his report about why the film was still not acceptable:

> No creo posible que, aún admitiendo las rectificaciones de diálogo propuestas por la casa importadora, pueda aprobarse esta película. Es una narración cruel, despiadada, escalofriante de una juventud femenina, rota o aplastada por conseguir 'su hombre' como imperativo máximo de su ser, como razón exclusiva de su vida. Quizá en la realidad de la sociedad norteamericana, pueda ser ejemplar esta película: pero ese supuesto implicaría una terrible realidad que no es posible admitir en España, ni aún en el juicio más pesimista. (Censorship report by Don Antonio Fraguas, 10 October 1960)

[I don't think it possible, even if the modifications in the dialogue proposed by the importers were admitted, for this film to be approved. It is a cruel, merciless, horrifying narration of a young woman, broken or smashed because of the fact that obtaining 'her man' is her main duty, the sole *raison d'etre* of her life. Maybe in the reality of North American society, this film can be considered to be exemplary: but this conjecture would imply a terrible reality which is not possible to admit in Spain, not even under the most pessimistic judgement.]

With the Spanish title *Mujeres frente al amor* ('Women opposing love'), the ban on the film was confirmed by the new *Junta de Clasificación y Censura* on 9 November 1962. In a letter addressed to the *Junta de Clasificación y Censura* dated 25 October 1960, A.S. Films S.A. had declared that the film was being presented 'without any modifications either to the image or the dialogue' – although the earlier letter of 10 October 1960 had reported some preliminary changes – on the grounds that the American League of Decency had classified it for adults without objections. This time, however, there were more differences of opinion among the censors, six of whom thought that the film could be approved for adults over the age of 16 and seven of whom thought that it should be banned again because of the immoral attitude of the characters. On 12 November 1962, the distributors again insisted on the possibility of changing the dialogue to achieve greater acceptance on the part of the authorities. The two-page list of changes to the dubbed screenplay suggested by the distributors and recorded in the censorship file included:

DIÁLOGO ACTUAL. **APRIL**: Mi madre nunca dice nada del amor. No se le ocurriría decirme que no tuviera un amante, como tampoco me diría que no robase un coche.

DIÁLOGO QUE SE PROPONE. **APRIL**: Mi madre nunca me dice nada del amor. Cree que viene y se va como un pájaro. Pero los pájaros también tienen sus nidos. Yo los he visto hacerse el amor.

[CURRENT DIALOGUE. **APRIL**: *My mother never says anything about love. She wouldn't think of telling me not to have a lover, as she wouldn't tell me not to rob a car.*

SUGGESTED DIALOGUE. **APRIL**: *My mother never tells me anything about love. She thinks it comes and goes like a bird. But birds also have their nests. I've seen them making love.*]

DIÁLOGO ACTUAL. **CAROLINE**: Abrazame [sic] Mike. Hazme el amor, te lo ruego. Aunque no me quieras nada.

DIÁLOGO QUE SE PROPONE. **CAROLINE:** Abrazame [sic], Mike. Lo necesito, te lo ruego. Aunque no me quieras nada.

[CURRENT DIALOGUE. CAROLINE: Hold me Mike. Make love to me, I beg you. Even if you don't love me.

SUGGESTED DIALOGUE. CAROLINE: Hold me, Mike. I need it, I beg you. Even if you don't love me.]

DIÁLOGO ACTUAL. **SHALIMAR:** Pero tu [sic] no debes olvidarte de que soy un hombre casado.

DIÁLOGO QUE SE PROPONE. **SHALIMAR:** Pero tu [sic] no debes olvidarte de que yo no soy libre.

[CURRENT DIALOGUE. SHALIMAR: But you mustn't forget I'm a married man.

SUGGESTED DIALOGUE. SHALIMAR: But you mustn't forget I'm not free.]

As can be seen above, in order to please the most conservative members of the censorship board, the suggested changes to the translated dialogue tend to avoid specific words and expressions considered highly immoral and dangerous, such as *amante* ('lover'), *hazme el amor* ('make love to me') and the open reference to marriage in the words of the two lovers, *soy un hombre casado* ('I am a married man').[8] These changes in the translation of the dialogue, together with the new more liberal approach in official circles, allowed the new *Junta de Clasificación y Censura* to approve the film on 29 November 1962. Nevertheless, there were still some noticeable differences of opinion among the censors, eight of whom thought that the film could be approved for adults over the age of 16 (prior to the age change to 18) and six of whom thought it should be banned. According to the reports kept in the censorship file, all members of the new *Junta* produced very carefully justified written evidence of the reasons for their verdicts, which reflect the special interest they took in this controversial film. Those in favour of the banning of this 'immoral film' still argued that it was *peligrosa y nociva, sobre todo para muchachas jóvenes* ('dangerous and harmful, especially for young women') (Censorship report by Srta. Elisa de Lara, 29 November 1962). On the other hand, those in favour of its approval, in accordance with García Escudero's more liberal views, explained that *esta película es un testimonio social de EEUU* ('this film is a social testimony of the USA') (Censorship report by Don Juan Miguel Lamet, 29 November 1962) and *el público comprenderá y repudiará la situación, las muchachas jóvenes sobre todo* ('the audience will understand and repudiate the situation, young women especially') (Censorship report by Don Juan Miguel Lamet, 29 November 1962). So, among other things, the approval was now being justified on the grounds that the action did not take place in Spain and, therefore, that that kind of behaviour was not characteristic of Spanish society. Finally, almost half a year later, after the adult age limit had been raised from 16 to 18, A.S. Films S.A. applied for a new classification of this film, which was certified by the new *Junta* on 2 April 1963 for adults over the age of 18.

Conclusion

The case study on *Mujeres frente al amor* reported above is highly representative of the film censorship situation of the 1960s in Spain: the moral tolerance threshold was gradually being raised, causing many differences of opinion between the more conservative and the more liberal censors, and leading the distributors to endless negotiations with the censorship boards in order to have their films approved. The appearance in film of themes such as infidelity, adultery, broken marriages, and so on was frequently justified on the grounds that the reprehensible behaviour depicted in the film was 'foreign', not Spanish. These topics started to be considered acceptable and became common in imported films which were permitted to be shown in cinemas, as long as there were no explicit references to these topics by means of specific words and expressions. Therefore, in order to avoid the film being banned, both translators and distributors made changes to the screenplay before seeking the approval of the censorship board. Other parts of the dialogue left unaltered in the translated version were, however, later revised and changed by the censors.

One of the main impediments to the process of liberalization in Spain in the 1960s was that it was still based on the same old legal, administrative and political mechanisms that had been at work for decades. As a result of this anachronistic situation, 'there was a feeling of widespread insecurity among artists and intellectuals on the grounds that non-conformism could be legally repressed by the prevailing apparatus at any time' (Gutiérrez Lanza, 2002: 155). However, although conservative forces regained some power during the final years of the Franco regime, thanks to the degree of liberalization which had been achieved in Spanish society in the previous years, attempts to restore the initial power of the censorship apparatus did not succeed.

Notes

1. Research for this article has been undertaken as part of the TRACE project, funded by the regional government of Castilla y León, Spain [LE020A09] and the Ministry of Science and Innovation [FFI2008-05479-C02-01/FILO]. The acronym stands for *Traducciones censuradas*/Censored translations. See http://trace.unileon.es/; http://www.ehu.es/trace/inicio.html.
2. All translations are my own.
3. The *Comisión Nacional de Censura Cinematográfica* consisted of the so-called Presidente and five other members: a representative of the military, of the ecclesiastic authority, of the Ministry of National Education, of the Ministry of Industry and Commerce, and of the Department of Cinematography (*BOE* 26 November 1942).
4. The *Ordinario Diocesano* is the member of the Catholic Church who, among other duties, oversees the selection of school teachers of the Catholic religion.
5. The new *Junta de Clasificación y Censura de Películas Cinematográficas* consisted of a *Rama de Censura* ('Censorship Branch'), a *Rama de Clasificación* ('Classification Branch'), and a Board of Directors common to both branches. According to the *Orden* issued by the MIT on 3 December 1962 (*BOE* 11 December 1962), the members of the Board of Directors were: *Presidente, Director General de Cinematografía y Teatro; Vicepresidente primero, Subdirector General de Cinematografía y Teatro; Vicepresidente segundo, Secretario general de Cinematografía y Teatro; Secretario, don Sebastián Bautista de la Torre; Vocal nato de las dos Ramas, Jefe de Servicios de Cine de la Dirección General de Cinematografía y Teatro*.
6. For more information about the changes brought about by the new 'spirit of aperture' towards a more lenient control of English–Spanish translated theatre or narrative, please refer to the (un)published works of other members of the TRACE research team (see http://trace.unileon.es/; http://www.ehu.es/trace/inicio.html).
7. I would like to thank Dr Raquel Merino (Universidad del País Vasco) for providing me with the unpublished *Informe sobre la Censura Cinematográfica y Teatral* and *Mis siete vidas: de las brigadas anarquistas a juez del 23-F* by García Escudero (1995) for the purposes of this chapter.
8. These are examples of suggested changes made by the distributors. Other case studies have also confirmed that censorship was mainly implemented before the translations reached the censorship boards, because of opposition of the censors to the use of what they considered to be morally incorrect words or expressions. This was the case not only for English–Spanish cinema translation but also in other textual areas such as narrative and theatre. For more information about this, please refer to the (un)published works of the members of the TRACE research team (see http://trace.unileon.es/; http://www.ehu.es/trace/inicio.html).

References

Anonymous (1967) *Cine asesor. Hojas archivables de información – exclusivas para empresas*. Madrid.

García Escudero, J.M. (1970) *Vamos a hablar de cine.* Madrid: Biblioteca Básica Salvat.
García Escudero, J.M. (1995) *Mis siete vidas: de las brigadas anarquistas a juez del 23-F.* Barcelona: Editorial Planeta, S.A.
Gutiérrez Lanza, C. (2002) Spanish film translation and cultural patronage: The filtering and manipulation of imported material during Franco's dictatorship. In M. Tymoczko and E. Gentzler (eds) *Translation and Power* (pp. 141–159). Amherst/Boston: University of Massachusetts Press.
Lleonart Amsélem, A.J. (1995) El ingreso de España en la ONU: Obstáculos e impulsos. *Cuadernos de Historia Contemporánea* 17, 101–119.
Martínez Bretón, J.A. (1988) *Influencia de la Iglesia Católica en la cinematografía española (1951–1962).* Madrid: Harofarma.
Ministerio de Cultura. Archivo General de la Administración. *Mujeres frente al amor.* Expediente No. 20.996. SIGNAGA 36/03987.
MIT (Ministerio de Información y Turismo). Dirección General de Cinematografía y Teatro. (1963) Informe sobre la Censura Cinematográfica y Teatral. Unpublished.
Pérez Merinero, C. and Pérez Merinero, D. (1975) *Cine y control.* Madrid: Miguel Castellote.
Pius XI (1936) *Vigilanti Cura.* On WWW at http://www.vatican.va/holy_father/pius_xi/encyclicals/documents/hf_p-xi_enc_29061936_vigilanti-cura_en.html. Accessed 7.10.2009.
Pius XII (1957) Miranda Prorsus. On WWW at http://www.vatican.va/holy_father/pius_xii/encyclicals/documents/hf_p-xii_enc_08091957_miranda prorsus_en.html. Accessed 7.10.09.

Index

Abkhazian 104-6
Academy of Basque Language 256
adaptation 11, 13, 40, 80, 82-5, 87-8, 117, 122, 130-1, 139, 252
Aeschylus 11-2, 77-83, 85-8, 254
agency 6-7, 12, 14-6, 19-21, 31-2, 113, 183-4, 195, 197, 241
alliteration 276
anarchy 4-5, 10, 197
ancient Greek 2, 4-5, 10, 85
anti-Semitism 299
apertura 27, 305, 308
Appiah, Kwame Anthony 114
audience design 21
audiovisual 30-1
authorship 11, 61, 63, 72-3, 115, 182, 186
autonomy 23, 25-6
Azeri 67

Baker, Mona 5, 28, 49, 113, 225, 291
Barthes, Roland 95, 118
Basque 26-7, 247-59, 261-2
Bastin, Georges 113, 117
Bhabha, Homi 163, 261
bilingualism 257
blogging 2
Blum-Kulka, Shoshana 192
Boratav, Pertev Naili 60-1, 63, 67-8
borrowing 96, 120, 166
Bosnian 285, 283, 291
Bourdieu, Pierre 15, 23-5, 84, 268, 270
Butler, Judith 140

canonical literature 63
capital
– cultural capital 23, 84, 86
– economic capital 23, 25
– social capital 223
– symbolic capital 23, 254, 270
capitalism 47, 205, 210, 216
Carlist War 250
Casanova, Pascale 249-50, 258
Catholicism 20, 186-7, 189, 191, 196-7, 249, 252, 286-7
censorship 17, 30, 114, 207, 252-4, 266, 268, 278-9, 305-8, 310-8
chauvinism 83, 198
Chesterman, Andrew 6, 14, 31-2, 111, 114, 117
children's literature 260, 301
Chinese 49
classicism 79, 255
code-switching 12, 19, 96, 163-9, 173, 175-7
coherence 190, 192, 199
cohesion 21, 27, 32, 192, 198-9, 259
colonization 93, 99, 192
comics 9
Communist Manifesto 204-6, 209-12, 217-9
Communist Party 21, 204-5, 207
compensation 175
conflict 2, 6, 106, 132-3, 162, 255, 262, 278, 285, 287, 291-3, 295
contextualization cue 19
Croatian 29, 31, 283, 285, 287-91
Cronin, Michael 19, 163, 225-6, 239, 241
cultural adaptation 253
cultural field 15, 24-5
Cyrillic 285
Czech 22, 225, 235

Derrida, Jacques 40, 95, 118, 138-9, 287, 289
dialect 17, 19, 22, 130, 132, 162-3, 166, 170, 173-5, 250, 257-8, 284-6, 291
diaspora 163
dictatorship 261, 268, 295
diglossia 247
discourse marker 166, 168-9
Dostoevsky, Fyodor 94, 96
dubbed films 30, 305

emigration 191, 247
erotic 27-8, 70, 265-70, 272-5, 277, 279
ethics 14, 224
Even-Zohar, Itamar 8, 60, 66
explicitation 21, 192-3, 195

Fairclough, Norman 21

Fascist 29, 266, 295-9, 301-3
Fawcett, Peter 112, 117
feminist 115, 267-8
fidelity 13, 42, 111-2, 116-9, 122
film classification 308
fluency 96
focalization 19-20, 164-5, 167, 169, 173, 176
formal equivalence 215
Franco, Francisco 248, 253, 258, 261, 268-9, 278, 305-7, 318
French 12, 19, 22, 94-7, 99, 102, 114, 154-5, 157, 163, 166, 193, 198, 200, 214-5, 226, 231, 235, 248, 251, 257-60, 262
Freud, Sigmund 105-6, 120, 286-7

Gambier, Yves 117
gate-keeping 6, 26
gay 16, 129-30, 273-4
gender 16, 27-8, 50, 135, 140-1, 162, 269-70, 278-9
Genette, Gérard 4, 164-5, 211-2
German 22, 95-6, 115-6, 119, 166, 172, 183, 205, 209, 214-5, 225-9, 231, 234-5, 237-8, 240, 259, 289, 291, 296
Gouanvic, Jean-Marc 15, 24-6
Gramsci, Antonio 204-5
Greek 2, 4, 22, 79, 85-6, 119, 204, 206, 209, 214, 217, 254, 266
Grimm Brothers 60
Gumperz, John Joseph 19, 163-4
Gutt, Ernst-August 118

habitus 15-9, 21-4
Harvey, Keith 16, 137, 211
hegemony 82, 204-5, 256, 295
Hermans, Theo 8, 15, 111, 122, 185, 199-200
heteroglossia 12, 291
heteronomy 1, 26-8
homology 23
homosexuality 16, 130, 133, 136
House, Juliane 40-2, 48, 51, 67, 161, 249
humour 104, 131, 148
Hungarian 226
hybridity 6, 19, 176

Ibsen, Henrik 10-1, 39-55
identity 6-7, 12, 14, 16-7, 21, 26, 28, 31-2, 72, 84, 87-8, 94-5, 97, 104-6, 111, 115, 122, 133, 136, 140, 163-6, 171-2, 176, 182, 184, 190, 216, 218-9, 247-8, 250-1, 253, 261, 283-5, 288, 290, 292
ideological 1, 8-12, 19-21, 24, 40, 42-3, 46-7, 50-2, 55, 61, 68-70, 73-4, 83, 86, 88, 100, 113, 147, 150, 157, 165, 184, 192, 198, 204-11, 213, 216, 218-9, 247, 251, 253, 259-60, 268, 271, 278-9, 298, 303
ideology 6, 10-1, 17, 22, 39, 42, 47, 50, 54, 64, 66-7, 72, 121, 130, 185, 205, 302
immigrant 1, 19, 146, 161-2, 166, 170, 172, 176
indirect translation 41, 259
indirectness 168, 175
intensifier 274
interdialectal translation 249
interlinear translation 102, 112
interlingual translation 118
interpreting 22-3, 30, 32, 41, 47, 223-4, 227, 239, 241-2
intersemiotic translation 2, 62
intertextuality 62-3, 118
intralingual translation 11, 17, 62, 118
irony 13, 99-100, 148, 171, 185, 200, 289
Italian 19-20, 161-3, 165-7, 170, 172, -6, 198, 225, 239, 291, 297, 300

Jakobson, Roman 2, 62, 118, 130, 154-5
Jones, Francis 185, 201, 292

kathareuousa 79, 84
Kosofsky Sedgwick, Eve 134

Lambert, José 8, 15, 122
Latin 93, 98, 105, 198, 216, 250-1, 254-5, 275, 285, 288, 291
Lefevere, André 7, 10, 39-40, 42, 48-49, 51, 53-4, 113, 200, 258, 271
Lenin, Vladimir Ilyich 50, 209
Lermontov, Mikhail 13, 94, 98-100
Levine, Suzanne Jill 113, 115
lingua franca 28, 271, 283
literal translation 112, 173, 200
Lodge, David 154-5

Marx, Karl 50, 205, 209, 212-3, 217, 255
Marxism 204-5, 207-4, 216-9
Mason, Ian 9-10, 21, 114, 289
Meylaerts, Reine 12, 24
migrant 152, 155, 176-7
migration 10, 21, 55, 161, 163
minority 17, 19, 103, 106, 143, 176, 259
(mis)translation 12, 31, 97-100, 106-7
monolingualism 260-1, 286
Montenegrin 283, 291
multilingualism 94, 97, 163, 173, 177

Nabokov, Vladimir 97-9, 103-4, 111, 117
narrative: (text type) 19, 65, 67, 95, 98, 104, 129, 133, 146, 148, 149, 150, 156, 157, 158, 163, 164, 165, 167, 172, 176, 177, 269

Index

narrative: (theory) 5, 29, 291-292
narratology 164-5
nationalism 54, 78, 83, 86, 98, 100, 251, 255-6, 287
nationalist 84, 198, 286-9, 292-3
Nazi 185, 224-5, 240, 266
neoclassical 78, 83-4
neologisms 255
Newmark, Peter 112, 117
Nida, Eugene 115, 214
Nietzsche, Friedrich 255
Niranjana, Tejaswini 93, 113
norms 10-11, 16-7, 24, 40, 45, 50, 88, 113, 117, 185, 200, 224, 241, 248, 274, 278, 308, 313
Norwegian 41-2, 45, 60

obscenity 27, 142, 266-8
Ossetian 94
O'Sullivan, Carol 20, 115, 185, 198, 200
Ottoman 11, 59, 61-2, 67-8, 70, 73, 77-8

Paker, Saliha 18-9, 59, 153
Paloposki, Outi 7, 73
paratext 137, 157, 192, 198
paratextual 20-2, 31, 191, 204, 253
patronage 7, 26, 49, 84, 257-8, 261, 271
performativity 77
pivot language 41, 259-60
poetry 16-7, 41, 51, 101-3, 129-31, 133-6, 143-4, 182, 255
Polish 22, 225-6, 228-9, 233, 235, 237
politeness 166, 168-9
political texts 21, 204-5, 211
pornography 27, 265-8
postmodern 144
poststructuralist 165, 167
propaganda 45-7, 54, 70, 113, 208, 295
Protestantism 189, 249
pseudo-translation 121
Pushkin, Alexander 98
Pym, Anthony 113-4, 117, 120

queer 16-8, 135, 137, 140-1, 143-4, 277-8

Rabadán, Rosa 266
racist 295, 297, 299-300, 302
Reiss, Katharina 116
religion 8, 27, 54, 67, 70-2, 113, 191, 255, 266, 286
republican 59-64, 66-8, 72
retranslation 21, 59, 73, 199, 206-7, 209, 213
rewriting 10-11, 13, 31, 39-40, 43-5, 49-50, 53, 55, 59-60, 63, 65-66, 71, 74, 122, 258
Rheingold, Howard 2

rhetorical 5, 10, 135, 191-3, 196, 201, 260, 272
Robinson, Douglas 118-9
Robyns Clem 8, 21
Romanticist 11, 82-8
Rundle, Chris 29, 295
Russian 12, 22, 94, 96-9, 101-2, 104, 106, 209, 225, 234-6

samizdat, 101
sarcasm 189
satirical 72
Schäffner, Christina 204
Scots 17-8, 135-7, 139
self-translation 116, 258
Serbian 283, 285, 288-91
Serbo-Croatian 28, 283-5, 287, 289, 290-3
sexuality 18, 134, 137, 167, 255, 265-9, 274, 278-9
Shaw, George Bernard 10, 42-8, 52, 54
Silesian 226, 228, 230
Simeoni, Daniel 15-6, 25-6
Simms, Karl 279
Simon, Sherry 163
skopos 17, 199
Slavic 29, 107, 284-7, 290, 292-3
Snell-Hornby, Mary 117, 120
socialist 10, 45-7, 103, 133, 150, 206-7, 209-10, 255, 262
sociological 14, 39, 163-164
sociology 14
Sophocles 84-7, 252, 254
Soviet 13, 93, 100-7, 134
Spanish 115, 172, 175, 248, 250, 255-60, 262, 270, 273-9, 306, 308-9, 311-2, 315-6
Spanish Civil War 26, 247-8, 251, 253
Stalin, Joseph 208-10
Standard English 132
standardization 26, 29, 258
Steiner, George 272
stereotypes 116, 164, 166, 172, 268
subtitles 29, 312
systemic approaches 7

taboo 269, 274
Tolstoy, Leo 12, 95-7
Tongor 102-3
totalitarian 29, 295
Toury, Gideon 40, 102, 259
tragedy 11-2, 48, 77-80, 82-8
Trotsky, Leon 208
Trotskyism 210, 217
Turkish 18, 62, 64, 67-8, 150-1, 154-5, 157
Tymoczko, Maria 93, 117, 154, 163, 184

Van Leeuwen, Theo 10
Van Steen, Gonda 11, 77-9
Venuti, Lawrence 9, 17, 20-1, 40, 73, 93, 95, 106, 111, 117, 182-3, 213-4, 248
Verschueren, Jef 10
voice 4- 5, 19, 47, 131-3, 135, 137, 140, 143-4, 150, 164-5, 167, 185
Voloshinov, Valentin 213
Von Flotow, Luise 21, 114, 120

vulgarity 273-4, 278

Wadensjö, Cecilia 240
World War I 297
World War II 207, 224

Yiddish 226

zero translation 12, 96-7

For Product Safety Concerns and Information please contact our EU Authorised Representative:

Easy Access System Europe

Mustamäe tee 50

10621 Tallinn

Estonia

gpsr.requests@easproject.com